Tar Heel History on Foot

Tar Heel History on Foot

Great Walks through 400 Years of

North Carolina's Fascinating Past

Lynn Setzer

UNIVERSITY OF NORTH CAROLINA PRESS

CHAPEL HILL

A SOUTHERN GATEWAYS GUIDE

© 2013 The University of North Carolina Press
All rights reserved
Set in Caecilia LT
Manufactured in the United States of America

The paper in this book meets the guidelines for permanence and
durability of the Committee on Production Guidelines for Book
Longevity of the Council on Library Resources.

The University of North Carolina Press has been a member
of the Green Press Initiative since 2003.

Library of Congress Cataloging-in-Publication Data
Setzer, Lynn, 1955–
Tar Heel history on foot : great walks through
400 years of North Carolina's fascinating past / Lynn Setzer.
pages cm. — (A southern gateways guide)
Includes bibliographical references and index.
ISBN 978-1-4696-0889-1 (cloth : alk. paper)
ISBN 978-1-4696-0890-7 (pbk. : alk. paper)
1. North Carolina—Guidebooks. 2. Historic sites—North
Carolina—Guidebooks. 3. North Carolina—History, Local.
4. Parks—North Carolina—Guidebooks. 5. Walking—
North Carolina—Guidebooks. I. Title.
F252.3.S4863 2013   975.6—dc23
2013015618

Southern Gateways Guide™ is a
registered trademark of the University
of North Carolina Press.

17 16 15 14 13 5 4 3 2 1

This book is dedicated to all professional and hobby historians as well as the preservationists who have worked and continue to work very hard to keep the details of the past alive and accessible for the future. Without their efforts—be they scholarly or personal or simply all in a day's work—we would have only the dimmest ideas of how we got here from way back there. Their work enabled me to take some mighty fine walks. I hope that you enjoy them as well.

Contents

Discovering, Settling, and Forming a State

Living Our Lives

Important Firsts

Geographical Table of Contents

Coastal Plain

Piedmont

Mountains

Preface

The history of North Carolina, first as a colony and then as a state, stretches back more than 400 years. The land area of the state encompasses 48,711 miles (thanks, Rand McNally!). And according to the 2010 United States Census, North Carolina ranks as the tenth-most-populous state in the country, with a population that grows—and grows more diverse—by the day. As you might imagine, therefore, designing a collection of walks that tells our history—without making a tome so large that you need a wheelbarrow to cart it with you as you walk—was quite a difficult challenge.

I quickly discovered that no single book on "history walking" in North Carolina could capture all of the stories that our state contains and that no one chapter describing any one walk could possibly tell everything that should be told along that particular route. Thus, I hope that if you enjoy the sips of history this book contains, you will decide to drink more deeply of the details and complexity by reading some of the source material I have listed for you at the back of the book. Our history is rich and fascinating, and I am grateful to the professional historians who have dedicated their lives to shedding light on those details so that the rest of us can come to know our state a little bit better.

Having written many articles about walks and hikes where the payoff is a jaw-dropping view and, hopefully, a greater appreciation for the natural beauty of the earth, I approached this book with a different goal. Here I wanted to write a guide where the payoff would be a richer appreciation of a place and the lives of our forebears in that place. I also wanted to help make sure that we remember some of the details of life and living that, over time, people tend to forget.

While walking the routes and researching the stories, I discovered something about the topic we call "history." First, the obvious: history is indeed a record of what happened. Having that record helps us to marvel at our progress: the next time you download digitized music from the Internet, consider that Thomas A. Edison recorded the first playable sound on material that resembles aluminum foil. It's hard to appreciate that evolution in technology unless you visit the Henry Ford Museum in Dearborn, Michigan, to see Edison's fabulous recording machine. Likewise, it's hard to appreciate the meager beginnings of the Carolina colony until you visit Fort Raleigh. Despite the numbers of visits I have made there, I marvel every time I think about the pluck and faith the first colonists had.

But "history" is more than a timeline of events. It reminds us of how many people have lived here before us and have also called the territory home. Sometimes the process was sequential; one generation left a community before another one, perhaps quite different in its background or aspirations, arrived in its place. At other times, however, the stories overlap, sometimes bringing about positive outcomes and sometimes causing sorrow. One need only to consider the violent encounters of the Tuscarora tribes with European settlers near New Bern in the early eighteenth century, the struggle of Cherokee people as they adapted first to the arrival of colonial settlers in our western mountains and later to their forcible removal from their homes in the 1830s, or the long journey from slavery to freedom and full civil rights for black citizens in our state. Similarly, and on a lighter note, if you ever discuss the merits of western North Carolina barbeque over eastern (or vice versa!), you're discussing, in part, the overlap of English settlers in coastal regions of North Carolina with German immigrants in the Piedmont. I hope the walks gathered here will encourage you to think in new ways about how our personal stories are intertwined with the past and present of our neighbors, for we North Carolinians represent a multiplicity of histories.

Walking through history also reminds us that history is personal and inspiring. As I walked and recalled lessons from school days and then augmented those lessons with the new details I learned, I marveled at how individual lives do have the power, if not to change the world, then to contribute mightily to the changes that inevitably await us. In North Carolina, we are lucky to have many examples of how events that happened here really did change—or at least inspired change in—the world. These examples—some of them business ideas, some of them aspirations for justice—can motivate us to keep carrying the ball forward, to form that more perfect union.

How To Use This Book

The walks in this book include a few that might take a whole day, and at least one where you can see the end even from the beginning. (Both the longest and the shortest were two of my favorites.) Most, however, fall safely in the middle, somewhere in the two-to-three-mile length and requiring perhaps an hour or two to complete. For those that trace a city walk (and many do), I've included turn-by-turn directions using the available landmarks. I also tried very hard to augment, not duplicate, what local visitor centers provide in the way of walking tours. So, if you want to walk in, say, Hillsborough, and you wonder if you should step inside the visitor center to see what it has to offer, the answer is *Yes!* Their information will deepen even more the architectural and historical descriptions of some of the structures you will walk by. I'm sure that it will whet your appetite for more information. Also, even though the directions, phone numbers, web links and operating hours (when listed) were current as of July 2012, you might be wise to call ahead if you're planning a day trip. If writing this book taught me anything, it taught me that change is constant.

Each walk contains an overview that sets the theme for that walk and then a narrative about the context of the walk, the "backstory" as we like to say today. Then you'll find the directions for taking the walk. At the end, you'll find directions on how to find where the walk is, as well as other practical information about your footwear, parking, restrooms, and such. At the very end of some of the walks, you may see information that points you to even more walks and opportunities to expand your knowledge of the history of a people or place.

This book contains two tables of contents because I wanted to help walkers get to the information from two different points of view. The first table of contents lists the walks according to how people live their lives. When you look up into the glistening green needles of a longleaf pine tree on a warm March day, it's hard to remember that these beautiful trees were once as important to the state's economy as biomedical research is today. In addition, North Carolina lays claim to some important "firsts," and I wanted to make sure these firsts were highlighted. On the other hand, the geographical table of contents reflects the routine classification of North Carolina: Coastal Plain, Piedmont, Mountains. If you live in the Piedmont and want to start your walks close to home, you can see which walks are within easier reach. The only spot where this arrangement might be a tad confusing is the walk celebrating North Carolina's status as a prime tourist destination in the United States. This chapter describes walks in Pinehurst and Asheville, two destinations that are exceptionally well known outside the state lines, even if they are separated by 214 miles. (The chapter appears in the geographical table of contents listed under Piedmont, where Pine-hurst is located, though Asheville is actually in the Mountains.) With luck you'll find time to enjoy a walk around both.

A Word about the Walks Included in the Book

Writing this book posed challenges of several sorts, but nothing was as difficult as deciding which walks would actually come to populate the pages at production time. At times I wished that I could share with you everything I learned and every walk I walked—but doing so would have made the book unwieldy. In addition, some areas of North Carolina are so rich with stories that I had to carefully choose which details to include. For example, in sifting through the complexity of hundreds of years of history in Wilmington, I experienced moments when I thought that perhaps Wilmington deserved its own 300-page book. Likewise, as a native North Carolinian, I learned in school the standard information that some of the early governors appointed by King Charles II were "corrupt." Not until I read some of the stories of their perfidy did I appreciate just how truly awful some of them were—and how lucky we are as citizens that our ancestors overcame the bad behavior. However, as the book went through its editorial paces, I realized that adding too much information on this early corruption, while fascinating, meant squeezing out other essential and interesting details of our state's history. All this is to say that, as you will no doubt find when you begin your own "history walks," there is nearly always even more to the already-intriguing story than meets the eye.

Acknowledgments

This book represents a team effort, for there is no way I could have delivered it all on my own. People who need more thanks than ink on paper can convey include many people at UNC Press, first among them Mark Simpson-Vos, my editor. He was a most optimistic and patient helmsman through some stormy seas. Likewise Paul Betz, Zachary Read, and Liz Gray, who helped chase the details of presentation, editing, pictures, and style. They saw what my eyes could sometimes not see. The staff of the North Carolina Collection at the Wilson Library at the University of North Carolina at Chapel Hill—Margaretta Yarborough, Alison Murray, Jason Tomberlin, Bridget Madden, Karry McKown, Caroline Keizer—were likewise instrumental in helping this book come to life. They fetched mounds of materials for me and always smiled as they did so. Other advisers include Pamela Grundy, Vicky Jarrett, Michael Hill, head of the research branch at the North Carolina Division of Archives and History, as well as his colleague Ansley Wegner. They knew details large and small and helped me decide which details needed to be added to give more fullness to the stories. Other help from across the state came from Wanda Stalcup, Fred Heath, Jerry Span, John L. Durham, Christopher Ammons, Christopher Meekins, Mike Whaley, Aric Sanoff, and Meg Philbrook. Randall Washington, my husband, also deserves many thanks. He walked these walks with me, usually without complaint, sometimes two or three times as I went out to quality assure the route. He held cameras when I took notes, held notes when I took pictures. The twenty-degree day after Christmas when we walked about Salisbury for the nth time, as a frigid wind cut our faces, was a true test of perseverance.

I am profoundly grateful to all who helped this book come to life.

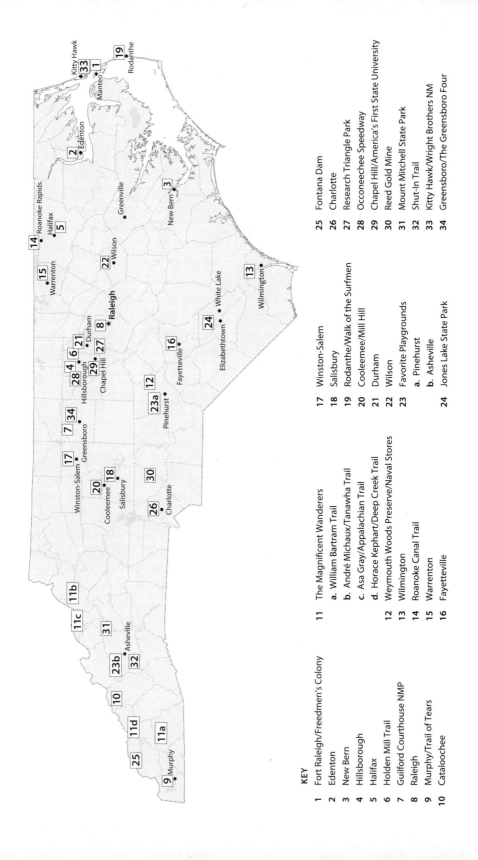

Kitty Hawk
33
1
Manteo
19
Rodanthe

2 Edenton

3 New Bern

Greenville

Roanoke Rapids
14
Halifax 5

Wilson
22

15
Warrenton

Durham
21
4 6
28 29 27
Hillsborough
Chapel Hill

★ Raleigh
8

16
Fayetteville

24
White Lake

13
Wilmington

Elizabethtown

12
23a
Pinehurst

7 34
Greensboro

17
Winston-Salem

18
20
Cooleemee Salisbury

30

26
Charlotte

11b

11c

31

23b
32
Asheville

10

11d

11a

25

9 Murphy

KEY

1 Fort Raleigh/Freedmen's Colony
2 Edenton
3 New Bern
4 Hillsborough
5 Halifax
6 Holden Mill Trail
7 Guilford Courthouse NMP
8 Raleigh
9 Murphy/Trail of Tears
10 Cataloochee
11 The Magnificent Wanderers
    a. William Bartram Trail
    b. André Michaux/Tanawha Trail
    c. Asa Gray/Appalachian Trail
    d. Horace Kephart/Deep Creek Trail
12 Weymouth Woods Preserve/Naval Stores
13 Wilmington
14 Roanoke Canal Trail
15 Warrenton
16 Fayetteville
17 Winston-Salem
18 Salisbury
19 Rodanthe/Walk of the Surfmen
20 Cooleemee/Mill Hill
21 Durham
22 Wilson
23 Favorite Playgrounds
    a. Pinehurst
    b. Asheville
24 Jones Lake State Park
25 Fontana Dam
26 Charlotte
27 Research Triangle Park
28 Occoneechee Speedway
29 Chapel Hill/America's First State University
30 Reed Gold Mine
31 Mount Mitchell State Park
32 Shut-In Trail
33 Kitty Hawk/Wright Brothers NM
34 Greensboro/The Greensboro Four

Discovering, Settling, and Forming a State

Fort Raleigh and the Freedmen's Colony

In 2011, the National Park Service reported that nearly 300,000 people visited Fort Raleigh National Historic Site. While some may have come because they were enjoying the magnificent Outer Banks and Cape Hatteras National Seashore, and they couldn't spend all day on the beach, others came, and will continue to come, because of the exquisite story of how the country we live in today tried to take shape here. When visitors arrive, they may know something about the role Fort Raleigh played in the first European attempts at settling the New World. But they may not be aware that hundreds of years later, during the Civil War era, this narrow strip of land also became meaningful for a colony of recently freed slaves who hoped the island would give them their own new beginning. In some ways, this walk has it all: an intersection of very different cultures, mystery, failure—and hope. It's a great place to begin your time travels through North Carolina history.

Historical Context

For ages, the Roanoke Island natives looked out to the east, over the water, perhaps on occasion admiring the sunrise. Then one day, big wooden ships appeared on the horizon. For the Native Americans on the island, perhaps the 1584 appearance of Arthur Barlowe and Philip Amadas, English sea captains charged with finding a good place to establish a colony for Queen Elizabeth I, was a harmless curiosity.

The newcomers offered gifts, the Indians offered fish, and over the ensuing days the two groups traded items. When the expedition returned to England later in the year, two natives, Manteo and Wanchese, sailed with it. The men were taught English and used to help generate excitement about the prospect of founding a permanent colony in the New World. When the captains reported what they had seen, they described "a most pleasant and fertile ground." Though scholars point out that Manteo developed a favorable opinion of England during this trip and that Wanchese did not, one can still wonder about their amazement upon experiencing life in England.

The Roanoke Indians lived in what scholars believe were one of the twenty Native American settlements that dotted that swath of the North American continent we call North Carolina. They are thought to be of the Algonquian culture, with language and other traits that connect them to other tribes along the Atlantic seaboard and into the continent's interior.

But in 1584, establishing a presence in the New World was a must for Queen Elizabeth I, and to that end, on March 25 she granted a royal patent to Sir Walter Raleigh, a favorite in her court. The document directed Raleigh to "discover, search, and finde out and view" any lands "not actually possessed by any Christian prince, nor inhabited by Christian people" and to "goe or travaile thither to inhabites or remained, there to build or fortifie." According to the contract, Raleigh had six years to show some results.

What motivated the queen and Raleigh? Some scholars assert that Raleigh was really a businessman pirate who believed that the New World would provide an outstanding base of operations to support his raids upon Spanish shipping, something the queen approved of. Others say that Raleigh craved attention from Queen Elizabeth and that helping her expand the influence of the English throne won him her approval. Still others suggest that both Raleigh and his queen were so full of religious fervor that they wanted to claim the New World for Protestantism. Another group suggests that Raleigh was a Renaissance man who savored adventure.

Likely the motivation included all of the above. Regardless, a pivotal moment in history's timeline had occurred, and life would forever be different for the natives who already lived on Roanoke Island and for the English who sought to expand the English-speaking world. After the 1584 expedition, two more would follow, one in 1585 and another in 1587.

The Walk

Begin behind the Fort Raleigh National Historic Site visitor center. Walk first to the restored Fort Raleigh. The mounds of dirt you see were reconstructed in 1950 after twelve years of archeological research; however, the ditches you see outlining the mounds are believed to be original. It is a tiny spot to begin colonizing the New World.

As you observe the reconstruction, consider why Darby Glande, Erasmus Clefs, Joyce Archard, and Audry Tappan, just to name a few men

These reconstructed earthworks suggest how the walls of Raleigh's original fort might have looked.

who signed up for the 1585 expedition, would want to spend eleven weeks being tossed about on the Atlantic Ocean in a small wooden boat to arrive here. The promise of opportunity and wealth clearly outweighed their fears.

Ultimately, however, the colonists begged their leader, Ralph Lane, to take them home. When Sir Francis Drake appeared in 1586, they departed. The colonists were absolutely separated from the rhythm of life in England and overwhelmed by the effort needed to establish a colony. The initially friendly relationships with the Roanoke Island Indians had soured: though the Indians had shared what food they could with the colonists, the colonists had not worked to plant their own food. When the Native Americans grew impatient with the dependent colonists, the colonists decided that perhaps the Indians meant to starve them at the very least, or wage war and kill them at the very worst. Lane, a military man, decided to kill the Native Americans before they killed him and his men. About a week later, Drake appeared and the expedition departed in failure.

With the 1587 expedition, Sir Raleigh tried a new model because the military model he had attempted in 1585 had so miserably failed. This time wives—two of whom were pregnant—and families came along, and each man was deeded a 500-acre plot. Under the best of circumstances in the 1500s, childbirth could kill a woman, so when Eleanor Dare gave birth to Virginia Dare, the first English child born in the New World, and Marger Harvye delivered her son Dyonis, prospects for success of the colony looked somewhat bright. The colonists built homes.

Nonetheless, records indicate that the 1587 expedition was troubled. Arriving in July, the colonists stepped into a hostile environment. Relations with Native Americans were uneasy because of the events of the 1585 expedition, and supplies were running short. After the birth of his granddaughter, Virginia, Governor John White returned to England for supplies. Though he intended to return quickly, Queen Elizabeth pressed his ship into service against the Spanish Armada. White could not return until 1590.

When White did return, the colonists of the 1587 expedition were gone. The now legendary clues they left behind—CRO carved on a tree, and CROATOAN carved on a palisade—came to naught. Moreover, the colonists had not carved the Maltese cross on something, the signal they had agreed to use if trouble arose. No one knows exactly what happened, but some historians think that the colonists were attacked by Indians, and those not killed were assimilated into area tribes. The question of what happened to the first English child born in the New World would never be answered, though theories would abound. While modern archaeologists have found bricks and roofing tiles, they have never actually uncovered home sites. While permanent English settlements would take root in Jamestown, Virginia, and in Plymouth, Massachusetts, another seventy years would pass before settlement would be attempted on Roanoke Island again.

Look to the left of the restored fort for signs to the Thomas Hariot Nature Trail. Thomas Hariot was, in 1586, one of England's leading scientists. He founded the English school of algebra—Manteo and Wanchese had been his students while they visited England—and was building telescopes about the time Galileo was doing likewise. Hariot also discovered the laws of refraction independently of Descartes. When selected to travel with the 1587 expedition, Hariot was living in Raleigh's home teaching math and navigation to would-be ship pilots.

Traveling with the second expedition, Hariot described what he saw; his notes reference much about the wonders and opportunities in the New World and little about the hardships. Yet hardships abounded. As you walk the Thomas Hariot Trail, consider the questions posed on the trail marker:

- How could you survive in these woods without outside supplies?
- What would you need to survive for several years?
- Are those necessities here?
- Do you know how to convert the resource into a usable form?

Subsequent markers give insight into how Native Americans could and did use the available resources. They ate medlars (persimmons) and acorns, and, perhaps surprisingly, they also ate greenbriar, that slightly heart-shaped, thorny vine many of us pull up as weeds from our gardens. They ate fish; they planted corn. In addition to discovering what the Native Americans ate, the first colonists discovered the native scuppernong grape, now recognized as North Carolina's state fruit. Colonists reported that they had found grapevines that "covered every shrub and climbed the tops of high cedars. In all the world a similar abundance was not to be found." Moreover, the Native Americans enjoyed a system of life not based upon property ownership and the drive to amass riches, a system unlike that which the colonists were accustomed to in England and had fully intended to model here.

This monument commemorates the Freedmen's Colony that once stood on Roanoke Island.

Return to the visitor center to walk to, and then through, the location of the Freedmen's Colony. Before leaving the visitor center, look for the large stone monument to the colony, erected in 2001. Next, cross the grass as if you're walking to the Elizabethan Gardens, but aim for the far side of the parking loop. Look for a sign marking the Freedom Trail. Green blazes also mark the way. As you walk to the water's edge, the trail travels along what was likely the southern edge of the Freedmen's Colony. (The center of the colony was further northwest on Roanoke Island.)

After the Civil War erupted in April 1861, the Confederacy assumed control of existing forts and built new ones to keep shipping lanes open for blockade runners. Union troops tried to strangle the Confederacy by capturing and closing the shipping lanes. Because Hatteras Inlet (to the south) was a major outlet for North Carolina ports to the Atlantic Ocean, fighting between Union and Confederate forces took place there first.

On August 29, 1861, when Forts Hatteras and Clark fell, pressure shifted north to Roanoke Island. Although Confederate forces tried to fortify the island, their efforts were ultimately doomed. On February 7, 1862, Union Brigadier General Ambrose E. Burnside landed with 7,500 men on the southwestern side of the island. On February 8, fighting began. Soon the Union forces won.

The Union victory enticed mainland slaves to flee to Roanoke Island, for they hoped to find freedom there. Union soldiers were aware of the coincidence of their surroundings and that of the first, failed colonists. Alfred S. Roe of the 24th Massachusetts wrote, "there was a charm in standing where the brave pioneers of Sir Walter may have been."

After he had taken Roanoke Island in 1862, General Burnside declared the 1,000 or so slaves on Roanoke Island free. Burnside's men started helping the freedmen build a new, hopefully permanent, community, complete with a school and churches. In April 1863, Major General John G. Foster appointed the Reverend Horace James from Massachusetts to be "Superintendent of all Blacks." Letters from James show that he clearly saw himself as helping to build a "New Social Order." In a letter to the *Congregationalist* dated September 5, 1863, James wrote, "We are beginning in the very wilderness, to lay the foundations of [a] new empire, but the results when carved out to their proper results no mortal mind can foresee. We sow in faith, and expect to reap in joy." By the summer of 1863, he and his assistants had laid out a New England–style village, stretching from Weir's Point to Pork Point on the Croatan Sound side of the island. The approximately 600 refugee families would be given one-acre lots. James foresaw light industry in the form of sawmills and fisheries and an agricultural trade in wine made from scuppernong grapes.

Life in the colony, however, was not good. Though missionaries arrived to help, they were overwhelmed. Estimates vary, but by the end of the war, the town contained anywhere from 3,500 to 6,000 residents. Missionaries thought they would be helping educate slaves and transition them to freedom but instead found themselves trying to nurse the

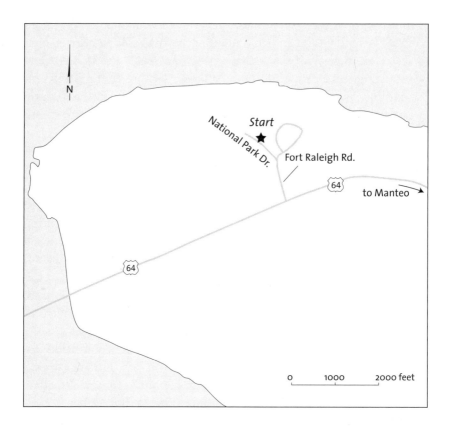

freedmen through smallpox, cholera, and dysentery. Because the colony wasn't yet self-supporting, the government and northern churches provided rations. Writes Patricia Click in *Time Full of Trial: The Roanoke Island Freedmen's Colony 1862–1867*, "the missionaries recognized that working for a wage so as to save and spend taught self-discipline and self-reliance, but these goals exceeded people's ability to pay."

Not long after the war ended, the white former owners of the land began petitioning the government to return their land, most noting that they hadn't really taken sides during the war. The light industry had not taken hold, and several shad seasons had proven scant. Scuppernong production hopes had not been met. When President Andrew Johnson restored the land to the prewar white owners and provided them amnesty, many freedmen slowly returned to the mainland to work as sharecroppers for their former owners. Vegetation eventually erased any signs of the town.

Near the water's edge, the trail loops. The right side leads to the water and the vicinity of Weir's Point. The left side leads to a picnic table and to the signs that mark the town and the former forts. Beyond the bridge remains is Pork Point. Not until the late 1980s and early 1990s were any remnants of the Freedmen's Colony uncovered.

Return to the visitor center by the same trail that brought you here.

Walk Details

HOW TO FIND IT: Fort Raleigh National Historic Site (1401 National Park Drive) is located on the coast of North Carolina in Manteo, on Roanoke Island. Signs on US 64 will direct you to the entrance.

LENGTH: 3 miles

SURFACE: Sand, coastal grasses

RESTROOMS: Located to the side of the visitor center

FOOTWEAR: Sneakers

PETS: OK on a leash

MAP: Available at the visitor center

BEWARE: Warm weather may bring snakes onto the trail.

GOOD TO KNOW: The town the freedmen built was one of three major colonies of newly freed slaves that developed in North Carolina in 1865. The other two freedmen's colonies were in the vicinity of Beaufort and New Bern.

Edenton

COLONIAL CAPITAL

To understand Edenton's place in North Carolina history, you must delve into the rich history of the Albemarle region. Known first as the Town on Queen Anne's Creek, Edenton was renamed at its incorporation in 1723 for Charles Eden, a proprietary governor whose administration was suspected of collaborating with the infamous pirate Blackbeard. After its founding, Edenton quickly surpassed Bath, North Carolina's oldest incorporated town and port, as the largest town in the colony and its de facto capital. Why? Among the reasons were its geographical blessings: Edenton's harbor was deeper than that of Bath, which meant that its harbor could accommodate larger ships and more commerce. In addition, Edenton lay sixty miles closer to the more stable Virginia colony than Bath did. Finally, northern Tuscarora Indians hadn't ravaged Edenton as the southern Tuscarora tribes had New Bern.

Although economic forces eventually dealt Edenton an unfavorable hand, a story in *Harper's Magazine* from 1857 opined that Edenton was "all the prettier" for it because old architecture had not been razed to make room for new. *Harper's* was right. Finding a more pleasant place to watch the sun sink over the water, especially during the winter, is difficult. Come spring, when flowers burst with color, walking Edenton and soaking in the wonderful architecture is an absolute joy. Even in the summer, breezes waft in from the bay, keeping days from becoming too oppressive. A jewel of stately, colonial beauty, Edenton produced some of the state's most influential colonial leaders. It also was the starting point for one of the most influential and widely read slave narratives in American literary history.

Historical Context

To understand the immense struggles of North Carolina's earliest years, think of our state as a start-up company. Like most start-up ventures, it experienced managerial challenges and damaging personnel issues.

The business venture we know today as North Carolina began in 1663, when Charles II of England thanked eight of his closest supporters with an enormous tract of land in the New World. (They had helped the monarchy regain the throne after a civil war and the beheading of Charles I in 1649.) That land, the Carolina Province, stretched from the south shore of the Albemarle Sound to about thirty miles north of St. Augustine, Florida. It stretched as far to the west as anyone knew.

These eight supporters, the Lords Proprietors, were free to manage the province and to reap its bounty as they saw fit, which is where the struggles began. Though accomplished and well connected, the original eight Proprietors were ill-suited to running a business that was 3,000 miles away. They were of different ages. They possessed different levels of education and sophistication. They had differing sensibilities. Their actions suggest that they had a high level of greed. In addition, for the sixty-seven years that the Carolina Province was a proprietary colony, fifty different men held the title of Proprietor, which resulted in instability in the managerial ranks.

Although the Proprietors may have disagreed on how to run the business, they did, for the most part, agree on one item: most had no desire to leave the good life in England for the wilds of Carolina. That being the case, they tried to find reliable men to govern the colony for them. In the sixty-seven years that the Carolina Province was a proprietary colony, twenty-four men governed the colony. Unfortunately, many of them were of questionable quality. Squabbles, intrigue, and mayhem followed them.

Some were bona fide scoundrels. Others were benignly inept. Still others were simply overwhelmed by challenges. Although they are little remembered today, their actions make for some astounding reading and may cause you to wonder how we ever managed to become a functioning colony at all, and to realize that the stability Edenton achieved was, in itself, a remarkable accomplishment.

Despite instability in its administration, the colony nevertheless grew over this period. Bath, North Carolina's first town, was established in 1705. In 1712, the colony was split, creating North Carolina and South Carolina. Then, in 1714, the Lords Proprietors sent North Carolina a governor who would guide the colony for over ten years: Charles Eden. With Eden, who owned property in Bath, at the helm, life slowly improved for the Albemarle region. In part, Eden was an amiable governor. He passed the Liberty of Conscience Act to protect the Quakers and met his first Assembly here in 1715. He tried to settle the ongoing boundary dispute with Virginia. But his administration's purported collusion with Edward Teach, better known as Blackbeard, proved scandalous.

The Mercy Act, promulgated in England by George I, said that pirates who were terrorizing ships in the Atlantic could surrender, throw themselves at the mercy of the Crown, and be pardoned. Teach, a shrewd opportunist, surrendered to Eden. At his trial, Teach was found to be a privateer—not a pirate. Thus transformed into an independent businessman, Teach received his pardon from Eden and settled into the good life in Bath.

Teach often claimed to travel to the West Indies "on business." When he returned, his ships full of cargo, he sold the goods to town residents. Though some residents were happy with this business model, others were not. Rumors abounded that Eden was on the take from Teach and that Teach had not really given up his pirating ways. Citizens tried to stop the racket, finally enlisting the help of Virginia governor Alexander Spotswood. Spotswood sent ships to battle Blackbeard. On November 22, 1718, Lieutenant Robert Maynard engaged the old pirate in the waters off Ocracoke Island, killing him and eighteen of his men.

Around this time, Eden sold his property in Bath and moved near the Chowan River, close to the Town on Queen Anne's Creek. Though implicated in wrongdoing related to Blackbeard, Eden was nonetheless popular. The colonists had lived well on his watch. To honor Eden after his death in 1722, the Town on Queen Anne's Creek renamed itself Edenton. Slowly the base of political power shifted from Bath to Edenton, despite the arrival of several more corrupt proprietary governors. (One of the last, George Burrington, was particularly vile. Ill-tempered and quarrelsome, Burrington assaulted a local merchant and tried to burn down his house. Within months of assuming his duties, he attacked Christopher Gale, the chief justice of the colony. Gale's deposition in England provides a remarkable picture of a governor out of control: Burrington had made several speeches in which he vowed to "slitt [Gale's] nose, crop his ears and lay him in irons." Though Gale returned from England with orders to oust the hated, volatile governor, Burrington did not leave Edenton immediately. He stayed and harassed the next governor, Richard Everard. In particular, Burrington tried goading Everard into a duel by calling him "a Noodle and an ape.")

In 1729 North Carolina ceased to be a proprietary colony. Seven of the Lords Proprietors transferred all of their rights in the colony back to the Crown, with only John Carteret, second Earl Granville, maintaining rights to his share of the land (though he had no say in the running of the government). Though Edenton vied to be the permanent capital of the colony, North Carolina citizens needed a more centrally located capital. When a 1795 hurricane decreased the navigability of the Roanoke Inlet such that ships couldn't reach Edenton as easily as they could other ports, Edenton's strength diminished. The construction of the Dismal Swamp Canal in 1805 proved even more deadly: it shifted commerce in northeastern North Carolina to the busier ports in Norfolk, Virginia. Soon, the Edenton wharves that had once been so busy fell quiet, and North Carolina's political battles shifted to other towns.

The Walk

This walk begins at Colonial Waterfront Park, which faces Edenton Bay at the end of Broad Street. Instead of seeing the pleasure boats, imagine a harbor busy with sloops, brigs, and schooners. As you enjoy the wonderful colonial architecture, be aware that Edenton's wealth was built largely on the backs of slaves whose labor was essential to the development of agriculture in the surrounding countryside.

Walk one block to Water Street. Look for the distinctive Cupola House (408 South Broad Street). Built sometime between 1724 and 1725 for ship owner Richard Sanderson and then updated in 1758 for Francis Corbin, Lord Granville's land agent in the colony, the Cupola House today is Edenton's most notable house and a contender for one of the most easily recognized in the state.

An influential man, Corbin was initially so respected that Hillsborough briefly called itself Corbinton. (Likewise, Salisbury has a Corbin Street.) Corbin was a friend of James Innes (for whom Salisbury's Innes Street is named), and after Innes died, Corbin married Innes's widow. Ultimately, Corbin later came under fire for land-grant abuses and was forcibly seized and taken under armed guard to Enfield.

The original woodwork in the first floor of the Cupola House, thought to be among the finest in the South, was sold to the Brooklyn Museum of Art in 1918. The museum bought the second floor also, but outraged Edenton citizens bought it back and reinstalled it. The house today is privately owned and managed by the Cupola House Association.

Turn right to walk along Water Street to the cannons. Brought to Edenton by William Borritz, captain of the French ship *Sacré Coeur de Jésus* in 1779, they were intended to arm the colonies in their revolt against England. The cannons were put out of commission nearly a century later by Union troops who quipped that the artillery held greater danger to the men who stood behind them than the men in front. The ship that

The Cupola House is one of the most distinctive houses in North Carolina.

brought them lies submerged in the bay. In 1980, underwater archeologists searched for it, locating hand-wrought spikes that likely secured wooden deck planks.

Near the cannons stands the Joseph Hewes monument. Joseph Hewes, a successful Edenton shipping merchant, represented North Carolina in the Continental Congress in Philadelphia. He later served as one of North Carolina's signers of the Declaration of Independence. Hewes put his entire fleet at the disposal of the Revolutionary cause, and some historians credit him with suggesting that the country needed a navy and with enlisting the services of John Paul Jones in the effort against the British navy. Hewes helped draft the state's constitution of 1776.

As the colony's leading political men met in Edenton in October 1774, they were openly defying royal governor Josiah Martin. In addition to selecting delegates to the upcoming Continental Congress, they passed a number of resolutions, one of which banned British cloth and tea. As the men passed their resolutions, some of their wives and daughters met in Penelope Barker's home (505 South Broad Street, alongside the bay) to show their support for the men's actions. Fifty-one women signed the pact to support the nonimportation act, agreeing that they would not "conform to the Pernicious Custom of Drinking Tea" and that they would not "promote ye wear of any manufacturer from England until such time that all acts which tend to enslave our Native country shall be repealed." In holding their "tea party," they became the first group of women in the colonies to take a political stand against the Crown, which was quite a shocking development at that time. In England, a political cartoonist satirized the women in a most unflattering way, giving them piggish faces. Arthur Iredell, whose brother James would soon join Edenton's pantheon of famous residents, sarcastically wrote that "there are few places in America which possesses so much female artillery as Edenton."

Walk through the village green to the Chowan County Courthouse on East King Street. Look for the Edenton Teapot, which commemorates the Edenton Tea Party.

The first Chowan Courthouse, built in 1728, was an unremarkable wooden structure—except for the smell. Virginia planter and surveyor William Byrd remarked that it held the "air of a Common Tobacco House." Today's courthouse dates to 1767. Historians suspect that John Hawks, architect of Tryon Palace, served as architect.

Courthouse records show that much of the courthouse business concerned land grants and survey requests. Here, citizens settled civil disputes and held religious meetings. Some records indicate they took dance lessons here, too. The General Assembly met at the courthouse for the last time in 1743. Since then, the building has served a variety of civic purposes, including hosting a dinner for President James Monroe, who visited Edenton in 1819.

Step behind the courthouse to see the 1825 Chowan County Jail, the jailer's house, and re-created stocks, pillory, and whipping post. This jail, the oldest documented jail in North Carolina, was used until the 1970s.

Return to King Street and turn right to walk to Broad Street. At Broad Street, turn right to walk to Church Street. At Church Street, turn right and walk one block to the Iredell House (105 East Church Street).

James Iredell might have stayed in England had his family not fallen on hard times. But they did, and he set out for the New World to earn his living as a customs collector at Port Roanoke. Because the job wasn't demanding, Iredell started studying law with Samuel Johnston, another

The Edenton Teapot stands on the village green and commemorates the Edenton Tea Party.

famous Edentonian. Records indicate that Iredell was a very serious, responsible young man, making sure to send much of his earnings back home to support his family. According to H. G. Connor, Iredell wrote in a 1770 diary entry that "indolence in any is shameful, but in a young man quite inexcusable. Let me consider for a moment whether it will be worth my while to attempt making a figure in life, or whether I will be content with mediocrity of fame and circumstances."

Iredell obviously decided to make something of himself, for within three years he was serving as the king's deputy attorney for Hertford, Perquimans, and Tyrrell Counties, mostly settling land disputes. As he traveled about he often wrote in his diary that he was "heartily tired of this cursed place."

As Revolution drew ever closer, Iredell became a political essayist, urging people to assert themselves but still support the Crown. He also helped establish the North Carolina court system, again necessitating that he travel the state as he toured North Carolina's court circuit, which included Wilmington, New Bern, Edenton, Halifax, Hillsborough, and Salisbury.

Ultimately, Iredell's political stance caused a rich uncle to disinherit him. But it also catapulted Iredell to both the state and national stages. During the war he litigated against Loyalists. Nearing the end of his private practice in 1780, Iredell had clients as far away as Petersburg, Virginia. His political views also brought him the notice of George Washington, who appointed Iredell to the first U.S. Supreme Court. The job had a familiar feel to Iredell, for in those days justices traveled a circuit to hear cases.

Among Iredell's most notable contributions to North Carolina is that, with William Davie, Iredell led the fight for North Carolina to ratify the U.S. Constitution. When the first attempt failed at the Hillsborough convention, Davie and Iredell published, at their own expense, the minutes of that meeting for the population to read for themselves. Later, in 1789, North Carolina voted to join the union. Iredell also espoused judicial review. In the case of *Calder vs. Bull* (1798), he argued against grounding the decisions of the court in the laws of nature. Instead, he argued that the only basis for invalidating a legislative statute, whether erected by Congress or any state legislature, was if it violated a provision of the U.S. Constitution.

Samuel Johnston, nephew of royal governor Gabriel Johnston, was Iredell's mentor. His service to the colony spanned the royal government, the American Revolution, the Articles of Confederation, and, finally, the federal government. In December 1770, Johnston supported the Crown and sponsored a bill to punish the Regulators (see chapter 4, Hillsborough, for more information about the Regulators). It asked the Regulators to turn themselves in or risk being shot on sight. In 1774, with Revolution plainly on the way, Johnston no longer supported the Crown. Writing to William Hooper, a North Carolina delegate to the Continental Congress and signer of the Declaration of Independence, Johnston said that "without courts to sustain the property and to exercise the talents of the Country, and the people alarmed and dissatisfied, we must do something to save ourselves." Within the next two years, Johnston served as North Carolina's acting governor when the last royal governor, Josiah Martin, fled. He later served as North Carolina's first state senator.

Return to Broad Street, cross Broad, and visit St. Paul's Church (100 West Church Street), the second-oldest church building in North Carolina. Even though the huge roots of the gnarly magnolia trees—not to mention the old, old boxwoods that are as tall as some of the trees—will draw your eye, look beyond them to the numerous headstones. Among the famous people buried here are proprietary governors Charles Eden and Walker Henderson and Thomas Pollock, who was acting governor at the close of the Tuscarora War and helped to rescue the embryonic

North Carolina colony on more than one occasion (see chapter 3, New Bern). As you enjoy the ambience here, appreciate that on June 19, 1776, less than a month before the country declared itself independent from England, several leading citizens met to assert their political stance. Minutes of the Vestry reveal that the citizens were struggling with how to be good subjects while at the same time asserting the right to govern themselves:

> We, the Subscribers, professing our Allegiance to the King and acknowledging the Constitutional executive power of Government do solemnly profess, testify and declare that we do absolutely believe that neither the Parliament of Great Britain nor any Member or constituent Branch thereof have a right to impose Taxes upon these Colonies to regulate the internal Policy thereof; and that all attempts by Fraud or Force to establish and exercise such claims & Powers are Violations of the Peace and Security of the People and ought to be resisted to the utmost, and that the People of this Province, singly and collectively, are bound by the Acts and Resolutions of the Continental and the Provincial Congresses because in both they are freely represented by persons chosen by themselves, and we do Solemnly and Sincerely promise and engage under the Sanction of Virtue, Honor and the Sacred Love of Liberty and our Country, to Maintain & Support all and every, the Acts, Resolutions & Regulations of the said Continental & Provincial Congresses to the utmost of our power and ability.

Exit the grounds of St. Paul's Church at Church Street, and turn right to walk to Granville Street. Turn left as if to return to the waterfront. Cross Queen Street and Eden Street, and then turn left onto King Street. Here you pass some of Edenton's beautiful homes. Their size and opulence indicate the affluence that Edenton enjoyed until the Dismal Swamp Canal was built. Of particular interest is Beverly Hall (114 West King Street). This house once held a private bank and for some time served as the branch office of the State Bank of North Carolina.

Editions of the *Edenton Gazette* from the 1830s provide insight into the lives of the local plantation society of the Albemarle region. Relaying the events of the day, the paper notes the passing of Revolutionary patriots, the arrival of ships from Boston, Philadelphia, and Baltimore, and the arrival in Boston of the first rhinoceros in America. Here and there the newspaper tells stories of duels and of love gone bad. One particularly gruesome story concerned a Miss Dolly Griffin who, according to the paper, "discarded" William Parker, a young man who had courted her for nearly three years and evidently expected to marry her. He arrived at a dinner party, treating Dolly "rudely." Later that evening he ambushed her and her friend on their ride home, killing both Dolly and himself. The paper also reports on the tensions that arose when Nat Turner led his uprising in southeastern Virginia.

At King Street, turn right to walk to Colonial Waterfront Park again, this time to consider it in a new light. As you look at the nooks and crannies of the water's edge, think of the story of Harriet Jacobs, born into slavery in Edenton in 1813. Her autobiography, *Incidents in the Life of a Slave Girl* (1860), is intimately tied to Edenton, and scholars consider it a significant work of African American literature. It provides a harrowing narrative of what life was like for slaves in early nineteenth-century North Carolina.

At her birth, Harriet became the property of Margaret Horniblow, though Harriet did not understand that she was a slave until the age of six. Harriet hoped that perhaps Margaret, having taught Harriet to read, write, and sew, might free her. Such was not the case. At her death in 1825, Margaret willed Harriet to her three-year-old niece, Mary Norcom, and Harriet moved into the home of Dr. James Norcom, where she lived under constant threat of sexual abuse by her new owner's father. For years, the harassment continued, even though Harriet sought a relationship with another local white man, with whom she had two children. Finally, Harriet went into hiding for six years, in the attic of the house of her grandmother, Molly Horniblow, a free black who lived near what is now Colonial Waterfront Park. Harriet eventually escaped to freedom, slipping away after hiding in the marshy areas of Edenton Bay. To do so, she had help from a free black man who identified a sea captain who would take her to freedom without reselling her into slavery or trying to collect a reward. The man arranged with two oarsmen with rowboats to meet Harriet at the wharf and posted lookouts to try to assure a successful escape. *Incidents in the Life of a Slave Girl* tells a frightening story of trying to avoid the snakes as they slithered over her while she waited for the boatman to ferry her to freedom. In New York, a friend helped Harriet purchase her freedom.

Walk along Water Street again, past the cannons and the village green, to Oakum Street. Bend left, and then turn right on King Street to walk to the Edenton Cotton Mill. At the Edenton Cotton Mill, look for an out-

and-back jaunt to Queen Anne Creek along a greenway path. This walk suggests what the Edenton Bay area looked like before it was ever settled. As you pass by the Edenton Cotton Mill, observe the modern preservation work taking place in town. The mill, built in 1898, supported over seventy homes in the nearby mill village.

Return to Oakum Street via King Street. At Oakum Street, turn right to walk to Gale Street. At Gale Street, turn left to pass by the house of Hannibal Badham Jr. (116 East Gale Street). Hannibal Sr. was a well-known African American builder in Edenton, and his wife Evelina opened the first recognized school for African Americans in Edenton. Badham built this house for his son.

Continue walking along Gale Street. Cross Broad Street. Look for the Kadesh AME Zion Church (119 East Gale Street). Behind this church the Edenton Normal and Industrial College once stood, organized by the congregation in 1895.

At the corner of Gale and Broad Streets, turn left to return to Colonial Waterfront Park. Before departing, look for the Roanoke River Lighthouse. This lighthouse dates to 1887 and gives an excellent idea of the living conditions for lighthouse keepers of the time. The lighthouse, in service until 1941, is thought to be the last original screw-pile lighthouse in the country.

Walk Details

HOW TO FIND IT: Edenton is located in northeastern North Carolina, on US 17. Colonial Waterfront Park is located at the end of Broad Street (US 17 Business).

LENGTH: About 3 miles

SURFACE: Paved

RESTROOMS: At the Historic Edenton visitor center (108 North Broad Street) and at Colonial Waterfront Park

FOOTWEAR: Sneakers

PETS: OK on a leash

MAP: Available at the visitor center

GOOD TO KNOW: Guided walking tours and trolley tours, available at the visitor center, further explain the beautiful architecture that abounds in Edenton.

For more information, visit www.edenton.nchistoricsites.org.

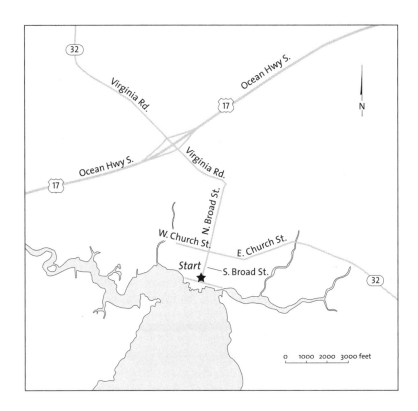

For More Exploration:
Bath, Original Anchor of the Albemarle Region

If time permits, take a side trip to Bath. The Historic Bath visitor center provides a brochure that details a one-mile walking tour of Bath's historic buildings. The town's Main Street is original.

Established in 1705, Bath was, by 1708, thriving, with twelve houses and about fifty residents. The town was also home to North Carolina's first library. Christopher Gale, North Carolina's first chief justice and the man who helped rid the colony of the reviled George Burrington, lived here, as did John Lawson, one of North Carolina's most famous early explorers and author of *A New Voyage to Carolina*. Make sure you see St. Thomas Church (Craven Street), the oldest church building in the state. No records exist that explain who financed the church or where the materials came from. However, church documents indicate that the church—with its paved floor, square pews, and high pulpit—is faithful to the style of Anglican churches built in England. Note the empty space to the right and somewhat behind the church. Early maps indicate that this spot was reserved for a courthouse, though one was never built there.

As you gaze out across the water, consider that not only did colonists fear attacks from the Tuscarora. They also feared attack by pirates. The early 1700s are often referred to as the golden age of pirates. Some estimates suggest that close to 1,500 pirates prowled the North American coastline. Whether Charles Eden was as much a crook as Edward Teach was we may never know. However, the working relationship between the two men helped pave the way for stability in the fledgling colony.

New Bern

ROYAL CAPITAL

The seat of North Carolina's royal government, New Bern lays claim to several firsts in the state: first newspaper, first bookstore, first post office, and first free school. The many beautiful mansions speak to New Bern's economic clout during the 1800s. No wonder, then, that in the 1940s the local boosters called their beloved town the "Athens of North Carolina."

Yet New Bern's riverside serenity masks an incredible spirit of determination and resilience. Settlers here withstood Tuscarora attacks and yellow fever epidemics. Later, they endured military occupation; they also rebuilt after devastating fires. Today the occasional hurricane tests their resolve. But New Bern survived—and thrives in a most gracious way.

Historical Context

New Bern's town flag, an eye-catching red and yellow banner, includes the image of a bear, a symbol that dates to the Middle Ages. Appearing on landscaping, city vehicles, and uniforms, the flag pays homage to Bern, Switzerland, home of Christoph Baron von Graffenried, the Swiss leader who founded New Bern in 1710.

Though well-connected in both Switzerland and England, Graffenried was in debt. When the Georg Ritter Company formed, Graffenried invested in it as a way to earn enough money to pay his creditors. The Ritter Company first planned to use Swiss paupers and Swiss Anabaptists to mine silver in the Pennsylvania and Virginia colonies. However, the company changed direction, buying 19,000 acres of the Carolina Province near the Neuse, Trent, and White Oak Rivers from the Lords Proprietors. The company also added some 650 German Palatines to the collection of colonists destined to settle in the area.

The Walk

From the Craven County Convention and Visitor Center (203 South Front Street), walk right to East Front Street. Turn left to walk about three and

one-half blocks along East Front Street to Council Bluff Green. Graffenried is believed to have landed near here with his colonists.

Even by standards of the day, their journey was difficult. The first group, the Palatines, left Gravesend, England, in January, enduring tainted food, disease, and pummeling winter storms. Only about half of them survived the trip across the Atlantic, and those who did had their clothes stolen by French pirates who plundered their ship as it arrived at the James River. Graffenried soon followed with a second group, 150 Swiss paupers.

Two men helped Graffenried establish New Bern. Thomas Pollock, without whom New Bern might not have survived, was a wealthy planter. Legend has it that Pollock saved King James VI of Scotland from death by a wild boar attack, and, in thanks, King James granted Pollock 40,000 acres near Bath—but this story is likely myth. After Graffenried had united his two groups in Hampton, Virginia, they traveled to Bath via cart and foot. Thomas Pollock, by then thriving in Albemarle, helped Graffenried secure water passage to complete the journey to the Neuse River area, and he sold much needed supplies to the survivors of the journey. John Lawson, who in 1700–1701 conducted a 57-day, 550-mile survey of the Carolina Province, also helped Graffenried lay the new town out in the shape of a cross on the site of the Neusioc town Chattooka. Graffenried called his town Bern on the Neuse.

Though well-prepared with colonists skilled in trades and agriculture, Graffenried was stepping into a complicated and dangerous situation. First among his troubles was the feud in Bath between Edward Hyde and Thomas Cary. Each man believed he was the rightfully appointed governor of the Lords Proprietors, and their feud diverted resources and energy away from New Bern. Compounding Graffenried's problems were increasing hostility with the Tuscarora Indians, whose well-established town sites and surrounding lands were being seized with regularity by encroaching colonists. In 1710 the Tuscarora petitioned the colonial government of Pennsylvania to protest the taking of their lands as well as the settlers' enslavement of Tuscarora people in the Carolina colony and to let the tribe move to Pennsylvania, but the petition fell on deaf ears. Skirmishes between the Tuscarora and colonists were escalating.

Complicating these tensions was a rift between Lawson and Graffenried that arose out of Lawson's site choice for Graffenried's settlement. Graffenried claimed Lawson said the area was uninhabited. But a southern Tuscarora tribe clearly lived there. Graffenried bought the land from the Tuscarora but reported that Lawson suggested that he not pay them. The tribe did leave, but they were not happy.

Within the year, their unhappiness erupted into warfare when Lawson invited Graffenried to explore the Neuse River with him in mid-September 1711. Within days, the aggrieved Tuscarora captured the men and took them to Chief Hancock's town of Catechna, not far from today's Snow Hill. They executed Lawson but let Graffenried go free.

Lawson's execution did not mark the end of the conflict, however, and, seeing that New Bern lacked support from Bath, the Tuscarora waged war on the settlers. In a sunrise attack on September 22, 1711, the Tuscarora tribe led by King Hancock swooped into the settlements along the Pamlico and Neuse Rivers, killing 130–40 colonists, slaughtering livestock, and burning homes. Not prepared for war, the colonists sought refuge in homes that they could quickly fortify. Graffenried had secured a promise from King Hancock that New Bern, and any Swiss or Palatine home bearing an N (for Neuse), would be spared.

The fighting raged into 1712. White settlers paid for scalps and sold captured Tuscarora into slavery; the Tuscarora slaughtered colonists and livestock. In late December, trying to help the North Carolina colonists, Col. John Barnwell of South Carolina marched with more than 300 Indians and 30 white militiamen. By April 1713, with the aid of North Carolina militia, he surrounded the Tuscarora at Fort Neoheroka, near Snow Hill.. After even more bloodshed, the Tuscarora could no longer fight. Thomas Pollock served as a key negotiator, enlisting King Tom Blunt of the northern tribes to subdue Chief Hancock of the southern tribes.

Though the Tuscarora wars were over, Graffenried had lost his motivation. He mortgaged the enterprise to Thomas Pollock and returned to Europe, saying "no good star shone for me" of his failed attempt to establish the colony.

Return to the visitor center. Turn right onto South Front Street and walk four blocks to Metcalf Street. The streets you cross—Craven, Middle, and Hancock—are among New Bern's oldest. (Hancock Street honors William Hancock, whose house served as a courthouse from 1715 until 1716, not Tuscarora chief King Hancock.)

After Thomas Pollock helped quell the Tuscarora attacks, the remaining colonists gutted out their tenuous circumstance until the town finally began to thrive. The source of early prosperity? The mighty Neuse River that you see along South Front Street. Because the Neuse reaches farther inland into North Carolina than does the Chowan River of Edenton, New Bern wharves busily shipped naval stores and lumber from the state's interior. Despite that advantage over Edenton, New Bern's commercial interests faced stiff competition from those in Wilmington. The Cape Fear also reached far into North Carolina's eastern plain, plus Wilmington had quicker and better access to the Atlantic. So, to woo commerce and thereby combat Wilmington's advantages, local businesses advertised New Bern's lower shipping fee. By 1769, at least six wharves dotted the New Bern riverfront.

At Metcalf Street, turn left and follow the arc of Front Street around Tyron Palace (610 Pollock Street). Where Front Street meets Eden Street, follow Eden Street to walk along the side of Tryon Palace to Pollock Street. Commerce wasn't the only thing New Bern wooed in the middle 1700s; the town wanted to be the seat of the royal government. Its bargaining chip was its location between Edenton and Wilmington. William Tryon, the governor after Arthur Dobbs, bought New Bern's sales pitch.

A man with a mixed legacy in North Carolina, Tryon had sailed to America on a ship named the *Friendship*. Despite that happy omen, Tryon found himself amid political tensions when he arrived. In 1765, the same year that Tryon assumed control, King George III enacted the Stamp Act to pay for the debt England had incurred in the French and Indian War. The Stamp Act required all legal documents in the colonies—permits, commercial contracts, newspapers, wills, pamphlets, and playing cards—to carry a tax stamp. The colonists responded with anger. This was taxation without representation! Records suggest that Tryon was against the tax because it would take much-needed currency out of the province, and when the English parliament repealed the tax the next year, Tryon gladly announced it to the colony.

Thinking that he had finally won the colonists' goodwill, Tryon went to work: he built roads into the Carolina backcountry, built a postal infrastructure, and tried to settle boundary disputes with Virginia and South Carolina. Tryon also announced plans to construct a governmental building in New Bern.

Though the colonists welcomed internal improvements, they were not happy to pay a new tax to defray the cost of what they termed a palace, and they were angry at the corruption they believed to be taking place. The Regulators, the citizen-radicals who formed near Hillsborough, were ready to do battle, ensuring that the rest of Tryon's tenure would be rocky (See chapter 4, Hillsborough, for more information about the Regulators). In the interim, Tryon subdued the Regulators in battle at Alamance. Tryon didn't live in his palace very long. It opened in 1770, and by 1771, Tryon was transferred to New York.

Josiah Martin, the last of the royal governors, did live in the palace. Although likeable, Martin was staunchly loyal to the Crown, and he inherited Tryon's unresolved border disputes with Virginia, the consequences of the Regulation, and rising tensions over taxation. He fled New Bern in 1775, staying first at Fort Johnston. Fearing attack, he removed to the HMS *Cruizer*, a ship anchored offshore. Later instrumental in rallying the Scots of Cross Creek to fight at Moores Creek Bridge, Martin joined Lord Cornwallis in Cornwallis's South Carolina campaign. He resigned as royal governor in 1781.

North Carolina's first four governors—Richard Caswell, Abner Nash, Richard Spaight, and Alexander Martin—also lived in the palace.

Today's palace is not the one that Tryon built. The original palace burned in 1798; only the kitchen and stable offices survived. Over the years, the stable served as an apartment, a school, and a church. By the 1940s, dilapidated buildings, including the west-wing stable, crowded the area. Chaired by Maude Moore Latham, who willed over $1 million of her money to the project in 1951, the Tryon Palace Commission began a massive renewal project, the first of its kind in North Carolina. The rebuilt palace is faithful to the original. In 1939, research revealed a copy of the original drawing in papers held by the New-York Historical Society. The final plans that King George had approved appeared in the British Public Records office. When the reconstructed palace opened in 1959, the General Assembly met here to honor the effort.

At the intersection of Eden and Pollock Streets, turn right to walk a few yards to George Street and to the John Wright Stanly House (307 George Street). New Bernians are proud of John Wright Stanly and his fine house. George Washington was entertained there during his southern tour in 1791. From 1935 until 1965, the house served as New Bern's library.

Stanly arrived in New Bern after being wrongly imprisoned in Philadelphia for debt. His résumé indicates that he was a ship owner, a merchant, and a molasses distiller. Part of the reason Washington stayed here was that the house was empty; Stanly and his wife had both fallen victim to the 1789 yellow fever epidemic that swept New Bern, and the house they left behind was indeed fit for a president. But another reason Washington lodged here was that Stanly was also a successful Revolutionary War privateer who plundered British ships. The Lady Blessington cannon, which is semi-buried at the corner of Pollock and Middle Streets, purportedly came from a British ship Stanly plundered.

John Wright Stanly's two sons, John Wright Stanly Jr. and John Carruthers Stanly, are also among New Bern's notables. John Wright Stanly Jr. had political differences with another New Bern son, Richard D. Spaight. Spaight represented North Carolina in the Constitutional Convention and helped find the compromise between people who wanted a strong centralized government and those who did not. The first native-born governor of North Carolina, Spaight served in the state legislature and in the U.S. House of Representatives. Stanly, an ardent Federalist, served as a congressman. Their differences about the need for a strong centralized government escalated from private argument to public acrimony. Spaight took to the newspaper saying that he would not "suffer any man to impugn [his] character," and Stanly countered by saying that Spaight wanted "to play the hero, strut the bravo, to ape the duelist." Eventually, the two met to duel (you'll pass near the spot later in the walk). After four rounds, Stanly killed Spaight. Spaight's death provoked antidueling laws; Stanly fled because he faced criminal proceedings. When Stanly Jr. died in 1833, the house passed out of family control. Future owners included, ironically, Spaight's descendants.

John Carruthers Stanly, generally acknowledged to be the son of the elder Stanly, was born a slave. However, he gained his freedom at age twenty-one, with the help of his owners, the Stewart family. He became a barber and earned the moniker "Barber Jack." So successful was Barber Jack that he went on to become a large-scale landowner, an entrepreneur, and one of the richest men in the area. Though he bought his own family out of slavery, he was also one of the largest slave owners in Craven County.

Although Stanly is often the mentioned as a notable free black man of New Bern, the African American history tour sponsored by the New Bern Tours and Convention Services likes to point out that before the Civil War, black citizens, some 25 percent of whom were free, made up half the town's population. These free blacks owned their homes, operated a wide variety of businesses, and worked as doctors, teachers, and religious leaders as well as in other professions.

Return to Pollock Street, turn left, and walk five blocks through downtown New Bern to Front Street. At least one house on this stretch, 605 Pollock, is purported to be haunted; listen carefully for eerie piano waltzes when you pass it.

Prime among downtown New Bern's many historical sites is Christ Episcopal Church, at the corner of Middle and Pollock Streets. Established in 1715, the church received from King George II a silver communion service, a Bible, and a Book of Common Prayer, which are displayed inside. The sanctuary, sometimes called the Third church, dates to 1874. Outside, the open-air chapel signals the site of the first sanctuary. Look for headstones; the churchyard surrounding Christ Church was once the town's principal cemetery. Cedar Grove Cemetery, which appears later in this walk, became the town's primary cemetery after the yellow fever epidemic of 1800. As you pass Christ Church, look across Middle and Pollock Streets to Bradham's Pharmacy. Here, Caleb Bradham concocted a winning recipe for a cola drink, which was marketed as Pepsi-Cola after 1898.

City Hall, a stunning example of Second Empire architecture, dates to the early 1880s. The brownstone used to build it came from outside Sanford. On display inside is a flag that Bern, Switzerland, gave to New Bern in 1896. Outside is the distinctive Baxter Street Clock, one of the few four-faced, turn-of-the-century clocks still in use in America.

At East Front Street, turn left to walk five blocks to Johnson Street. Beautiful mansions stud this stretch and speak to the wealth that accumulated here in the 1800s from naval stores, lumber, and agriculture. The Coor-Bishop House (501 East Front Street) is but one such example.

When civil war erupted, wealthy New Bern became an important link in President Abraham Lincoln's strategy to blockade the Southern coastline. By March 1862, Union general Ambrose Burnside had staged a large army—15,000 men, 12 steamers, 23 schooners, 4 barks, 4 ships, and 1 brig—further down the Neuse, after taking Roanoke Island in February. He prepared to take New Bern.

The March weather didn't favor battle, and a story in the *Narragansett Historical Register* from 1891 notes that the Union soldiers described themselves as a "congregation of flies making a pilgrimage through molasses," and that they called their feet "mudhooks." The Confederates resisted but quickly withdrew to Kinston, some thirty-five miles away, causing New Bern to be the first coastal Southern city to fall into Union hands. The easy Union victory also gave rise to a joke:

New Bern City Hall proudly displays the Baxter Street Clock, one of the few four-faced, turn-of-the-century clocks still in use in America.

So much beautiful architecture to enjoy in New Bern, a testament to the wealth that this riverside port town helped build in North Carolina.

What's the difference between a Newberne Fight and a Newberne Flight?

An l - (ell) of a difference!

Union troops began a three-year occupation. Rebels would try three times, unsuccessfully, to retake the town.

After Burnside and the Union army began its occupation of New Bern, fugitive slaves began crowding into the town. Burnside faced enormous problems trying to feed, clothe, and house the fugitives. Part of the solution Burnside enacted was to establish nearby James City as a camp. Joe A. Mobley's book *James City: A Black Community in North Carolina 1863–1900* provides more detail about this facet of the Civil War and its impact.

David Cecelski's book *The Waterman's Song* also delves deeply into the history of New Bern during this time. Describing the maritime slave culture of towns and cities along North Carolina's coast, it tells the story of Abraham Galloway, a black man born in 1838 in Smithville (now Southport), North Carolina. Because, in part, of the increased freedom maritime slaves experienced, Galloway was able to conceal himself among barrels of turpentine tar on a ship bound for Philadelphia in 1857. Because of federal fugitive laws in Philadelphia, abolitionists there helped Galloway escape further away, into Canada. There Galloway worked as a brick mason and devoted himself to the activities of the Underground Railroad. Soon after General Burnside occupied New Bern, Galloway convinced authorities that because he knew the area, he could work as a spy. Soon Galloway arrived in New Bern as a spy for General Benjamin T. Butler. As more and more fugitive slaves came to New Bern, Galloway emerged as their leader. He was keenly interested that black citizens get a better outcome than being used as cannon fodder in the fighting that was still taking place. In that spirit, he negotiated for education and equal voting privileges. After the war, Galloway returned to the Wilmington area to advance the cause of newly freed black people there. (To learn more about Galloway's remarkable story, see Cecelski's book *The Fire of Freedom: Abraham Galloway and the Slaves' Civil War*.)

Turn left onto Johnson Street and walk four and one-half blocks to Queen Street. Look for the Charles Slover House (201 Johnson Street), which served as Union general Burnside's headquarters during the occupation. (It was later purchased by Caleb Bradham.) Look also for a marker that signals the spot of the Spaight-Stanly duel.

What isn't marked, however, is the now-demolished factory where Pepsi-Cola syrup was first manufactured. Standing at the corner of Johnson and Hancock streets, the factory was, in 1919, producing 1,200 gallons of syrup an hour. Caleb D. Bradham did well for himself despite his rocky start in life. He had first enrolled at the University of North Carolina but transferred to the University of Maryland to attend medical school. After three years, however, he quit because he could no longer afford the tuition. After teaching at Vance Academy and saving his money to return to Maryland to study pharmacy, Bradham started reading trade publications and experimenting with various flavors and syrups. By 1890 he had concocted a winning recipe. (How winning? The 2011 Annual Report states that PepsiCo generated more than $300 million in retail sales *each day* due to the popularity of its many brands, in addition to the soft drinks.)

Look also for the George White House (519 Johnson) and King Solomon's Lodge Number One, the first black Masonic Lodge in North Carolina. The house honors George White, a free black educated at Howard University who became a lawyer, state legislator, and U.S. congressman.

The marl gate of Cedar Grove Cemetery absorbs rainwater and then "weeps."
Legend advises visitors to avoid being hit by a "graveyard tear," lest they
become the next resident!

Cross Queen Street and take a slight left to Cedar Grove Cemetery. In the mid-1700s, Queen Street marked the northern edge of town. The area now home to the cemetery originally housed a horse-racing track. Later, however, as malaria epidemics filled the burial grounds of Christ Church, the church bought land here for a cemetery. The 1864 epidemic proved to be especially deadly: in September and October, malaria took 1,300 people, mainly Union soldiers and their friends and families. Today Cedar Grove Cemetery is home to a splendid collection of funerary art. If you enter the cemetery, be aware that the marl gate through which you enter has a legend all its own: the marl absorbs rain but dries as the rain slowly seeps out. Don't let a "graveyard tear" hit you; otherwise, you'll become the next resident of the cemetery, or so legend has it.

Recross Queen Street to return to Johnson Street, noting St. Peter's AME Zion Church at 617 Queen Street. Founded by James Walker Hood in 1863, this church served the newly freed slaves of post–Civil War New

Bern. It began life as the Rue Chapel African-American Methodist Episcopal congregation, one of the two oldest congregations in North Carolina. Many consider the church as the mother church of AME Zion churches in the South. Today's building is not original, however. The Great Fire of 1922 destroyed that structure.

Many stories emanate from St. Peter's, among them Sarah Dudley Pettey's. Sarah was born in 1869 into a world where she thought she could expect full civil rights. Although her parents and grandparents were slaves, Sarah was born free. She attended Scotia Seminary (forerunner of today's Barber-Scotia College) and later returned home to work as principal of the black graded school in New Bern. She later married Charles Pettey, who had been born a slave in Wilkes County, educated at Biddle Memorial Institute (forerunner of today's Johnson C. Smith University), and became a bishop in the church. His job gave Sarah a reason to write a newsletter, the *Star of Zion*, for the church. Sarah soon gave voice to the concerns of black citizens, and of black women in particular. Challenging the notion of "place," Dudley Pettey wrote, "Some would say that a woman is good in her place. This reminds me of what some white people say of the Negro: that 'He is good in his place.'"

Unfortunately, Sarah watched as disfranchisement of the 1890s first eroded and then destroyed the hopes of black people for fair and equal treatment. As the color line continued to harden, Sarah chose to move north after the death of her husband. Sarah Dudley Pettey died in 1906.

Also nearby is the Isaac Smith House (607 Johnson Street), the home of one of New Bern's wealthiest black citizens. Smith served as a representative in the North Carolina House of Representatives in 1898.

Turn right onto Metcalf Street; walk one block to New Street. Before turning left on to New Street, look right to the home of John Carruthers Stanly (501 New Street).

Turn left onto New Street, and walk past New Bern Academy. The first school in North Carolina established by law, the New Bern Academy building served as a hospital during the Civil War. In 1881, it became part of the New Bern Graded School System. The original building burned in 1795. This brick building dates to 1810.

Still on New Street, cross Hancock Street. Walk two blocks to Craven Street. This section of New Street contains many of New Bern's oldest churches. The First Presbyterian Church served as a hospital for Union soldiers during the Civil War. Another interesting historical fact is that Drury Lacy, pastor of this church and one-time president of Davidson College, opened Peace Institute (now William Peace University) together with his wife. Next appear Centenary Methodist Church (right) and St. Paul's Catholic Church (left). Local legend says that when the Great Fire of 1936 erupted in the Methodist church, the Catholic nuns across the street prayed for divine intervention. Though the ceiling did burn and collapse, the beautiful stained glass windows inside the Methodist church were spared.

At Craven Street, turn right to walk four blocks to return to the Craven County Convention and Visitor Center. Look for the house of Judge William Gaston (421 Craven Street), whom some scholars consider one of North Carolina's most influential political leaders.

The first student admitted to Georgetown College, forerunner of today's Georgetown University, Gaston later graduated from Princeton at the top of his class. He was one of the first state leaders to speak against slavery, doing so as early as 1831. Historians speculate that Gaston more keenly felt the wrong in slavery because he was Catholic. (Few Catholics lived in North Carolina in the early 1800s; their sparse numbers meant that finding a place to worship was difficult. Gaston was one of five Catholics selected in North Carolina to be allowed to conduct services in his home.) A member of the North Carolina Supreme Court, Gaston ruled in 1834 that a slave had the right to defend himself if his master attacked him without justification. In 1838, Gaston ruled that black people were indeed citizens and protected by the state constitution. However, Gaston also owned slaves. Gaston also interceded for his friend John Stanly Jr. after his duel with Spaight, helping his friend to avoid criminal charges, and he was president of the Bank of New Bern. He turned down the offer to serve as attorney general for William Henry Harrison. In 1833, Gaston introduced the bill to charter the North Carolina Railroad.

Though details of Gaston's political legacy may be forgotten, most North Carolinians recognize his poetic legacy: In 1840 Gaston penned the poem that was later put to music and made our state song. Some historians think that Gaston wrote the poem to counter the charge that North Carolina merited its "Rip Van Winkle" label. Though difficult to sing, the song nonetheless celebrates what is good about our state.

Carolina! Carolina! Heaven's blessings attend her!
While we live we will cherish, protect and defend her;
Tho' the scorner may sneer at and witlings defame her,
Still our hearts swell with gladness whenever we name her.

Hurrah! Hurrah! The Old North State forever!
Hurrah! Hurrah! The good Old North State!

Tho' she envies not others, their merited glory,
Say whose name stands the foremost, in Liberty's story,
Tho' too true to herself e'er to crouch to oppression,
Who can yield to just rule a more loyal submission?

[Chorus]

Plain and artless her sons, but whose doors open faster
At the knock of a stranger, or the tale of disaster.
How like the rudeness of the dear native mountains,
With rich ore in their bosoms and life in their fountains.

[Chorus]

And her daughters, the Queen or the forest resembling
So graceful, so constant, yet the gentlest breath trembling.
And true lightwood at heart, let the match be applied them,
How they kindle and flame! Oh! none know but who've tried
    them.

[Chorus]

Then let all those who love us, love the land that we live in,
As happy a region as on this side of heaven,
Where plenty and peace, love and joy smile before us,
Raise aloud, raise together the heart thrilling chorus.

[Chorus]

Beyond Gaston's house stands the architecturally splendid Craven County Courthouse, where the Governor's Boulder honors the three North Carolina governors from New Bern: Richard Dobbs Spaight, Richard Dobbs Spaight Jr., and Abner Nash. (As of this writing, North Carolina's first female governor, Beverly Perdue, was yet to be listed on the rock.)

As you near the parking lot at the visitor center, note the castle-like spires of the First Baptist Church. Thomas Meredith and Richard

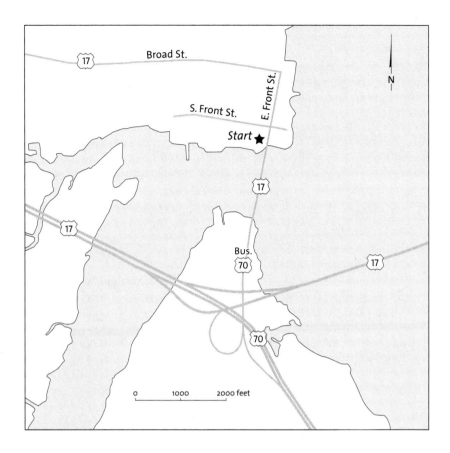

Furman, former pastors at the church, have colleges named for them, Meredith College in Raleigh and Furman University in Greenville, South Carolina. New Bernians also like to point out that just a few days after Harry Truman won his tight election against Thomas Dewey, Truman stopped here to attend services on his way to Florida for a fishing vacation.

Walk Details

HOW TO FIND IT: New Bern is located in eastern North Carolina, about midway between state lines. US 70 is the main thoroughfare to New Bern. As you near New Bern, signs will direct you to the Craven County Convention and Visitor Center (203 South Front Street), where this walk begins.

LENGTH: About 3.5 miles

SURFACE: Paved

RESTROOMS: At the visitor center

FOOTWEAR: Sneakers

PETS: OK on a leash

MAP: The visitor center provides maps for four walks that further describe New Bern's past: Civil War heritage, African American heritage, historic homes, and churches and cemeteries. You can pick up any of these maps to augment this walk.

BEWARE: Buckled cobblestone walks near Tryon Palace.

GOOD TO KNOW: Admission to the Tryon Palace complex allows you to tour the palace and several other historic homes. The complex is open 360 days a year, closing only for Thanksgiving, December 24, 25, and 26, and New Year's Day. Visiting the palace is always enjoyable, but an especially good time to visit is between Thanksgiving and Christmas, when the holiday decorations are fresh. Dozens of people work incredibly hard to create the fruit- and flower-laden adornments in just a few days. For more information, visit http://www.tryonpalace.org/index.php.

The New Bern Academy Museum is open Monday through Saturday from 1:00 P.M. until 4:00 P.M. and admission is charged.

Hillsborough

COLONIAL TOWN OF THE PIEDMONT

Don't let today's relative quiet of Hillsborough fool you. In the early days, Hillsborough was anything but. On the eve of the American Revolution, Hillsborough seethed with unrest, so much so that townspeople were occasionally afraid to leave their homes. During the Revolution in the spring of 1781, General Cornwallis occupied the town and tried to keep the citizens on the side of the English Crown. After the Revolution, feisty and outspoken politicians voted against ratifying the U.S. Constitution here. At one point, Hillsborough nearly became North Carolina's permanent capital. But Cape Fear politicians cut a deal with Guilford politicians, and Hillsborough lost its bid. Even so, given Hillsborough's colonial prominence, it's a safe bet that North Carolina's founding fathers spent time here.

Eventually, political power in North Carolina would find other towns to call home. Interestingly, in the 1960s, feisty Hillsborough, which had changed its name to Hillsboro in the nineteenth century, would honor its heritage by restoring the English spelling of its name, distinguishing itself from the other "-boro" towns in North Carolina.

Historical Context

The Occaneechi Indians lived here first along the banks of the Eno River, near an early commercial artery called the Great Trading Path. (Today Interstate 85 loosely follows parts of this path.). Documented by explorers John Lawson and John Lederer, these Native Americans conducted a lively trade with other tribes, travelers, and explorers, a fact verified in 1983 by a team of UNC archaeologists. As the archaeologists chipped and dug along the banks of the Eno, they found trash-filled storage pits, several small cemeteries, broken pottery, discarded stone tools, glass beads, and European bracelets adorned with Jesuit symbols.

To understand why Hillsborough came to life, examine the river systems of North Carolina. Somewhere underneath today's Falls Lake, three rivers—the Flat, the Little, and the Eno—join to form the Neuse River, a major artery for inland settlement that began in Beaufort. Though the Neuse was a mighty waterway, development into North Carolina's interior was slow, requiring, some have said, forty-one years—a generation in those days—to move the 116 miles from coastal Beaufort to Hillsborough. But as settlers pushed westward, they discovered that the area's terrain was higher and breezier than that of the coast. A higher, breezier terrain meant fewer mosquitoes, which in turn meant an escape from the malaria epidemics that plagued coastal towns.

The Walk

Begin at the Alexander Dickson House (150 East King Street), at the corner of Cameron and King Streets.

Walk two blocks south along Cameron Street to the Eno River. The flattish area where many Orange County government buildings now stand is where the 1983 UNC archaeology team unearthed the artifacts of two Occaneechi villages. One village dated from about 1500, and the other from about 1700. Historians think John Lawson visited the second village sometime between February 5 and February 18, 1701. These archaeological finds underscore that many Native American tribes called North Carolina home before Lawson and other explorers arrived.

Return to the Alexander Dickson House. At the corner of Cameron and King Streets, cross Cameron Street to the right and walk to St. Mary's Road, which angles off Cameron Street. St. Mary's Road roughly follows the old road to Halifax, another of North Carolina's early political centers. Walk through the parking lot of the Orange County Board of Education up the hill into Cameron Park to find a marker indicating where six Regulators were hanged on June 19, 1771.

As Revolution approached, Hillsborough was the primary population center of Orange County, a huge land area that included all of present-day Orange, Chatham, Caswell, Person, and Alamance Counties, as well as parts of present-day Wake, Guilford, Randolph, Rockingham, Durham, and Lee Counties. As a seat of administrative power, the thirty to forty residents of Hillsborough enjoyed close ties to the English Crown.

After Governor William Tryon assumed control of the colony in 1765 (see chapter 3, New Bern), he levied taxes to pay for public improvements. Needing men to serve as tax collectors, Tryon appointed Edmund Fanning to serve as the register of deeds—or as some perceived the job, the tax collector—of the large Orange County. Though townsfolk may have been happy with the royal connections of the town, the backwoods settlers of the county who detested paying the taxes were not. There was also a sense of outrage at the corruption they saw. From where they stood, they were only underwriting the construction of Tryon's "palace" in New Bern, the capital of the royal colony. Unrest built.

By 1768, the Regulators—the name these unhappy backwoods settlers gave themselves—had grown bold. They took over Hillsborough and for two days conducted mock trials, trying and finding Crown officials corrupt. They also shot through the roof of Fanning's house. No doubt that Fanning had grown rich in his job: he owned some 10,500 acres between New Bern and Charlotte, including so much land near Hillsborough that the Regulators contemptuously suggested the town be called Fanningsburg. Nonetheless, town residents were happy and continued supporting the Crown. In 1769, in what appears to be something of a thank-you gift for their support, King George gave the town a clock. Meanwhile, to divide the backcountry insurgents, Tryon hit upon the strategy of forming, in 1770, Guilford County from part of Orange and part of Rowan Counties.

Neither the gift nor the strategy worked. Later in 1770 the Regulators raided Hillsborough again, this time tying up the sheriff and taking his horse. Then they returned, smashing windows and dragging Fanning through town by his heels. By March 1771, even the Crown-appointed judges were afraid to go outside. Fanning begged Tryon for help.

Tryon left New Bern with 1,000 men, arriving in Hillsborough on May 9, 1771. After another week of posturing, the Regulators and Tryon battled in what is today Alamance County. Fewer than twenty people were killed, and Tryon pardoned most of the ones he captured after they pledged allegiance to the Crown. Tryon, however, hanged six Regulators for instigating the uprising.

Return to Cameron Street, cross it, and walk two blocks along King Street to Churton Street, which honors William Churton, the surveyor who platted the town. While the arrowhead marking the Great Trading Path is easy to see, remnants of colonial Hillsborough—the wooden market house and town water pump that once stood at this intersection—are gone.

Turn right and walk north one block along Churton Street to the Hillsborough Historical Museum (201 North Churton Street). Here, an abundance of historic markers pays homage to the Revolutionary leaders who made Hillsborough important.

One marker honors Thomas Burke, a man who met an exceedingly sad fate, given the work he did before and after the Revolution. Irish by birth, Burke moved to Hillsborough in 1774, representing the town in April 1776 when the provisional state government met in Halifax. While there, Burke helped draft the Halifax Resolves (see chapter 5, Halifax), the earliest such document in the colonies calling for independence. Later in 1776, Burke traveled to the Continental Congress to represent North Carolina; he served from 1777 to 1781. There he engaged in heated debates over the drafting of the Articles of Confederation, contributing language that helped make them acceptable to North Carolina by ensuring that powers not explicitly granted to the United States automatically went to the state governments. Whereas most of the congressional representatives fled Philadelphia in September 1777 to escape impending battle with the British, Burke went to fight with Francis Nash's North Carolina troops in the Battle of Brandywine. So highly esteemed was Burke that the newly formed Burke County was named in his honor, and in 1781 political leaders chose him to serve as the state's third governor. Although the Revolution was ending, tensions surrounding it still ran high. David Fanning, a Loyalist (but no relation to Edmund Fanning), captured Burke, first sending him to Wilmington and then to Charleston, where Burke was imprisoned on James Island. Burke successfully escaped and returned to Hillsborough in 1782, aiming to resume his gubernatorial responsibilities. However, many Hillsborough residents thought Burke had dishonored himself by the terms of his imprisonment! Their scorn so surprised Burke that he decided not to stand for governor again. Little more than a year later, Burke succumbed to alcohol and the strain of his imprisonment, dying at the age of thirty-six.

Another marker honors Francis Nash, a brigadier general under George Washington. Mortally wounded during the Battle of Germantown in 1777 as he commanded the 1st North Carolina Regiment, Nash inspired one friend to describe him as "one of the most enlightened, liberal and magnanimous gentlemen that ever sacrificed for his country." Nash County honors him (not North Carolina's second governor, Abner Nash) as does Fort Nashborough in Tennessee. Fort Nashborough was the forerunner of America's Music City, Nashville.

A third marker honors William Hooper, from Wilmington. Hooper came to Hillsborough to escape heat and mosquitoes. Though generally remembered as one of North Carolina's signers of the Declaration of Independence, Hooper at first supported Governor Tryon against the Regulators in 1771. His transition from supporting the Crown to sign-

This marker commemorates the Great Trading Path, a route Native Americans used in conducting trade and travel. Interstate 85 now follows parts of the route.

ing the Declaration was anything but easy. At one point, Hillsborough residents enraged over his support of the Crown dragged him through the streets and destroyed his home.

The contributions of Hillsborough residents who participated in the Continental Line explain a fourth historical marker noting the formation of the North Carolina chapter of the Society of the Cincinnati in Hillsborough in October 1783. The Society of the Cincinnati, the oldest military hereditary society in the United States, provided a social outlet for Revolutionary military men, reserving membership for those who had served as Continental Line officers during the war, and later their descendants. The society provided ongoing fellowship for members and helped provide pensions for veterans and funding for families in need. It could provide those funds because each original member agreed to pay his state chapter one month's officer's pay.

No marker along Churton Street pays homage to the legacy of British general Lord Cornwallis. Local legend has it that when Cornwallis came through Hillsborough in February 1781 on his way to Guilford Courthouse (see chapter 7, Guilford Courthouse), he directed his men to lay cobblestones on Churton Street. He hoped that by paving the muddy streets and improving life in Hillsborough, Cornwallis could convince the patriots to quit their rebellion. Cornwallis's gesture was appreciated but it held no sway with the patriots. Whether this story is historically accurate or not, the cobblestones stayed on Churton Street until 1909.

Hillsborough's energy didn't diminish with the ending of the Revolution. Having been so involved in colonial politics and the birthing of a new state and country, Hillsborough was selected as state capitol in 1782. The Cape Fear contingent protested, and by striking a deal that made Alexander Martin of Guilford County North Carolina's seventh governor, the vote making Hillsborough the state capitol was repealed.

Cross Churton Street to visit the graveyard behind the Hillsborough Historical Museum. William Hooper's grave rests in the upper right quadrant of the cemetery, at the end of a path lined with huge boxwoods. Where the Presbyterian Church now stands, an Episcopal church once stood. Here, the first state convention took place in 1788 to consider adopting the newly written U.S. Constitution. The vote didn't pass, largely because planters, who had financed the war, didn't want a strong centralized government that they believed would diminish their own power. Before exiting the graveyard, look also for monuments to other notable North Carolinians: Archibald D. Murphey, William A. Graham, and Thomas Ruffin.

Archibald D. Murphey was perhaps North Carolina's earliest visionary. A faculty member of the University of North Carolina—he was one of three at the time—Murphey led early efforts to motivate the state to build roads, canals, and public schools. His enthusiasm for educating the populace gave rise to the 1825 State Literacy Act and, fifteen years later, the first public schools. Like many other North Carolinians, Murphey was also a distiller, operating an eighty-gallon distillery on his 2,000 acre estate near Swepsonville. He was also the first major collector of North Carolina manuscripts. However, he was also prone to overextending himself financially to pay for his business ventures, and he once spent twenty-some days in a Greensboro jail for not paying off a note. The town of Murphy in western North Carolina honors him, albeit with a different spelling.

William A. Graham, whom Graham County honors, is notable for the irony of his political activities. He opposed Andrew Jackson and supported Henry Clay. Though never a seaman, Graham served as secretary of the navy under President Millard Fillmore, supporting Matthew Perry's proposal to open Japan to trade. He was the vice presidential candidate on the Whig ticket with Winfield Scott, once again making his dislike for Andrew Jackson and Jackson's policies evident. The

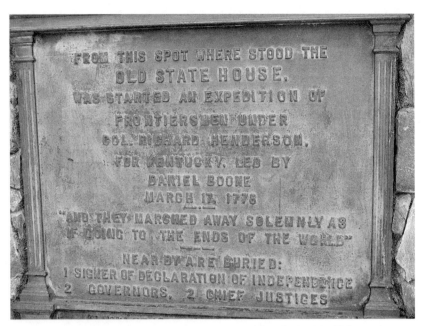

This marker speaks to the political vigor and activity of colonial Hillsborough—
as well as Hillsborough's claim to Daniel Boone.

Scott-Graham ticket lost, however, as James Buchanan won the race. Later, after Abraham Lincoln won the election of 1860, Lincoln considered Graham for a cabinet post. The irony of Graham's political life culminated in the marriages of his three nieces. Graham was an ardent Unionist, but his nieces married Confederate generals: one wed Rufus Barrington, one D. H. Hill, and one Stonewall Jackson.

A classmate of Winfield Scott and a law student of Archibald Murphey, Thomas Ruffin represented North Carolina at the February 1861 Washington Peace Conference, a last-ditch effort to avoid civil war. Ruffin served as chief justice of the North Carolina Supreme Court from 1833 to 1852, and again from 1858 to 1859, writing opinions on over 1,400 cases. An irony of Ruffin's career is that in 1830, while acting as a judge for North Carolina, Ruffin handed down the decision that the slave master must have absolute power over his slaves. Harriet Beecher Stowe later immortalized the judicial decision in her novel *Dred*.

Exit the graveyard by returning to Tryon Street. Turn right to walk one block west. The Nash-Hooper House (118 West Tryon Street) is the only remaining home of any signer of the Declaration of Independence from

North Carolina. Francis Nash built the house in 1777; William Hooper bought it in 1781.

At the corner of Tryon and Wake Streets, turn right to walk north three blocks along Wake Street. At Union Street, turn right and walk one block to Churton Street and past Burwell School (319 North Churton Street), one of the longest-lived female academies in North Carolina. Also look for the historical marker to Elizabeth Keckly, a slave who bought her freedom and later worked as dressmaker to Mary Todd Lincoln.

At Churton Street, turn right and walk three blocks to King Street. Here you can observe how Hillsborough businesses have adapted old store-fronts into interesting shops and cafés.

At the corner of King and Churton Streets, turn right and walk one block west along King Street to Wake Street. The Masonic Hall (142 West King Street) is on the site of the house of the much-reviled Edmund Fanning. Look for the Colonial Inn (153 West King Street). Records indicate that an inn has sat here since 1838. The stones out front are said to be like those Cornwallis used as pavers. Long a favorite local eatery, the build-ing is now in disrepair.

At Wake Street, turn left and walk toward the Eno River. When Cornwal-lis visited in 1781, his troops camped on the knoll across the river.

At Margaret Lane, turn left to walk one block east to Churton Street. As you do, you will have a wonderful view of the clock that King George gave Hillsborough in 1769. It is now in the cupola of the old courthouse. Cross Churton Street and walk to the Alexander Dickson House, which is now to your left. Along the way, look for the Norwood Law Office (131 Court Street), the only remaining office of three that once lined Court Street in the late 1700s.

Hillsborough's history certainly contains a healthy dose of colonial history, but when you return to the Alexander Dickson House, where this walks started, you can ponder a final tidbit: This house is where General Joseph E. Johnston ("Fighting Joe") of the Confederacy first met with Union general William Tecumseh Sherman to discuss terms of surrender on April 17 and 18, 1865 (see chapter 16, Fayetteville).

Walk Details

HOW TO FIND IT: Hillsborough is in central North Carolina, just off
  I-85. To find the Alexander Dickson House (150 East King Street), fol-
  low Churton Street (also called US 70) into town and turn right onto
  King Street.

LENGTH: About 2.75 miles

SURFACE: Mostly sidewalk

RESTROOMS: At the visitor center in the Alexander Dickson House

FOOTWEAR: Sneakers

PETS: OK on a leash

MAP: Available from the Alliance for Historic Hillsborough at the
  Alexander Dickson House (www.historichillsborough.org or at 919-
  732-7741). The alliance publishes a pamphlet that provides a deeper
  explanation of Hillsborough's many historic buildings.

GOOD TO KNOW: To explore the remnants of the Great Trading Path,
  contact www.tradingpath.org/. The 350-foot high Occoneechee
  Mountain, which rises just outside Hillsborough adjacent I-85,

served as a major landmark along the path. You can visit the state natural area there to get a sense for what the Eno River Valley once looked like. For more information, see http://www.ncparks.gov/ Visit/parks/ocmo/main.php.

The Orange County Historical Museum is open 11 A.M.–4 P.M. Tuesday through Saturday, 1–4 P.M. Sundays. The museum closes Mondays.

In June, the Alliance for Historic Hillsborough sponsors a Walkable Hillsborough Day.

The Occaneechi Band of the Saponi Nation have undertaken the Occaneechi Homeland Preservation Project. Working with the Landscape Architecture Department of North Carolina A&T and the Rural Incentive Project, Inc., of Winston-Salem, the tribe hopes to reconstruct a village and build a museum and walking trails off Daily Store Road outside nearby Mebane on north NC 119.

Halifax

WITH RESOLVE

For eleven momentous days in April and again for about six weeks in December 1776, the quiet little town you see today was anything but serene, as leaders throughout the colony flocked here to attend the Fourth and Fifth Provincial Congresses, where North Carolina took some of its first major steps in transforming itself from a colony into a state. On April 12, 1776, about a week after the meeting began, the Fourth Provincial Congress approved the Halifax Resolves, the first formal sanction of American independence; in doing so, they gave North Carolina an early voice in the politics of the new nation and distinguished a date that would one day appear on our state flag. Our first non-royal governor, Richard Caswell, was appointed here. After the Revolution, the General Assembly met twice here.

The men attending the Fourth Provincial Congress were an illustrious group: Cornelius Harnett and Thomas Person had counties later named for them. Two men, Thomas Burke and Abner Nash, would become governors. Three others, William Hooper, Joseph Hewes, and John Penn, would travel to Philadelphia to sign the Declaration of Independence. Later, when they met again in December for the Fifth Provincial Congress, these men would write our first state constitution. (See chapter 4, Hillsborough, for more information about these men.)

Historical Context

To understand the events of Halifax in 1776, begin a few years earlier with the Boston Tea Party, which took place in December 1773 and ignited tensions across the colonies.

North Carolina's First Provincial Congress met in New Bern in August 1774, eight months after the Boston incident. Ben Patton from Mecklenburg reportedly walked the 280 miles to New Bern to attend. There, colony leaders elected North Carolina representatives to attend the Continental Congress, set to convene in September in Philadelphia. They also approved a trade boycott. Further, they approved the call to raise 1,500 minutemen from Edenton, New Bern, Halifax, and Wilmington. Then, in

October, the ladies of Edenton staged their own tea party and circulated a petition regarding the tax on tea.

Tensions across the colonies worsened. Soon Patrick Henry was calling for liberty or death; Paul Revere was galloping through Lexington and Concord on his midnight ride; the New York Provincial Congress formed and mobilized 13,600 soldiers; and the Virginia governor was hiding gunpowder from colonists there. In North Carolina, between April 3 and April 7, 1775, the Second Provincial Congress met, again in New Bern. And on April 23 that year the royal governor of North Carolina, Josiah Martin, fled his palace in New Bern, preferring the relative safety of British ships on the Cape Fear River.

The rest of 1775 was equally tense. During the spring and summer, North Carolina colonists drafted the Mecklenburg Resolves, the New Hanover Resolves, the Liberty Point Resolves, and the Pitt County Resolves. When the Third Provincial Congress met in Hillsborough between August 20 and September 10, 1775, the state's leaders decided to divide North Carolina into six military districts and to raise two regiments of Continental troops and the money to support them. In New York, the Provincial Congress was pledging obedience to the Continental Congress; meanwhile Connecticut raised troops.

A couple of intriguing, if unlikely, stories come out of the revolution fever in Halifax. The first curiosity is said to have occurred in 1775. That summer, a young man named John Paul reportedly visited the town, meeting with North Carolina politician Willie Jones (see chapter 8, Raleigh, for more information about Jones), for whom Jones County is named, and General Allen Jones of Northampton County. So taken with these men was John Paul that he purportedly adopted "Jones" as his last name, thus becoming the John Paul Jones known today as the father of the U.S. Navy. Apparently Joseph Hewes helped John Paul Jones receive his first commission. The other story of how John Paul Jones adopted his name says that John Paul fled his brother's home in Fredericksburg, Virginia. He had been accused of murdering a sailor under his command and was headed for the hangman's noose. In this version of the story, John Paul took the last name Jones at the prompting of his brother. Given, however, the close ties between this part of North Carolina and Virginia, the visit to Halifax seems plausible.

The increasing tensions in the run-up to the Revolution thus poised Halifax to attain immortality in 1776. New Hampshire started the year by preparing the first independent state constitution in January. In February, Richard Caswell led North Carolina militia in battle against

Scots Loyalists from present-day Fayetteville at Moores Creek Bridge. Among the Loyalists captured at Moores Creek Bridge was Allan Mac-Donald, husband to a legendary woman from North Carolina's colonial history, Flora MacDonald; Allan MacDonald was jailed in Halifax after the battle. (See chapter 16, Fayetteville, for more information about the MacDonalds).

By April, North Carolina leaders had written, approved, and announced the Halifax Resolves, which authorized the state's delegates to vote for independence. In addition to writing the Halifax Resolves, the Fourth Provincial Congress reorganized the troops that had mustered the previous fall, started drafting the state constitution, and elected Richard Caswell North Carolina's first governor.

The Halifax Resolves certainly read as a forerunner of the Declaration of Independence:

> The Select Committee taking into Consideration the usurpations and violences attempted and committed by the King and Parliament of Britain against America, and the further Measures to be taken for frustrating the same, and for the better defence of this province reported as follows, to wit,
>
> It appears to your Committee that pursuant to the Plan concerted by the British ministry for subjugating America, the King and parliament of Great Britain have usurped a power over the Persons and Properties of the People unlimited and uncontrouled; and disregarding their humble Petitions for Peace, Liberty and safety, have made divers Legislative Acts, denouncing War Famine and every Species of Calamity against the Continent in General. That British Fleets and Armies have been and still are daily employed in destroying the People and committing the most horrid devastations on the Country. That Governors in different Colonies have declared Protection to Slaves who should imbrue their Hands in the Blood of their Masters. That the Ships belonging to America are declared prizes of War and many of them have been violently seized and confiscated in consequence of which multitudes of the people have been destroyed or from easy Circumstances reduced to the most Lamentable distress.
>
> And whereas the moderation hitherto manifested by the United Colonies and their sincere desire to be reconciled to the mother Country on Constitutional Principles, have procured no mitigation of the aforesaid Wrongs and usurpations, and no

hopes remain of obtaining redress by those Means alone which have been hitherto tried, Your Committee are of Opinion that the house should enter into the following Resolve to wit,

Resolved that the delegates for this Colony in the Continental Congress be impowered to concur with the delegates of the other Colonies in declaring Independency, and forming foreign Alliances, reserving to this Colony the Sole, and Exclusive right of forming a Constitution and Laws for this Colony, and of appointing delegates from time to time (under the direction of a general Representation thereof) to meet the delegates of the other Colonies for such purposes as shall be hereafter pointed out.

Later that summer, when the Declaration of Independence came to North Carolina, Cornelius Harnett, who has often been called the "Sam Adams of North Carolina," read it to the crowd assembled in Halifax (see chapter 13, Wilmington, for more information about Harnett). He was the first North Carolinian to read the document in public, and did so, presumably, because he had chaired the committee that had produced the Halifax Resolves. Stories indicate that cannons thundered when each of the North Carolina signers' names was read.

In November 1776, the Fifth Provincial Congress met to finish drafting the state constitution. Modeled after English law, the first constitution set property requirements for the governor (£1,000) and land requirements for senators and representatives to the House of Commons (300 acres and 100 acres, respectively). Voters for state senators had to have fifty acres in freehold, while male taxpayers were allowed to vote for representatives to the House of Commons. Neither Roman Catholics nor Jews could hold office. One senator and two Commoners would come from each county. Borough towns—Edenton, Halifax, New Bern, Wilmington, Hillsborough, and Salisbury—could send a representative. The legislature would choose the governor and all judicial officers. Clearly the first government of North Carolina was a property owner's government.

This first constitution would undergo revision in 1835. In 1861, when the state flag was established, one of the two dates inscribed on the flag was May 20, 1775, that of the purported Mecklenburg Declaration of Independence, a much-disputed document. Some argue that the Mecklenburg Declaration of Independence predated the Mecklenburg Resolves by eleven days. However, there exists no official evidence that a Mecklenburg Declaration of Independence was ever drafted, and many consider the drafting of such a document unlikely. The date of North

Carolina's secession, May 21, 1861, was the second date inscribed on the flag. On February 5, 1885, the North Carolina flag that we know was designed. Instead of the date of secession, the second date commemorated the Halifax Resolves, April 12, 1776.

Halifax's status as an inland port town on the Roanoke River, the number of wealthy residents living there, and the town's proximity to Virginia helps to explain why the small town was the scene of such political activity. Down at the river, warehouses abounded. In town, visitors had a choice of taverns. Beginning in the 1830s, however, as railroads arrived and surpassed the speed of river commerce, Halifax started its transformation to the serene little town you see today.

The Walk

Begin at the Historic Halifax visitor center to watch a short film that discusses Halifax's role in the fight for independence.

From the visitor center, walk left along St. David Street, turning left onto King Street. When you turn, look for the Tap Room directly across the street. This tavern was built between 1760 and 1810. The Eagle Tavern, which is now to your left, was built around 1790. Walk King Street all the way to the Roanoke River. On the left is the town jail; below that, the clerk's office. The large open area to your right is the site of the market square. As you pass through the wooded section, try to imagine that the wooded area was once full of warehouses.

From the River Overlook, turn around, and retrace your steps to Fishing Club Road. Walk Fishing Club Road to the Sally-Billy Plantation house, a tripartite house built about 1808.

Return to King Street, cross King Street, turn left on Dobbs Street and walk to Market Street. Turn left onto Market Street, passing by the site of the former courthouse on the left and Dudley's Tavern to the right. Once you reach King Street, you can turn right to return to the visitor center, or cross the street to walk down to where Old Granville Street once ran and where the Burgess Law Office stood.

To add about three-quarters of a mile to the distance, walk up to the corner of St. David and Norman Streets, to the house of William R. Davie, one of North Carolina's most active and illustrious founding fathers. Davie lived here from 1785 to 1805. (See chapter 29, University of North Carolina, for more information about Davie.)

The Eagle Tavern in Halifax likely witnessed many serious political discussions as leaders debated whether and how to declare independence from England.

The home of William Davie, one of the state's most important colonial leaders.

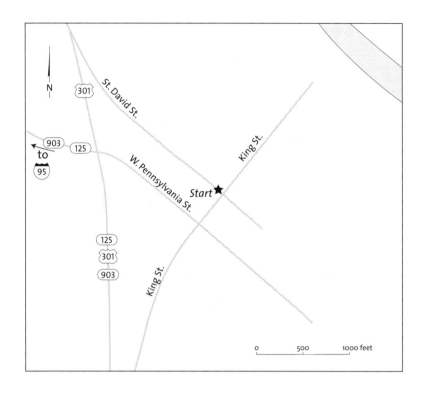

Walk Details

HOW TO FIND IT: Halifax is located in northeastern North Carolina just east of I-95 and US 301. The Historic Halifax visitor center is located at 25 St. David Street.

LENGTH: About two miles depending upon your exact route

SURFACE: Pavement

RESTROOMS: At the visitor center

FOOTWEAR: Sneakers

PETS: No

MAP: Available at the visitor center

GOOD TO KNOW: April 12 is Halifax Day.

For additional information about Flora MacDonald, see http://ncmu seumofhistory.org/workshops/womenshistory/flora.html

Building Infrastructure

HOLDEN MILL TRAIL

Many people think history is about the big moments that define a generation: walking on the moon, or refusing to sit at the back of the bus, or fighting the great wars. Plus, given how convenient our lives are in a land of plenty—how fast can you get to the grocery store nearest your house to buy a loaf of bread?—we tend to forget about just how hard and time consuming the work of daily life once was.

Yet history doesn't always take place against the backdrop of the big moment. Nor is history the sole province of bigger-than-life people on the public stage. History is often mundane and basic, the stuff of daily life. This walk celebrates just such a humble historical emblem of daily life: the gristmill. Without the gristmill, the basic act of eating would have been far more difficult—and boring! Moreover, the gristmill was a place where "social networking," as we think of it today, took place. It created communities and brought people together. And as people formed their communities, they shared ideas, made plans, lived lives . . . and created family narratives.

Historical Context

Historians disagree about where the first American gristmill appeared: was it in Jamestown, Virginia, in 1621? Or in Plymouth, Massachusetts, in 1636? In North Carolina, historians think, the first grist mill was built in Bath in 1707, two years after the town, our state's first, was established.

In the early days colonists used wind and tidal action to power the mills. Tides, because they occur twice a day, were more reliable than winds. However, as settlers moved inward from the coast, they started erecting water-powered gristmills.

In 1715, just eight years after Bath was established, North Carolina's royal government encouraged colonists to build an infrastructure by granting fifty acres of land and exemptions from both taxes and service in the state militia to men who would build and operate grist- and sawmills. The law also contained incentives for roads, bridges and ferries.

The incentives were successful: settlers started moving inland from the coastal creeks. By the 1800s, over 1,000 gristmills were operating.

Throughout North Carolina, gristmill enthusiasts have preserved the old mills. Yates Pond Mill outside Raleigh and the Old Mill in Cedarock Park near Burlington are two examples. Moreover, when you drive the county roads of the state, you can sometimes spot the remnants of old gristmill. Just keep a sharp eye for the stone foundation of the millhouse sitting at a river bank, or perhaps the millrace, the channel that water ran through to power the mill.

The Walk

The Eno River Association believes that the forty-mile Eno River has been the home of thirty-two different mills. Historians believe that the first mill there dates from 1752. Holden Mill, the remnants of which you see on this walk, dates from 1811.

From the Few's Ford Access parking lot at the visitor center, follow the Buckquarter Creek Trail down to the Eno River. At the riverside, look left to the flattish area along the river. This is Few's Ford. The shallow spot is notable for three reasons: first, it is a natural river ford. Second, William Few, who moved from Maryland to North Carolina in the 1760s, once owned this land. His son James was one of the Regulators hanged by royal governor William Tryon after the battle at Alamance Courthouse (see chapter 4, Hillsborough). Third, across the river you can see the remains of the old Hillsborough-Halifax coach road (see chapter 5, Halifax).

Turn right to begin hiking the red-blazed Buckquarter Creek Trail. Almost immediately, you'll climb and then descend a wooden staircase over a rock formation. The view of the rapids below is quite impressive. As you walk alongside the river, mind your footing. The tangle of roots across the trail can be slippery from rain and high river water! Look also for the gnawed-off tree stumps, a clear signal of beaver activity.

As you walk, observe the river. To build a gristmill, a man had to understand the lay of the land so as to build a dam, a headrace, and a tailrace. The dam made the water more powerful by giving it speed, the headrace channeled and transported water to the water wheel, and the tailrace removed it. A miller also needed a sizable community to support his mill: the cost of constructing a mill was not trivial. Jean Anderson, author of A *Community of Men and Mills*, reports that the up-front capital investment needed ranged from $1,000 to $6,500, nearly $500,000 in today's money. Costs included hand digging waterways, building the millhouse, and dressing the stones, all hard jobs.

Initially, colonists brought millstones with them; later they made them. Once a carver had obtained two round stones he would dress them, that is, cut furrows in the stone. Millers sometimes did this work, but if the area had a cluster of mills, a man might work as an itinerant stone dresser, going from mill to mill to dress or re-dress (freshen) the millstones.

Millstones always come in twos: the bedstone and the runner. The bedstone is fixed. The runner whirls on top of, but does not touch, the bedstone. If the runner stone touches the bedstone, then the meal and flour will contain stone dust. The two stones might also spark, cause the grain dust to explode, and thus torch the millhouse.

A mill builder also had to understand the different types of rock. A riverbed cut in the shape of a V, the result when the rock is hard, produces naturally faster, more powerful water. A meandering river, the result of softer rock, produces less powerful water—and more engineering challenges for the builder. Between Hillsborough and Durham, the Eno River flows over hard igneous rock, creating a V-cut riverbed. Beginning in the Durham basin, the rock is sedimentary and softer, making a gentler river. The difference in rock helps explain why the upper section of the Eno was home to many gristmills.

In about .75 mile, after scrambling over another large rock outcropping, you'll see Buckquarter Creek. Cross the creek and begin walking on the Holden Mill Trail. Start looking for the remnants of the headrace that led to Holden Mill.

Isaac Holden built the mill in 1811. When he died nine years later, he left the mill to his son Thomas, who later left it to a son-in-law, John F. Lyon. According to park ranger Christopher Ammon, Holden Mill was the largest enterprise in the Eno River Valley. It employed seven, possibly eight, people.

It also helped form a community that included threshing machines, a sawmill, a cotton gin, two wool-carding machines, and an oil mill, along with several homes and a schoolhouse. In 1845, when the mill went up for sale, it was advertised as coming with 300 acres, a six-room dwelling house with three fireplaces, and all of the necessary outhouses.

While this area may look faded today, in the 1800s milling provided a way to improve one's financial success and social standing. William

A moderate hike will bring you to these remnants of Holden Mill, one of several gristmills that once stood in the Eno River Valley.

Woods Holden, one of North Carolina's more controversial governors, is one such example. Son of Thomas Holden, the second owner of the mill, W. W. Holden is principally known for his uneasy relationship with the Democratic Party as civil war approached. Though he voted for secession in 1861, he criticized Zebulon B. Vance and the Confederacy, and he led the North Carolina peace movement. After the war, President Andrew Johnson appointed Holden as North Carolina's provisional governor. After Holden was elected governor in 1868, he became embroiled in the increasingly violent relations between white North Carolinians, primarily the newly formed Ku Klux Klan, and newly freed black North Carolinians. The result was the brief standoff known as the Kirk-Holden War and Holden's eventual impeachment. He was convicted in March 1871, the first governor in the United States to be not only impeached but also convicted and removed from office.

As Jean Anderson notes, any mill was vulnerable to flooding. Heavy rains could put a man out of business, which is what happened to Holden Mill. Lyon lost the mill in 1868 due to financial difficulties. Samuel Cole reopened the mill sometime after 1882 and ran it until his death in 1893. In 1908, a flood washed away the dam and the mill.

After inspecting what remains of Holden Mill, continue walking alongside the Eno. The trail soon curves to return to the park office. As you walk here, you'll see old road beds that attest to the lively community that was once here.

Walk Details

HOW TO FIND IT: The Few's Ford section of Eno River State Park is located between Durham and Hillsborough. From I-85 exit 173, take Cole Mill Road northwest away from Durham. After five miles, Cole Mill Road will end at the park's Few's Ford Access (6101 Cole Mill Road, Durham).

From I-85 exit 170, take US 70 west to Pleasant Green Road. Turn right and follow Pleasant Green 2.2 miles, then turn left on Cole Mill Road. After one mile, Cole Mill Road will enter the park's Few's Ford Access.

LENGTH: Buckquarter Creek Trail is about 1.5 miles long. Hiking the Holden Mill Trail adds another 2.6 miles, for a total of 4.1 miles

SURFACE: Woods trail, some rock scrambles

RESTROOMS: At the visitor center

FOOTWEAR: Boots recommended

PETS: OK on a leash

MAP: Available at visitor center kiosk and at www.ncparks.gov/Visit/parks/enri/main.php

GOOD TO KNOW: This walk is best when leaves are down so that you can more easily see the remnants of Holden Mill.

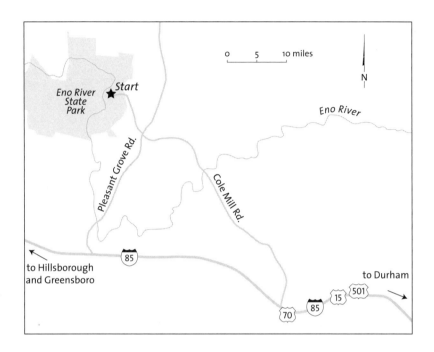

For More Exploration

West Point on the Eno, a Durham city park, is home to a classic mill with the vertical wheel, with many of the machine parts and stones on display. The mill dates from 1778. To see a gristmill with a horizontal wheel, visit Merchants Millpond State Park, located near Gatesville. That mill dates to 1811.

In service since 1812, House-Autry Mill in Four Oaks claims to be the oldest still-operating gristmill in North Carolina. The original location for House Mill was Newton Grove. The original millstones came from England and were transported via oxcart to the mill site. In 1967, House Mill merged with the Autry Brothers Mill Company. The company moved to its present location in 2001.

You can find meal and flours at other gristmills in North Carolina, including

- Cottonman Mill in Edenton
- Old Mill of Guilford, north of Greensboro
- Dellinger Grist Mill outside Bakersville
- Bost Grist Mill located in Cabarrus County
- Murray's Mill outside Catawba

Guilford Courthouse

WHERE A DEFEAT BECAME A VICTORY

Both Revolutionary War and Civil War battles took place in North Carolina. One such battle, that of Guilford Courthouse, holds two distinctions: it is the first Revolutionary War conflict whose battlefield was preserved as a national park, and it is where the British army won what some call its worst victory.

A ruinous victory? Yes, because the definition of victory can depend upon the price a general pays. And make no mistake: British general Lord Cornwallis paid dearly at Guilford Courthouse: he lost 27 percent of his army. Even worse, he lost 29 percent of his experienced officers. Although the first and second lines of the American Continental forces turned and ran—and General Nathanael Greene ordered the third line to withdraw–the Americans suffered only a 6 percent loss.

On March 15, 1781, approximately 4,400 Americans and 2,000 British fought at Guilford Courthouse, a number comparable to the current undergraduate enrollment at Wake Forest University. As measured by the number of men who fought in the major battles of the American Revolution, only the battles at Monmouth, New Jersey; Brandywine, Pennsylvania; Germantown, Pennsylvania; and Yorktown, Virginia, were larger than Guilford Courthouse.

This walk surrounds the battlefield where the British army began spiraling toward its demise. When news of the victory reached London, Charles Fox, a leading politician in the British House of Commons, quipped that "another such victory would ruin the British Army." Fox was right: the losses Cornwallis incurred here were so severe that he surrendered at Yorktown seven months later.

Historical Context

Some might think that because New England and the mid-Atlantic states are home to some of the American Revolution's most stirring stories—the Boston Tea Party, Paul Revere's midnight ride, and Nathan Hale's giving of his life for his country—all of the fighting took place there. Not so. North Carolina had its share of skirmishes in the run-up to war. Some of the violence in the pre–Revolutionary War years was not directly related to what would become revolution, but contributed to the tumultuous era nonetheless. In May 1771, royal governor Tryon and the Regulators fought near Alamance Creek, near present-day Burlington (see chapter 4, Hillsborough). In October 1774, about nine months after the Boston Tea Party, Revolutionary fever struck several upper-class women in Edenton who hosted their own tea party (see chapter 2, Edenton). In February 1776, only months before the Continental Congress produced the Declaration of Independence, Scots Loyalists mustered in the area that would become Fayetteville to march to Moores Creek Bridge to attempt to unite with a British fleet that intended to land at Wilmington (see chapter 16, Fayetteville). Their goal was to subdue patriotic North Carolina colonists with their broadswords.

After we Americans declared our independence, the British strategy focused, naturally, on Boston, New York, and Philadelphia. But after four years, although each of the cities had fallen at one time or another, the British still had not gained firm control of the northeastern colonies, which forced a turn to the southern colonies, populated with Loyalists who were eager to side with the Crown.

Sir Henry Clinton laid siege to Charleston in 1780; the city fell quickly. Buoyed by his success, Lord Cornwallis, having received command of the southern theater from Clinton, marched to Camden, South Carolina, where he defeated an American army commanded by Horatio Gates in August 1780. When Cornwallis entered Charlotte in September 1780, something had to be done, so groups of militia from west of the Blue Ridge formed, calling themselves the Overmountain Men.

In October 1780, the Overmountain Men delivered that "something": a decisive and much-needed victory at the Battle of Kings Mountain. After that battle, Cornwallis withdrew to Winnsboro, South Carolina, with his sick, decimated, and increasingly hungry army that, interestingly, was composed of North Carolinians.

Meanwhile, George Washington appointed Nathanael Greene commander of the Southern Department of the Continental army. When Greene assumed command in Charlotte in the winter of 1780, he found an army that was not much healthier than Cornwallis's. Yet Greene had two advantages: he could more easily find food and clothing for his troops in the North and South Carolina countryside than could Cornwallis. Moreover, Greene was a brilliant strategic thinker, supported by seasoned Patriot fighters.

As Greene commissioned Moravian craftsmen to make shoes and Salisbury residents to sew linen cloth into clothing, Cornwallis fended off raids by the Patriots. American Daniel Morgan, for whom Morganton is named, was one such raider, and a brilliant combat commander. Cornwallis sent his able lieutenant colonel Banastre Tarleton and all of the army's infantrymen to hunt down and destroy Morgan. But Morgan set a trap for the British at Cowpens, South Carolina. When that battle ended on January 17, the American forces, an effective mix of the Continental army and frontier militiamen, claimed victory.

After Cowpens, instead of resting his army, the stubborn Cornwallis chased Greene across the western North Carolina Piedmont—from Ramsour's Mill (in present-day Lincolnton) to Cowan's Ford in Mecklenburg County and the Dan River in Virginia and east into Hillsborough. So dogged was Cornwallis that Greene dubbed him the "modern Hannibal." Cold winter rain, rutted and muddy roads, and swollen rivers took their toll on Cornwallis's tired men. When Greene withdrew his army into Virginia, he appeared to have given up North Carolina without a real fight. However, Greene was protecting his supplies and his ragtag army, waiting for the prospects for battle to become clear.

By late February, those prospects were clear. Greene's army was poised near Troublesome Creek, near northwestern Guilford and southern Rockingham Counties. Cornwallis was encamped near Stinking Creek in southwestern Guilford County near NC 62. Guilford Courthouse lay between them, on New Garden Road.

The Walk

This walk follows the perimeter walk, which surrounds much of the original battlefield, on a counterclockwise circuit.

Begin at the Guilford Courthouse National Military Park (2332 New Garden Road). With the visitor center behind you, walk right to New Garden Road and then left about thirty yards toward Tannenbaum Historic Park. Watch for traffic. As you do, imagine that the only thoroughfare in the area is New Garden Road.

Today's Tannenbaum Park was originally the farm of Joseph Hoskins, who had come to North Carolina to escape the war; in 1777 Sir William Howe, commander of the British army, had damaged Hoskins's Pennsylvania farm during the Philadelphia campaign. Now, four years later in March 1781, General Cornwallis readied his troops for the battle here after they had skirmished their way across the Piedmont. These men were tired and hungry. They had been sleeping in the winter cold and rain, and now the time had come to fight in the hilly woods generally behind you and to your right.

One more practicality to consider before you circle the battlefield. The flintlock musket, which had an effective range of roughly fifty to seventy-five yards, was the weapon of choice for armies in those days. The farther the distance the shot traveled, the more inaccurate it became. The result? The field of battle will strike you as being small. Combat was bloody and horrible because it was held at close quarters, with bayonet charges generally following close-range musket volleys.

Return toward the visitor center parking lot and look for signs that point to the paved auto path. On its left side, the auto path contains a lane for walkers. Here is where Hoskins's cornfield lay, muddy from recent rains, and where the American first line stood, generally in the open.

Composed of about 1,000 North Carolina militiamen, Greene's first line stretched across New Garden Road. Greene's best hope was that these untested citizen-soldiers could slow the British attack. That didn't happen. Around 1 P.M. on March 15, as the British began their uphill march along New Garden Road—the developed area you drove through on the way in—the citizen-soldiers poised in the center of the line fired their muskets, but then fled into the woods. These men were not professional soldiers accustomed to battle. Later mocked as the "Guilford Run-Aways," these fighters nonetheless inflicted casualties on the British.

The path begins to bend left. As it does, you enter the area where the left flank of the North Carolina militia fought. Although the center of the line had dissolved, either end continued fighting. Marker 2 describes the action along the American left flank. Some North Carolina units withdrew and joined the men commanded by "Light-Horse" Harry Lee and William Campbell. Two British regiments followed the Americans and suffered more casualties. As you walk, notice that the terrain rolls up and down, gradually rising toward the right.

Cross Old Battleground Road to approach the area where the American second line stood. Two brigades of Virginia militiamen composed the American second line. These men benefited from nearly a half-mile of thick woods standing between them and the oncoming British. Historian Thomas Baker states that the woods "accomplished what the North

These cannons, tucked in the wooded, ravine-marked terrain north of downtown Greensboro, speak to how Continental troops used natural features to their advantage.

Carolina militia had not." By concealing the Americans and fragmenting the British advance, the woods changed the battle from one of large units engaging each other to one of small pockets of fierce, squad-level fighting among the trees. If you step from the auto path at tour stop 3 to walk onto the battlefield and toward the Nathanael Greene monument near tour stop 8, you'll roughly trace where the American second line stood. The Greene monument is roughly the midpoint of the line. Again, note how the land rolls now both left and right.

Return to the auto path and continue walking uphill toward the site of the Guilford Courthouse. Here the terrain grows hillier. Forget the open area you see today. When battle took place, the area was wooded; the Park Service is restoring the area to its former wooded state. Though many of the Virginians had scattered through these woods, some of them engaged the British in running firefights, uphill and through the woods, wearing the redcoats down. The British soldiers not killed or still fighting in broken pockets of battle now faced the American third line, the seasoned Continental army, which stood at the top of a gentle ridge in the open area around the courthouse. As you approach the site of the courthouse, look for New Garden Road.

The auto path crosses the top of the battleground. Here the 1st Maryland regiment and William Washington's cavalry fought valiantly in the

Battle raged on both sides of New Garden Road, part of the Great Salisbury Road that connected Guilford Courthouse to Salisbury.

third line, taking on the 2nd Guards, one of the best units in the British army. Reports say that the 2nd Maryland regiment fired a single round and bolted for the woods. Fighting was a furious mix of shooting, clubbing, and stabbing; one American soldier, Peter Francisco, achieved notoriety here. An aura of myth surrounded Francisco in the aftermath of the war, as reports said that he may have hacked to death as many as eleven British soldiers, including the guard who severely injured his leg. Nursed back to health by the local Quakers, Francisco returned to

Virginia in time to see Cornwallis surrender at Yorktown. Later in his life, Francisco's own account painted a different picture, acknowledging that he was "seen to kill two men."

As the auto path begins its return to the visitor center, look for the creek, another obstacle the British faced. You'll cross once again the American second line, Old Battleground Road, and the American first line.

Walking at a moderate pace, you can circle the perimeter of the battlefield in about forty-five minutes or so, depending on how long you linger at signboards and how often you take the trails that piece the battlefield. The battle of Guilford Courthouse took about two and a half hours. Having lost over a quarter of his army, Cornwallis chose not to pursue the retreating rebels. Later, after burying the dead, he marched his army to British-held Wilmington to refit. Soon after that, Cornwallis left North Carolina for Virginia, having decided the Carolinas could not be taken. Seven months later, with his men exhausted, hungry, and surrounded at Yorktown, Cornwallis surrendered.

After the battle ended, local residents moved away, claiming that the area smelled foul and that ghosts haunted the battlefield. The Guilford Courthouse community ceased to exist when the North Carolina General Assembly chartered a new town, called Martinsville, at the old county seat. But Martinsville failed to survive, and in 1809, the new county seat moved down the road to Greensboro.

As you near the visitor center, look for a monument to and a parking lot named for David Schenck. In 1857, efforts to preserve the battlefield began, but the Civil War stopped them. In 1876, the effort resumed. Congress, flush with the centennial of the Declaration of Independence, set aside $244,000 for monuments at several Revolutionary War sites, Guilford Courthouse among them.

David Schenck, a Superior Court judge and general counsel for the Richmond and Danville Railroad who moved into the area in 1882, became interested in the battle. Eventually he found a local resident who could help him understand where it had taken place. Using historical accounts, he located where major events of the battle had occurred. Schenck also began buying parcels of land where the American third line had fought.

But Schenck couldn't afford to buy all of the land and so established the Guilford Battle Ground Company in March 1887. The company cleared away undergrowth and planned monuments. It also planned a lake and constructed two springhouses and a restaurant to serve the

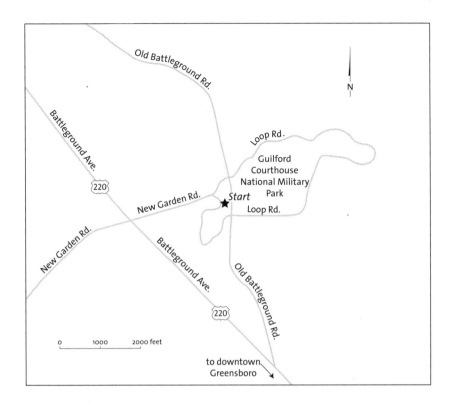

visitors who came. However, interest in the company waned, and the company could not preserve the area without help from the government.

The first attempts to federalize Guilford Courthouse failed. Bill after bill was introduced in Congress to erect a monument to Nathanael Greene, all to no avail. Finally in 1910, Congress approved the monument. Then, in March 1917, Congress voted to establish Guilford Courthouse as a national military park, the first Revolutionary War battlefield to be so preserved.

Walk Details

HOW TO FIND IT: Guilford Courthouse National Military Park
(2332 New Garden Road) is in Greensboro, off US Business 220
North, which is also called Battleground Avenue. Park in the visitor
center lot.
LENGTH: The perimeter is roughly 2.25 miles. You can add in the gravel

Historic New Garden Road, which splits the battlefield roughly in half, and the footpaths that interlace the battlefield for more mileage.

SURFACE: The perimeter walk is paved, as are the footpaths traversing the battlefield. New Garden Road is gravel.

RESTROOMS: At the visitor center

FOOTWEAR: Sneakers

PETS: OK on a leash

MAP: Available at the visitor center. Be sure to get the Park Service map in addition to the black-and-white walking tour guide.

BEWARE: Watch for traffic when you cross Old Battleground Road. This road carries upwards of 20,000 cars a day.

GOOD TO KNOW: The best time to enjoy this walk is during the winter; that way, the terrain looks the way it did the day of the battle, March 15, 1781. Summertime walking is deceptive because fully leaved trees hide the moderately hilly terrain and the creek the British had to slosh across to reach the American third line.

Raleigh

THE DEBATE ENDED HERE

Surveyed by a man named Christmas on a fine April day, Raleigh is something of a gift to North Carolina citizens.

Our early political leaders wanted to end the decades-long debate about which already-established North Carolina city should become the state's capital. New Bern, Wilmington, Edenton, Hillsborough, Salem, Fayetteville, and Salisbury all made good arguments as to why one of them should become North Carolina's capital. Yet just as many arguments existed as to why none of them should.

To find peace, our leaders—an interesting mix of men—agreed to carve a city out of the backwoods where no city previously existed. As they did, they honored established cities with street names. In addition, they named streets for the state's early military leaders, legal minds, and judicial districts. Finally, they named streets for themselves, presumably to honor their own bold decision.

This walk, which traverses the original settlement, tells only some of the stories of the men who founded Raleigh and of the sites you see.

Historical Context

The debate about where to locate North Carolina's permanent capital started in 1744 when royal governor Gabriel Johnston remarked, "We have tried every town in the colony and it is high time to settle somewhere." With that, he moved the colony's government from Edenton to Wilmington. In those days, "every town in the colony" meant Bath and Edenton, the thriving commercial centers of the Albemarle region, where settlement had first taken root. The Albemarle delegates to the General Assembly responded by boycotting legislative sessions.

But Wilmington's service as state capital was short lived. In the 1760s royal governor William Tryon moved the government to New Bern (see chapter 3, New Bern). In addition, he commissioned a fine building: Tryon Palace. You might think that with such a splendid new building, New Bern would remain the capital. You would be wrong. After the

Revolution, North Carolina's argumentative leaders met in Fayetteville, Halifax, Hillsborough, Smithfield, Salem, New Bern, Edenton, and Tarboro—hauling the state's founding documents from town to town in the back of a cart.

Finally, in 1788, after sixteen years of slogging across the state, James Iredell of Edenton suggested that the General Assembly fix the state capital within ten miles of Isaac Hunter's Tavern, which sat along the Petersburg Road, roughly where Raleigh Community Hospital sits today on Wake Forest Road. (See chapter 2, Edenton, for more information about Iredell.) Four years later, the unthinkable actually happened: North Carolina had a fixed state capital.

The Walk

This walk starts at the corner of Hargett Street and Boylan Avenue, roughly the location of the original Wake County Courthouse. The Bloomsbury Estates condominiums dominate the corner today, so look carefully for the granite marker noting the site of the original courthouse.

Before Raleigh was ever formed, the Wake County Courthouse already had a place in history: just two months after Wake County was established in 1771, the courthouse marked a rendezvous spot for royal governor William Tryon's troops as they marched from the coast to battle the Regulators in Orange County (see chapter 4, Hillsborough). In 1781, the North Carolina Revolutionary Assembly met there.

The log courthouse stood at a crossroad. Running through Cross Creek (today's Fayetteville), the Petersburg Road connected Petersburg to Charleston. The other main road in the colony roughly followed today's US 70, connecting New Bern to Hillsborough. The first name of this new county seat was Bloomsbury, adopted from Joel Lane's homestead, which stood close by. As the crow flies, Isaac Hunter's Tavern sat only seven miles or so from the Bloomsbury crossroads.

Walk one block along Hargett Street to St. Mary's Street and the Joel Lane House (728 West Hargett Street). Thought to be the grandson of Ralph Lane, Sir Walter's appointed governor of the original Carolina colony (See chapter 1, Fort Raleigh), Joel Lane settled here in August 1769. Lane had already served as sheriff of Halifax; here he served in the House of Commons, where he introduced the bill to form Wake County. History suggests that Lane picked the sites for the courthouse, jail, and stocks.

The home of Joel Lane, who is often called the Father of Raleigh.

Before the courthouse was built, Wake County's first court session met in his home, a tavern, on June 4, 1771.

On December 5, 1791, three years after James Iredell's suggestion to establish a state capital within ten miles of Isaac Hunter's Tavern, nine men formed a commission. They were Thomas Blount, William Dawson, Frederick Hargett, Henry William Harrington, Willie Jones, James Martin, Joseph McDowell, Timothy Bloodworth, and Thomas Person. Three months later, in March 1792, six of the nine men, Hargett, Dawson, McDowell, Martin, Jones, and Blount, met at Hunter's tavern to discuss the specifics. The next day they moved to Lane's tavern, where they stayed for two weeks.

During those two weeks, the committee reviewed seventeen pieces of property. Three tracts rose to the top: a tract near present-day Cary owned by Nathanial Jones, a tract on the north side of the Neuse River called Milburnie, owned by John Hinton, and 1,000 acres offered by Joel Lane east of the Wake County Courthouse. On March 22, 1792, the commission decided to buy Lane's land for $2,756. Governor Alexander Martin suggested naming the capital Raleigh. James Martin made the purchase and took the deed for the land on the state's behalf. William Christmas surveyed and platted the tract in April, and on December

31, 1792, the General Assembly confirmed the proceedings. Raleigh was born.

From the Joel Lane House, walk along St. Mary's Street to Hillsborough Street. At Hillsborough Street, turn right and walk to Union Square. When you cross West Street, you enter the original town limits.

Cross Salisbury Street, enter Union Square, and walk to the upper-right side at the corner of Morgan and Wilmington Streets. Look for three large stones. Surveyor Christmas used these stones to begin his survey of the first 400 acres composing Raleigh.

North, East, South and West Streets formed Raleigh's town limits. Inside those boundaries lay four public squares: Nash, Caswell, Moore, and Burke. Caswell, Nash, and Burke Squares honored North Carolina's first three governors; Moore honored Alfred Moore, a state attorney general. Today only Nash and Moore remain. In the center of the new town, the statehouse stood in Union Square. The streets bounding Union Square honored the judicial districts of the day: Edenton, Wilmington, Salisbury, and Morgan. Intersecting the boundary streets were streets honoring the towns that had served as state capitals: Halifax, New Bern, Fayetteville, and Hillsborough. Then came the streets the commissioners named for themselves. The last four original streets honored William Lenoir, speaker of the Senate; Stephen Cabarrus, speaker of the House of Commons; Joel Lane; and William Davie. This original design held intact for sixty years.

Turn around and approach the front door of the 1840 Capitol, the second structure on this spot. As was the custom of the day, lots in town were auctioned to raise money to build a statehouse; lot prices ranged from $60 to $254. However, when the first statehouse was built, a Massachusetts architect described it as a plain brick structure, a "huge misshapen pile." The 1840 Capitol is, of course, anything but plain or misshapen.

The General Assembly met here beginning in 1794. Like the Chowan County Courthouse in Edenton, the building had a multipurpose life. It opened for July 4th dinners, theatrical performances, and religious services. In time, the statehouse was enlarged and upgraded. One of the upgrades included a domed rotunda to house a marble sculpture of George Washington carved by Antonio Canova. In 1831, however, the original statehouse caught fire and burned to the ground. Ironically, the fire may have been started by workmen who were installing a zinc roof to help fireproof the building. The marble statue of Washington, surrounded by flame, turned white hot and shattered as burning timbers fell upon it. Fragments, however, were preserved.

Almost immediately after the fire, Fayetteville angled to become the state capital. Not until December 1832, when the General Assembly approved a new capitol, the one you see today, was Raleigh's destiny of being the state capital truly fixed. Completed in 1840, the new capitol cost about $532,682. The exterior granite, quarried in southeast Raleigh, arrived in Union Square hauled by the state's first railroad. A lead box in the cornerstone contains a copy of the journal of the Provincial Congress of North Carolina dated April 4, 1776, a copy of the Mecklenburg Declaration, documents of the Cumberland Association, and a copy of each newspaper published in North Carolina at the time. The General Assembly met here from 1840 until 1963.

At first, churches and inns, not governmental buildings, studded the streets closest to Union Square. Where today's Department of Agriculture stands, the Eagle Tavern once stood. A market house appeared on Hargett Street between Fayetteville and Wilmington Streets, in an area called "grog alley." And, as grog arrived, so did traveling preachers, among them Francis Asbury (see chapter 10, Cataloochee) and John Chavis. While Asbury's legacy is well known, Chavis's is less so.

Debate surrounds Chavis's life. Where he was born? How he was educated? Some scholars speculate that he was born in the West Indies; others think Granville County. Some believe he was self-taught; others think Chavis attended Princeton. Regardless, records agree that he was a free black man who studied at Washington Academy (forerunner of today's Washington and Lee University) and was, in his day, the most learned black man in the nation. He fought in the Revolution in the Fifth Regiment of Virginia and was licensed to preach in 1799. From 1801 until 1807, he preached in Maryland, Virginia, and North Carolina, concentrating here in 1807.

Preaching mainly to black congregations in Granville, Orange, and Wake Counties, Chavis was ordered to stop after Nat Turner's 1831 uprising in southeastern Virginia. Chavis then turned his efforts to education, teaching white children by day and black children at night. Some of the most powerful white men in North Carolina learned their Latin and Greek from Chavis.

As stately as Union Square is today, Frederick Law Olmsted harrumphed at it during a mid-1850s visit to Raleigh. Noting that the town was "pleasing," he observed that Union Square remained "in a state of undressed nature and is used as a hog pasture." At the time, Olmsted worked as a journalist; his contribution as a landscape architect was yet to come.

In the early 1900s, the Italian government gave North Carolina a plaster cast of Canova's statue. In 1970, Romano Vio, an Italian artist, used the cast to create the plaster replica that stands in the rotunda today.

Walk past the monument of the three presidents with North Carolina roots, Andrew Jackson, Andrew Johnson, and James K. Polk. Exit Union Square, cross Wilmington Street, and traverse New Bern Place, which was once part of New Bern Avenue.

Cross Blount Street and look for the original State Bank building and Haywood Hall. Now occupied by the State Employees Credit Union, the State Bank building (123 New Bern Avenue) is Raleigh's oldest financial building. Haywood Hall (211 New Bern Place), the home of John Haywood, the first state treasurer, is the oldest house in Raleigh. Thomas Blount, one of the nine men who helped locate Raleigh, was a mercantile operator and one of the original trustees for UNC. Serving in the 5th Regiment of the North Carolina Continental Line, Blount served time as a prisoner of war in England.

Return to Wilmington Street. Turn left to walk two blocks to Hargett Street. An ardent Anti-Federalist, Frederick Hargett descended from the German Palatines of New Bern. He served in the 8th North Carolina Continental Line, which fought at Moores Creek Bridge, an early Revolutionary War skirmish. An original UNC trustee, Hargett donated land for a public school in Onslow County.

As you walk along Wilmington Street, note the First Baptist Church (101 South Wilmington Street). When the original First Baptist Church formed in 1812, the charter committee contained twenty-three people, fourteen of whom were black and nine who were white. The congregation grew to about 436 people by 1859, relocating several times. In June 1868, due to internal strife following the Civil War, the black congregation split from the white, asking to worship under the name the First Colored Baptist Church. Eventually, the name became, like that of the white congregation, the First Baptist Church. (The other First Baptist Church sits at 99 North Salisbury Street.)

Cross Hargett Street, then turn left to walk one block to Blount Street. At Blount Street, turn right to walk two blocks to Davie Street. Moore Square is to your left. A schoolhouse once sat here. At one point, town residents called it Baptist Square, named for the Tabernacle Baptist Church, which stands on the corner of Hargett and Person Streets. Alfred Moore, whom the square honors, was the second and so far the last North Carolinian to serve on the Supreme Court. (James Iredell of Edenton was the first.) Today the square is home to Raleigh's favorite symbol, the bronze acorn. Symbolizing the City of Oaks, the acorn drops each New Year's Eve at midnight.

The next structure on the left is the 1914 City Market. Before the City Market relocated from Fayetteville Street, the North Carolina state fair took place here from 1853 until 1872.

Davie Street honors William Davie, a titan among North Carolina founders (see chapter 29, University of North Carolina). Though most often remembered for sponsoring the bill to found the University of North Carolina—and for designating the spot where the university would be built—Davie was an accomplished war hero. His most notable contribution came in the waning days of the Revolution in Charlotte. Ordered to harass the British as they entered North Carolina after the battle of Camden, South Carolina, Davie and his 150 men positioned themselves in the center of town (near where the Bank of America building now stands) on September 26, 1780. Around noon, General Cornwallis entered town with a force of about 2,000. Clearly outnumbered, Davie and his men nonetheless made the British charge three times before he and his men retreated toward Salisbury. Even though the British did occupy the town, Cornwallis did not stay long. Davie kept harassing the redcoats, causing Cornwallis to label Charlotte a "hornet's nest." Davie later served as our tenth governor.

Cross Davie and walk three blocks to South Street. To your left is Shaw University, started in 1865 by Henry Martin Tupper, a Baptist minister from Massachusetts. Calling the school the Raleigh Institute, Tupper intended the institution to teach freedmen how to read, and he used Bible classes to begin the work. This was one of several such schools founded in the region in the years after the Civil War, dramatically expanding educational opportunity for black citizens. (Another was the St. Augustine's Normal School and Collegiate Institute, founded nearby in 1867 and making Raleigh a hub for the education of freed slaves; among St. Augustine's most famous early students was Anna Julia Cooper, who became a prominent author and educator in her own right as one of the first black women to earn a Ph.D.) At first, the classes took place in a hotel that stood where the North Carolina Museum of History now stands. Later, Tupper used money he had saved during his time in the Union army to purchase the land where Shaw stands today. Students built the original buildings with red clay found on campus grounds. Ten years later, the school changed its name to honor Elijah Shaw, a Massachusetts textile manufacturer who funded the first building. The striking building you see, Estey Hall, served as the first women's dormitory on a coeducational campus in the United States when it opened in 1873.

At South Street, turn right, walk one block, cross Wilmington Street, and then turn left to see another of Shaw's notable buildings, Leonard Hall (which has twin turrets). Built in 1881 and named for Tupper's brother-in-law Judson Wade Leonard, the structure housed the Leonard Medical School, the first medical school in the United States for black citizens. The first class, a group of six black men, graduated in 1886. Tyler Hall, which stands next to Leonard Hall, served as the hospital.

Retrace your steps to South Street, turn right and walk to the planters. A marker in front of Meymandi Concert Hall (the former Memorial Auditorium) signals where the first Governor's Palace stood. Before the palace opened in 1816, governors rented lodging in downtown boardinghouses when they came to town. Governor William Miller, the eighteenth governor, was the first to live in the building, which likely resembled Tyron Palace in New Bern. This palace was razed after the Civil War. Union general Grant stayed a few nights there, apparently tainting it in the eyes of future governors.

Turn right at the planters and cross Lenoir Street. William Lenoir, who distinguished himself at the Battle of Kings Mountain, later served as speaker of the North Carolina Senate from 1790 to 1795. A French Huguenot from Virginia, Lenoir was a self-taught man. Among his many accomplishments was surveying, which acquainted him with western North Carolina, where he eventually settled.

Walk five blocks along Fayetteville Street to Union Square. Fayetteville Street was the heart of Raleigh's original business district. The Raleigh City Museum, located in the 1874 Briggs Hardware Building (220 Fayetteville Street), has a brochure that explains the buildings and history here. (The Raleigh City Museum is open Tuesday–Friday, 10 A.M.–4 P.M., and Saturdays 1–4 P.M. Free admission.)

One of two cannons that once protected Edenton. They were cast in France before the Revolutionary War.

Cross Morgan Street to reenter Union Square. Exit the square on the north side and walk toward the new Legislative Building. In doing so, you will traverse the museum complex, where several markers explain events in Raleigh during the waning days of the Civil War.

Cross Jones Street. Take a moment to observe the "new" Legislative Building, which opened in 1964. Then take another moment to consider the contributions of Willie Jones, whose name appears throughout this book. Just who was he?

Virtually no decision was made in the early days of North Carolina—about anything—that didn't involve Willie Jones. He was well connected to the Earl of Granville, and his home, located near the southern end of Halifax, was a focal point for colonial society. It sported one of the finest horse-racing tracks anywhere in the colonies. He was a significant landowner, holding 9,942 acres. He marched with William Tryon to Alamance. He led the fight against adopting the U.S. Constitution, and he was a friend to Thomas Jefferson. He traveled with William Davie to locate the University of North Carolina. He served in the North Carolina Senate and unsuccessfully ran for president in the 1790s. When Raleigh was platted in 1792, Jones erected for himself a summerhouse on land just north of town, where St. Augustine's College stands today. Although Jones is buried on the property, no marker signals the grave, and it's a mystery as to what happened to Willie Jones. Nonetheless, it's fitting that both the new Legislative Building and the Department of Administration stand on Jones Street.

Turn right. Walk to and then cross Wilmington Street. Turn left and walk two blocks to North Street, crossing Lane Street. Modern-day governmental buildings fill the area. Beyond them stands the main building of William Peace University (formerly Peace College), which served as a hospital for the Confederate army in 1865. Though the school was chartered in 1857, the building wasn't quite finished when war erupted. After the war, it served as the Freedman's Bureau. During Reconstruction, Henry Tupper, founder of Shaw University, created a stock corporation to reclaim the land for use as a girls' school.

Turn right on North Street to enter the Raleigh of the 1890s. Carefully cross Blount Street (there is no traffic light here). Walk one block to Person Street. Most people who travel Person Street likely don't realize how important Thomas Person was to the formation of North Carolina. Early on, he served the Earl of Granville as surveyor. In doing so, Person learned about choice land across the state. By 1788, he owned 82,358 taxable aces. As a landowner, he attended all of North Carolina's provincial congresses.

Person's political activism erupted when he helped lead the Regulators against William Tryon in 1771 (See chapter 3, New Bern, and chapter 4, Hillsborough). Tryon's troops seized Person and put him under the care of the Reverend George Micklejohn in Hillsborough. During that first night of captivity, knowing that he had incriminating papers at home in his desk, Person somehow convinced the reverend to let him go, promising to return by dawn. In a mad nighttime dash, Person galloped from Hillsborough to his home in western Granville County, a distance of nearly seventy miles roundtrip, to retrieve the papers and burn them. He returned to Micklejohn as promised. When Tryon's troops arrived at Person's home the next morning, they hacked open Person's desk, finding only ashes. Tryon's troops then returned to Micklejohn, who replied only that he had "supped and breakfasted with" Person. Person spent three weeks in irons anyway and was at one point marched to the gallows. Ultimately Tryon had to free Person as he had no evidence against him. The experience indelibly marked Person, so much so that some scholars believe that the language of the Halifax Resolves is largely Person's work. When North Carolina became a state, Thomas Person was one of its most generous benefactors, loaning money to Governor Burke and underwriting UNC.

Cross Person Street. Turn left, and then turn right onto Oakwood Street. Walk two blocks to East Street, crossing Bloodworth Street. Some records suggest that Bloodworth Street honors James Bloodworth, but it's possible the name honors Timothy Bloodworth. Active in Wilmington politics, Timothy Bloodworth helped form the Wilmington Safety Committee and was so harsh to Wilmington-area Loyalists that some people accused him of trying to depopulate New Hanover County. After North Carolina joined the Union, Bloodworth served one term as a U.S. senator.

At East Street, turn right for a sampling of Raleigh's Victorian architecture. At Lane Street, turn right and walk two blocks to Person Street, crossing Bloodworth again. Lane Street is the only original Raleigh street named for a Wake County resident.

Cross Person Street and walk to Blount Street. The Governor's Mansion, which stands where Burke Square once stood (See chapter 4, Hillsborough, for more information about Thomas Burke), appears to your left.

The 1891 Governor's Mansion, built in the Queen Anne style. The first Governor's Mansion sat near today's Meymandi Concert Hall (formerly Memorial Auditorium).

Turn left at Blount Street to walk in front of the Governor's Mansion, which was built with convict labor. The first governor to live here was Daniel G. Fowle, beginning in 1891. Though the quarters have been renovated several times, the exterior has been altered very little.

At the intersection of Blount and Jones Streets, you'll see the NC Museum/Government Center Parking lot.

Walk Details

HOW TO FIND IT: Raleigh is located in the east-central portion of North Carolina, off I-40. If possible, park in the NC Museum/Government Center Parking lot (100 East Jones Street). This walk ends there. Once you park, follow the directions below to the original Bloomsbury crossroads, where this walk begins.

1. From the parking lot, walk south along Wilmington Street toward the old State Capitol building.

2. At the corner of Wilmington and Edenton Streets, cross Wilmington Street. With the 1840 Capitol to your left, walk Edenton Street to Salisbury Street. Don't tarry at the old Capitol now; you'll return soon.

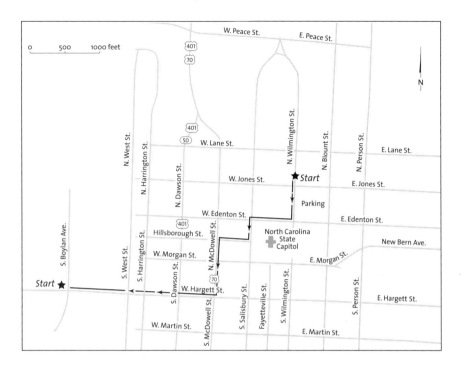

3. Cross Salisbury Street and turn left to walk to Hillsborough Street.

4. Cross Hillsborough Street. Turn right, and walk away from the Capitol along Hillsborough Street.

5. Turn left at McDowell Street, and walk two blocks to Hargett Street.

6. Cross Hargett Street and turn right. On your left you'll see a park, Nash Square, one of Raleigh's two original remaining public squares.

7. Walk west three blocks along Hargett Street, crossing Dawson, Harrington, and West Streets. This short stretch is scruffy, but improvements are on the way. Cross the railroad track and ascend the short hill to the intersection of Hargett and Boylan Streets. The walk begins here.

LENGTH: About 3.25 miles

SURFACE: Paved

RESTROOMS: At the Raleigh City Museum located at 220 Fayetteville Street, inside the old Briggs Hardware Building

FOOTWEAR: Sneakers

PETS: OK on a leash

MAP: For more information about Raleigh architecture or other sites on this route, visit www.visitraleigh.com/visitors/things_to_do/downtownwalkingtour.

GOOD TO KNOW: For information about parking in downtown Raleigh, see http://www.godowntownraleigh.com/get-around/parking.

For information about the Joel Lane House, see http://www.joellane.org/.

Capital Area Visitor Services, located in the lobby of the North Carolina Museum of History, provides information about touring Raleigh's state-owned attractions. For more information, call 919-807-7950 or 866-724-8687 or visit http://ncmuseumofhistory.org.

For information about touring Oakwood homes and gardens, see www.historicoakwood.org/history.php.

The first floor of the Governor's Mansion is open for tours, most often during the holiday season. Call 919-807-7950 for tour times.

Murphy

THE TRAIL OF TEARS

Our southern mountains are rich with the history of the Cherokee. Long before white settlers first explored the backcountry of the southeastern United States, the seven clans of the Cherokee people had established a network of communities that stretched over the entire region. But the mountains of western North Carolina are the heart of the Cherokee homeland. As Brett Riggs and Barbara Duncan write in their *Cherokee Heritage Trails Guidebook*, "The Cherokees say that they have always been here in the southern mountains, that the Creator put them here." Cherokee creation stories say that their first village was at the Kituwah Mound, near today's Bryson City, and that the surrounding mountains and valleys are full of spiritual and cultural significance.

In 1540, when Spanish explorer Hernando de Soto and his men traveled through the edges of Cherokee territory, cautious trade between the Cherokee and Spanish explorers was punctuated with violence, as de Soto's men executed those who would not help guide them to the next village. These first encounters foreshadowed the long and increasingly difficult history between Cherokees and white settlers. At times, relations between settlers and Native Americans were friendly; over time, however, they turned tragic.

This walk takes you to an emblem of that tragedy, the site of Fort Butler, in Murphy. Fort Butler served as the headquarters for the Eastern Division of the U.S. Army when, in 1838, some 16,000 Cherokee were removed from the southeastern United States on a forced march that came to be known as the Trail of Tears. In 1987 the National Park Service established the Trail of Tears National Historic Trail to commemorate the Cherokee's forced migration. The trail stretches across nine states and includes thousands of miles of land and water routes.

The phrase "Trail of Tears" comes from the Cherokee *Nunna Daul Tsunny*, or "the trail where they cried." It's easy to feel the heartbreak when you read the words of one survivor: "Long time we travel on way to new land. People feel bad when they leave Old Nation. Womens cry and make sad wails. Children cry and many men cry . . . but they say nothing and just put heads down and keep on go towards West. Many days pass and people die very much."

From mid-June until mid-July 1838, over 3,000 Cherokee passed through the Fort Butler depot on their journey west.

Historical Context

When historians and anthropologists refer to Native American tribes before European contact, they often do so by language group. Tribes of the Algonquian language family such as the Neusioc and Roanoac lived in coastal North Carolina, and tribes of the Siouan language family such as the Saura, Occaneechi, Catawba, and Cheraw lived in central North Carolina. The Cherokee, however, belonged to the Iroquoian language family, linked to Native American tribes of the Great Lakes region. (Many archaeologists and historians believe the ancestors of the Cherokee migrated to the southeast from the Great Lakes.) By the late 1600s, Europeans and Cherokees clearly knew of each other. The word *Charaquie* appeared in French documents by 1699, and Cherokees provided British traders with deer hides as they continued their inland settlement. Sharyn Kane and Richard Keeton, authors of *Beneath These Waters: Archaeological and Historical Studies of 11,500 Years along the Savannah River*, believe that in 1707, over 121,000 deer hides were traded in South Carolina alone.

Beyond being trading partners with European explorers, Native Americans were a source of slaves to early settlers. Though the Lords Proprietors (see chapter 2, Edenton) had issued an edict in 1677 stating that only colonial governments could engage in the slave trade, white settlers took advantage of long-standing disputes between Native American tribes and pitted tribes against each other. By trafficking in slaves, Native Americans could get guns and gunpowder, something that made their quarrels with each other—in particular the fractious relationship between the Creek and the Cherokee—even more troublesome. The Cherokee, who had largely avoided the slave trade, sent a delegation to Charleston in 1693 to offer "friendship, coupled with pleas for protection from other Indians hunting slaves" to get their share of the English guns.

The Cherokee, the friendliest of the southern tribes, also insulated the British colonies in the east from the French and Indians to the west. This usefulness was in part why the British colonel George Chicken visited the area near Murphy in 1725. During the Revolution, the Cherokee generally supported the British. During the War of 1812, however, the Cherokee supported the Americans. The military alliance between the Cherokee and the Americans reached its high point when, in 1814, the Cherokee helped General Andrew Jackson defeat a portion of the Creek tribe known as the Red Sticks in the Battle of Horseshoe Bend. The battle effectively ended the military struggle between the United States and the Creeks, who were forced to sign a treaty surrendering more than 20 million acres of land. Legend has it that Cherokee Chief Junaluska personally saved Jackson's life during the battle.

Trusting their white allies during the eighteenth and early nineteenth centuries, the Cherokee adopted European ways and eased into a trade-based economy. They intermarried with white settlers, adopted the English language, and used European tools in their farming. Their cabins and homesteads came to resemble those of whites, and some Cherokee planters owned slaves. In some cases, they managed way stations along the Unicoi Turnpike, a trail that matured into the main thoroughfare between north Georgia and the Smoky Mountains.

The Walk

Begin at the Cherokee County Historical Museum (87 Peachtree Street), next door to North Carolina's only blue marble courthouse. This courthouse, dedicated in 1927, is the fifth structure built here for use as a courthouse.

Walk past the courthouse into town and cross Peachtree Street at the first traffic light. Continue walking right to the intersection of US 19 Business, Valley River Avenue, and Peachtree Street. Two markers note Spanish interest in the area. Hernando de Soto wandered through in 1540 looking for gold. Juan Pardo, who came through twenty-seven years later, was to claim the interior of the New World for Spain and convert the natives to Catholicism. In addition, he was to find a quick route to the silver mines in Mexico. Mexico, however, is nearly 2,000 land miles away, and Pardo left disappointed.

At the marker noting the visit of British colonel George Chicken, turn left and walk downhill across the Hiwassee River. Pass the old L&N Depot and walk over the W. Frank Forsyth Bridge.

The friendship between the Cherokee and the white settlers unraveled due to the settlers' appetite for land. Though a 1785 treaty established recognized borders between the two nations, other treaties

The distinctive blue marble courthouse of Cherokee County, the fifth such structure built here. Fire destroyed the first four wooden courthouses.

chipped away at Cherokee land. At one point, Thomas Jefferson tried to induce the Creek, Choctaw, Chickasaw, Seminole, and Cherokee to leave by offering to leave them alone if they would go west across the Mississippi into land acquired by the Louisiana Purchase.

Some Cherokee migrated. Most, however, did not. They were happy and prosperous where they were, even though by 1819, 90 percent of their land was gone. By the mid-1820s many Cherokees could read using the alphabet Sequoyah had developed. (By 1830, the Cherokee literacy rate would be higher than that of the United States.) Modeling their government on that of the United States, they elected a chief, a senate, and a house of representatives. They had a constitution that incorporated them as the Cherokee Nation. Article 1, Section 1 describes what the Cherokee believed was their country according to the current treaties: north Georgia, eastern Tennessee, and southwestern North Carolina. It was their legal attempt to protect what land they still possessed.

It's impossible to say what the story would have been had gold not been discovered in 1828 in the north Georgia mountains near present-day Dahlonega, an area inside the Cherokee boundary. Legal maneuvering had started before the discovery of gold when, in 1819, Georgia asked the federal government to remove the Cherokee. The appeal failed. When news leaked out of the discovery of gold, tensions between white settlers and the Cherokee exploded.

In 1828, Georgia outlawed the Cherokee government, taking tribal lands. The Cherokee National Council responded in 1829 with a law making cession of tribal land a capital offense. In 1830, President Andrew Jackson, a firm believer in Manifest Destiny, pushed the Indian Removal Act through Congress.

Jackson's action, though generally popular, drew criticism from four notable men: Henry Clay, Daniel Webster, Ralph Waldo Emerson, and Davy Crockett. In his 1834 autobiography, Crockett wrote: "I believed it was a wicked, unjust measure and that I should go against it, let the cost to myself be what it might . . . I voted against this Indian bill, and my conscience yet tells me that I gave a good honest vote and that I believe will not make me ashamed in the day of judgement."

Some credit Crockett's break with Jackson with ruining Crockett's political career and prompting his journey to the Alamo.

Legal maneuvering escalated, and two factions of Cherokees emerged. A small group agreed with Major Ridge, John Ridge, and Elias Boudinot, editor of the Cherokee paper *Phoenix*. The majority agreed with John Ross, principal chief of the Cherokee. Everything broke apart in 1835 when the Ridge-led faction of the Cherokee signed the corrupt Treaty of New Echota.

The Ridge-led Cherokee believed that they were going to lose their land anyway and that the way to avoid doing so at a complete loss was to sign the treaty. They believed that the federal government would pay $4.5 million for the land they left, assume the cost of relocation, and give them land in Oklahoma. Twenty Cherokees signed the treaty. However, the overwhelming majority of Cherokees did not support the treaty and refused to move.

Legal maneuvering continued, but in 1836 Congress ratified the treaty anyway—by one vote. John Ross presented Congress with a petition containing over 15,000 signatures, asking that the treaty be voided. It was not. The Cherokee had two years to move. They did not.

At the corner of Valley River Avenue and Lakeside Street, cross Lakeside onto Hunter Street. Turn left onto Cherokee Street and walk to Fort Butler Street. Near the end of Fort Butler Street, look for a monument marking where Fort Butler once stood.

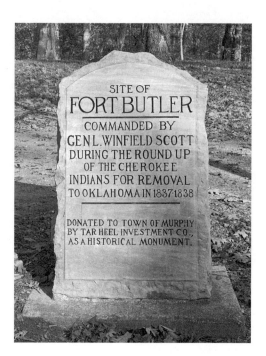

This marker commemorates Fort Butler, a collection fort and the place where the Trail of Tears began for the Cherokee Nation.

Western North Carolina was full of forts meant to keep order after the Treaty of New Echota was ratified. Fort Lindsay (near present-day Almond), Fort Hembree (near present-day Hayesville), Fort Delany (near present-day Andrews), Fort Montgomery (near present-day Robbinsville), and Camp Scott (flooded by the manmade Nantahala Lake) were among them. Fort Butler served as the collection depot for these other forts.

In late May 1838, the forced removal started. It was ugly. State militia in Georgia harassed the Cherokee. Freeman Owle, an elder and storyteller from the Eastern Band of Cherokee Indians, recalled a story from his great-great grandfather:

> Early one morning he heard a knock on the door. He and his wife and a small baby named David were in the house. Opened the door and six or eight bayonets were instantly stuck in his face. The Georgia Guard had arrived. Told him to get out of the house and he asked them why. They said it belonged to them. It was Georgia property and they were taking it. . . . So they marched him out of the house under fire, burned down the cabin, killed all of the livestock and marched him into Murphy to Fort Butler.

Reports from soldiers support Cherokee accounts. Evan Jones, a soldier in the Georgia militia, said the Cherokee "were driven before the soldiers, through mud and water, with whopping and hallowing like droves of cattle."

President Martin Van Buren asked U.S. general Winfield Scott to take over. Called "Old Fuss and Feathers" because he insisted on discipline and liked gaudy uniforms, Scott set about his job. Although the direct harassment ended, the stories about the removal are no less painful. Reported Captain L. B. Webster, an officer of the 4th Artillery on June 7, 1838: "There are about six thousand in our neighborhood—their houses are quite thick about us, and they all remain quietly at home at work on their little farms, as though no evil was intended them. They sell us very cheaply anything they have to spare, and look upon the regular troops as their friends. . . . They have no idea of fighting, but submit quietly to be tied and led away."

The first Cherokee to leave suffered greatly. They left at the height of summer; the heat killed many people and livestock. Federal government estimates indicate that three to five deaths occurred each day. It also did not help that collection forts allowed diseases to breed. Appealing to General Scott, the Cherokee asked to delay the removal until the cooler months. Scott agreed. He also agreed to allow Cherokee chiefs instead of U.S. Army personnel to lead the remaining groups. Former President Jackson protested Scott's action but did nothing.

Still, some of Cherokee resisted the relocation, and what happened next has become an enduring Cherokee legend of martyrdom, the legend of Tsali.

Was Tsali a bachelor or an old man? Was he defending his wife against the abuse or just trying to escape? The traditional account is that Tsali was removed from his cabin by force and became angry when a soldier prodded his wife, telling her to walk faster. Speaking in Cherokee to his sons, Tsali hatched a plan to create a scuffle and take the soldier's rifle. Somehow in the scuffle, the soldier shot himself. Tsali and his sons (and maybe as many as 1,000 like-minded Cherokee) fled into the Snowbird Mountains, where they would be impossible to find. Scott offered a deal: if Tsali and his sons came forward, the remaining Cherokee could stay in North Carolina. Official reports say that Tsali came forward but that the Cherokee who stayed had to serve in the firing squad that executed him in November 1838.

By 1839, the removal was done. The Cherokee were in Oklahoma and a new North Carolina county, called Cherokee County, was formed out of the existing Franklin County. The county seat would be Murphy; some factions in town, however, wrote Governor E. B. Dudley suggesting that the new county seat be named Junaluska.

Upon hearing what Jackson had done to his people, Chief Junaluska, who had been given 337 acres of ground in 1847 in present-day Robbinsville for saving Jackson's life at Horseshoe Bend—and who walked from Oklahoma back to North Carolina to live on that ground—was often heard to say, "If I had known that Jackson would drive us from our homes, I would have killed him that day at the Horseshoe." Junaluska's grave in Robbinsville is marked by a plaque, placed there by the Joseph Winston Chapter of the Daughters of the American Revolution.

Retrace your path from Fort Butler Street to Cherokee Street. This time, walk all the way up Cherokee Street, turning left onto 5th Street. At the turn, look for what looks like an unused roadbed. This roadbed is part of the old Unicoi Turnpike. You'll see a sizeable monument on the right in a large flat area. This monument commemorates A. R. S Hunter, the first white settler in the area. Hunter operated a ferry across the confluence of the Hiawassee and Valley Rivers. The flat area on which the monument stands was the site of the hospital area that served Fort Butler.

Return to Hunter Avenue, cross Lakeside Street and walk to the left. The Unicoi Turnpike becomes very obvious. About 0.3 of a mile from the corner, where the curb flattens into a gravel pull-out, look for a pipe in a small, wet area on the side of the hill, across Lakeside Street. This pipe marks the spring where the Cherokee got water while at Fort Butler and as they left town along the turnpike.

Return to the corner of Lakeside and Valley River Avenue. Turn left and walk back up the hill into town. Though the history of Cherokee removal is tragic, it is not the end of the story. Treaties between the Cherokee people and the United States in 1817 and 1819 allowed Cherokee families to leave tribal lands in exchange for the right to apply for citizenship and their own plot of 640 acres. After removal, when Cherokee landowners in North Carolina resisted attempts to seize their land, North Carolina courts upheld the Cherokees' claims. This remnant of some sixty families became known as the Oconaluftee Citizen Indians, and they remained as farmers, day laborers, and traders. In 1868, the federal government recognized the descendants of this community as the Eastern Band of Cherokee Indians, and today they are one of three federally recognized tribes of Cherokee people. The living culture of this

This monument, sitting near the Unicoi Turnpike, honors
A. R. S. Hunter, the first white settler in the area.

small but vital community, centered on what is known today as the Qualla Boundary, reminds us that North Carolina's Native American heritage is as much a part of its present and future as its past.

Walk Details

HOW TO FIND IT: Murphy is located in the far western tip of North Carolina. At the intersection of US 74, 64, and 19, look for Peachtree Street. This street passes the Cherokee County Historical Museum (87 Peachtree Street), where this walk starts.

LENGTH: 3.2 miles roundtrip

SURFACE: Concrete

RESTROOMS: None

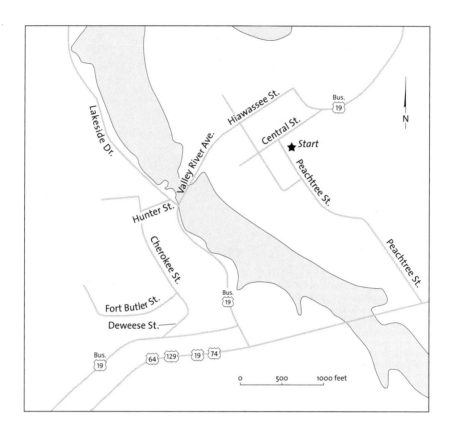

FOOTWEAR: Sneakers

PETS: Not advised; outdoor dogs live at private homes along the way.

MAP: None available

GOOD TO KNOW: The Cherokee County Historical Museum houses the Trail of Tears Interpretive Center, which provides an excellent, in-depth explanation of the Cherokee Nation before and just after the Cherokee removal. It also provides other information about the town. The museum asks a modest entrance fee.

Upon reaching the Cherokee County Historical Museum, Abraham Lincoln buffs might want to continue walking up Peachtree Street, turning right to visit Harshaw Chapel. Here Abram Enloe is buried, whom some people say is the father of Abraham Lincoln. Lincoln's mother, Nancy Hanks, had been taken in by the Enloe family to work as a housemaid.

The walk passes private residences. Please respect them.

For More Exploration

To learn more about the history of the Cherokee, consider visiting the Museum of the Cherokee, located at 589 Tsali Boulevard in Cherokee. Though sixty miles separate Murphy from Cherokee, the drive along US 74 East (assuming you're coming from Murphy) will allow you to enjoy the western North Carolina mountains. For more information about the museum's hours, exhibits, and admission fee, visit http://www.cherokeemuseum.org.

If your travels take you through Robbinsville, look for the brown signs on US 129 that point the way to Chief Junaluska's grave.

Cataloochee

GHOST OF A REMOTE MOUNTAIN COMMUNITY

Time was when "going to the mountains" was a major undertaking. Towns were remote and mountain driving required formidable skill on the twisty, curvy roads. Today, however, the western mountains don't feel terribly remote anymore, and some people find enough hours on the weekend to enjoy a daytrip to the high ground.

To recall, then, the days when mountain communities were isolated and the roads to them demanded serious driving skills—and driver courtesy to negotiate blind curves on steep cliffs—visit Cataloochee, a community preserved in Great Smoky Mountains National Park.

Even today, Cataloochee Valley is a world apart; to reach the high valley, you must travel a gravel road carved onto the side of a mountain. Once there, however, you can marvel at the world of the mountain people. Here, men showed their measure by the bears they killed, bears that they had named: Honest John never killed more than he could eat. Old Kettlefoot killed for the sake of killing. Cataloochee women were healers: boneset tea made a good spring tonic. Groundhog grease could ease a chest cold. Everyone watched for bell-tails—rattlesnakes—and if a person weren't careful, a run-in with an animal could mark him for life, as Polecat John Cagle and Turkey George Palmer discovered.

Historical Context

The Cherokee hunted and fished here first, naming the area *Gadalutsi* to describe a place where trees "stood erect." To reach the high valley, they used a footpath later called the Cataloochee Trail.

One of the earliest travelers of the Cataloochee Trail was Francis Asbury, father of the American Methodist Church. He documented the day he followed the Cataloochee Trail, November 29, 1810, writing, "Friday, our troubles began at the foaming, roaring stream, which hid the rocks. At Cataloochee I walked over a log. But O, the mountains, height after height, and five miles over! After crossing other streams, and losing ourselves in the woods, we came in, about nine o'clock. . . . What an awful day!" Asbury says further that the trip left him "strongly afflicted with pain." That's no surprise: the steep ascents and descents of today's gravel road into Cataloochee are breathtaking. Later Asbury would recall his trip, writing, "I rode, I walked, I sweated, I trembled and my old knees failed; here are gullies, and rocks, and precipices." Yet Asbury found settlers in Cataloochee to whom he could preach. Plentiful wild game, beautiful vistas, sparkling streams and creeks: the early settlers must have thought they lived in Eden.

The earliest recorded white settler in Cataloochee was Henry Colwell, who bought land there in 1814, intending to graze cattle. Twenty-two years later, his grandson Levi Caldwell arrived to homestead. By then, Cataloochee Trail had matured into the Cataloochee Turnpike, a toll road used by drovers. Today, NC 284, Tennessee 32, and Cove Creek Road follow parts of the historic turnpike.

Better transportation brought more families into this Eden, and for almost one hundred years they prospered. When the Park Service announced that it intended to buy parcels to help form Great Smoky Mountains National Park, the area population numbered nearly 1,300, making it the largest settlement in the Smokies. Residents who heard the news, which was announced in Palmer's Chapel, couldn't believe their ears. Firsthand accounts tell of women holding their babies, tears running down their faces, wondering where they would go and what they would do. Menfolk threatened to fight. Some even talked of blowing up the road leading to Cataloochee. Reluctantly the residents moved.

Understanding their reluctance to leave is easy when you visit here. So is understanding why even today the descendants of the families return to tidy the cemeteries, attend services in Palmer Chapel, and have dinner on the grounds. The beautiful valley is its own world.

The Walk

From the parking area at Pretty Hollow Gap, step over to Beech Grove School, several yards beyond the rhododendrons. Beech Grove School dates to 1907. Its story speaks to the tenacity of Cataloochee residents.

North Carolina's 1838 public school law required counties to provide schooling, but provided no funding for schoolhouses. Nor did that law say what to teach, how long the school term should be, or what qualified a person to teach. So, until 1868, whatever Cataloochee residents learned—cooking, weaving, hunting, farming skills, Bible verses, and music—they learned at home or in church. When, in 1868, a new state

Inside Beech Grove School, where the children of Cataloochee learned their ABCs.

constitution required the General Assembly to educate, tuition free, all children between the ages of six and twenty-one, life started changing in Cataloochee.

By 1880, eighty-five children were crowding into Beech Grove School. The term ran from November through January; if enough local taxes could be collected, a spring term ran from February through March. For years, the school coped with serious overcrowding until finally, in 1905, the Cataloochee School Board—Steve Woody, Hiram Caldwell, and George Caldwell—traveled by horseback to Waynesville to ask the Haywood County commissioners for a new, larger school. The twenty-five-mile round-trip distance required three days. But the commissioners turned them down, saying that the residents didn't pay enough taxes to warrant a new school building.

Resilient in finding ways to get things done, the angry men bought a bottle of whiskey and started talking. They didn't want to tell Cataloochee residents about their failure; besides, they needed a new school. A plan took shape: because "the law" required the children go to school, if the school burnt down, they reasoned, the county would have to build a new school. Making a solemn pact not to tell anyone of their plan until only one was left alive, the three men removed the contents of the school—the desks, the books, the lunch buckets, everything—

hiding it all in the nearby woods—and then burned the schoolhouse. When the structure you're standing in opened for class in 1907, the contents and furnishings mysteriously reappeared. As you imagine eighty-five school-aged children in here, remember that this schoolhouse is bigger than the one that burned in 1905.

To visit a preserved Cataloochee farmhouse, walk left along the last half mile of Cataloochee Road to Hiram Caldwell's house and barn. In 1836, Levi Caldwell arrived in Cataloochee with his family, ready to homestead on his grandfather's property. Until 1903, Levi and his family lived in Grandfather Henry's log house here. Legend says that Mary Ann, Levi's wife, had a thrilling encounter with a panther in that cabin. She was cooking pork in a big pot in the fireplace while Levi was away. He had taken sacks of corn over the mountain to a mill. Because he didn't have a horse, Levi put a sack on each shoulder and started walking.

Smelling the pork, the hungry panther circled the cabin, striking terror with its bloodcurdling shrieks. Other panthers came out of the night to circle the cabin, too, and Mary Ann later told of the panthers jumping on the roof, clawing at the wooden shingles. She feared that a panther might come down the chimney, so she built a large fire in the fireplace. Just before daylight Mary Ann fell asleep. The fire, unattended, burned out. She heard scratching; a rock fell into the fireplace. The panther was coming down the flue! Mary Ann grabbed a string of dried peppers, threw them in the embers, and fanned the embers for all she was worth. When the peppers caught fire and flamed up, their gases burned the panther's eyes. He crawled out of the flue and left.

You won't see any panthers here today—they were extinct by 1950 or so—but you may see elk. In spring 2001, the National Park Service released twenty-five elk into Cataloochee, making it the first time elk had roamed the Smokies in nearly 200 years. The elk came from the Land Between the Lakes National Recreation Area along the Kentucky-Tennessee border. To date, they have successfully established themselves.

Architectural details of the house reveal that Hiram Caldwell was wealthy. Lumber, not rough-hewn logs, skins the house. Bead board serves as interior paneling.

To see another preserved Cataloochee house and enjoy a woods walk, walk two miles to Steve Woody's house, which sits adjacent to Rough Fork Trail. Rough Fork Trail follows an old railroad bed and crosses a creek several times on foot logs.

The home of Hiram Caldwell, a descendant of one of the first white families to settle in Cataloochee.

Steve Woody was likely the last resident to leave Cataloochee after it became part of the Great Smoky Mountains National Park. Most families had left by 1937, but records indicate that Woody stayed until 1944. Woody's house began as a one-room log cabin, but he expanded it several times between 1901 and 1910 as he raised eight children there. As the mountain economy slowly changed from subsistence farming to tourism, Woody adapted: he allowed sightseers and trout fishers to sleep in his house and barn and to fish the streams on his property. Other stories indicate that Woody shrewdly earned a living in other ways: an apple buyer once arrived looking for his neighbor, Hiram Caldwell. Woody told him that Caldwell had already sold his apples, but that the buyer could buy Woody's apples so as not to leave with an empty wagon.

Return to Pretty Hollow Gap. Walk about .7 mile along Pretty Hollow Gap Trail, a gently rising old roadbed, to Little Cataloochee Trail. Today a horse camp stands were Jesse Palmer's house once stood.

Little Cataloochee Trail appears about a half mile later on the right. The major path between the early-settled Big Cataloochee and the later-

The home of Steve Woody, likely the last person to leave Cataloochee settlement after the federal government established Great Smoky Mountains National Park.

settled Little Cataloochee, this path requires now, as then, a full day to walk the round-trip, eleven-mile distance. However, if you walk about twenty minutes up the mild ascent to Davidson Gap, you can see the remains of a homestead on the left. Look trailside left for a small rock wall and small yucca plants; these signal the remains of a house foundation. Further up the trail are remnants of the Cook cabin, little Cataloochee Church, and the Hannah cabin.

Return to Pretty Hollow Gap Trail. For another two miles of easy walking, turn right for an out-and-back jaunt to Indian Flats, where Turkey George Palmer lived. Palmer Creek, the stream that you hike along, was famous for its trout population. Stories say that a man once caught ninety-seven brook trout in it. Today the stream is closed to fishing to protect the declining trout population. On the right side of the trail, look for the home of Turkey George Palmer.

Turkey George Palmer was the son of Jesse Palmer and the great-grandson of George Palmer. The eldest Palmer arrived in Cataloochee in 1848, apparently trying to start his life over. He had fallen in with the wrong crowd somewhere in Buncombe County, losing all of his money in gambling and drinking. He needed a place to start over, one where there weren't many people; Cataloochee fit the bill. By 1858, Palmer was a prosperous farmer, making good on the lessons of his earlier mistakes. The Palmer family was among the most successful in Cataloochee, giving their name to the chapel where Methodist circuit-riding preachers visited each month. The ranger station you passed on the way in once belonged to Jarvis Palmer, George Palmer's grandson.

Turkey George, a most colorful and legendary figure in Cataloochee, earned his nickname in an incident with wild turkeys. Once he had trapped nine big turkeys in a pen so as to keep them out of his cornfield. When he came to the pen to kill the turkeys, the turkeys turned on him. Reported Turkey George, "they riz up an' mighty nigh killed me instead." When he died, Turkey George was buried in a steel casket bought in Waynesville. Having killed 106 bears—some accounts say 105, a minor quibbling point—Turkey George wanted to make sure that the bears still in Cataloochee didn't dig him up out of revenge.

Once you reach Indian Flats, return to the parking area at Pretty Hollow Gap. Cataloochee was truly a world of its own. As Elizabeth Powers notes in *Cataloochee, Lost Settlement of the Smokies*, "Archdukes were assassinated, ships were blown up, volcanoes erupted, bathtub gin was invented, the Charleston was danced, fortunes were lost, tycoons flung themselves to death while Cataloochee followed the slow round of seasons, planting and harvesting, wedding, birthing and burying, with a time to dance as well."

Walk Details

HOW TO FIND IT: Reaching Cataloochee takes steely nerves and perseverance. From Waynesville, travel US 276 North to Cove Creek Road. Just before US 276 merges onto I-40, Cove Creek Road appears to the left. Turn and follow Cove Creek Road into Great Smoky Mountains National Park. At the park boundary, the road changes from paved to gravel. The total distance from US 276 to Cataloochee Valley is about 13 miles. When the gravel road ends in the parking lot, look for the trailhead for Pretty Hollow Gap trail.

LENGTH: This walk has four components:

- Pretty Hollow Gap parking area to Caldwell House, about 1 mile round trip.
- Caldwell House to Woody House, about 4 miles roundtrip.
- Pretty Hollow Gap to Little Cataloochee Trail, you can see remnants of a cabin, about 2.8 miles round-trip

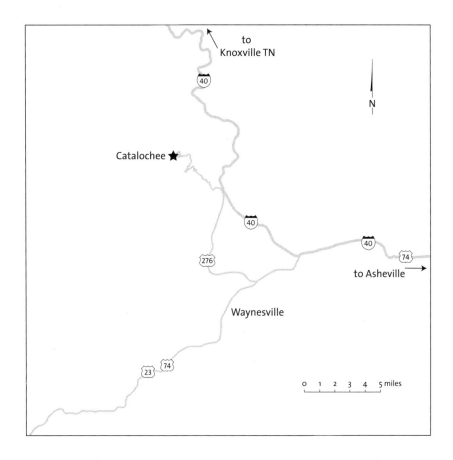

to
Knoxville TN

40

N

Catalochee ★

40

40

74

276

to Asheville

Waynesville

74

23

0   1   2   3   4   5 miles

- Pretty Hollow Gap to remnants of Jesse Palmer's corn mill and
  Turkey George Palmer's house, about 1.5 miles, round-trip.

SURFACE: Woods trail, some road walking, flat or very gentle grades

RESTROOMS: Available at Cataloochee campground, which you pass on
the way to Pretty Hollow Gap

FOOTWEAR: Boots; hiking stick recommended

PETS: Not allowed on park trails. You are in bear and wild boar country
when you're in the Smokies, and you don't want your pet to strike
up a fight with the wildlife.

MAP: None available for this walk because it is an amalgam of several
trails. However, if you want a map, see *Hiking Trails of the Smokies*,
published by the Great Smoky Mountains Natural History Association.

GOOD TO KNOW: You may see wildlife. Give all wild animals a wide
berth, and remember that the animal gets to decide what is wide

enough. If an animal stops feeding it is likely concerned about your presence.

The best time to see the unpreserved sites of cabins is when the leaves are down and undergrowth has died back.

The historic Asbury Trail follows the road into Cataloochee from Cove Creek Baptist Church to the park line. You can pick up the Asbury Trail for foot travel at the park line.

Mountain Discoverers

THE MAGNIFICENT WANDERERS

Since before the American Revolution, wilderness wanderers have visited North Carolina to catalogue and otherwise enjoy our natural landscape. It is indeed a wonderful landscape, even though it has challenged people as they tried to settle a state. Through their writing, these wanderers, William Bartram, André Michaux, Asa Gray, and Horace Kephart, helped us understand our state, in addition to telling the world that our western mountains are wonderful places to walk, full of beautiful plants and animals and, best of all, splendid distant vistas.

This collection of walks celebrates where these four men roamed our mountains. In some cases, the walks follow their actual paths.

Historical Context

Nearly 158 years intervene between the visits of William Bartram and Horace Kephart. Nonetheless, these men form a time-spanning wilderness society. William Bartram first tramped through the state in 1773. André Michaux, a friend of Bartram's, arrived in 1794. Asa Gray, a Harvard professor, was studying Michaux's work in 1839 when he found a strange omission of data. Horace Kephart, a librarian-turned-outdoorsman, was inspired by all three and came to the Smokies seeking to restore his health in 1931.

William Bartram

Son of John Bartram, America's first botanist, the well-educated William Bartram had trouble finding his place in the world. He tried being a merchant but fled his creditors. He tried farming rice and indigo but endured crop failures. He tried map-making; that didn't stick either. Some historians speculate that the father despised the son. However, both father and son may have just been eccentric: they reportedly horrified George Washington by refusing to weed their gardens.

Dr. Samuel Fothergill, the father's patron, took an interest in William, noting his superb ability to draw birds and plants. Fothergill wrote

John Bartram saying, "it is a pity that such a genius should sink under distress." So, in 1773, at age thirty-six, William Bartram came south at Fothergill's behest to catalog plants and send specimens back to England. Wandering alone throughout the southeast and into the mountains for the next four years—missing the American Revolution—Bartram became a roving botanical reporter. As he did, he gained a new name: the Cherokee called him *Puc-Puggy,* "Flower Hunter."

His book *Travels of William Bartram through North and South Carolina, Georgia, East and West Florida,* published in 1791, describes everything Bartram saw, from his encounters with the Cherokee to his discovery of the flame azalea. Some think that the book, a classic of naturalist writing, inspired passages in S. T. Coleridge's poems "Kubla Khan" and "The Rime of the Ancient Mariner." Though the book is more a catalog than a narrative, Bartram's drawings are exquisite. Where he does narrate, the prose is positively rhapsodic, for Bartram saw the soul and beauty of everything.

André Michaux

André Michaux was well educated, but he was also a farmer's son. And at age fourteen, his father removed him from school to accustom his son to a farmer's hard life. The experience resulted in Michaux gaining a reputation for being able to grow even the most difficult plants. Given the importance of agriculture in the late 1700s, Michaux's gift brought him the notice of Louis XVI.

Were it not for the death of his young wife days after giving birth to their only child, Michaux might have happily become the royal gardener. Instead, the physician for Louis XVI noticed Michaux's grief as well as his botanical gift and encouraged the young man to travel to foreign lands to collect plants and then return with them to France to see if he could make them grow. Putting his son in the care of his family, Michaux did exactly that. After traveling to Persia to study plants, Michaux arrived in America in 1783. Once here, Michaux met William Bartram, who inspired Michaux to visit the forests of the southern Appalachians. France, having depleted its forests in building ships to wage war against the English, needed its forests restored. Michaux came south, bringing with him plants that southerners would come to love: crape myrtle and camellias.

Like Bartram, Michaux wandered about, "herborizing." He passed through present-day Belmont, near today's Daniel Stowe Botanical Garden, and Lincolnton and Morganton. His journals speak of seven journeys through the Piedmont, where he discovered the rare, bigleaf magnolia, which would become the rage of Europe. The Empress Josephine was among the first to have one in her garden. One wonders if Michaux also brought to Josephine another plant: the rhododendron catawbiense. Discovering it in the headwaters of the Catawba River, likely near Linville Gorge, Michaux named this purple-blooming shrub that North Carolinians adore.

Asa Gray

A New Yorker, Asa Gray attended Harvard to become a medical doctor. But soon he left medicine for botany, and by age thirty-two, Gray was a professor of natural history at Harvard. Given the link between America and France with regard to botanical research, Gray started traveling to France to study collections there, André Michaux's foremost among them. In 1839, Gray discovered one specimen Michaux had not named. Gray became obsessed with finding and naming it.

Thus to the North Carolina mountains Gray came. For decades Gray roamed the mountains, hunting the plant. He never found it. He did, however, find other plants as well as high adventure. His notes are full of stories of difficult mountain treks and of roads so rocky that they pitched him and his horse into the trees. Among the new plants Gray found was a beautiful orange-red lily, later named Gray's lily, which today grows on Roan Mountain, one of Gray's favorite spots.

Not until 1877 did a seventeen-year-old boy find Michaux's plant on a riverbank in McDowell County. He sent a specimen to a skeptical Gray. Gray returned to North Carolina, but the plant wasn't blooming at the time and Gray could not find it. In 1886, another Harvard professor traveled to North Carolina looking for the plant, and was spectacularly lucky in the original colony that Michaux had described. The flower? The beautiful Oconee bells.

Horace Kephart

Horace Kephart, a professional writer and librarian, didn't set out to save the Smokies or to create a national park, but because of his energy in the effort, the National Park Service today watches over some one hundred species of native trees, more than in any other North American national park. Almost 95 percent of the park is forested, and about 25 percent of that area is old-growth forest—one of the largest blocks of deciduous, temperate, old-growth forest remaining in North America. Over 1,500 additional flowering plant species beautify the park. More than 200 species of birds, 66 types of mammals, 50 native fish species, 39 varieties of reptiles, and 43 species of amphibians call the park home, as do lungless salamanders and a record-breaking variety of mollusks, millipedes, and mushrooms.

In 1913, when Kephart wrote *Our Southern Highlanders*, he provided the first in-depth study of the people of the Smoky Mountains, calling the area the "back of the beyond." Historians later criticized Kephart's study, calling it overly romantic. Kephart's anecdote about making kraut supports their assertion, for apparently he didn't see the poverty: "Once I helped make kraut. We chopped up a hundred pounds of cabbage with no cutter but a tin coffee-can, holding this in two hands and chopping downward with the edge." Even Kephart himself recorded that one mountaineer remarked, "The people around hyur is so pore that if free silver war shipped in by the carload, we-uns couldn't pay the freight."

Kephart's writing about the Smokies suggests that he seemed sure that the unfamiliar terrain and people of the Smokies would stay that way. "The backcountry is rough," he wrote, "No bicycle nor automobile can enter it. No coach can endure its roads."

But Kephart was wrong. When he returned to the area a second time, this time intending to live in the mountains and heal himself from his alcoholism, he saw that the rich forests of region had indeed been found—by loggers. So denuded were the mountains that Kephart became one of the most vocal advocates for a national park. In the *Asheville Citizen* on July 25, 1925, Kephart wrote, "When I came to the Smokies, the whole region was one of superb forest primeval. . . . Not long ago I went to that same place again. It was wrecked, ruined, desecrated, turned into a thousand rubbish heaps, utterly vile and mean."

To see the Smokies today is to see Kephart's belief in the power of regeneration. Like Thoreau, who went to the woods because he wanted to "live deliberately," Kephart believed in the power of nature to regenerate. Though Kephart was unsuccessful in fighting his private demons—he was killed in a car crash between Ela and Bryson City while driving under the influence—he did help create a magnificent national park for all to enjoy.

An interesting outcome of Kephart's time in the Smokies is that in addition to developing a deep and abiding love of the Smokies, he became a skilled outdoorsman, known as the "Dean of American Campers." Outfitters such as Abercrombie and Fitch routinely sought Kephart's opinions on the gear they sold. (Like retailer Eddie Bauer, Ab-

Hike a bit in Great Smoky Mountains National Park and you will likely see remnants of life from early settlers.

ercrombie and Fitch originally sold outdoor clothing to elite sportsmen. Theodore Roosevelt and Amelia Earhart were among the customers.) Kephart's other book, *Camping and Woodcraft: A Handbook for Vacation Campers and for Travelers in the Wilderness*, was for years the gold standard for camping advice. An exuberant and practical book, it offers advice—about everything. On snakes, Kephart notes that "copperheads are more dangerous than rattlers . . . it gives no warning of its presence, nor according to my observation does it try to get out of the way, but holds its ground and springs at any intruder." In explaining how to cope with injury, if such should befall, Kephart advises, "as for the patient . . . let him never say die. Pluck has carried many a man triumphantly through what seemed the forlornest hope."

This millstone marks the favorite campsite of Horace Kephart, who was instrumental in building interest to establish Great Smoky Mountains National Park.

Walk Details

William Bartram

Inspired by Bartram's words, eleven North Carolina citizens formed, in 1977, the North Carolina Bartram Trail Society. They maintain a trail that follows, as closely as possible, Bartram's original route through western North Carolina. This walk follows a section of the William Bartram National Recreation Trail, where you can see Bartram's "sublimely awful scene of power and magnificence" where there is a "world of mountains piled on mountains." Bartram visited the area May 23–27, 1775.

HOW TO FIND IT: The section of trail runs between Wayah Fire Tower and Wine Spring Bald outside Franklin. From Franklin, travel US 64 West about five miles. Turn right onto SR 1442; look for a sign for Wayah Bald. Turn left onto SR 1310. Follow Wayah Road approximately nine miles to Wayah Gap. Turn right onto the gravel Wayah Bald Road, FR 69. Drive 4.5 miles up the Forest Service road to a small parking area at the top. Be sure to climb the Wayah Bald Fire Tower to see a magnificent view, and then follow southward the white rectangle blazes of the Appalachian Trail, which runs concurrent with the Bartram Trail here.

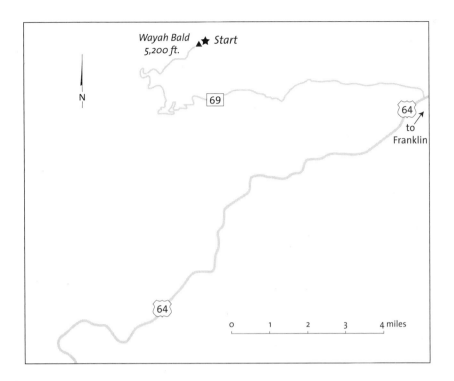

LENGTH: 4 miles round trip
SURFACE: Woods trail
RESTROOMS: Pit toilets
FOOTWEAR: Boots
PETS: No
MAP: Often available at gear shops

André Michaux

One detail forever endears André Michaux to anyone who walks or hikes. In 1794, as he climbed what he believed to be the highest mountain in North America—Grandfather Mountain—Michaux apparently started signing the Marseillaise and shouting, "Long live America and the Republic of France, long live liberty!" You have to love a man who breaks into song when climbing one of North Carolina's most distinctive peaks. To experience Michaux's exhilaration when he climbed Grandfather Mountain on August 30, 1794, walk a highly engineered but spectacular section of the Tanawha Trail near Grandfather Mountain. You may break into song also; the views are among the best in the state, especially at dawn.

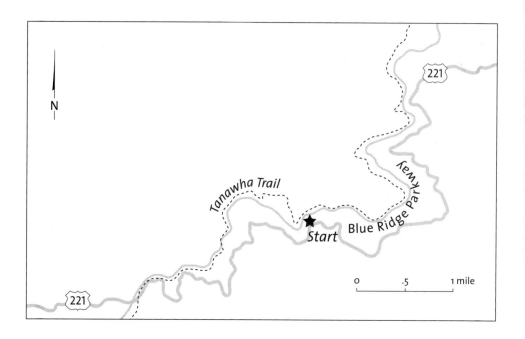

HOW TO FIND IT: Rough Ridge Parking area, Blue Ridge Parkway, milepost 302.8

LENGTH: Almost 3 miles

SURFACE: Rocks, boardwalk

RESTROOMS: None

FOOTWEAR: Boots

PETS: No

MAP: None available

Asa Gray

To see (but not pick) the beautiful but endangered Gray's lily, go to Carver's Gap, at Roan Mountain, and hike north on the Appalachian Trail.
The lily usually blooms in late June.

HOW TO FIND IT: Carver's Gap is located north of Bakersville, where NC
261 becomes Tennessee 143.

LENGTH: 3.5 miles roundtrip if you hike all three balds, Round Bald,
Jane Bald, and Grassy Ridge Bald.

SURFACE: Grassy

RESTROOMS: At the paved parking lot on the Roan Mountain side of
Carver's Gap.

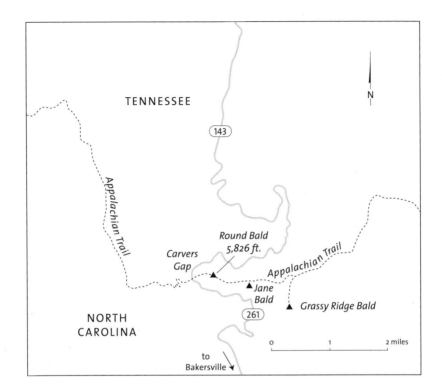

FOOTWEAR: Sneakers OK, boots better

PETS: No

MAP: None available

GOOD TO KNOW: Even if the day is warm, hike with a jacket. These balds are nearly 6,000 feet high, and you'll likely be glad for the warmth.

The lily grows on Jane and Grassy Ridge Balds.

Horace Kephart

You can visit Horace Kephart's last-known permanent campsite, which is located on the Deep Creek Trail.

HOW TO FIND IT: From downtown Bryson City, follow national park signs to the Deep Creek section of Great Smoky Mountain National Park. Once you arrive in the parking area, trail signs will signal the Deep Creek Trailhead.

LENGTH: 12 miles round-trip; strenuous due to length, not elevation gain

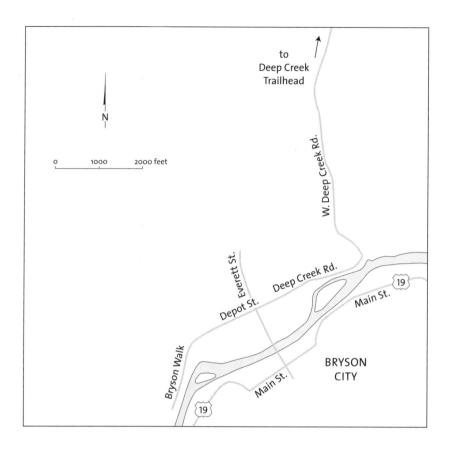

SURFACE: Woods trail

RESTROOMS: At the Deep Creek picnic area

FOOTWEAR: Boots

PETS: No

MAP: See *Hiking Trails of the Smokies*, published by the Great Smoky
Mountain Natural History Association.

BEWARE: Be prepared to navigate several stream crossings.

GOOD TO KNOW: You can most easily find the grindstone that marks
Kephart's last campsite if you walk to Martin's Gap but do not cross
the stream. Instead, turn around, retrace your steps about 75 yards
and then look to your right about 50 yards for the millstone, placed
in 1931 under the evergreens, that marks Kephart's campsite.

You can visit Kephart's grave while in Bryson City. See the visitor
center on Main Street for directions.

Living Our Lives

Colonial Industry of the Sandhills

NAVAL STORES

While North Carolina's economic engine hasn't always been technical and diverse, it has always been global. How so? Through those gorgeous longleaf pine trees, whose long, spiky evergreen needles glisten in the sun and make the wind whisper that formed our first major industry: supplying naval stores to Europe. No wonder that our state toast celebrates these wonderful trees! Likewise, this early industry provided us our nickname: the Tar Heel State.

To enjoy the trees that provided our first big-name export, walk in Weymouth Woods–Sandhills Nature Preserve. Here our longleaf pines filter the sunlight so that you can inspect the scars left by the harvesting of pine rosin, the sap that became tar, pitch, and turpentine.

Historical Context

Many scholars believe that naval stores represent the oldest chemical industry in the world: Genesis 6:14 records that when God asked Noah to build his ark, He also instructed Noah to use pitch to seal it. Evidence suggests that Egyptians used such products to embalm their mummies and that the Phoenicians used them to make their ships watertight. An ancient Greek scientist, Theophrastus (372–287 B.C.), is thought to have discussed the usefulness of the products.

When the New World was being settled, Sweden was a major source of tar and pitch, its trees producing a quality not found in the resinous products of other nations. As Spain and England battled for sea supremacy, Sweden prospered by selling both sides the products that kept the two countries' fleets afloat.

In time, Sweden and England experienced trade difficulties. Naval stores in Sweden had been taken over by a single company, which raised prices, and the decision was made that sales of tar and pitch would no longer be done on Swedish soil, thereby upsetting the British, whose need for naval stores was great and who wanted to be able to sail to Sweden and then bring back tar and pitch in English vessels to cut costs.

Sweden's unpredictability as a supplier was nothing new. The possibility of securing another source for tar and pitch was among the reasons Queen Elizabeth I supported Sir Walter Raleigh's efforts in the New World. As Carroll Butler notes in *Treasures of the Long Leaf Pines*, when Amadas and Barlowe, leaders of Raleigh's 1584 New World expedition, returned to England, they described the prospects for producing tar and pitch: "There are those kinds of tree which yield them [pitch, tar, rosin, and turpentine] abundantly in great stor. In the very same island where we were seated, being fifteen miles in length and five or six miles in breadth, there are few trees else but of the same kind, the whole island being full."

Just how eager was England to find a new supplier of naval stores and quit doing business with Sweden? Jamestown was settled in 1607; in 1608, the first shipment of naval stores left Virginia bound for England. In 1704 England instituted an incentive program to try to get the American colonies to produce more naval stores.

Production of naval stores rose steadily. In 1701, the colonies produced 177 barrels of the stuff. By 1718, production reached 82,084 barrels and represented 90 percent of British imports. Production was so fierce that in 1715 Massachusetts passed what may have been the first conservation law in the New World. Its trees were nearly exhausted, tapped out, you could rightly say.

More people than the British valued the products. Currency was scare in the colonies, and several colonies, North Carolina among them, used naval stores as legal tender. In 1723, the Assembly of North Carolina passed the following law: "Whereas through the great Industry of divers of the Inhabitants of the Province the making of Hemp Rice and Turpentine are much Improved and would become valuable species in Trade in this Government if due Encouragement were given making them equal in their Currency with the Staple commodity of this Government."

As New England exhausted its trees, a business migration foreshadowing that of textiles took place: the industry came south. North Carolina pines were not exhausted. Moreover, to the industry's delight, producers soon learned that the longleaf pine, which grew over 90 million acres from North Carolina to Texas, produced a superior product.

During the American Revolution, North Carolina took the lead in producing naval stores, a position we kept for nearly one hundred years. In 1840, production came to 593,451 barrels—the output of some 1,526 turpentine operations. The output was valued at over $5 million.

At some point during this time, our state nickname began to emerge. According to William S. Powell, professor emeritus of history at the University of North Carolina at Chapel Hill, the first incarnation of our nickname was "Tar boiler," referring to the messy process of cooking pine resin into pitch and tar. His research finds two sources of the disparaging name: an Ohio journal published in 1845 and a poem by Walt Whitman published in 1888. Powell also cites evidence that in 1856 *Harper's Magazine* called North Carolina the "tar and turpentine state."

Given North Carolina's public position as the leader of the naval stores industry, it isn't hard, then, to believe the other story that explains how we came by our nickname. During the 1863 Battle of Chancellorsville, when other divisions ran from the field, North Carolina troops stood alone to fight, standing their ground as though stuck to it with tar. When reports of the battle made their way to Robert E. Lee's notice, Lee reportedly said, "God bless the Tar Heel boys." Over time, the name changed from being derogatory to being loved, and in 1893, when the University of North Carolina established a newspaper, the students decided to call it the *Tar Heel*.

Though the work of distilling resin into tar, pitch, and turpentine would nearly cease during the Civil War, the industry would bounce back. Wooden ships still sailed, and those ships still needed to be watertight. Between 1870 and 1880, North Carolina reached its maximum output of naval stores.

By 1885 our pines were tired and damaged; by 1890 Georgia was leading production. In 1957, with North Carolina's days of leading the naval stores industry well behind her, the General Assembly passed general statute 149–2 establishing our state toast, forever honoring our earliest commercial resource:

Here's to the land of the long leaf pine,
The summer land where the sun doth shine,
Where the weak grow strong and the strong grow great,
Here's to "Down Home," the Old North State!

Here's to the land of the cotton bloom white,
Where the scuppernong perfumes the breeze at night,
Where the soft southern moss and jessamine mate,
'Neath the murmuring pines of the Old North State!

Here's to the land where the galax grows,
Where the rhododendron's rosette glows,

Where soars Mount Mitchell's summit great,
In the "Land of the Sky," in the Old North State!

Here's to the land where maidens are fair,
Where friends are true and cold hearts rare,
The near land, the dear land whatever fate,
The blest land, the best land, the Old North State!

The Walk

Pines bearing the scars of collecting pine resin abound throughout Weymouth Woods trails. However, the best trail to observe the effects of resin harvesting is the Lighter Stump Trail.

Harvesting pine resin was a relatively simply process. All a person needed was a tree, an axe, a bucket, a dipping ladle, and a very strong back.

The first step was to "box" the tree. Usually this step took place in November. The cut would be made about three to six inches above the ground. The width of the box would be determined by the width of the tree, usually about eight to sixteen inches. Boxing would continue until the middle to end of March.

Chips would then be removed above the box to induce the resin to flow from the veins of the tree. The resin would be collected in a bucket, poured into barrels, and hauled to a distillery. Often a distillery would sit next to a river for easier transportation to the port.

Because a tree will try to heal itself, the resin naturally clots, compelling the harvester to re-chip the tree to keep the resin flowing. In effect, tree and man do battle for the lifeblood of the pine.

Today we have a different sensibility to the longleaf pines and the importance of trees in general. Many people react with horror when they consider how pine resin was harvested, and they are very pleased that today we have a new attitude toward using this beautiful natural resource. The buzzwords "renewable" and "sustainable" take on new meaning.

To the earliest residents of the Carolina colony, however, and to many generations afterward, these scarred trees you walk underneath represented the straightest path to wealth.

This longleaf pine still bears scars from cuts made to collect sap, the raw material used in the manufacture of naval stores.

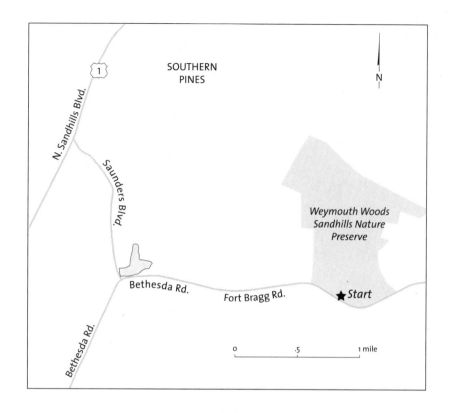

Walk Details

HOW TO FIND IT: Weymouth Woods–Sandhills Nature Preserve (1024
Ft. Bragg Road) is just east of Southern Pines. Signs point the way
from US 1.

LENGTH: 0.5 mile, but easily combined with other trails for more mileage. Use the signboard to design your own walk.

SURFACE: Sand, pine needles

RESTROOMS: At the visitor center

FOOTWEAR: Sneakers

PETS: OK on a leash

MAP: Available at the signboard near park office

BEWARE: Look out for poison ivy. Most of the trails are free of the
noxious vine, but some, in particular the Pine Island Trail, are not.

GOOD TO KNOW: Hours of the park office are November–March, 8 A.M.–
6 P.M.; April–October, 9 A.M.–7 P.M. Exhibits inside further discuss
the preserve. Try your upper body strength by attempting to stir the
sticky goo in the pine resin bucket.

Wilmington

A GRAND PORT CITY

Amid the azaleas and wrought iron, the mansions and church steeples, beautiful Wilmington exudes a vibrant, cosmopolitan flavor.

The roster of famous people who visited here runs long: William Tryon, General Lord Cornwallis, George Washington, Henry Clay, Daniel Webster, James K. Polk, Millard Fillmore, Thomas Edison, William H. Taft, and Jim Thorpe. The list of movies and television shows made here is impressive: *Firestarter*, *Dawson's Creek*, *Weekend at Bernie's*, *The Hudsucker Proxy*, *Touched by an Angel*, *One Tree Hill*, and *Matlock*. The roster of talented people born here is cause for serious state pride: David Brinkley, Charlie Daniels, Roman Gabriel, Michael Jordan, Charles Kuralt, Meadowlark Lemon, and Sugar Ray Leonard.

Yet Wilmington is more than a marriage of antebellum wealth and modern star power. Underneath the beauty is a complex city that has seen and survived much.

Historical Context

The first European to see the beauty of the area was Giovanni da Verrazano. Sailing for the King of France, he described the region in 1524 as "pleasant and delectable." Yet early attempts to settle this pleasant and delectable area failed. The Spanish arrived in 1525 but quit by 1561. In 1663 a group of New England Puritans arrived, intending to raise cattle, but they left within four months. In 1664, colonists from Barbados established a settlement called Charles Town, and within two years there were about 800 people living in the vicinity. They, too, left quickly, going south within six years to establish a new Charles Town, today's Charleston, South Carolina. Not until 1732 would the settlement appear that would one day grow up to become Wilmington.

The Walk

Start at the foot of Market Street at Riverfront Park. Imagine the view without the USS *North Carolina*. This is the oldest of the settled areas of Wilmington. On the marshy land across the river, New Liverpool was established in 1730. New Town—later Newton—where you stand now, was established in 1732. By 1739 royal governor Gabriel Johnston had renamed the settlement Wilmington to honor his friend Spencer Compton, the Earl of Wilmington. The swampy area across the river eventually became part of a rice plantation owned by Richard Eagles.

Today Riverfront Park is a pleasant place to linger. Early on, however, this area was as seedy as a waterfront could be, as bawdy saloon wenches solicited the arriving sailors. Local lore says that Gallus Meg—her name an abomination of "Gallows Meg"—tended bar in the Blue Post pub. She stood over six feet tall and weighed nearly 350 pounds. And Gallus Meg had her standards: she routinely bit the ears from sailors who harassed her "ladies," taking care to spit the ear into a pickling jar that sat upon her bar.

As Revolution fever began to spread, Wilmington was reaching its stride as a city. A monument at the base of Market Street where William Tryon's house sits speaks to the energy that enveloped the city during this time. As Tryon was assuming control of the colony, local citizens—nearly 500 of them according to the *North Carolina Gazette*—were protesting the 1765 Stamp Act. After quelling the disturbance, Tryon moved the seat of government to New Bern (see chapter 3, New Bern). Nonetheless, anti-British fervor continued to grow in Wilmington: when the Battle of Moores Creek Bridge occurred in February 1776, a militia unit mustered here.

With the river to your right, walk along the cobblestoned Water Street to Orange Street. By 1765, Wilmington had nearly 2,000 residents, almost two-thirds of whom were black. Men built wealth in rice, the "sticky gold" of naval stores (see chapter 12 on the colonial naval stores industry), and shipbuilding. Imagine a riverfront crowded with barrels of resin and turpentine ready to be shipped out and warehouses full of ice imported from New England, signs of the city's energetic and far-ranging economic life. Imagine, too, that Orange Street would in time become a departure point for slaves seeking freedom via what came to be called the Underground Railroad. Across the river, swampy Eagles Island provided a somewhat safe haven.

Turn left onto Orange Street and walk to Front Street. The 1740 Mitchell Anderson House (102 Orange Street) is likely the oldest surviving structure in Wilmington.

Cross Front Street, turn left, and walk to Market Street. At Market Street, turn right to walk to Fourth Street and to St. James Church. Revolutionary War activity permeated this area. The Bull Pen, a prison for military and political prisoners, stood near Second and Third Streets. One prisoner held there was Governor Thomas Burke (see chapter 4, Hillsborough). The Burgwin-Wright House (224 Market Street) served as Lord Cornwallis's headquarters in January 1781. Its basement also served as a prison. Among its prisoners was Cornelius Harnett (see chapter 5, Halifax).

Nearly forgotten today, Harnett was a titan of political leadership before and during the Revolutionary War. He represented Wilmington in the General Assembly, chaired the Sons of Liberty's Wilmington chapter, presided over the first North Carolina Provincial Congress, and represented North Carolina in the Continental Congress of 1777–79. No wonder that Harnett was chosen to read the Declaration of Independence when it arrived in Halifax in 1776 and that the men carried Harnett about town upon their shoulders when he finished.

When Cornwallis arrived in Wilmington in January 1781, Harnett fled to Onslow County; he knew that his actions had roused British anger. Cornwallis's men captured Harnett and returned him to Wilmington, carried, reports say, like a sack of meal on horseback. Already in failing health, Harnett was imprisoned, though soon released. He died April 28, 1781, and is buried in St. James Church's graveyard. (Look for Thomas Godfrey's tombstone; Harnett's is behind it, slightly to the right.) An obelisk at Fourth and Market Streets honors Cornelius Harnett. Harnett County (established 1855) is named in his honor.

But not all Wilmingtonians supported the Revolutionary cause. Tom Peters, a fugitive slave living near Wilmington, joined the British army and served in a unit called the Black Pioneers. In 1783 he went with the Black Pioneers to Nova Scotia. While there, he earned the respect of other black Loyalists who had become angry when the British reneged on their promises of land grants and fair treatment. Acting on behalf of more than one hundred black families, Peters negotiated with British authorities in London, drawing the attention of the Sierra Leone Company, which needed people to help rebuild settlements there. The British eventually agreed to give the black Loyalists their freedom and grant them the right of self-governance in Sierra Leone. Eventually, Peters and the contingent he led realized that many of the promises made to them would go unfulfilled.

Return to Third Street, cross it, and then turn left to walk along Third Street. As you walk Third Street, observe evidence of the wealth that accumulated in Wilmington. Blessed with the state's best harbor and a mighty river into the state's interior and surrounded by productive plantations, Wilmington thrived. With newspapers, schools, shipyards, railroads, and theater groups: antebellum Wilmington enjoyed great prosperity. A scan of newspapers in the late 1850s shows an exceptionally brisk business in men's hats and walking canes.

At Nun Street, turn right, walk two blocks to Front Street. Cross Front Street and walk left a few steps to see the Governor Dudley–James Sprunt House (400 Front Street). The lives of these two men personify Wilmington's early 1800s history.

Edward Bishop Dudley came from Wilmington wealth: his father owned 10,000 acres and eighty-seven slaves. Dudley served in the state legislature for many years, as well as in the U.S. Congress. After one term there, he declined reelection, saying that Congress was no place for an honest man.

Dudley then set about diversifying the family wealth. Chief among his activities was encouraging government support of the Wilmington and Raleigh Railroad (later the Wilmington and Weldon Railroad). When the 1835 Constitution stated that the people would now elect governors rather than the General Assembly appointing them, Dudley became North Carolina's first popularly elected governor. However, he had just won office as president of the Wilmington and Raleigh Railroad. Though he resigned that position, he continued efforts to expand rail lines, returning to the job after serving two two-year terms.

James Sprunt, purchaser of Dudley's mansion, was a Wilmington businessman—and blockade runner during the Civil War. From a business point of view, blockade running was understandable: cotton that sold for .03 cents per pound in Wilmington fetched .43 cents per pound in Liverpool. In Wilmington, the Confederacy's thirteenth-largest city, 260 blockade runners entered the port between mid-1863 and late 1864. And though blockade running suggests romance and drama, the reality Sprunt described in his book *Chronicles of the Cape Fear River* was somewhat different:

> Sometimes [blockaders] got in or out by boldly running through the blockading fleet itself, but that was hazardous; for, if discovered, the ocean was alive with rockets and lights, and it was no pleasant thing to have shells and ball whistling over you and

around you. The chances were then that if you were not caught you had, in spite of your speed, to throw a good many bales of cotton overboard. . . .

The wreck of these blockade runners . . . occurred by being stranded or beached, and highly diverting skirmishes would occur between the blockaders and the garrisons of the forts . . . a wreck was a most demoralizing affair. The whole garrison generally got drunk and stayed drunk for a week or so afterward. Brandy and fine wines flowed like water; and it was a month perhaps before matters could be got straight."

Return to Third Street, turn right, and walk to Castle Street. Look for the historical marker to Alex Manly. With the Civil War, the slave-labor economy ended. Moreover, as people shifted from agrarian to industrial lives, they started experiencing cycles of business booms and busts. No longer battling weather and pestilence to create wealth from the ground, people now competed with each other for jobs and wages. But after the war, jobs were scarce in Wilmington, as elsewhere. While available jobs represented a step up to newly freed slaves, these jobs were many steps down to wealthy whites. Resentment festered as Reconstruction took shape. Battle lines hardened: whites, wanting their old way of life back, supported the Democrats. Newly freed slaves and freemen supported the Republicans. The 1896 landmark decision upholding the constitutionality of racial segregation, *Plessy v. Ferguson*, further poisoned the tangled, smoldering relationships between white and black citizens.

Alex Manly, editor of the *Wilmington Daily Record* and generally acknowledged to be the black son of Governor Charles Manly, put himself in the center of the gathering storm with an editorial in November 1898 when he responded to a speech made by Rebecca Felton at the Georgia Agricultural Society. Felton had asserted that the greatest threat farm wives faced was the threat of black rapists.

"Tell your men," wrote Manly, "that it is no worse for a black man to be intimate with a white woman than for a white man to be intimate with a colored woman . . . you set yourselves down as a lot of carping hypocrites; in fact, you cry aloud for the virtue of your women while you seek to destroy the morality of ours. Don't even think that your women will remain pure while you are debauching ours. You sow the seed—the harvest will come in due time." The editorial was reproduced in newspapers around the state, enflaming racial tensions. It was like throwing gasoline on live embers. The rioting that followed Election Day of 1898 and the white supremacy campaign of the era were extraordinary setbacks for race relations, both in Wilmington and across the state. To learn more about these events and their legacy, read *Democracy Betrayed: The Wilmington Race Riot of 1898 and Its Legacy*, edited by David Cecelski and Timothy Tyson, or Rob Christensen's book, *The Paradox of Tar Heel Politics*.

Cross Third Street at Castle Street. walk toward Market Street, turning right at Nun Street. Walk to Sixth Street, cross, and walk just past Gregory Congregational Church to a marker noting Gregory Normal School. After the Civil War, the American Missionary Association supported two schools for black children, Williston Graded School and Gregory Normal School, named for J. J. Howard Gregory, a philanthropist from Marblehead, Massachusetts. Despite appeals for local support, Gregory School closed. Williston Graded School closed also, after suffering three arson attempts in 1897. In 1915, however, a new school emerged, Williston Industrial Institute. It taught skilled trades such as bricklaying, carpentry, and tailoring, a curriculum espoused by Booker T. Washington. This institute was the forerunner of Williston High School, Wilmington's much-beloved and respected all-black high school.

But the 1898 riots so damaged Wilmington that anger still smoldered into the 1960s and 1970s. One young Wilmington man affected by the legacy of racial segregation was Joseph McNeill, one of the Greensboro Four who sat at the lunch counter in Woolworth's in Greensboro (see chapter 34 on the Greensboro Four).

In February 1971, violence erupted again in Wilmington, as students struggled with poorly handled desegregation that closed Williston High School. The firebombing of a grocery store and the resulting arrest of nine black men and one white woman, who came to be called the Wilmington Ten, caused violence to erupt across town. The Ku Klux Klan patrolled the town, and black activists holed up in Gregory Congregational Church. When firemen arrived at the church, snipers shot at them. Fighting raged for about two days. Two people were killed. When the Wilmington Ten came to trial, they received a combined 282 years in prison. But in 1980 the convictions were overturned, and at the end of 2012 Governor Bev Perdue issued full pardons to all of the members of the group. Among the Wilmington Ten was Ben Chavis, descendant of John Chavis, a free black who moved to Raleigh and served as an educator and Presbyterian minister preaching both to blacks and whites.

Gregory Congregational Church stands near a marker noting the location of Gregory Normal School, one of two schools built for black children after the Civil War.

(Raleigh's Chavis Park, built for African Americans during segregation, was named for him. See chapter 8, Raleigh, for more of the story of early attempts to educate freed black citizens.)

Return to Fifth Street. Turn left and walk to Market Street. Cross Market Street and turn right to walk to Eighth Street. Look for the Kenan Fountain, the Bellamy Mansion, and a marker honoring James Shober, the first known black physician in North Carolina. A graduate of Howard University, Shober was the son of Francis Edwin Shober, a lawyer from Salisbury and director of the Western North Carolina Rail Road, and Betsy Ann Waugh, a slave from Salem.

Turn left onto Eighth Street to walk one block to Princess Street. Before you do, note that the Cape Fear Museum of History and Science (814 Market Street) sits diagonally across this intersection. Along the way, look for the Giblem Masonic Lodge. This building once served as the library for Wilmington's black population.

At Princess Street, turn left. Walk one block to Seventh Street, cross it, and then cross Princess Street to walk to Grace Street. Turn left. On your left is St. Mark's Episcopal Church, which welcomed its first black minister in 1869.

Walk Grace Street to Fifth Street. Turn left. Walk to Chestnut Street and turn right. Follow Chestnut Street to Water Street. When you cross Third Street, look left to Thalian Hall and City Hall. When you cross Second Street, look for the Cape Fear Club. A men's club dating to the 1860s, the Cape Fear Club is notable for its powerful Cape Fear Punch, which includes bourbon, rum, cognac, and champagne—among other ingredients.

Cross Water Street, and then turn right to walk to the Coast Line Center. Look for the Cotton Exchange, where the downtown waterfront revitalization efforts started in 1972. At the Coast Line Center, note the adaptive reuse at work with Cape Fear Community College and the Wilmington Railroad Museum.

Turn left to walk the Riverfront Boardwalk and see (as if you could avoid it) the battleship. Commissioned in April 1941, the USS *North Carolina* entered Pearl Harbor in April 1942 to much cheering. Recalled Admiral Charles Nimitz, "our strength and fortunes were at a low ebb . . . and her mere presence in a task force was enough to keep morale at a peak." By the war's end, having performed admirably in every major naval of-

The Bellamy Mansion catches the eye of drivers and pedestrians alike.

fensive in the South Pacific, including the attack on Iwo Jima, the USS *North Carolina* was the most decorated U.S. battleship in World War II.

She was mothballed in 1947; for thirteen years she rusted. In 1960, a statewide subscription drive was launched to save her. Schoolchildren raised over $325,000 in dimes and nickels to help bring "The Showboat" to the harbor to serve as a memorial to the 10,000 North Carolina men and women who gave their lives in World War II.

The nickname "The Showboat" comes from the memoir of Francis E. Tellier, a sailor who served on the USS *Washington*. The story arises out of competition between the newly commissioned USS *North Carolina* and the USS *Washington*. While the *North Carolina* had received much good press, the *Washington* had not. Moreover, Chesterfield cigarette ads featured the *North Carolina,* further wounding the pride of the sailors assigned to the *Washington*.

One day the two ships happened both to be in the Chesapeake Bay at the same time. The *North Carolina* sent the message to the *Washington* that it intended to sail by at 1300 hours and that it expected to receive full honors.

The chaplain of the *Washington*, who also served as the band director, told his band to play "Here Comes That Showboat" when the *North Carolina* passed by, which they did.

The matter might have been forgotten had the *Cougar Scream*, a weekly

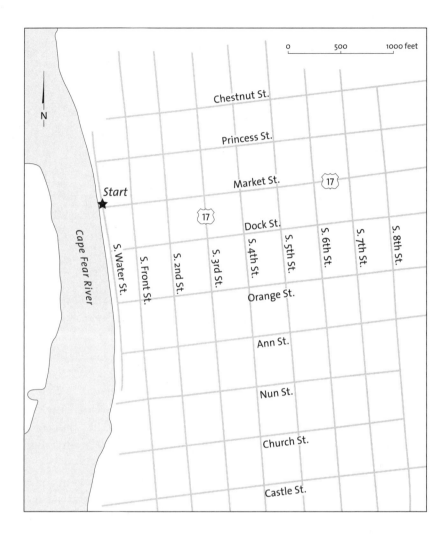

publication on the *Washington*, not captured the story—and had the captain of the *Washington* not tried to squelch the story. Ultimately, the captain was unsuccessful. When the captain saw the story, he recalled the newspaper immediately. But some of the sailors had already stashed the papers in a locker. When a reissue of the *Cougar Scream* came out, several sailors noted that the article about "The Showboat" was missing. Over time the story spread throughout the fleet and the nickname stuck. The captain, in trying to squelch the story of "The Showboat," did more to nickname the *North Carolina* than any other person.

After passing the USS *North Carolina*, you'll return to the base of Market Street.

Walk Details

HOW TO FIND IT: Wilmington is located in southeastern North
Carolina, off US 17 and US 74. Signs will direct you to the waterfront.

LENGTH: About 3 miles

SURFACE: Paved

RESTROOMS: At the visitor center located at 505 Nutt Street

FOOTWEAR: Sneakers

PETS: OK on a leash

MAP: None available

GOOD TO KNOW: To learn more of Wilmington's history, visit the Cape
Fear Museum of History and Science. See www.capefearmuseum
.com.

Ghost walks, pub crawls, Hollywood studio tours, and historic homes tours abound. See www.cape-fear.nc.us/ more information.

Two other books also explain the white supremacy campaign that exploded in Wilmington in November 1898: H. Leon Prather Sr.'s *We Have Taken A City: The Wilmington Racial Massacre and Coup of 1898*, and LeRae Umfleet's *A Day of Blood: The 1898 Wilmington Race Riot*.

The Roanoke Canal Trail

NORTH CAROLINA'S FIRST BUSINESS CORRIDOR

It's 1790, the Revolution is over, and you're a North Carolina farmer somewhere near the Virginia state line. How do you get your crops to market? You can, of course, use what few roads exist to haul your crops to the coast, assuming you have a horse. But covering that distance with a horse will take seven, maybe fourteen, days. (Today the trip along US 158 from Reidsville to Elizabeth City takes about five hours.) As you and your horse and cart plod along somewhere in northern Caswell County, your crops perishing in the heat, you mutter, "If only I had a faster way to get this corn to the markets." If only, indeed.

Solving this problem is the reason the Roanoke Canal came into being. After the Revolution, North Carolina desperately needed a better way for farmers to get their wares to the markets. Indeed, with a better way to get goods to markets, the markets themselves would be more commercially strong. Goods and profits wouldn't be going out of state enriching transportation interests in Virginia, strengthening Virginia.

The answer? The Roanoke Canal, one of North Carolina's earliest attempts at interstate commerce. To walk the trail there today is to get a lesson in how North Carolina struggled to overcome the state's natural barriers so that its citizens could prosper.

Historical Context

Three formidable topographical features—the Outer Banks, the shallow sound waters, and the Fall Line—caused North Carolina to develop much more slowly than did her sister colonies. The Outer Banks seriously handicapped growth due to the shifting—and sometimes disappearing—inlets from the Atlantic Ocean. The shallow sound waters proved difficult for ships to navigate. The Fall Line, running from Maryland to Georgia, describes the jamming of the flat Coastal Plain against the rolling, hilly Piedmont. Rivers that cross this abutment—the Haw and the Cape Fear, for example—usually have rapids and, sometimes, waterfalls. Today these rocky intersections provide fun places to play in our canoes and kayaks; in earlier times, however, the Fall Line made

One of the preserved locks along the Roanoke Canal.

river transportation difficult for boat pilots, usually a job done by male slaves. Navigating a bateau loaded with crops through foamy whitewater isn't a recipe for high profit. One or two overturned boats spell ruin.

In addition, the Roanoke River, the earliest commercially valuable, long-distance river in North Carolina, rises in Virginia's Blue Ridge and serves a large number of that state's farmers. But the Roanoke eventually empties beyond the North Carolina state line and is, therefore, a "North Carolina river." Not surprisingly, the river became a political football as Virginia and North Carolina fought to answer a simple but difficult question: who controls a river? More important, how do you control a force of nature as brawny as the Roanoke River?

The Walk

From the Aqueduct parking lot (off Ponderosa Road), walk east. Controlling the Roanoke started in 1783, when Patrick "Give me Liberty or Give Me Death" Henry supported a Virginia law making it illegal for anyone to obstruct the Roanoke River. The rivers that form the Roanoke, the Dan and the Staunton, bounded his plantation, Red Hill. Like any other planter, Henry needed to get his crops to market.

With laws guaranteeing that the Roanoke would flow freely through Virginia, focus turned to other transportation obstacles: the distance between where the Roanoke emptied into the Albemarle Sound and Norfolk, the nearest port city. Norfolk wasn't easy to reach: the Great Dismal Swamp was in the way. Moreover, before the Roanoke emptied into the Albemarle Sound, the river thundered over a formation called the Great Falls.

How to get around these obstacles? Virginia's government, in place longer than North Carolina's, grew impatient with North Carolina's slow pace of progress and passed a measure to build a canal through the Dismal Swamp. This action distressed North Carolina's government because a canal meant faster transport of North Carolina products out of the state to enrich the Norfolk market.

Cooperation between the two states halted. In 1787 North Carolina started plans to build an Outer Banks canal through a reef near Roanoke Island. Seventy years would pass before work ever started on that canal (work that was ultimately fruitless). In 1790 the two states resumed talks on how to build the Dismal Swamp Canal.

North Carolina agreed to help fund the construction, but in truth our state dragged its feet. The Dismal Swamp Canal would benefit North Carolinians, but it would benefit Virginia more. Virginia, ever impatient with the slow progress, started seriously considering building canals from that part of the Roanoke River in Virginia to the Meherrin River so as to dodge the Great Falls and North Carolina politics altogether.

Outspoken North Carolina senator Archibald D. Murphey tried to rouse the state to action. He believed that North Carolina could improve her fortunes dramatically if the Albemarle Sound could be linked to the Roanoke River, thus bypassing the Great Falls of the Roanoke.

Real progress came when both states realized that a serious percentage of North Carolina products had no port at which to land. Thus, thirty years after Virginia enacted its first laws regarding the river, the North Carolina legislature finally started a public works project: it passed an act to raise money to build a canal to bypass nine miles of treacherous rapids.

The business model was simple: wealthy men could buy shares in the Roanoke Navigation Company to supplement the shares that the state would buy. The company would charge tolls to those wanting to use the river to transport goods. Through subscription and tolls, the company would raise the cash needed to build the canal.

Like other public works projects during that time, the first attempts to conquer the Roanoke River stumbled. Despite initial enthusiasm, many subscribers didn't pay for their stock. Though the Roanoke Navigation Company raised enough money to purchase land for the canal, build houses to lodge the workers, and dig 978 yards of canal—roughly one-half mile—progress ground to a halt. With North Carolina slow to help, the Roanoke Navigation Company turned to the Virginia legislature for help. Virginia entered into a plan much like the one in North Carolina. Still, progress was slow.

Soon you'll arrive at the Aqueduct, an outstanding example of canal engineering from the 1800s. In 1819, the future for the canal brightened because the state took money from the sale of acquired Cherokee lands to create the Fund for Internal Improvements and a board to oversee projects. The money also paid for the services of Hamilton Fulton, a twenty-three-year-old Scottish civil engineer who stepped in to save the stalled, troubled project. Fulton slowly turned the project around.

Still, problems abounded. One concerned labor. In 1822, James Olcott of New York was hired to finish the stonework using Portuguese stonemasons. Whether the stonemasons were actually from Portugal remains open to debate; what is sure is that after a few weeks on the job, Olcott left, stealing everything of value. His workers stayed about another month before they too left. North Carolina and Virginia discussed what to do next and how to pay for it and whose engineering advice to follow. Meanwhile, company-owned slaves dug the canal with axes, shovels, and picks. Stone slabs for canal locks and the aqueduct had to be fashioned not with dynamite but with dozens of smaller holes drilled in lines and then split. Fulton's aqueduct over Chockoyotte Creek is a particularly good spot to look for these holes. As you examine the remnants of the work, know that digging the canals was deadly labor for whoever did it, often slaves. Malaria was a likely plague during the "sickly season," as David Cecelski reports in *The Waterman's Song*. Beyond that mosquito-borne disease, workers had to watch for copperheads and rattlesnakes as they cut a path through the thick undergrowth. Encounters with eastern black bears were also a possibility. Slaves were often flogged to make them work harder, and sometimes, after the flogging, had to endure pork or beef brine poured on the open welts. The only thing that may have made digging these canals more tolerable than other canal projects (like those at Somerset Plantation, for example) was that here there was less need for workers to stand in the muck of swamps to dig and drain them.

Follow the trail to Weldon, just a little more than a mile and a half away. When the Aqueduct was completed in 1823, attention turned to the interchange in Weldon. Because the Weldon basin didn't lock into the river, goods had to be taken from larger vessels and placed on bateaux, or vice versa.

As progress on the canal became visible, land speculators, anticipating all of the commerce about to travel down the Roanoke, started buying land and developing towns. Although several towns were planned, only two ever appeared on maps: Rock Landing and Weldon. Today, only Weldon survives, due in large part to a thriving warehouse district that served river commerce.

By the late 1820s, over forty years after Patrick Henry made sure no one would obstruct the Roanoke, life was finally good for the region. Farmers as far away as Salem, Virginia, could get crops to market in as little as four days. The Dismal Swamp Canal, which had also been plagued with problems and delays had opened, thirty-six years after work had started. How could life possibly be better?

As you enter the Weldon basin, look for train tracks. A new technology, the steam locomotive, was about to exponentially improve, and change, life here. In 1833 the Halifax and Weldon Railroad was chartered, and by 1836 this railroad was part of the 161-mile-long Weldon-to-Wilmington Railroad, in its day the longest rail line in the world. Ground access was now as fast, if not faster, than river transportation.

As you arrive at River Falls Park, look for the remnants of warehouses. In time, Weldon became a major rail hub. The arrival of the railroads, however, started killing river commerce, which had always been dicey. Sometimes water levels were too low for river travel. Sometimes heavy rain damaged the locks. At other times, hurricanes pushed water and debris into the river. Steamboats were proving problematic, too. Iron horses didn't have these problems. By 1836, stockholders in the Roanoke Navigation Company knew that railroads would be serious competitors to the canal. By 1855, river commerce was all but over. Too many storms had damaged the locks; railroads were more reliable.

Because of the strength of the railroads, and of the Weldon-to-Wilmington Railroad in particular, the area saw significant Civil War activity. General Robert E. Lee's supply line ran to nearby Petersburg, Virginia. The railroad connected it with the blockade runners who sailed into Wilmington. The Union army tried mightily to put the railroad, and Roanoke River towns, out of business.

After enjoying the sights of the Great Rapids in Weldon—and marveling at the skill the boat pilots required to stay alive and keep the cargo from going into the river—it's time to return to your car. After the Civil War, water power from the canals brought a milling community to life in Weldon. The Industrial Revolution had arrived! And as the automobile arrived, people even talked of building car factories, though that vision was never realized.

Because designers of the Roanoke Canal had planned with an eye both to navigation and to water power, by 1890, the Roanoke Navigation and Water Power Company was generating electricity. Again life looked promising. In fact, life looked so good that a competitor arrived, the Great Falls Water Power Manufacturing and Improvement Company. This company intended to harness the water power of the Roanoke River also. Relations between the two competitors were fractious, confusing, and difficult to sort out. Lawsuits ensued, and by 1925 the forerunner of VEPCO (Virginia Electric Power Company) owned what was left of the enterprises.

Walk Details

HOW TO FIND IT: Roanoke Rapids is located in northeastern North Carolina. The Aqueduct parking area is just off Ponderosa Road, which is off US 158 East outside Roanoke Rapids.
LENGTH: 3.2 miles round-trip
SURFACE: Gravel, dirt, grass, some asphalt.
RESTROOMS: At River Falls Park in Weldon, the eastern terminus
FOOTWEAR: Sneakers

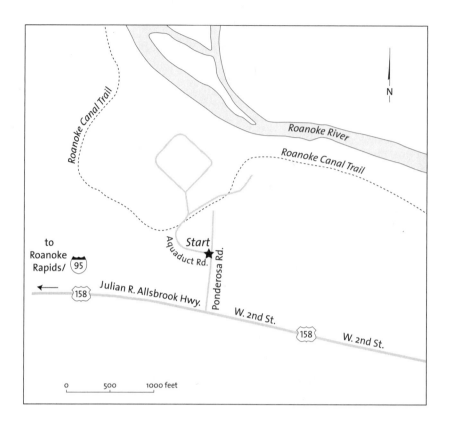

PETS: OK on a leash

MAP: A map is available at the Roanoke Canal Museum. Signboards at the western terminus at Oakwood Avenue, at the Aqueduct, and at River Falls Park also show the route.

Beware: In summer this walk entails wading through the sorts of grassy spots snakes like to hide in. You might prefer to walk in the fall or spring when vegetation isn't quite so lush.

GOOD TO KNOW: The Roanoke Canal Trail is 7.8 miles long, one way. You can ride a mountain bike if you want to see it all but don't want to walk the 15.6 round-trip length.

The Roanoke Canal Museum is located in downtown Roanoke Rapids on NC 48. Visit www.roanokecanal.com for more information.

Warrenton

ANTEBELLUM TOWN

Two state historic sites, Somerset Place (near Creswell) and Stagville (outside Durham) provide a glimpse into plantation life in our state. But because these plantations speak to the wealth of only two families, you might think that North Carolina didn't depend as heavily on slave labor as other states. While it's true that slave labor wasn't as central to North Carolina's economy as it was to the rest of the South, we still had a sizable plantation society.

To get a sense of the degree to which North Carolina did have a plantation society, as well as a sense of the political clout of that society, travel to Warrenton, a town so full of antebellum homes that a mid-1950s visitor once described it as a "casket of architectural jewels." As you walk about Warrenton and see the peeling paint, the weathered Greek columns, and the fading opulence of the mansions, you may find it hard to believe that the town was, on the eve of the Civil War, the wealthiest and one of the most politically powerful in North Carolina. The 1860 census reveals that Warrenton was home to eighteen merchants, fifteen seamstresses, eleven lawyers, eight tailors, eight shoemakers, five doctors, and four dentists, in addition to several theatrical groups. Numerous gristmills dotted the countryside, and two sawmills operated. And almost from the beginning, the town sent political leaders to state and national positions.

After the Civil War, the old way of life in Warrenton never recovered. How could it? The wealth of the 4,293 white people who lived in the area was built upon the labor of 10,777 slaves.

Warrenton seemed destined to fade. Then, in the 1960s, Warrenton's energy seemed poised to reemerge, this time in the form of black activism. Area residents, some of them likely descendants of Warrenton's slave population, worked to create Soul City, a nearby planned urban area that would become an economic engine for black people. Although the dream of such a community quickened the pulse of the region, funding problems and claims of corruption kept the vision from being fully realized.

Historical Context

Why did people settle in this area? Good question, for Warrenton is no coastal port town.

Warrenton arose because of the massive spring floods of the Roanoke River, which lies thirty-eight miles east of Halifax. Though the floods caused Native Americans to call the Roanoke the "River of Death," the floods also brought life in the form of rich soil from the Virginia mountains and piedmont. In a day when 95 percent of Americans farmed, rich soil meant prosperity.

Because Virginia was permanently settled so much earlier than North Carolina, Tidewater farmland was, by the 1770s, exhausted. To maintain their fortunes, Virginians came south and formed a plantation society in the floodplain of the Roanoke River, growing rich on tobacco and cotton. As you walk about Warrenton, note the abundance of low stone walls, a sign of Virginian sensibilities.

Another Virginian sensibility—appetite for revolution—helps explain how the town and county got their permanent names. Originally honoring the Earl of Bute, the county became a target for a name change when planters learned that the Earl of Bute may have, in 1765, authored the hated Stamp Act. By 1779, in the thick of the Revolutionary War, the planters were successful. Bute County became two counties, Franklin and Warren. One honored Benjamin Franklin, the other Joseph Warren, the Massachusetts doctor who sent Paul Revere on his famous ride in 1775 and who died in the battle of Bunker Hill. Curiously, no one in the county is believed to have actually known Warren.

Beyond changing the county name, planters supported the Revolution by keeping Continental troops in clothing and shoes. Accounts indicate that the plantation tradesmen of Warren County produced 76 hats, 315 yards of linen, 152 yards of wool, and 152 pairs of shoes for the effort.

Because Warren County escaped much of the damage British troops inflicted elsewhere in North Carolina and Virginia in the waning days of the Revolution, the already-thriving plantation society was poised to grow even stronger, which it did.

The Walk

A kiosk near the visitor center contains the brochure *Walking Tour of Warrenton*, which describes many of the beautiful homes in town. Jacob

Holt, Warrenton's builder of note, built not only the home that serves as the visitor center but also many of the homes and churches you'll pass.

Begin with the visitor center (122 South Bragg Street) behind you and walk left on Bragg Street. Cross Franklin Street and continue one long block to Plummer Street. At the corner of Plummer and Bragg Streets, turn right to walk one block to Main Street. Across the street to the left a historical marker remembers Benjamin Hawkins, one of Warrenton's earliest politically powerful citizens.

Benjamin Hawkins, an interpreter in George Washington's field staff, as well as North Carolina's commercial agent to Holland, France, and Spain during the Revolution, served in the Continental Congress of 1781–82 and 1786–87. He was North Carolina's first senator under the U.S. Constitution and is notable for introducing a resolution to the House of Commons excusing Moravians from the legal requirement of military service. Interestingly, Hawkins spent the majority of his career as the United States' agent to the Creek Indian Nation, giving up his life of relative ease in Warrenton to transition Native Americans living south of the Ohio River from their life of hunting to one of farming.

Turn right to walk along Main Street to Macon Street, a distance of three blocks. A boyhood friend to Benjamin Hawkins, Nathaniel Macon is another Warren County son. Some might argue that Macon was the most important politician North Carolina ever produced. Certainly he is among the most intriguing. Counties in Alabama, Georgia, Illinois, Missouri, and Tennessee honor him, as does Fort Macon, outside Beaufort.

Schooled by a private tutor with his friend Ben (and later taught in a makeshift school run by Charles Pettigrew), Macon became a landowner at age five when he inherited 500 acres and three slaves from his father. When Macon died in 1837, his estate included 1,945 acres of land and almost eighty slaves. How Macon won his wife, Hannah Plummer, sounds like a scene from *Gone with the Wind*: he competed for her in a card game. Though he lost the game, and therefore Hannah, Macon refused to give her up, or so suggests Manly Wellman in *The County of Warren*. Hannah, suitably wooed, fell into Macon's arms; the winner of the card game took his hat and left. Wellman, a writer of speculative fiction, may have exaggerated the story or even made it up; however, it speaks to the plantation society of the day.

In many ways, Macon typified a planter's life. He enjoyed cockfights and horse races, and some historians think he watched the famous

Sir Archie race. Sir Archie, a thoroughbred and bloodline contributor to many well-known champions—including Man-O-War and Secretariat —was at one point owned by William R. Davie of Halifax, who was influential in the founding of the University of North Carolina. Curiously, Macon reportedly worked in his fields alongside his slaves when at home at Buck Springs, his plantation.

Macon's political views were typical of planters: he was an ardent Anti-Federalist. Opposing the U.S. Constitution, Macon believed that a national government would be too big to understand local needs. He hated taxes, thought college-educated people pretentious, favored militias over free-standing armies and navies, and advocated for the Bill of Rights. Some credit him with giving North Carolina its Rip Van Winkle image as a state that would rather have a sleeping economy than one flourishing at the hands of the national government. At one point he suggested moving the University of North Carolina from Chapel Hill to Raleigh because "the manners of boys should be attended to as well as their minds."

Anti-Federalist that he was, however, Macon served in the U.S. House of Representatives for twenty-four years and in the U.S. Senate for thirteen years, proud that he never campaigned for a vote. In the House he served as Speaker. He declined cabinet appointments twice. In the Senate he chaired the Foreign Relations Committee, a distinction he shares with Senator Jesse Helms. Like Helms, who carried the moniker "Senator No," Macon had a reputation for casting many negative votes. He read law but never practiced. Macon voted against federal government funding for a tomb for Washington. He was a close friend of Thomas Jefferson's, and reports indicate that some 1,500 people reportedly attended Macon's funeral.

As you pass through the center of town, don't let the quiet fool you. Newspapers of the early 1800s speak to the wealth here. Pianofortes costing $500 commonly appeared in advertisements. Residents enjoyed coffee from Costa Rica, bacon from Cincinnati, Cuban molasses, and Puerto Rican sugar. About six miles south of town, Shocco Springs and Jones Springs welcomed tourists to the mineral waters. Halls, pavilions, and clusters of cottages provided lodging there. Horseracing provided diversion.

Cross Macon Street and continue walking north three blocks on Main Street to Wilcox Street. Here you can admire Jacob Holt's work. Not only do historians believe Holt built nearly eighty homes in the area, he also

The gravesite of Nathaniel Macon, one of North Carolina's most important political leaders, rests a short drive outside Warrenton.

gained a commission for carpentry and brickwork for Peace Institute (now William Peace University) in Raleigh and for Trinity College (predecessor of Duke University) in Randolph County.

Look for the historical marker noting Warren Academy. (The building behind the marker is not Warren Academy; it once was Warrenton's high school). Warren Academy, a boarding school for young men, opened in 1788 and provided an upscale education. Tuition was $20 a year in 1804, compared to the $5 charged at UNC in 1795. Room and board cost another $75. Illustrious graduates included William Miller, a state attorney general in 1810 and governor from 1814 to 1817. The Warrenton Female Academy (also known as the Mordecai School for Girls), established by Jacob Mordecai in 1809, attracted Yale-educated teachers, among them Bronson Alcott, the father of Louisa May Alcott. Women studied landscape drawing, oil and water color painting, voice, and flower arranging there.

At Wilcox Street, cross over North Main. Turn right and walk along Main Street one block to Academy Street. Turn left and walk one block to Bragg Street. Look for the white clapboard Bragg House (236 North Bragg Street). Thomas Bragg built homes in Warren, Halifax, and Northampton Counties. He also worked as assistant superintendent of construction on the state capitol in Raleigh for two months. His sons, Thomas, John, and Braxton, rose to political prominence, distinguishing themselves throughout the southeast. John Bragg moved to Alabama, serving there as a judge and U.S. congressman. Thomas served as a U.S. senator and as governor of North Carolina just before the Civil War, in addition to serving as the attorney general of the Confederacy. Though he resigned from the U.S. Senate to stand with his southern friends, he wrote privately that he considered seceding impractical. Braxton, a West Point cadet, graduated near the top of his class. A U.S. Army base in Fayetteville honors his conduct in the Mexican War. When civil war erupted, Bragg served as one of Jefferson Davis's generals. His tenure with Davis was fractious: though he resigned from the job in 1863, he later rejoined Davis's staff and was with him as the Confederate president fled Richmond and was captured. While at West Point, Bragg became friends with W. T. Sherman, the man who would become a Union general and to whom Confederate general Joseph Johnston would surrender at Bennett Place, outside of Durham (see chapter 16, Fayetteville).

Turn around and return to Main Street. Then turn left and walk six blocks to Marshall Street. Continue taking in the beautiful homes, especially the Eaton House (210 North Main). The calm beauty of these homes belies how brightly secession fever burned and tempers flared in Warrenton in the days before civil war. Northern-educated school teachers talked of abolition. One Pennsylvania jeweler living in Warrenton defiantly helped a slave boy, John Hyman, learn to read. To retaliate, local residents broke into the jewelry shop one night, plundering the display cases. Quickly sold to a new master in Alabama, Hyman would later become a U.S. congressman representing our state. Warrenton Academy alumnus Weldon Edwards, a state senator, led the call for secession at the Southern Rights Convention in Goldsboro in March 1861. In nearby Ridgeway, the Warren Rifles formed, a troop of nearly 1,017 white men.

After the war started, local losses ran high. In addition, Warrenton's way of life diminished. According to accounts in *The County of Warren*, one resident lamented in the summer of 1862 that "the watermelons are coming on fine, I believe, and will soon be on hand, but who is to eat them?"

At the corner of Marshall and Main Streets, turn left to walk one block to Eaton Street. A historic marker commemorates John White, a real-life Rhett Butler who was appointed by Governor Zebulon Vance to represent North Carolina as its agent to England during the Civil War. In that role, White purchased North Carolina's first blockade runner, the *Lord Clyde*. Renamed the *Ad-Vance*, the ship successfully pierced the blockade eleven times between July 3, 1863, and September 1864, bringing $12 million worth of supplies, mostly medicine and shoes, to North Carolina troops. But Federal troops captured the *Ad-Vance* in September 1864 as the ship tried to run the Cape Fear inlet. Federal troops renamed the boat the *Frolic* and then used it to intercept other blockade-running ships.

Given Warrenton's political prominence in North Carolina, Sherman's army eventually arrived here. According to some accounts, they passed through town quickly. According to Wellman's account in *The County of Warren*, families hid smoked hams underneath the floorboards of their houses and in their ceilings, where grease stains eventually bled through. Reports state that Sherman's troops tried to be nice, mainly due to Sherman's friendship with Bragg and because the war was nearly over. For their part, town residents were practical and accommodating: they needed the hard currency the Federal troops carried to jump start the local economy.

At the corner of Marshall and Eaton Streets, turn left on Bragg Street to walk one block to Halifax Street. Turn right to walk two blocks to the end of the sidewalk. More plantation homes appear, the most notable of which is Engleside (203 Halifax Road; the road name may also appear as Baltimore Road). A story surrounding Engleside illustrates the depth of Confederate loyalties in the town.

In 1862, Mrs. Robert E. Lee came to Warrenton to visit Jones Springs to take the waters for her rheumatism and to escape the war. With her traveled her four daughters. While in Warrenton, one daughter, Annie, caught typhoid fever and died. Mrs. Lee, unable to take the child home for burial, buried her in the family cemetery of the resort owner. General Lee could not attend the funeral due to the demands of war. After the war, Lee was often sick, and from 1865 until 1869, he could not leave Virginia due to the terms of his parole. After he had finished his parole, Lee embarked on a trip to Georgia to seek a warmer climate. On his way south, Lee and his daughter Agnes stopped in Warrenton to visit Annie's grave. Willie White, son of blockade runner John White, happened to be at the train station awaiting the arrival of his sister. Recognizing Lee, White invited him to Engleside. Lee, having no reservations at the local hotel, agreed. The next morning, as the White family readied their carriage to take Lee to Annie's gravesite, people lined the town streets, bringing flowers from their private gardens to pay tribute to the general. Lee died six months later.

Cross Halifax Street/Baltimore Road, turn left and follow Halifax Street to Franklin Street. Turn left and walk three blocks to Main Street. On Main Street, look for the historic marker to John Hyman, the slave whom the jeweler taught to read. Hyman eventually returned to Warrenton as a freeman and won election to the North Carolina senate in 1868. In 1874 he was the first black man to represent North Carolina in the U.S. House. Hyman's accomplishment helped established Warrenton as a cradle of black activism in North Carolina.

At Main Street, turn right to walk three blocks to Church Street. Turn right onto Church Street and walk two blocks to the Boyd-Kerr House (216 North Church Street). This neoclassical revival house was named for its original owner, tobacconist Walter Boyd, and its later owner, John Kerr, who served in the U.S. House of Representatives for three decades. The Boyd-Kerr family represents a modern chapter of North Carolina political influence based in Warrenton.

After the war, residents rebuilt their lives by farming tobacco. But by the early 1930s, tobacco farmers found themselves in difficult circumstances. The better their harvest, the less they profited due to oversupply. In 1919, tobacco sold for .41 cents a pound. By 1934, the price was .10 cents a pound. Prices dropped so low that then governor Ehringhaus closed the tobacco markets until a price system could be worked out and farmers taught not to overproduce.

In addition to the supply and demand problems that farmers created for themselves, the federal government was increasing tobacco taxes. A political cartoon from the *Warren Record* shows the farmers' reaction to the taxes: a huge thumb is dropping out of the sky with the words UNFAIR FLAT CIGARETTE TAX 6¢ PER PACKAGE on the neck of an overall-wearing farmer whose nose is bent to a grindstone.

Testifying before the House Ways and Means Subcommittee in the spring of 1934, John Kerr complained that tobacco taxes confiscated "the wealth and initiative and the industry of 400,000 farmers in America whose principal crop is tobacco." He further advocated "a flat reduction of the tax to be fixed . . . so that we can contemplate the possibility of keeping our great industry active and allowing everybody engaged in it to make an honest living and get the proper return for their activity." To farmers whose tobacco leaves were rotting in the fields, Kerr's frank language was heroic. It also laid the groundwork for the Kerr-Smith Tobacco Act, as well as other agricultural adjustment legislation that became the basis for farm policy in the United States for the next seventy years.

The Kerr Mansion is but one of the many beautiful homes in Warrenton.

When the Roanoke River flooded in 1940, destroying all of the crops in the Roanoke Valley, John Kerr led the way to impound the river. In 1953, nearby Kerr Lake was born.

Retrace your steps to Main Street and turn left to walk to Franklin Street to return to your car.

Walk Details

HOW TO FIND IT: Warrenton is located in northeast North Carolina on US 401, about 15 miles from the Virginia line. To find the visitor center, enter town on US 401. Turn onto East Franklin Street. The Visitor Center sits at 122 South Bragg Street.

LENGTH: About 3.5 miles, more if you wander the side streets to see other homes

SURFACE: Sidewalk

RESTROOMS: At the visitor center

FOOTWEAR: Sneakers

PETS: OK on a leash

MAP: Usually available at the visitor center

GOOD TO KNOW: If you really enjoy studying the architecture of the town, you might like to have a copy of Catherine Bishir and Michael

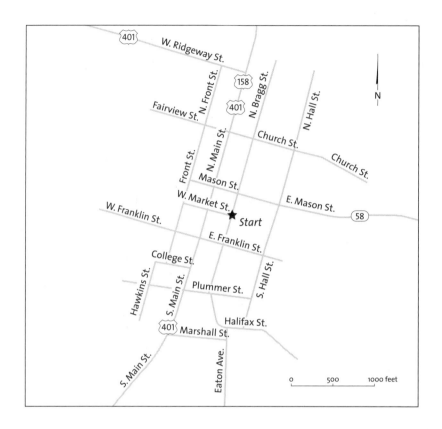

Southern's *Guide to the Historic Architecture of Piedmont North Carolina*, which offers excellent detail about the historic structures of Warrenton and many other towns and cities. Bishir and Southern have also written similar guides to the eastern and western parts of the state.

Nathaniel Macon's home is located about 12 miles outside Warrenton off US 158 east. To find it, follow Macon Street from Warrenton to the town of Vaughn. Turn left opposite a historic marker remembering Macon. Follow Eaton Ferry Road; it will make a right turn. Eventually a brown sign signals Macon's grave, off SR 1348. In about a mile or so, the humble rock pile that marks Macon's grave appears. Across the road from the parking area stand Macon's reconstructed home and original smokehouse and corncrib. It's worth the drive to see the utter lack of pretention this giant of North Carolina politics possessed.

To find Soul City, drive US 158 West 10 miles out of Warrenton. Turn left onto SR 1151. When SR 1151 runs into SR 1100, turn left. Soul City will appear shortly.

Fayetteville

VIBRANT QUEEN OF THE COASTAL PLAIN

Fayetteville's outward patina is that of a military town. The active military population of Fort Bragg exceeds 50,000; the base employs more than 8,000 civilians, and upwards of 65,000 active-duty family members live nearby. Close to 100,000 retirees and their families live here too. Yet the post is a relatively new addition to Fayetteville's heritage; it arrived in 1918, when the U.S. Army decided that the surrounding area met criteria for a year-round training facility.

Underneath Fayetteville's outward visage is a heritage that may qualify as the most complex in all of North Carolina. When you walk about Fayetteville, you must be mentally ready to travel across decades, almost as if you're a hummingbird going from flower to flower. It's a rare walk that encompasses Flora MacDonald, Union general William Tecumseh Sherman, Babe Ruth, and Charles Chesnutt.

Historical Context

At the invitation of royal governor Gabriel Johnston, Scots Highlanders began migrating to the area in 1738 when Johnston, himself a native Scot, gave 360 Scots a ten-year tax exemption and land grants. But Fayetteville didn't arise as one town: it started as separate inland port communities, the town of Campbellton (1762) and the settlement of Cross Creek (ca. 1760). In 1778 the communities merged, and in 1783 the town was renamed Fayetteville.

Well situated along the upper reaches of the Cape Fear River, Fayetteville soon hummed with commerce as naval stores wrought from longleaf pines made their way to Wilmington. In time, a 130-mile plank road, the longest in the state, connected Fayetteville to Salem, putting Fayetteville squarely between Wilmington, North Carolina's biggest port city, and the backcountry.

With commerce came political strength, so much so that North Carolina's ratification of the U.S. Constitution took place in Fayetteville in November 1789. Fayetteville also made a serious bid to be North Carolina's state capital, both before and after Raleigh received the nod.

The political vigor brought Fayetteville favorable national attention: a branch of the Second Bank of the United States arrived in 1820. The Marquis de Lafayette visited in 1825. In 1838, the U.S. government chose Fayetteville as the site to build an arsenal. Certainly life was good in Fayetteville and the region surrounding it in the first half of the 1800s.

One wonders what Fayetteville's story would be had the arsenal not been built here. As Union general Sherman split the Confederacy, Fayetteville was clearly in his sight, and he made sure that Field Order #2 put the prosperous, feisty town on its knees. His order to destroy all railroad property, shops, factories, tanneries—and all gristmills save one of sufficient capacity to grind corn for all of the people of Fayetteville—dealt the town a mighty blow. Fayetteville eventually recovered, though life was decidedly different.

The Walk

This walk starts at Fayetteville's most distinctive symbol, the Market House, the second such structure to stand at the intersection of Green, Hay, Gillespie and Person Streets. The first one, called the State House, burned in 1831 in Fayetteville's Great Fire.

The first State House witnessed big events: state leaders ratified the U.S. Constitution here after the newly added Bill of Rights made the Constitution more palatable to them. State leaders chartered the University of North Carolina here less than a month later. As North Carolina's leadership struggled to fix a state capital, they occasionally met here. Here, North Carolina became a smaller state when leaders ceded the land that became Tennessee. And, as was the practice of the day, planters bought and sold slaves here.

Fayetteville's Great Fire of 1831 started near the northwest corner of Market Square and burned over 600 structures. It left citizens in such dire straits that, according to the newspaper, Raleigh citizens raised $500 to help relieve the suffering. Wilmington citizens sent three boatloads of groceries and dry goods up the Cape Fear River. Within a week of the fire, however, the newspaper was asserting that "no time will be lost" rebuilding and that "the spirit of enterprise is very far from being crushed." It welcomed all masons and carpenters.

From the Market House, walk south along Person Street to Cool Spring Street, just past the Fayetteville Convention and Visitor Bureau (245 Person Street). The several old buildings you pass, collectively called Lib-

The distinctive symbol of Fayetteville, the Market House. Important events took place here, among them the vote to ratify the U.S. Constitution.

erty Row, were built just after the Great Fire. At the corner of Person and Bow Streets, a granite monument marks Liberty Point. Here, in 1755, a group of fifty-five patriots met to pledge their lives and fortunes to the "preservation of peace and good order, and the safety of individual and private property." Calling themselves the Cumberland Association, these men drafted the Liberty Point Resolves, a document in the spirit of the Halifax and Mecklenburg Resolves. Although the men wished for reconciliation with Great Britain, they vowed to fight on behalf of the colonies if necessary. Another marker notes the First Presbyterian Church. Burned in the Great Fire, the church rebuilt on what was left of its original foundation.

If you were to continue walking along Person Street to the bridge spanning the Cape Fear River, you would arrive near the original site of Campbellton. This distance traverses a warehouse district and adds a total of two miles to your walk.

Turn left onto Cool Spring Street and walk two long blocks to Grove Street. (Be advised that, as of this writing, Cool Spring Street has no sidewalks.) Though this segment of the walk is short, it is long in stories.

First among the stories is that of Flora and Allan MacDonald. When the MacDonalds arrived in Fayetteville, Flora was already the stuff of romantic legend. She had helped Prince Charles Edward Stuart, commonly known as Bonnie Prince Charlie, escape English forces after his defeat at the Battle of Culloden in 1745. She was jailed in the Tower of London for doing so. Allan MacDonald's dance with fame came after he led the largely Highland Scots Loyalist militia into battle at Moores Creek Bridge in 1776 to defend the English Crown, an action for which he was later captured and jailed. After her husband's arrest, Flora returned to Scotland; Allan joined her in 1781. A marker to the right recalls the approximate spot where Flora MacDonald bade her husband Allan goodbye as the loyal Scots, led by Donald MacDonald, prepared to march to Moores Creek Bridge.

To the left is the old parade ground and monuments for the Fayetteville Independent Light Infantry (FILI), a state militia group formed in 1793 as a response to President Washington's Militia Act of 1792. The oldest southern militia unit in continuous existence, the unit first fought in the War of 1812. It fought again in the Battle of Bethel on June 10, 1861, early in the Civil War. FILI would later send regiments to fight in the Spanish-American War and in World War I. Today it is a ceremonial organization. Interestingly, FILI member Charles M. Stedman was one of ten North Carolinians to be at both Bethel and Appomattox, the site of Confederate general Lee's surrender to Union general Grant. After the Civil War, Stedman served in the U.S. House. When he died at age ninety, he was the last surviving Confederate veteran in Congress.

As you pass the FILI monument, look right to Cross Creek Cemetery. It's the oldest public cemetery in Fayetteville, with the first graves dating to 1785. The Confederate Burial Ground was started soon after Sherman left Fayetteville in 1865, and the oldest Confederate monument in North Carolina was erected on this site in 1868.

On the left stands Evans AME Zion Church (301 North Cool Springs Street). Henry Evans left his mark on Fayetteville just as surely as Flora MacDonald did. Evans, a young black man, was traveling to Charleston, South Carolina, circa 1780, when he saw the condition of the area slaves and was inspired to stay and preach. At first the townsfolk thought him an agitator and sent him outside the town limits to preach. Word of his message and of his eloquence grew, however, and soon the town welcomed him. People of all colors came to hear him speak, even Francis Asbury, the leading bishop and one of the founders of American Methodism. When Evans died in 1810, his passing was reported in both the *Charlotte Observer* and in the *Raleigh Minerva*.

At Grove Avenue, turn left to walk two blocks to Green Street. To the right, a marker remembers Warren Winslow, who served briefly as governor in 1854–55. Winslow would go on to become a member of the House of Representatives. He is notable for negotiating the surrender of the U.S. Arsenal at Fayetteville in 1861, thereby putting the 37,000 arms and munitions into southern hands. The Fayetteville Arsenal and Armory, as it was later named, would be a major source of arms for the Confederacy, thus positioning the town to receive General Sherman's fury four years later.

At Green Street, turn left to walk three blocks to the Market House. Here again numerous historical markers attest to Fayetteville's rich heritage. At the Old Town Hall, the North Carolina Convention gathered to ratify the Federal Constitution in 1789. Fayetteville Academy opened in 1791, its mission to educate both boys and girls. As you approach the Market House, look left into Cross Creek Park to the statue honoring Lafayette. Local lore says that, although dozens of towns have honored Lafayette by adopting his name, Fayetteville is the only so-named town that the Marquis actually ever visited.

As you pass the park, look for the Fascinate-U Children's Museum. The offices of the *Fayetteville Observer* once stood here. Of the over 2,000 newspapers that have been published in North Carolina, the *Fayetteville Observer* lays claim to being the oldest. Had General Sherman not burned the newspaper offices when he occupied Fayetteville in March 1865, the *Observer* could also claim status as North Carolina's oldest continuously published newspaper, a distinction that instead belongs to the *Wilmington Star-News*.

The first newspaper appeared in North Carolina in 1751, in New Bern, making our state the eighth colony to have a newspaper. Royal governor Gabriel Johnston had earlier hired printer James Davis to publish the royal laws and announcements and, likely, the colony's currency. Over time, Davis started publishing on the side. His four-page sheet, the *North Carolina Gazette*, sold for four shillings per quarter. Eventually the paper appeared weekly. That the royal printer had the audacity to publish "public" news eventually caused Arthur Dobbs, the royal governor who succeeded Johnston, to replace Davis.

Publishing ceased during the Revolution, due to a lack of paper. After the war, Halifax, Hillsborough, Wilmington, Edenton, and New Bern all had newspapers, though none survived. In August 1789, Caleb Howard, publisher of a Wilmington newspaper, started publishing the *Fayetteville Gazette*. This paper lasted until 1791. In 1816, the *Carolina Observer* began publication, eventually becoming the *Fayetteville Observer*.

The publisher of the *Fayetteville Observer* was an open, ardent supporter of the Confederate cause, likely provoking Sherman's rage as much as the takeover of the arsenal had. On February 6, 1865, the *Observer* proclaimed, "The idea of any further connexion with the United State is abhorrent to our every proper feeling." The paper further reported that peace commissioners had passed through the line of Union general Grant in Petersburg, Virginia, to ask Lincoln to allow North Carolina to be its own country. Apparently the peace commissioners failed to persuade Lincoln, and on February 20, Governor Zebulon B. Vance used the *Observer* to rouse the citizens of Fayetteville to fight: "The enemy marched triumphantly through the heart of our sister Georgia and is she conquered? . . . Therefore, I now appeal to you by everything held sacred among men to prevent the degradation of your country."

On March 6, five days before General Sherman marched into Fayetteville and little more than thirty days before the surrender at Appomattox, the *Observer* still called for southern independence: "let the Confederacy but establish its Independence and there will be indeed what we all pray for, a lasting Peace!" When Sherman arrived in Fayetteville, so records Joey Powell in *Cumberland County*, the Union army band played *Dixie* as it entered town. Once in town, Sherman's troops burned the newspaper offices and the federal arsenal. On February 8, 1883, nearly eighteen years later, the offices reopened. The paper carried a note about the destruction "by the orders of General Sherman."

At Market Square, cross Green Street to the right and then cross Hay Street, walking toward a marker indicating the establishment of the University of North Carolina. Walk Gillespie Street three blocks to Blount Street to a marker honoring Charles Chesnutt, Fayetteville's greatest literary notable. A child of free parents, Chesnutt attended the Howard School, forerunner of Fayetteville State University, the second-oldest public institution of higher learning in North Carolina. Beginning professional life as an educator then trying his hand as a Wall Street reporter, Chesnutt then studied law and passed the Ohio bar exam. Later, however, Chesnutt found his voice as a writer, becoming the first black person published in the *Atlantic Monthly*. In 1899 Houghton Mifflin published *The Conjure Woman*, a collection of stories that depicted slave life in central North Carolina. Chesnutt's third novel drew upon the 1898 Wilmington uprising.

If you walk another two blocks along Gillespie Street, you can see the marker commemorating George Herman "Babe" Ruth. Ruth hit his first home run as a professional baseball player in an exhibition game in Fayetteville, prompting his teammates to nickname him "Babe."

At the light, cross Gillespie Street. Turn left as if to return toward the Market House. When you reach Halliday Street, turn right. Walk toward an enormous mansion, the Sandford House (225 Dick Street). Built in 1797, this property became, in 1820, the Second Bank of the United States.

In the early days, colonies created their own currencies, banks, and financial practices: they saw no need for a centralized bank. When the First Bank of the United States was chartered in 1791, North Carolina didn't get a branch; however, when the second national bank was chartered in 1816, we did. Although Raleigh and Wilmington vied for the bank, Fayetteville got it. In 1827, the bank relocated to Hay Street, which turned out to be an unfortunate move because it, along with the Bank of Cape Fear, was one of the 600 buildings destroyed in the Great Fire of 1831. Eventually Andrew Jackson vetoed any extension of the First Bank of the United States' charter, believing the bank to be exceptionally corrupt. He also removed federal deposits, which caused the bank to falter. By 1835, the Fayetteville branch had negotiated a sale of its existing loans and was rechartered as the Bank of North Carolina.

Turn left to walk along Dick Street one block to Russell Street. At Russell, turn left to return to Gillespie Street. Cross Gillespie Street, walk one block right toward the Market House. However, before reaching the Market House, turn left to walk three blocks along Franklin Street to the historic Fayetteville Depot (325 Franklin Street). This gorgeous brick building, once home to the Cape Fear and Yadkin Valley Railroad, is today home to the Fayetteville Area Transportation Museum. The first rail line in Fayetteville was the Western Railroad, chartered in 1852 to build a forty-three-mile line from Fayetteville northwest to a coal mine which lay about seven miles beyond Sanford near the present-day community of Cumnock. Bringing coal to Fayetteville took on special importance during the Civil War. From Fayetteville, coal traveled down the Cape Fear to Wilmington to the blockade runners. General Sherman, of course, wreaked great damage upon the line. But because Confederates

Bank architecture has certainly changed since 1820 when the Sandford House served as the location of the Second Bank of the United States.

hid the locomotives and rolling stock in Egypt, a small community near Sanford, and because Sherman chose not to go there, they were available for use after the rail line was rebuilt in 1868. By 1879, the Western Railroad was merged with the Mt. Airy and Ore Knob Railroad to form the Cape Fear and Yadkin Valley Railroad. In 1893, a financial depression put the railroad into receivership. Until that happened, however, area residents found respite from the summer heat by traveling the Cape Fear and Yadkin Valley Rail to the cooler, breezier Mt. Airy.

From the corner of Maxwell and Franklin Streets, walk one block to Hay Street. At Hay Street, you can either turn left to walk another 0.6 mile up the hill to the Haymount Historic District, the Museum of the Cape Fear, and the remains of the Fayetteville Arsenal (this out-and-back segment adds 1.2 miles to the distance), or you can turn right to return to the Market House.

Holding the opinion that "the United States should never again confide such valuable property to a people who have betrayed a trust," General Sherman ordered Colonel Orlando M. Poe to "batter the arsenal building into piles of rubble and then burn and blow up the ruins." Poe did just that.

If you walk to the remains of the Fayetteville Arsenal, you'll pass the 82nd Airborne and Special Operations Museum, a must-see for anyone

The foundation remnants of the Fayetteville Arsenal, a structure that Union general William T. Sherman made sure to burn when he and the Union army passed through Fayetteville in the waning days of the Civil War.

interested in military history. Displays of military technology provide an interesting juxtaposition to Fayetteville's humble beginnings as a port town. At the arsenal, you can also visit the Museum of the Cape Fear.

Whether you climb the hill to the arsenal or turn right to return to the Market House, when you reach the Market House again, step inside it a final time to look for bullet marks and scuffs left by General Sherman on the great wooden columns.

Walk Details

HOW TO FIND IT: Fayetteville is located in the southeastern Piedmont, just west of I-95. Signs point the way into downtown, but be sure to look for NC 24, also known as Rowan Street. Turn onto Green Street and drive to the Market House, which sits at the intersection of Green, Hay, Gillespie, and Person Streets. On-street parking is usually available in the area, or you can park in the lot of the Fayetteville Convention and Visitor Bureau (245 Person Street).

LENGTH: About 3.5 miles, with potential for 6 miles

SURFACE: Paved

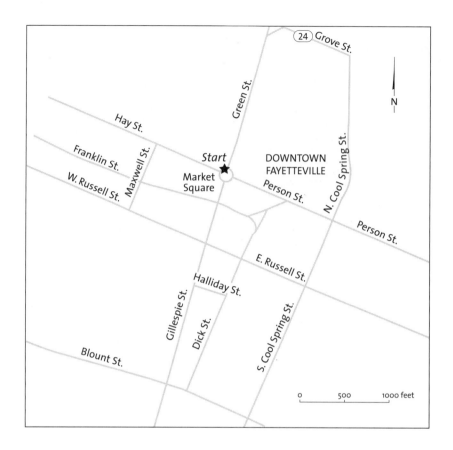

RESTROOMS: At the convention and visitor bureau

FOOTWEAR: Sneakers

PETS: OK on a leash

MAP: None available

GOOD TO KNOW: In April, Fayetteville hosts the Dogwood Festival.

For More Exploration: Bentonville Battlefield

Given the impact General Sherman had on Fayetteville, Civil War buffs might enjoy a side trip to visit a state historic site commemorating the Battle of Bentonville. Much of the 6,000 acre battlefield is not walkable because of private ownership. However, you can stroll a small portion of the area across the road from the visitor center to see the remnants of breastworks dug by the 1st Michigan Engineers, the same unit that torched the Fayetteville arsenal. You can also walk several yards to the Harper House, which stands to the left of the museum. It served as a field hospital during the battle. Most people who visit, however, take the driving tour, which is marked by the North Carolina Division of State Historic Sites.

In going to Bentonville, you visit an area where 80,000 hungry, weary men fought and where, when the shooting stopped, the war that was nearly a hundred years in the making finally ended. What follows is a brief history of the months leading up to the battle that took place here.

Before General Sherman occupied Savannah on December 21, 1864, and sent word that the proud city was President Lincoln's Christmas gift, General Grant had planned to transport Sherman and his troops to Virginia by sea so that the two armies could together smash Confederate general Lee in Petersburg. Yet when Grant saw how quickly Sherman crossed Georgia—Sherman left Atlanta on November 15 and covered the 250 miles in little more than a month—Grant decided that the better course of action was to have Sherman continue ripping the Confederacy apart by marching up through Georgia and then into the Carolinas.

Sherman knew exactly what he wanted to accomplish when he headed north: "The utter destruction of the enemy's arsenals of Columbia, Cheraw, and Fayetteville are the principals of the movement." Furthermore, Sherman wanted to destroy the railroad depot in Goldsboro. Thus, Sherman intended to cover the 465 miles between Savannah and Goldsboro as fast as possible, destroy the railroad, and then get to Virginia to witness Lee's surrender. Historians suggest that Sherman was keenly interested in seeing Lee surrender.

Sherman's March to the Sea and the ensuing Carolinas Campaign are marvels of military logistical transport. Sherman's army was 60,000 men strong. It included sixty-eight guns—thirty-four twelve-pounders and thirty-four three-inch rifle cannons. He had 2,500 supply wagons and 600 ambulances. This collection of matériel traveled roughly ten miles a day, often in the rain and usually near and through the swamps of South Carolina. Even more amazing, as the army slogged northward in the rain, army engineers had to "corduroy" the roads. They felled trees, placing them across muddy, rutted roads, and then covered the new roadbed with sand so as to provide a better surface on which to travel.

In addition, as Sherman and his army trudged along, it picked up thousands of refugees: former slaves happy to be walking to freedom and white plantation owners riding along in their worn carriages in what was left of their top hats, silk dresses, and festive bonnets.

Sherman's letters indicate that he intended to treat North Carolina differently than he had South Carolina. Sherman intended to destroy South Carolina because it had led the secession of the southern states. North Carolina "may be of political consequence," Sherman wrote. He forbade foraging, and he directed that the people of North Carolina be paid for supplies needed by the army. He also intended to keep his army together, "compact," to use Sherman's words.

When Sherman's tattered army reached Fayetteville on March 11, 1865, he sent the refugees to Wilmington. He also rested and resupplied his troops, and his men enjoyed the first mail delivery they had had in months, eagerly reading newspapers that were three months old. Sherman had earlier requested 40,000 pairs of shoes; his men's shoes were worn or rotted from the constant dampness. What he received on a second barge from Wilmington, however, was a cargo of oats.

Though Sherman intended to rest his army, he didn't want to spend a lot of time in Fayetteville. "We must not give time for Jos. Johnston to concentrate at Goldsboro," Sherman wrote to Major General Terry in Wilmington. "We cannot prevent his concentrating in Raleigh, but he shall have no rest." In a letter to General Grant, Sherman reemphasized his plan: "If I can now add Goldsboro without too much cost, I will be in a position to aid you materially in the Spring campaign." Sherman's plan was to feint battle to the north and west toward Smithfield, while saving his main troops for a run to Goldsboro, a decision that ultimately would not keep his army "compact."

Only thirty days earlier, Jefferson Davis, president of the Confederacy, had returned General Joseph E. Johnston to command duty. Davis didn't like Johnston's cat-and-mouse style of battle; today, analysts would say that he micromanaged his generals. But Davis had no choice. Braxton Bragg was ordered to defend Fort Fisher and Wilmington. By January, however, Fort Fisher had fallen. Something needed to be done, and at General Robert E. Lee's suggestion, Davis asked Johnston to command the Army of Tennessee.

The army, however, was fragmented, and desertion ran high. But when the men heard that Johnston was back, the army collected itself into a fighting force of about 20,000. In addition, Johnston had the services of Lt. General W. J. Hardee at his disposal. Hardee, whose nickname was "Old Reliable," possessed a reputation commensurate with Generals Stonewall Jackson and James P. Longstreet. Johnston then set about planning his strategy. Would Sherman go to Raleigh and destroy a state capital as he had in Georgia and South Carolina? Or would he go somewhere else? Johnston decided to position his army near Smithfield to try to trick Sherman into revealing his plans.

Though Sherman had learned that Johnston had reassumed command, Sherman didn't know how large the Army of Tennessee was. Moreover, some historians suggest that because Sherman had had such a relatively easy time ripping the South apart, the general had become lax. Plus, the end of the war was clearly at hand. Finally, whatever charm the endless destruction may have had for the Union troops when Sherman's army began its march, their appetite for destruction was dwindling.

Thus the two armies drew closer to battle. Sherman split his troops: the bulk of his men went north and east Goldsboro, while a smaller contingent went north and west under the command of Major General Henry Slocum to harass Johnston in Raleigh. Meanwhile, Johnston was close by in Smithfield. This time, Johnston decided he wouldn't play cat-and-mouse.

Depending upon whose history you read, the purpose of the fighting that occurred on March 15–16 in Averasboro, a town between Fayetteville and Bentonville, was meant to elicit from Sherman clues as to what his plan was, or it was a Confederate attempt to slow Sherman's advance. Regardless, once the fighting in Averasboro ended, Johnston set an ambush for the Federal army by placing his troops around Bentonville in a sickle-shaped trap on the night of March 18.

On Sunday morning, March 19, the rain stopped and the day was warm. The sky was cloudless. And Slocum's unit stumbled into Johnston's trap.

Sherman was resting in his tent at Falling Creek Church when he learned of Johnston's trap. In his memoirs, Sherman wrote that "a messenger overtook me, and notified me that near Bentonville, General Slocum had run up against *Johnston's whole army*." So surprised was Sherman when he learned about Johnston's successful gamble, he rushed out to a campfire near his tent, wearing nothing but a red flannel undershirt and his drawers. He started barking orders to rush the army to Slocum's aid.

When battle ended that day, the Confederacy had reason to hope; perhaps its gamble was successful. On day two, however, the two armies battled to a determined stalemate. By day three, Sherman had collected his forces and overpowered the Confederate troops. In little more than thirty days, Johnston surrendered to Sherman at Bennett Place outside Durham.

History suggests that Sherman and Johnston held each other in high esteem after the war ended and that Johnston attended Sherman's funeral. As Sherman's casket passed, Johnston took off his hat. Some in Johnston's group pleaded with the man to put his hat back on, but Johnston replied that if he were in the casket and Sherman were paying his respects, Sherman would remove his hat. Sadly, during the funeral Johnston caught pneumonia and died just a few weeks later.

Bentonville Battlefield is located in Four Oaks. From Fayetteville, travel north on I-95 to US 13 North. Travel US 13 North to US 701 in Newton Grove. In Newton Grove, signs will point the way to the battlefield and visitor center. For more information, visit www.nchistoricsites.org/Bentonvi/Bentonvi.HTM.

Winston-Salem

RELIGIOUS FREEDOM AND INDUSTRY
SIDE BY SIDE

If you've visited Winston-Salem, what do you think of first? The tin coffee pot in Old Salem that symbolizes the industriousness of the Moravians who settled here first? The red-brick stacks emblazoned with the initials RJR, marking the global tobacco industry that came to life in Winston? Krispy Kreme's beloved neon sign announcing that the doughnuts are HOT NOW?

Maybe. Then again, maybe you think of the tiny punctuation mark that the local baseball team has adopted as its name: the Dash.

The dash, you see, links two very different towns. One town, Salem, reminds us why people were willing to risk everything to come to America. The other, Winston, shows what happens when business vision intersects with human energy. Together these towns created a city steeped with self-reliance and forward-looking energy. If you don't agree, then consider this: on this walk you can marvel at a village restored to its mid-1700s feel and then pass by the prototype of the Empire State Building.

Historical Context

The story of Winston-Salem begins in Europe in the 1400s with Jan Hus. Predating Martin Luther, Hus inspired believers who lived across central Europe with his ideas about religious reformation. But the Catholic Church branded him a heretic, burning him at the stake for his beliefs.

His followers took their religion underground, enduring severe persecution over the next 265 years, and were it not for the Austrian Count Nicholas Ludwig von Zinzendorf, who felt that people should not be persecuted for pursuing their religious beliefs, these early Protestants might have disappeared altogether. But in 1722, Zinzendorf allowed a few families to live safely on his estate. There, under the count's ideals—"in essentials, Unity; in nonessentials, Liberty; in all things, Love"—they thrived. At first calling themselves Unitas Fratrum, the Unity of the

Brethren, they became known as Moravians, named for Moravia, a region in today's Czech Republic with which they were most identified.

Zinzendorf had a missionary bent. In 1741, he helped the Moravians come to the Pennsylvania colony and to establish the towns of Bethlehem, Nazareth, and Lititz. Although Pennsylvania offered some degree of religious tolerance, land there was expensive. Moreover, the numbers of German immigrants dismayed some Pennsylvanians, prompting even Ben Franklin to question why the colony should "become a colony of aliens." In little more than a decade, Count Zinzendorf directed Bishop Augustus Gottlieb Spangenberg to explore the Carolina backwoods to find yet another new home for the Moravians. The land in Carolina was more affordable, and the Moravians had gained the reputation of being good settlers. After the English Parliament gave the Moravians official recognition in the colonies, John Carteret, second Earl Granville, offered nearly 100,000 acres of land, at a very reasonable price, to the Moravians.

After sailing from Philadelphia to Edenton in 1752, Spangenberg and his explorers spent over four months traveling the Carolina backwoods—Granville District, or the upper one-half of North Carolina—going as far west as Quaker Meadows, outside Morganton.

Some historians have said that Spangenberg and his group stopped somewhere on a mountaintop between Boone and Blowing Rock in December 1752 and, looking east, saw the land where they would settle. Describing the chosen area, Spangenberg wrote: "The hills are not large and not to be compared with those in other tracts. . . . Most of it is flat, level land; the air is fresh and healthful, the water good." Zinzendorf bought nearly 100,000 acres from John Carteret, and Spangenberg named the tract of land Der Wachau, after Zinzendorf's estate in Austria.

Thus the Moravians joined the early wave of German immigrants leaving Pennsylvania along the Great Wagon Road. In 1753, fifteen unmarried men, Spangenberg's "little Pilgrim Band," arrived in the Wachovia tract to build their carefully planned utopia. Having been persecuted, they now wished to be isolated and self-sufficient. Their first community, Bethabara, served as a staging ground for the capital they planned to build. Though the French and Indian War hindered their progress, the Moravians stabilized themselves and by 1764 were planning Salem, the seat of government for their country.

On February 19, 1766, eight men from Bethabara arrived near Salem

Creek. For the next six years, these highly motivated, detailed-oriented Germans erected their town.

The Walk

Walk up the hill on Academy Street into Old Salem to Main Street. Look for the Salt Street gardens on both your left and right. The orderliness and productivity of the gardens—even in the winter months—speaks volumes about the orderliness and productivity of life in Salem.

At the corner of Academy and Main streets, turn left to walk one long block along Main Street. Salem's first houses stood here. Fourth House, at 438 South Main, is the oldest surviving original house built in Salem (the others are reconstructions). As you study the houses, note the half-timbering technique used to build them. Area clay couldn't make strong enough bricks, so the Moravians used the European technique of interspersing timbers in the walls to strengthen the brick work. Also note the kick eaves on the buildings. Kick eaves, a raised angle at the roofline, help a roof shed water better.

Moravian archives report that the day the brethren "cut down trees on the place where the first house was to stand," they sang "several stanzas as they worked." Though a theocracy, Salem was not terribly repressive. The Moravians thought music a necessity; they enjoyed alcohol in moderation; and women could wear clothes of colors, not just black. They respected tradesmen, for in the Moravian view, everyone had an opportunity to serve God in some way.

At the corner of Bank Street, cross Main Street and walk to the Winkler Bakery (521 South Main Street). Stand so that you can see the large Single Brothers' House (600 South Main Street). Although Salem wasn't terribly repressive, the town *was* a theocracy, and rules did govern life there. For example, unmarried men and women didn't socialize; at least once, this particular custom gave rise to a great social dilemma.

The rules governing an adolescent boy's life stated that at age fourteen or so he would go to live in the Single Brothers' House to learn a trade. There, boys answered to the Master Teacher—not their parents. Without the Master Teacher's consent, for example, parents could not give their sons even so much as an item of clothing. After serving as apprentices and learning a trade—shoemaking, tin smithing, bread baking, leather tanning—young men became journeymen. Later, to have

This winter garden behind the Single Brothers' House in Old Salem speaks to Moravian industry and self-sufficiency.

his own shop, a journeyman needed the church's permission. Moreover, until a Brother had mastered his trade and was self-sufficient, he could not marry. And, yes, the church approved every marriage. (Interestingly, although the church approved marriages, it did not require a woman to marry against her will.) The lives of young women were likewise rule-bound. They lived in the Single Sisters' house and learned to contribute to the community.

And the great social dilemma? In early Salem, the Single Brothers made bread, and for the Single Sisters to have bread they had to buy it from the Single Brothers.

This situation concerned congregational leaders, who recruited the married Brother Thomas Butner to serve as baker. However, Butner didn't like being a baker; he preferred farming and shoemaking to baking. By 1807, church leaders hired Christopher Winkler to be the baker.

But Winkler was single, and so for him to serve as the baker, he had to marry. The elders proposed Elizabeth Danz as a wife; the two agreed to marry; and for the next thirty years, Salem enjoyed both tasty bread and proper behavior at the Winkler Bakery.

Walk four blocks south along Main Street (passing the Single Brothers' House) to the town square. Navigate the sidewalks carefully; tree roots have seriously uplifted the cobbles and bricks. Note the details of North Carolina's first planned community: the Market Fire House, the many buildings devoted to trades, and North Carolina's first municipal water system, the water pump at the corner of the square. (A wooden spigot in the Single Brothers' House also still works.)

On the labor of its tradesmen, Salem thrived: by 1815, the Bank of Cape Fear in Wilmington had opened a branch in Brother Blum's house, and by 1835 Salem had three hatters, three gunsmiths, two clockmakers, and several confectioners. As Salem thrived, more non-Moravians, whom the congregation called Strangers, came to the surrounding area to live.

Continue walking south to the Salem Tavern (736 South Main Street). The tavern once marked the edge of town. It sat on the boundary to protect the congregation from the worldly influences of travelers who stayed here. Today's tavern, renovated several times, dates to 1785. When George Washington stayed here on his southern tour, he called Salem an "oasis in the wilderness."

At Race Street, turn left and walk one block to Church Street. The Museum of Early Southern Decorative Arts (MESDA) is to your right. It houses splendid recreations of how people lived, from the most Spartan cabin to the most opulent Charleston manor house. As you walk this block, look for the archaeology project at the Reich-Hege House.

Turn left onto Church Street to walk six long blocks to the gates of God's Acre. The first structures you'll likely notice are a reconstructed log cabin and St. Philips Church (911 and 913 South Church Street), the home church of the Moravian community's black population and North Carolina's oldest standing black church. The Moravians had an uneasy relationship with slavery. They didn't approve of the practice, and the church did not want congregants to think themselves above manual labor. But they wanted the labor to help build their town. In addition, although the Moravians believed that everyone had a way to serve God through their labor, they also believed that after death, everyone was equal spiritually. The result of this tangle of sensibilities was that in Salem's earliest days, Brother Traugott Bagge, Salem's first storekeeper, purchased slaves for the church to rent out as laborers. Although not equal in the eyes of the church in that day, the enslaved Moravians fared somewhat better than did other slaves in the colony. Some of the slaves learned to speak German as well as English, and some attended school with the white Moravians. In the earliest days, slaves who died were buried alongside the Moravians in the town cemetery. By the mid 1820s, however, attitudes had hardened, with the black community forming its own church, St. Philips, and starting its own cemetery. One of the slaves rented out by Brother Bagge to the settlement's doctor was a gardener known as Davy. (The foundation remains of his small house are located further up Church Street.) Later christened Christian David, in honor of the Christian David who led the exiled Moravians to count Zinzendorf's estate, Salem's Christian David was an enthusiastic supporter of the division of the church groups and ultimately served as St. Phillips's sexton.

Look next for Salem College, which includes the Single Sisters' House (601 South Church Street).

According to the American Council on Education, Salem College is the oldest women's college in the country (by founding date) and thirteenth oldest overall. Started in 1772 as the "Little Girls' School" by the Single Sisters as a school to educate young girls in Salem—a seriously radical idea for its time—the school had, within thirty-five years, become a boarding school for other girls. Records show that the school educated young black girls and that in the 1820s the daughter of a Cherokee chief attended school here before departing on the Trail of Tears. The first teacher at the school, Elisabeth Oesterlein, walked with fifteen other girls and women 500 miles from Bethlehem, Pennsylvania, to be part of this new community that believed women deserved to be educated. Just over 1,000 young women attend classes here today.

Beyond Salem College is Home Moravian Church (529 South Church Street), built in 1800. The front door lists hours that the church is open to tours. Adjacent are several church offices.

Past the church, you can see Gottes Acker, or God's Acre, the cemetery. Near the cemetery gates, a marker signals the foundation remains of Christian David's house.

The first burial took place in God's Acre in June 1771. If you wander through the graveyard, you'll see that even in death the Moravians abided their social customs: men and women, be they young or old, married or widowed, each have their own area, called a "choir," where they are buried.

Turn around and walk to Bank Street. Turn right onto Bank Street and walk one block to Main Street. From the beginning, Salem's Moravians were something of an enigma. Although they had no particular quarrel with the British Crown and were not interested in revolution, when peace returned, Salem was the first town in North Carolina to celebrate the 4th of July. A Salem diary indicates that the day started with trombone music and continued with prayers.

But, as more people came to the surrounding area, the Moravians tried several times to persuade the General Assembly to let them be a country, separate from North Carolina. On January 16, 1849, the General Assembly granted part of the Moravians' wishes: the General Assembly decided to give the Moravians their own county by carving a new one out of Stokes County. They named it Forsyth, to honor the military exploits of Benjamin Forsyth. Forsyth, a daring guerilla leader in the War of 1812, led a group of volunteers on a twelve-mile march up the frozen St. Lawrence River on a raid against the British, capturing 52 British soldiers and 134 stands of arms and liberating several prisoners.

As Michael Bricker writes in *Winston-Salem: A Twin City History*, the formation of this new county was both good and bad news for the Moravians. On the one hand, they were glad for the separation. On the other hand, the new county needed a county seat, something church leaders did not want Salem to be. They didn't approve of trial by jury, and they disapproved of the riotous atmosphere that occurred when trials were conducted. Worse than the bad behavior, however, they feared God's wrath—in the form of a tornado.

Before officials carved Forsyth County out of Stokes County, there was the original Surry County, which included present-day Wilkes, Stokes, Forsyth, and Yadkin Counties. A town called Old Richmond served as county seat. Not long after Old Richmond formed, a tornado struck it, destroying the town. Salem Moravians took this event as a divine signal that being a county seat was bad. What to do?

Church leaders suggested that the community next door to Salem become the county seat, and then helped the cause by selling 51.25 acres for $256.25 to officially form a county seat. The name of the new county seat was Winston, honoring Joseph Winston, who fought at Moores Creek Bridge and at King's Mountain during the Revolutionary War, and served as a state legislator and congressman.

At Main Street, turn right to walk Main Street into Winston. Look for the coffee pot. While Salem was a model of piety and hard work, Winston was mostly a mill town studded by saloons. As you walk past the coffee pot, notice the mills to your left, now adapted for modern use. The Winston-Salem Visitor Center, which you pass later, has offices there.

One story associated with the coffee pot claims that a Yankee soldier hid inside it to escape a gang of Rebels.

Walk three blocks and cross the bridge over Business I-40. Watch for cars coming up the exit ramp. The differences between the two town's personalities didn't matter much after the Civil War, however, because the war had devastated both towns. Both needed something to bring prosperity back. According to Bricker, mutual prosperity arrived in the form of fruits and berries. The orchards and gardens of Salem produced as much fruit as ever, while over in Winston, the Pfhol and Stockton business dried and shipped the fruits and berries. Soon the two mutually advantageous activities revitalized the area. By the 1870s, the call for one city had started.

Walk one more block to First Street. Cross Main Street to the left. Just a few steps along First Street stands a granite monument marking the original dividing line between Winston and Salem.

Cross First Street and walk one block to Second Street. Across Second Street, another granite marker indicates where the first house in Winston once stood.

Cross Main Street again to arrive at a statue of Richard Joshua Reynolds. The 1870s saw the rise of the tobacco industry. In 1870, Major Hamilton Scales opened the first tobacco factory. Then, in 1874, Richard Joshua Reynolds arrived, purchasing from the Moravian Brethren a lot on Depot Street for $388.50 and building a tobacco factory there. It was no bigger than a tennis court.

Walk south along Main Street one block to First Street. At First Street, turn left to walk one block to Chestnut Street. This area, today's Piedmont Triad Park, is on the fringe of the original R. J. Reynolds complex.

At Chestnut Street, turn left and walk three blocks to Fourth Street, past Albert Hall. If as a child you ever participated in the phone prank of asking the person who answered if he had Prince Albert in a can, pay homage to this plain brick building where R. J. Reynolds Tobacco Company did indeed produce Prince Albert tobacco. Note that Victoria Hall, presumably named to honor Queen Victoria, stands next to Albert Hall.

At Fourth Street, turn left and walk two blocks to Main Street. After you do, turn around to look at the RJR complex, signaled by the stacks emblazoned with RJR. Then look across Fourth Street to the original head-

What's in a dash? The joining of two different communities into the city we call Winston-Salem.

quarters of R. J. Reynolds Tobacco. Built in 1929, this building served as a prototype for the Empire State Building, which was built two years later. Designed by New York architects Shreve and Lamb, this building was for a long time the tallest building in the Southeast.

Turn left onto Main Street to walk one block to Third Street. Though R. J. Reynolds became the biggest name in tobacco in town, his wasn't the only tobacco business here. In 1890 at least thirty-one tobacco companies were doing business in Winston. Among them were brothers Pleasant Henderson and John Wesley Hanes, who later sold their tobacco business to R. J. Reynolds, split up, and went into separate business: P. H. into knitting and J. W. into hosiery. In 1965 the two companies united to form Hanes Corporation. The prosperity in Winston-Salem also gave rise to one of North Carolina's most respected banks: Wachovia (now Wells Fargo). Look for the original headquarters building of Wachovia at the corner of Third and Main Streets.

Cross Main Street and walk along Third Street two blocks to Tower Run Lane. Turn left on Tower Run Lane to enter the Downtown Strollway. The Strollway provides excellent views of the Winston-Salem skyline, particularly the 1965 Winston Tower, the 1995 Wachovia Building, now the Wells Fargo Center, purportedly the world's only granite-domed skyscraper. After crossing under Business I-40, the Strollway passes

*Look for artistic whimsy while walking in Winston-Salem,
North Carolina's City of the Arts.*

through the area that once housed the textile mills. As you cross Brook-stown Avenue, look to your left to the area where the first outlet for Krispy Kreme doughnuts once stood.

Within about six long blocks (about half a mile), the Strollway will pass the parking area at the corner of Academy Street and Old Salem Road where this walk began.

Walk Details

HOW TO FIND IT: Business I-40 passes through downtown Winston-Salem. Brown signs will direct you to Old Salem. Although you can park within Old Salem, easier parking is available at the corner of Academy Street and Old Salem Road.

LENGTH: About 2.75 miles

SURFACE: Sidewalks, some cobblestones

RESTROOMS: At the Winston-Salem Visitor Center (200 Brookstown Avenue)

FOOTWEAR: Sneakers

PETS: OK on a leash but not allowed in buildings

MAP: You can find a map of the downtown area Winston-Salem at
   http://www.dwsp.org/downtown_info/DTparking-map10.pdf.
GOOD TO KNOW: The Winkler Bakery is open to the public.

Guided tours are available, and many of the historic buildings in Old
Salem are open to touring with admission. See www.oldsalem.org for
more information.

Salisbury

PIEDMONT EMBLEM

What is the essence of a Piedmont town? Unlike coastal towns, a Piedmont town cannot point to a harbor or a river and say, "This is what gave us life." Unlike a mountain town, a Piedmont town cannot say, "People came here to escape the heat and to rest from their toil."

To understand a Piedmont town, you must use a different lens: why did people collect here to make a life for themselves? How did they trade with others to create an economy? You must think about how an ever-evolving web of transportation—rivers, Native American paths, primitive roads, and railroads—impacted how and where settlers and citizens invested their energy into earning their living. Sometimes, as in the case of Burlington, Gastonia, or Greensboro, a Piedmont town came to life because of the industry it supported. Sometimes, as in the case of Statesville, a Piedmont town came to life because it once marked the edge of wilderness.

To be sure, every Piedmont town has its own particular history. One town, however, seems to have captured it all: Salisbury. To walk about Salisbury is to be absolutely wowed by how a river, an ancient path, a primitive road, a plank road, and a railroad coupled with both industry and agriculture—not to mention hard-working everyday people—transformed a frontier outpost into a jewel of prosperity.

Historical Context

Eastern and Piedmont North Carolina divide along a topographical feature called the Fall Line. East of the Fall Line, the state's commercial prospects were initially better because navigable rivers flowed easily to coastal ports, decreasing the time getting goods to market. For that reason English and Scots settlers, colonizing from the east, stopped at the Fall Line, content to make their fortunes in agriculture and naval stores. West of the Fall Line agricultural prospects dimmed because land was rockier and the rivers were harder to navigate, especially over the waterfalls that signal the Fall Line.

Where the English and Scots colonists declined to go, however, Pennsylvania Dutch and newly arrived Germans migrating from Pennsylvania went. By way of the Great Pennsylvania Wagon Road (also called the Great Philadelphia Wagon Road, the Great Wagon Road, and the Carolina Road), these immigrants dropped into the Piedmont. Along the way, they found the 203-mile-long Yadkin River, which rises outside Blowing Rock and quickly turns south. These immigrants knew a good river when they saw it: the Yadkin emptied into the Pee Dee, which met the Atlantic Ocean in Georgetown, South Carolina. Thus, this great interior river became a lifeline of the North Carolina Piedmont.

The Walk

From the Visitor Information Center (204 East Innes Street), turn right onto Innes Street and walk to the intersection of Innes and Main Streets, also called the Square. When you reach the Square, look to the right down North Main Street. About six miles away is the Yadkin River and the spot where the Native American Great Trading Path crossed the river. From the late 1740s into the early 1750s, immigrants from Pennsylvania settled there, calling the spot the Trading Ford. By 1753, these settlers were asking royal governor Matthew Rowan for their own county. Rowan obliged them, splitting a county out of Anson. This new county, named Rowan, was huge: it stretched north to Virginia and south to South Carolina. It shared an eastern border with Orange County and stretched west as far as anyone knew.

On February 11, 1755, Salisbury was established as the county seat; Squire Boone (Daniel's father) helped plat the town on an area called the Trader's Camping Ground, which lay adjacent to the Great Trading Path. Most think that Salisbury's name comes from a similar town in England, but it is possible that Salisbury, Maryland, inspired the name. Town fathers decided to name the main thoroughfare in town Innes Street to honor the accomplishments of James Innes, a friend of royal governor Rowan. Innes had led a contingent of North Carolina militia to help Governor Dinwiddie of Virginia in the Braddock Expedition, a failed attempt by the British to fight the French and Indians at Fort Necessity, Pennsylvania.

Though remote, Salisbury became a focal point for people living in the then-backwoods of central North Carolina.

Cross Main Street, and walk one block to Church Street to the Confederate monument. Cross Church Street. Then cross Innes Street to the left and walk to the Henderson Law Office (202 South Church Street). Built in 1795 and perhaps the oldest structure in Salisbury, this building speaks to Salisbury's importance as a frontier town. By 1800, Salisbury was the sixth-largest town in North Carolina, behind New Bern, Wilmington, Edenton and Fayetteville (which were tied), and Raleigh. For a time after the turn of the nineteenth century, Salisbury was the only town west of Fayetteville that had a bank.

Not only had Salisbury become a commercial hub, the town had become a frontier judicial hub, due in part to the many notable leaders the town produced: William Davie, who helped create the University of North Carolina (see chapter 29), studied law here, as did Andrew Jackson. Other Salisbury citizens also ascended the national stage: John Steele, a U.S. comptroller appointed by George Washington; Colonel John Stokes, North Carolina's first federal judge; Colonel Alexander Martin, a state governor and U.S. senator; and Waightstill Avery, North Carolina's first attorney general. Of all of the distinguished men to live and study in Salisbury during the period, Andrew Jackson likely had the wildest reputation. James Brawley, author of *The Rowan Story: 1753–1953*, described our seventh president as "the most roaring, rollicking, game-cooking, card-playing, mischievous fellow that ever lived in the South."

Continue walking South Church Street to Bank Street. At Bank Street, turn right and walk one block to Jackson Street. When gold was discovered in nearby Gold Hill in 1824, local papers began calling for improved transportation. When the plank road arrived in the 1840s, the town hummed with commerce. Slowly, agrarian life changed to industrial: gristmills, mining, and tobacco manufacturing gained the upper hand, as did distilling and selling whiskey. One historian called Salisbury the "wettest and wickedest" town in the state. This block of historic homes speaks to how prosperous antebellum Salisbury was.

Life became even better when the railroad arrived in Salisbury in January 1855. The citizenry, eager to let the good times roll, celebrated with a parade from the courthouse to the depot, speeches by Judge John Ellis and John Motley Morehead, brass bands, and a barbeque. Nearly 15,000 people braved the January weather to turn out for the party. The list of meats cooked that day in Salisbury indicates the unbridled joy at the railroad's arrival: twenty-four hogs, sixteen sheep, six "beeves," and ten opossums fed the crowd.

Salisbury's mural on Fisher Street may make you look twice to see who's real and who is a portrait!

Turn left onto Jackson Street and walk one block to Horah Street. Turn left and walk two blocks to South Main Street. Turn left and walk two blocks to Fisher Street. Turn left onto Fisher. The Empire Hotel (212 South Main Street), built in 1855, illustrates Salisbury's antebellum wealth. This magnificent building once had a domed ballroom on its top floor. Look also for the Conrad Brem House (205 South Main), the oldest structure in the downtown area. Of course, not all of Salisbury's notable downtown buildings qualify as antebellum. The Meroney Theater (213 South Main) dates to 1905.

Walk one block along Fisher Street, to Lee Street. Turn right onto Lee Street and walk one block to Bank Street. At Bank Street, turn left and walk to and cross over the railroad track until you arrive at Long Street. Now you enter the sixteen-acre area where a Confederate prison once stood. All that remains today of the prison is the Garrison House, which you pass just before you walk over the train track.

The Civil War indelibly marked Salisbury as it did Fayetteville and Warrenton. Though citizens of Salisbury first rejoiced at the attack on Fort Sumter in April 1861, the town soon grasped what war would mean. When asked to send troops to the Federal cause, Governor John Ellis (the same man who spoke when the railroad arrived) refused, saying, "You can get no troops from North Carolina." Ellis died in office just a few months later on July 7. On July 9, Henry T. Clark, the new governor, agreed to turn over a textile mill for use as a prison. By December 1861, 120 Union prisoners had arrived.

Early on, life wasn't completely bad for the prisoners; records show that to beat the boredom, prisoners played baseball in the compound. However, by the end of the war, the prison was seriously overcrowded, the conditions dismal and unsanitary, the food meager. Prisoners lived through the winter wet and cold in tents. Some tried to burrow in the ground to stay warm. Others tried to escape. Salisbury citizens brought food and clothing to the prisoners, and one woman opened her door to soldiers who needed convalescent care.

Turn right onto Long Street. At Monroe Street, turn right. The textile-mill-turned prison stood generally to your right. Historians debate whether the number of incarcerated men was 5,000 or upwards of 11,000. What they don't debate is the death rate: it jumped to 28 percent in October 1864. The dead were buried in mass graves in a nearby cornfield—the origin of Salisbury National Cemetery, to your left. By the time the war ended, eighteen trenches contained the bodies. Three days after Lee surrendered to Grant at Appomattox, Union general George Stoneman arrived in Salisbury to free the Federal prisoners, burn the prison, and burn a nearby arsenal. In 1868, the U.S. government assumed responsibility for the cemetery and in 1870, the cemetery became a memorial to those who died while in prison.

To find where the eighteen trenches lay, turn left onto Railroad Street and walk toward Military Street to the entrance of Salisbury National Cemetery. Follow the cemetery road all the way to the end.

Return to Monroe Street and turn left. Cross the railroad track and then walk to Craig Street, eight blocks away. Arrive at Livingstone College. This stretch traverses part of the West Square Historic District. Filled with beautiful homes, the district speaks to turn-of-the-century prosperity in Salisbury that returned due in large part to the railroad. The 1896 North Carolina Business Directory cites seventeen manufacturing firms, fifteen grocers, the headquarters of the Western North Carolina Railroad company, and seven hotels in Salisbury and thirty-six gold mines in Rowan County. A 1912 business directory cites twelve department stores, seven butchers, three architects, and two brick manufacturers. Judging by their homes, this mercantile class lived well.

Established in 1879, Livingstone College was first located in Concord. The school, first named the Zion Wesley Institute, was meant to train ministers. After three terms, the school closed. Later Rowan County gave the trustees a $1,000 donation and invited the school to reopen in Salisbury. Under the guidance of Joseph C. Price, whose mantra was "the Head, the Hand, and the Heart," Livingstone College, an affiliate of the AME Zion Church, offered North Carolina's black citizens a classical education, rather than the vocational education Booker T. Washington espoused. Today Livingstone College enrolls about 1,000 students and continues to prepare them with a liberal arts education. On a less serious note in the college's history, a marker in the center of the campus notes the first football game between two historically black colleges to take place in the United States. Livingstone's opponent was Biddle College, which would later become Johnson C. Smith University.

At Craig Street, turn left to walk one block to Monroe Street, to a marker noting North Carolina's plank roads. The construction of plank roads, North Carolina's first commercial attempt at road improvement, reached its height in the 1850s. In 1852, the state legislature granted thirty-nine charters for road-building companies; in 1854 it granted thirty-two. This primitive intrastate highway system soon met its demise because not only was road building difficult and costly work—road-building crews could manage about one mile a week—maintenance costs soared. In addition, plank roads were no match for the railroads. The plank road commemorated here ran to North Wilkesboro.

Turn around to retrace your steps to Monroe Street. Turn right onto Monroe and walk two blocks to Innes Street. Once again you will pass by many of Salisbury's beautiful homes. At Fisher Street, look left to see the home of John Ellis (200 South Ellis Street).

On Innes Street, turn right to walk downtown. You will pass several of Salisbury's famous monuments: Bell Tower Park, the Session House, the Wren House, the Confederate monument, and St. John's Lutheran Church, established in 1747.

Turn left onto North Main Street. Then turn right onto Council Street. Walk south three blocks to Depot Street. Along the way, look for the 1857 Rowan County Courthouse. Spared by General Stoneman, today this Greek Revival building houses the Rowan Museum.

The differing styles of architecture at the Salisbury station hint at the plethora of building styles you will see along this walk.

Once at Depot Street, it's time to consider the depot itself. Today's depot is the second such structure at that site. Built in 1908 in the Mission style, by 1911 this depot was welcoming forty-four trains a day as they passed through on their way between Washington, D.C., and Atlanta, Georgia. It has, on occasion, been featured in Hollywood movies.

Like other economic engines of the Piedmont, railroads lost the upper hand of commerce, causing growth in Salisbury to level. Instead, cities such as Charlotte and Raleigh became the growth centers due to new industries such as banking and technology. By 2000, Salisbury was usually ranked in the mid-twenties in terms of population.

Walk Details

HOW TO FIND IT: Salisbury is located off I-85, about 40 miles west of Charlotte. This walk starts at the visitor information center (204 East Innes Street).

LENGTH: About 4.75 miles

SURFACE: Paved

RESTROOMS: At the visitor information center

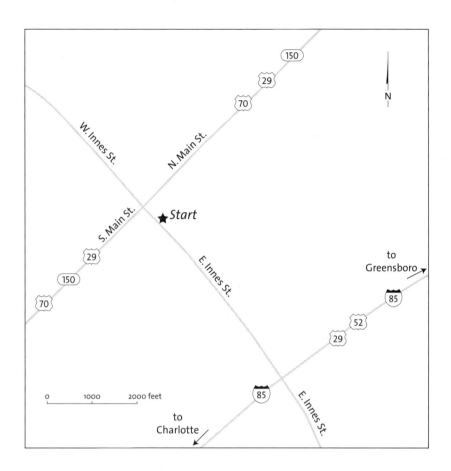

FOOTWEAR: Sneakers

PETS: OK on a leash

MAP: You can find an online map of Salisbury at www.visitsalisburync
.com/plan-your-trip/maps-directions/default.aspx. Look for the link
Plan Your Trip.

Beware: Sidewalks are available for most of this route, but occasionally
you will have to cross the street.

GOOD TO KNOW: Salisbury hosts a tour of historic homes during the
second weekend of October.

If you love architecture, get the Salisbury Heritage Tour brochure
from the visitor information center; it discusses many, many more of
the historic homes in town.

Walk the Walk of the Surfmen

Imagine walking along the surf line at night carrying a lantern, your eyes squinting into the darkness, your ears straining to hear the screams of shipwreck survivors above the roaring waves. Imagine wind and rain swirling about your body as you walk. Imagine that your work manual states that you're obliged to row your way out into the ocean to rescue people, but that you don't "have to come back."

Such were the working conditions of the surfmen, members of the U.S. Lifesaving Service and forerunners of today's U.S. Coast Guard.

Though today we take for granted that the U.S. Coast Guard will rescue people whose ocean-going trips have gone badly, such was not always the case. The push to protect the Atlantic coastline grew slowly and in piecemeal fashion. Were it not for several spectacular wrecks along the North Carolina coast, the realization of such an agency might have been even slower than it was.

The next time you visit the beach, especially if you visit the Outer Banks, use your beach walk to remember the North Carolina surfmen. Theirs is a most heroic story.

Historical Context

Our coast earned the name Graveyard of the Atlantic for a reason. Shipwreck counts differ; David Stick, author of *Graveyard of the Atlantic*, believes that 650 wrecks lie just offshore. Others say that unverified wrecks could push the number to 2,000. As coastal residents like to say, Who knows what the next storm will uncover?

Why is the North Carolina coastline so dangerous? At Cape Hatteras, the cold, northern Labrador Current and the warm, southern Gulf Stream collide. This collision makes for great fishing, but it creates great turbulence. Add in the elbows of Capes Hatteras, Lookout, and Fear—and the shifting sands of Diamond Shoals, Cape Lookout Shoals, and Frying Pan Shoals—and you have maritime disaster waiting to happen.

Sea captains, of course, knew these facts, but they were not sailing for pleasure. They sailed for business, and in business the old saw holds true: time is money. A steely nerved captain who dared to sail closer to

The life-saving station at Chicamacomico now serves as a museum to the surfmen.

shore—outwitting the wind, outmaneuvering the turbulence, and out-racing the storms—could complete his trip more quickly. Faster trips meant more income.

But sailing closer to the coast increased the likelihood of wrecking. In the beginning coastal residents risked their own lives to rescue victims —drying them, warming them, and feeding them with their own scant resources. No one else was there to do it. (Not that altruism was the sole motivation of coastal residents: they also scavenged the wrecks for us-able items that washed ashore.)

North Carolina's first attempt to provide safe passage along our coast-line came in the form of two lighthouses. Protecting Ocracoke Inlet, the colony's principal port of entry, these wooden towers appear on a 1733 map. English newspapers indicate, however, that the towers didn't pre-vent ships from wrecking.

Although the United States created the Revenue Marine Service 1789, this agency didn't rescue shipwrecked sailors. It enforced customs laws and collected taxes. Not until 1791 did a privately funded organization, the Massachusetts Humane Society, provide the country's first organized service to help shipwreck victims. In time, the federal government agreed to allow the Revenue Marine Service cutters to rescue survivors, and by 1854, the federal government had empowered the secretary of the treasury to build stations along Long Island and New Jersey. Though the 1854 measure funded station keepers, it did not pay for life-saving crews. Keepers relied upon volunteers. Joe A. Mobley's book *Ship Ashore!* provides a detailed history of the evolution of the U.S. Coast Guard.

Despite these advances, ships still wrecked along the North Carolina coast, some dramatically, as when the *Pulaski* wrecked near New River Inlet in 1838, its boiler exploding. Other wrecks were heartbreaking, like the 1837 wreck of the *Home* near Ocracoke, in which ninety passengers lost their lives, their bodies washing ashore, some still wearing their jewelry. Few weeks passed when coastal newspapers didn't carry a story of yet another shipwreck.

After the Civil War, commercial traffic increased, as did the shipwrecks. The pressure to do something likewise mounted. New lighthouses, including today's Cape Hatteras, Bodie Island, and Currituck Beach lights, were built, as were new life-saving stations. By 1874, nine new stations in the northern Outer Banks were under construction. Paid surfmen now manned the stations; however, they were not full-time employees.

The surfmen worked only during the storm-active months, December through March, and their job involved healthy doses of standing and walking. During the day, when sailing was smooth, they stood a four-hour watch in an open tower of the station, calmly logging the ships that passed by. At night, and during the day when visibility was poor, they walked the beach. At each station, usually spaced about five to seven miles apart, two surfmen left, one walking north, the other south. The two would eventually meet. Exchanging tokens to prove that he had indeed patrolled his area, each man would then turn around to return to his home station. As he walked, a surfman carried a lantern to light his way. If a surfman spotted a wrecked ship, he used the flares he carried to signal that help was on the way. Sailors were routinely admonished to let help come to them rather than try to reach shore on their own if their ship did indeed wreck.

"Help is on the way" hardly describes the surfmen's job when wrecks did occur. If the wreck was close, the surfmen fired a life-saving line and a breeches buoy to haul survivors to shore. If the wreck was farther out, the surfmen faced a multistep procedure requiring great strength and fortitude.

This kitchen served many a hungry surfman.

First, a team of surfmen lugged their wooden rescue boat via a cart often a mile or more across soft sand. The boat was typically about twenty-six feet long, and six to seven feet wide. It weighed anywhere from 700 to 11,000 pounds. (Remember this the next time you complain about hauling a beach tote and an aluminum chair to the surf's edge.)

Once at the water's edge, the surfmen then boarded their boat, grabbed their oars, and muscle-oared their way through the breakers to reach the wreck. Splashing through crashing, angry, open waves, salt water burning their eyes and noses, the brave surfmen would eventually reach the wreck and set about pulling survivors to safety.

The Walk

Walking along a beach doesn't require much in the way of directions, so this space will tell a brief story of the wrecks of the USS *Huron* and of the steamer *Metropolis*, the two wrecks that focused federal attention on North Carolina's dangerous coastline and helped make the U.S. Life-Saving Service, predecessor to the present-day U.S. Coast Guard, its own entity. These wrecks also caused the federal government to build more life-saving stations and to reevaluate the methods and tools used in the service.

In November 1877, just days before the stations were to open for the season, the *Huron,* a warship, departed New York for a leisurely expedition to reconnoiter the Cuban coastline. After a stop in Hampton Roads, Virginia, the ship continued its journey south on November 23. Late in the evening, and pushing into early morning on the 24th, the ship's captain sailed close to the coastline to avoid a strong, northward-pushing current of the Gulf Stream, the result of a heavy storm. The storm and a faulty compass caused the *Huron* to run aground near Nags Head. Sailors hung perilously to the damaged rigging, waiting for the flares that signaled that help was on the way. For over a day, the cold waves pounded the sailors. Fatigue took over, and the weakened men, unable to hold on to the rigging, dropped into the ocean. Local residents who stood at the surf line couldn't help, and the life-saving station wasn't due to open until December. Nearly one hundred sailors were lost.

Thomas Nast, America's first political cartoonist, heard of the tragedy and turned his pen to the story. The *Harper's Weekly* sketch shows a mildly dismayed Uncle Sam standing in the surf, with the *Huron* in the background and dead bodies in the foreground. The caption was deadly: "I suppose I must spend a little on life-saving . . ."

Little more than two months later, the steamer *Metropolis* wrecked near Currituck Beach, about halfway between two existing lifesaving stations, losing another eighty-five people. Though rumors suggested that the *Metropolis* was rotten, mistakes and bad luck doomed the rescue attempt. The surfmen pulled their cart through soft sand for over a mile. When they fired safety lines, the first shot went beyond the wreck. On the second shot, the apparatus broke. After a quick repair, the surfmen prepared for a third shot but realized that the cart carried only enough gunpowder for two shots. Accounts say that life savers, volunteers, and recovered victims stretched for over a mile along the shore trying to rescue *Metropolis* passengers.

A great public discussion arose. Were North Carolina surfmen competent? Was the service adequately funded? Should the service continue as part of the Revenue Marine Service in the Treasury Department, or should it be its own entity? When the political dust settled, the U. S. Lifesaving Service became its own entity, more life-saving stations were built, and the methods and tools of life saving were reevaluated.

Joe Mobley, author of *Ship Ashore!* describes in vivid detail the he-

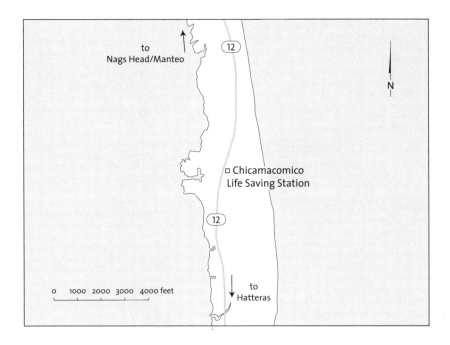

roics of North Carolina's surfmen after the 1878 reorganization. The all-black crew of the Pea Island station, led by Richard Etheridge, routinely distinguished itself, particularly with the rescue of *M&E Henderson*, which, in addition to being rotten, may have witnessed a mutiny. Rasmus Midgett, patrolling the beach during the hurricane San Ciriaco, single-handedly saved ten people from the *Priscilla*. John Allen Midgett, keeper of Chicamacomico Station, led a rescue of the *Mirlo* that would astound even Hollywood filmmakers. The ship had been torpedoed by a German U-boat. Three attempts were required to launch the life-saving boat against the furious ocean. To rescue the sailors, Midgett instructed his men to row through flames to reach capsized lifeboats that the *Mirlo* sailors clung to.

Walk Details

HOW TO FIND IT: Given that anywhere from 650 to 2,000 ship lay wrecked off the North Carolina coast, this walk is beachcomber's choice! To combine your walk with the opportunity to see a life-saving station and some of the apparatus the surfmen used, visit the restored Chicamacomico Lighthouse in Rodanthe.

The steamer *Metropolis* wrecked further north, near Currituck. The

USS *Huron* wrecked in Nags Head, near where Bladen Street intersects US 158.

LENGTH: As long as you want

SURFACE: Sand

FOOTWEAR: Bare feet or sandals

PETS: Depends upon local beach regulations; leashes may be required.

MAP: Not needed

BEWARE: Sharp-edged shells

GOOD TO KNOW: To be sure to see a shipwreck, park at the Coquina
Beach lot on NC 12, across from the Bodie Island Lighthouse. You can
see the remains of the *Laura Barnes* there.

Cooleemee

MILL HILL

Linthead was what you were and *mill hill* was where you lived if you were one of the hundreds of thousands of textile workers in North Carolina. The Piedmont, sometimes called the "backwater of the South," was home to hundreds of textile mills. Of course, mills appeared along the coast and in the mountains, but more than anywhere else, the mill village defined the North Carolina Piedmont during the late 1800s and throughout the 1900s.

The Piedmont's hilly terrain and moving water formed a landscape made for the mills. Interestingly, mills mimicked the rivers they sat beside, their long, narrow buildings conforming to the rivers that powered them. Multiple floors better allowed an efficient transfer of power to the numerous belts and pulleys. Visit a Piedmont town today—Kannapolis, Cramerton, Belmont, Glencoe, Mebane, Ramseur, Saxapahaw, Mount Holly, or Rutherfordton, just to name a very, very few—and you'll likely see the remains of a textile mill, where the ornamental trappings of the central towers speak to the textile barons' grand visions.

While today a mill might stand empty as a forgotten bucket, it may also have been restored to serve as lofts, offices, shops, or public spaces. In June 2012, Davie County officials announced that they had received grants from the Environmental Protection Agency and the National Endowment of the Arts to examine whether the Cooleemee Mill (the location of this walk) could undergo revitalization.

Regardless, the mills that dot North Carolina testify to one of the most significant economic drivers the state has ever seen. In 1973, the height of mill employment, some 293,600 people worked in North Carolina textile mills. Cooleemee, once home to about 348 mill families, represents this slice of North Carolina life.

Historical Context

The first textile mill in North Carolina is believed to be the Schenck Mill built in 1813 on the banks of Mill-branch, a fork of the Catawba River, about two miles east of Lincolnton. The second and third mills appeared in Edgecombe and Cumberland Counties, respectively. By 1860 the state was home to forty-six water-powered textile mills (thirty-nine producing cotton yarns and seven producing woolen). During those days, mills produced yarn that went north to be woven into cloth.

The Civil War, however, changed the model. Instead of shipping yarns northward, mills kept the yarns at home, weaving the cloth to produce uniforms for the war effort. In the last several months of the war, however, Union forces burned many of the mills; those that survived likely had worn out machines. The future looked bleak.

However, the First Cotton Mill Campaign, an industrial push arising during Reconstruction to rebuild the South, helped the industry rebound. By 1870, eighty-five North Carolina mills employed 3,000 workers. In addition, the mills put other people to work: farmers grew cotton to satisfy the mills' appetite for raw product, and machinists arrived to maintain the mills and to supply parts.

The hilly terrain enticed the northern mill owners to come south, as did the cheap labor they found here. In outsourcing textile production to the South, owners sometimes named the new mill towns after the recently departed New England towns. Lowell is one such instance. Steadily, the number of mills and millhands rose. Not even the rise of women's hemlines in the Roaring Twenties—and the resulting lessened demand for cloth—could slow the mills for long. The demand for cloth uniforms for World War I uniforms spiked production; by 1923 North Carolina was ahead of Massachusetts in textile manufacturing.

Who worked in the mills? From the mountains came men and women left unemployed by the departing logging companies. Entire families moved away from farms, flocking to the mills because a weekly wage from the mill was more appealing than farming.

The Walk

With the Zachary House (131 Church Street) behind you, walk Church Street one-half block to the left to Cross Street, where a restored mill house (Old #14) stands. Compare the Zachary House, where the general manager of the mill lived, to the restored mill house, typical of where millhands lived. The large, grand home of the manager, sitting up on the hill, clearly shows the social stratification of life in the mill village.

Textile barons, like lumber barons and plantation owners before them, controlled most aspects of mill workers' lives. Life in the mill village was about as self-contained as you will ever find in North Carolina. At first, millhands rented their houses from mill owners, the rent usually deducted from the week's wages; later mill owners let workers buy their homes outright. Companies provided water at centralized hydrants, coal, and electricity. Companies also built schools, churches, pools, and parks. In addition, they usually hired a doctor and a nurse, all to keep workers happy, healthy, dependent, and working. In the mill village, the mill whistle governed all life. Mothers even nursed babies according to the mill schedule.

On the mill worker's house, notice the lack of "underpinning" in the foundation. The brick piers, the typical construction technique of mill-village homes, did indeed put a floor under mill workers' feet. But it also allowed cold winter air to make those floors cold. As people born in the mill village went on to other types of jobs, having an enclosed foundation under their houses became a symbol of their success.

The open foundation of the mill house, however, meant that families could keep chickens, an often-cherished reminder of the farms they had left behind and a cheap food source. The large backyard behind the mill house, often devoted to a vegetable garden, is also typical. Note, too, the front window underneath the porch eave. Called a "coffin window," this window, with easy-to-remove panes, allowed a coffin to come inside the house for the wake of a loved one. In the era before funeral homes, people commonly held wakes in the family home.

If you visit Cooleemee when the restored mill house is open, you'll see remnants of mill-village living inside: linoleum "carpets," tiny fireplaces and coal hoods, and kitchen appliances like ice boxes and cast-iron stoves. The four rooms include a kitchen, a bedroom for the parents, a bedroom for the daughters, and a bedroom for the sons. There is no dining room. The inside toilet of the house indicates that the house had been up-fitted: in the early days of mill-village living, a row of outhouses edged the backyards. The interior paint is the same used in the mills. You'll also see a favorite boys' game: hoopstick, also known as hoop rolling. The simple game involved only two pieces of gear, a hoop and a stick. The aim? To see who could roll the hoop the longest with the stick.

With the mill house behind you, turn left to walk three blocks to Main Street, where a marker notes the location of the old Riverside Hotel. The styles of mill-village houses usually reflect one of two facts of mill-village life. For every room the mill house had, the family had to supply a worker. Thus, a four-room house had to supply at least four mill workers. Or, it could be that the worker had attained a high-status job, in which case, his house was a bit larger.

The 1899 wood-framed Riverside Hotel served several purposes. Traveling salesmen and visiting mill executives stayed there when in town. It also housed schoolteachers because Cooleemee did not have a freestanding teacherage, housing for the single women who taught school. Occasionally, to celebrate loyal, long-employed workers, the mill held banquets in the hotel and allowed the hands to experience the white linen and silver service. Local legend says that the Riverside served a wonderful chocolate pie.

Turn left onto Main Street to walk one long block to Cooleemee Town Square, passing the former Riverside Park. Though Erwin Mills demolished the Town Square in 1963, a mural on the walls of the now-defunct mill shows how the town looked. J. N. Ledford's, usually called the company store, supplied whatever millhands needed, making sure that millhands didn't spend their money elsewhere. Above the company store was a beauty salon, thought to be the first in Davie County. Below the company store were a barber shop and a men's shower. The shower, complete with hot water, let the men wash the lint from their bodies after a day's work before going home. A drug store, Dr. A. B. Byerly's office, a bank, and a movie theater completed the mix.

The land the mill sits on is off limits, so you'll have to imagine how the mill abutted the town. On the far side of the mill and generally out of sight, a 422-foot dam spanned the Yadkin River. A mill race diverted water to the waterwheel that powered the mill. The dam also created a pool of water where doffer boys, young boys who removed full bobbins and replaced them with empty ones, could sneak a quick, refreshing swim in the Yadkin River and rinse the lint from their bodies.

The descriptions of mill jobs denoted either a step in the process of spinning yarn or a machine part. *Openers* opened bales of cotton, and *pickers* picked debris from the raw cotton. *Card hands* hand-fed cotton into the carding machine, and *weavers* operated a loom. Little children worked in the mill alongside adults, their employment eventually prompting child labor laws. *Spinner girls*, usually the youngest female workers, walked up and down the bank of looms looking for threads that had snapped apart to tie the broken threads together. Any mill job could be either boring or dangerous or both, especially as fatigue accumulated during the twelve-hour shifts. In 1904, an opener likely earned about $4.50 a week for seventy-two hours of work.

This mural recalls the bustling downtown square adjacent the mill in Cooleemee.

As you study the abandoned mill, notice that the windows are bricked shut. Although the windows provided ventilation, mill operators learned that in the humid South, fibers absorb the water that's in the air. Varying levels of absorption cause the fibers to behave unpredictably and break as they spin furiously onto the bobbins. In addition, workers looking out windows to escape the boredom of their jobs might injure themselves. Thus, companies bricked the windows to control humidity and boost productivity. But, as bricked windows solved one problem, they exacerbated another, that of the lint flying about in the air. Unable to escape to the outside, the cloud of lint thickened as each week progressed. Many workers whose lungs cleared somewhat during a day off on Sunday started coughing furiously Monday when they returned to work. Monday morning sickness eventually came to be known as brown lung disease.

Turn a hard left onto Duke Street to walk one very long block back to Cross Street. At Cross Street, turn right and walk one block to a marker describing the original wooden schoolhouse. The two-story, eight-classroom wooden building opened in 1902, soon after the mill did. Each room contained a pot-bellied stove for heating. Toilets were outside, as was the water fountain: a cast-iron pipe and a gourd dipper. Though mill companies offered to educate the workers, many workers recall that after a day spent working in the mill, they were too tired to study.

Like the hotel, the school building had multiple uses. Millhands might enjoy a cakewalk or a covered dish supper there, or perhaps a skit or play put on by schoolchildren. (My grandfather, a doffer boy in a mill, met his bride-to-be, a spinner girl, at such a cakewalk, putting an outrageously high bid on one of the young woman's pies to draw her favorable notice.)

At the marker, turn left to walk one long block along Watt Street to Marginal Street. To the right, a marker describing the new schoolhouse explains how this building served as a community cannery where women could work together to help each other put up the bounty of their backyard vegetable gardens. Research into mill life often reveals its hardships. But despite the hardships—or, perhaps, because of them—mill villagers developed quite a sense of family and of relying upon each other.

Standing at the marker describing the new schoolhouse, look across NC 801 to a little cluster of mill houses there. Those houses mark where black mill workers lived, attended school, and went to church, forming their own sub-community. As historian Jacquelyn Hall and her coauthors point out in *Like A Family: The Making of a Southern Cotton Mill World*, although slaves had worked in the mills before the Civil War, mill owners increasingly turned to poor white farmers for labor because slaves were becoming expensive. As mill owners shifted their labor model in this way, they helped deepen segregation. In the mills, certain jobs were done by men or by women, and certain jobs were done by white workers and by black workers. When the shift was done, mill workers went home to their assigned area.

Between you and the houses of black mill workers, a ball park once stood. Over the years, Cooleemee sported several minor league baseball teams. Their names? The Cooleemee Cards, the Weavers, and the Cooleemee Cools. These teams did not merely provide entertainment; they also provided excellent talent-hunting grounds for professional scouts. In addition, sometimes a man could get a relatively good job in the mill if he had a good batting average. Shoeless Joe Jackson was a product of textile-mill baseball.

Turn around, walk two blocks along Marginal Street to Church Street to return to the Zachary House. At the Zachary House, plaques honor the men who died in World Wars I and II, Korea, and Vietnam. Many sons and daughters left the mill village to serve their country and did not return, some because they became casualties of war. Many more

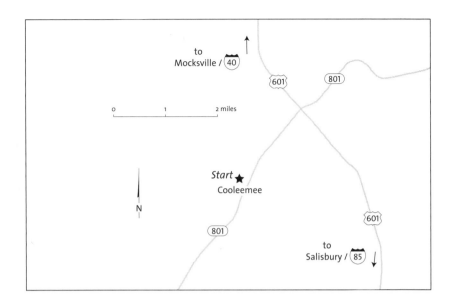

thousands used military service to launch themselves into other lines of work and escape the mill village.

Walk Details

HOW TO FIND IT: Cooleemee is located in central North Carolina, near the intersection of US 601 and NC 801 South. From NC 801, turn right onto Marginal Street, and then left onto Church Street to find the Zachary House (131 Church Street), home of the Mill Village Museum, where this walk starts.

LENGTH: 2 miles

SURFACE: Asphalt

RESTROOMS: At the Mill Village Museum, which is open Wednesday–Saturday, 10 A.M.–4 P.M.

FOOTWEAR: Sneakers

PETS: OK on a leash. Expect neighborhood dogs to bark and defend their turf.

MAP: Available at the Mill Village Museum

GOOD TO KNOW: You can visit the restored mill house described above when the Mill Village Museum is open.

Respect the property and privacy of Cooleemee residents as you walk about their village.

For more information, visit http://www.textileheritage.org.

Durham

THE BULL CITY

Every basketball season, some television sports announcer will refer to Durham as "Tobacco Road," as if that quickie description explains everything one should know about the city or the region. Wrong!

Durham's history is as diverse as that of any North Carolina city and includes a wide cast of characters, from the Occaneechi Indians who once lived in the vicinity, to the white entrepreneurs such as W. T. Blackwell and Julian Carr who made Durham a home to tobacco manufacturing, to the black entrepreneurs such John Merritt and Aaron Moore who turned their energy to helping establish a thriving black middle class in North Carolina after the Civil War. In 1901, the *Durham Sun* encouraged citizens to "make it your policy to talk Durham, act Durham, sleep Durham, wear Durham, smoke Durham—if you smoke; chew Durham, come to Durham, and patronize Durham. Every man for the town and you will see things hum." By 1913, that spirit must have taken root, for a large electric sign near the train station proclaimed, "Durham Renowned the World Around." The closure of tobacco manufacturing plants that dominated the downtown's economic and physical landscape dealt a blow to that spirit for a time, but like other cities in North Carolina's Piedmont, the city center has enjoyed a considerable resurgence. Today when you walk downtown you'll see that Durham still exudes the energy that drove its growth at the turn of the twentieth century.

Historical Context

Outside North Carolina, most people know Durham in one of two ways: either as the home of Duke University and its renowned Blue Devils, or through one of the most beloved sports movies of all time, *Bull Durham*, which featured a fictional version of the city's rough-and-tumble minor league baseball franchise. But Durham's civic energy doesn't start with basketball, bulls, or baseball.

Well before the arrival of white settlers in the mid-1700s, Native American people known as Occaneechi, Eno, and Shakori had established substantial villages in the area. In his *New Voyage to Carolina*, early explorer John Lawson wrote of a Native American settlement called Adshusheer that archaeologists believe is near present-day Durham. As North Carolina's backcountry was settled by whites from the 1700s until the 1840s, the area was a collection of farms and settlements, most of which have been lost to time. In addition, farms, factories, and taverns dotted the area, in part because the land wasn't that well suited for agriculture and because travelers were passing through the area on their way to somewhere else, often Hillsborough or Oxford. But in 1848 the state legislature chartered the North Carolina Rail Road, planning a route from Goldsboro, through Raleigh, Hillsborough, Greensboro, and Salisbury, and then finally to Charlotte. Those plans would create the Piedmont Crescent, a string of towns arcing through North Carolina.

One of the towns brought about by the railroad was Durham. Railroads needed stations thirty or so miles apart for water and coal stops. Railroad officials approached William Pratt of nearby Prattsburg, but Pratt wouldn't grant a right of way. He asked a big price for his land, using as a bargaining chip his worry that a railroad would scare his horses. The officials wouldn't pay. Dr. Bartlett Durham then offered them four acres of ground near the foot of today's Corcoran Street. (Pratt's land was just east of today's Church Street.) The station opened in 1854. Students who went to school at UNC and arrived by train boarded wagons for transport to Chapel Hill here.

Soon after the station opened, Robert Morris and his son moved nearby to begin the manufacture of tobacco products. In 1862, John Ruffin Green bought Morris's tobacco "manufactory" and created a brand of tobacco that was described as being "Spanish flavored." It was reportedly very popular with UNC students as well as others. Thus, available transportation and a popular product give rise to a thriving commercial endeavor that enticed others to come here.

After the Civil War, among the others to find a home in Durham were newly freed black citizens. As Jeffrey Crow, Paul Escott, and Tom Hatley explain in *A History of African-Americans in North Carolina*, Durham arose as a city after the Civil War in part because it didn't have an antebellum aristocracy struggling to adapt to the profound changes in their world. In Durham, the tobacco business was booming and workers were needed, which meant that black citizens had more of a chance to distance themselves from slavery. Although southern workplaces were consistently segregated, as historians Leslie Brown, Jacquelyn Hall, and Robert Korstad point out—and the color line and segregation would harden in the late 1890s and explode in Wilmington—Durham was a better place for black North Carolinians to be than other towns because tobacco factories offered somewhat more opportunity for black women and men than did the region's textile mills.

The Walk

This walk starts at the entrance of the parking deck located at Rigsbee Avenue and East Chapel Hill Street. Rigsbee Avenue once led to the heart of Tobacco Row, a collection of twelve auction warehouses (the last one closed in 1986). The street, named for Atlas Rigsbee, predates the town. Rigsbee was one of Durham's original aldermen, and his farm lay at the end of the lane to the southwest.

To begin the first section of this walk, turn left from the parking deck to walk along East Chapel Hill Street to Corcoran Street. At Corcoran, turn left to walk past the bronze bull. How the bull came to be Durham's emblem is an oft-told tale, with ties to the final days of the Civil War and the city's role as a hub of tobacco production.

The final surrender of Confederate general Joseph Johnston to Union general William T. Sherman was negotiated in April 1865 just miles from downtown Durham, at the farmhouse now known as the Bennett Place historic site. This meant scores of soldiers were encamped near Durham Station, where they discovered what UNC students and other locals already knew: John Ruffin Green's tobacco was highly appealing. Union troops eventually raided his factory looking for more of the tobacco, almost ruining him. When they returned to their northern homes, they wrote to Durham Station asking for more of the flavorful bright leaf. As other manufacturers tried to capitalize on the demand for the tobacco, Green searched for a way to set his product apart from the others.

One version of the story says that a friend told Green that another man, James R. Day, had a new bull. "Why not have a picture of the bull and you on its back as your brand?" The other version suggests that Green was dining with a friend, John Y. Whitted, when Whitted pointed to a jar of Coleman's mustard, noting, "there is a condiment that is, as you see by the label, manufactured in Durham, England. It bears the sign of a Durham bull's neck. Why not name your product Bull Durham Smoking Tobacco and adopt a whole bull as a trademark?" Apparently following his friends' advice, Green launched a memorable brand. In

This bronze sculpture of a wheat penny, one of six along the walk, speaks to the thrift encouraged by Mechanics and Farmers Bank.

time, Bull Durham Tobacco became so popular that ads featuring the famous bull appeared all over the world, including on the pyramids in Egypt. Lore also states that Alfred, Lord Tennyson, poet laureate of England, enjoyed smoking the tobacco. Some people also believe the bull gave rise to such popular phrases as "bullpen" (from a Bull Durham ad painted behind the Yankee's dugout) and "shooting the bull" (from chewing tobacco).

Whatever the exact truth, the popularity of the product and the appeal of the branding helped loosen the grip that Virginia had on the tobacco business. Durham Station became crowded with tobacco warehouses. In a day when property values were half of what they were before the war and banks that had invested in Confederate bonds had failed, the tobacco business was a way to reclaim prosperity and build a thriving city.

Continue walking to Parrish Street. Turn left to walk the entire length of Parrish Street. As you walk this segment, read the commentary at the six bronze sculptures along the way and study the photographs in the former North Carolina Mutual Life Insurance building at 114–16 West Parrish Street. Here along Parrish Street, the nuanced history of Durham's black and white citizens intersects.

Shown on early maps as Clay Street, by 1887 the corridor became known as Parrish Street, honoring Edward J. Parrish, a Methodist lay preacher and successful auctioneer in W. T. Blackwell's warehouse. Within eight years, Parrish opened his own warehouse, a 65,000-square-foot behemoth that stood between Mangum and Church Streets, roughly where you stand now. The financial panic of 1893 (when a series of bank failures occurred because of the overbuilding of and investment in railroads) resulted in Parrish selling his property at a sheriff's auction in 1901. John Merrick, one of Durham's black citizens, bought one of the lots; over the next several years, as Merrick bought several more parcels, Parrish eventually recovered a measure of his wealth as an employee of James Duke's American Tobacco Company.

John Merrick's impact on Durham's history cannot be overstated. Accounts differ as to whether Merrick was born a slave or to a free black woman shortly before the Civil War. But accounts agree that after working as a brick mason, and possibly having laid bricks at Shaw University, Merrick became a barber, opening a chain of barber shops in Durham. Among his customers were Washington Duke and Julian S. Carr, who was both a brother-in-law to Parrish and one of his creditors, and who had a role in the repossession of Parrish's property.

Duke and Carr mentored Merrick in his business efforts. While the specific advice shared among the men may be lost to time, Merrick was clearly a quick study. In 1898, he diversified into insurance and cofounded, along with Aaron M. Moore, a company that would later be known as North Carolina Mutual Life Insurance Company. The company's first motto was "merciful to all."

Moore, born during the Civil War to free parents, trained to teach and then worked in a high school for several years. Later he entered the Leonard Medical School at Shaw University in Raleigh (see chapter 8, Raleigh), becoming the first black physician in Durham. Moore believed that the black citizens of Durham should have their own hospital where black doctors and nurses could practice, and he persuaded the Duke family to back such an institution. Lincoln Hospital opened in 1901. The original structure, the fourth hospital in North Carolina established to respond to medical needs of black citizens, stood at the northwest corner of Proctor and Cozart Streets. In 1905 the hospital added a nursing school. After a 1922 fire, a new eighty-six-bed Lincoln Hospital was built at 1301 Fayetteville Street. Later, Lincoln Hospital merged with Watts Hospital to become Durham Regional Hospital. (Although the structure on Fayetteville Street was eventually razed, the Watts Hospital campus is today the home of the North Carolina School of Science and Math.)

Although Merrick, Moore, and the black community benefited from the mentoring by Duke and Carr, the white men's motivation was perhaps not completely altruistic. Some historians suggest that it represents how segregation was established through institutions as well as everyday interactions between white and black citizens.

Having bought property along Parrish Street, Merrick moved the Mutual offices to a stylish, yellow brick building there. Now a national historic landmark, the building's prominent facade and relative height exude optimism. Some seventeen years later, an employee who shared Merrick's work ethic—he worked first as a janitor for the Mutual, as well as a clerk, part-time agent, agent, and general manager—would be promoted to the office of president of the company. Under the leadership of C. C. Spaulding, the Mutual gained national recognition for itself and for Durham. One of America's leading black businessmen, Spaulding earned national recognition for his ability to navigate the often-treacherous waters of racial uplift, business, education, and philanthropy.

As Merrick, Moore, and Spaulding led the way, several more black-owned business moved to Parrish Street, Moore's Bull City Drug Company and the Mechanics and Farmers Bank among them. As entrepreneurial and professional efforts concentrated here, the area grew and thrived, so much so that in 1912 W. E. B. Dubois visited and observed that "it is precisely the opposite in spirit in places like Atlanta." In 1949 *Ebony Magazine* declared the area to be the "Wall Street of Negro America." Near the center of Parrish Street, a historical marker commemorates the efforts of these men.

Even though opportunities for black citizens were more open in Durham than in other places in North Carolina, race relations here have still been marked with strife, as one marker off the path of this walk (the intersection of Roxboro and Dowd Streets) indicates. The Royal Ice Cream sit-in predates the sit-in at the Woolworth lunch counter in Greensboro by three years. The ice cream parlor's Dowd Street entrance was for blacks; its Roxboro Street entrance was for whites. In June 1957, several black youths protested. Eventually found guilty of trespassing, the youths paid their fines even as their lawyers appealed to higher courts. Ultimately, the U.S. Supreme Court refused to hear the case, but it is nevertheless recognized today as an important precursor to the Civil Rights activism of the 1960s.

At Roxboro Street, turn left to take a few steps up Roxboro to see the Durham County Public Library. Opening in 1898, the library was the first local library supported by tax funds, opening ahead of the public libraries in Raleigh (1901) and Charlotte (1903).

Return to Parrish Street, turn right and walk along Parrish until you reach Mangum Street. At Mangum, turn left to walk one block to better see the Kress Building, which faces Main Street. On the return trip through town, be sure to note the advertising murals on some of the brick store sides. Historians think that parts of Main Street followed the old wagon road between Hillsborough and Raleigh. As in the case of Rigsbee Avenue, they think the path Main Street follows predates the town. The Kress Building, opened in 1933, housed an important department store in its day. Today it is home to luxury condos and is just one of the many instances of successful adaptive reuse in Durham.

To being the second section of this walk, return to Parrish Street, turn left, and walk to the bronze bull. Walk then to East Chapel Hill Street, turning left to walk to West Main. Cross the intersection of Morris and Main and Chapel Hill Streets very carefully. Getting to West Main requires a soft right turn, not a hard right, and vigilance always with turning vehicles.

Follow West Main to North Duke Street to see some of the warehouse district that what was once the American Tobacco Company and, later, Liggett and Myers. You may even catch the sweet wafting scent of cured tobacco along the street as Brightleaf Square comes into view.

Washington Duke's life fills volumes, from his time as a tenant farmer, to being a Union prisoner of war detained in Richmond, to walking home from New Bern to Durham, to building a business that one day would become the American Tobacco Company, one of the twelve original companies on the New York Stock Exchange. (The American Tobacco complex is located on Blackwell Street, on the south side of the railroad tracks. Some Durhamites fondly argue that the Lucky Strike Tower, not the bull, is the prime landmark in downtown Durham today.) The Duke University archives indicate that Duke "considered himself very poor twice in his life—first, when he began making a living with nothing but 'willing hands and a stout heart' and second, upon returning to his home after the Civil War."

After the return from the war, the entire Duke family turned their attention to the manufacture of tobacco products. At first, the work meant beating the cured bright leaf tobacco by hand with sticks, sifting it, and packing it into bags for sale. Then the men would hit the road, selling the tobacco. Over time, they traveled through thirty-two states. Then they would return home to produce more of the bagged tobacco. In time, son James B. Duke realized the significant labor savings they could attain if they switched from hand-produced bagged tobacco to a new product, cigarettes, produced by machine. The mechanization of the production process and demand for the product built the Duke family's wealth, a portion of which family members funneled into many and various causes, from relocating Trinity College (outside High Point) and transforming it into Duke University, to making large contributions to preserve historic mansions of Newport, Rhode Island.

Brightleaf Square, diagonally across from the corner where you will turn, is another defining visual emblem of Durham. Thank goodness for the massive 1970s renovation project initiated by Terry Sanford Jr. and Clay Hamner. While admiring the striking architecture of Brightleaf Square people today can shop, have a meal, or head to the offices housed within these historic buildings, built in the early 1900s. If you want to step inside the reclaimed tobacco warehouses, do. Return to this corner when you're ready to continue the walk.

At Duke Street, turn right. As you walk three blocks to Corporation Street, be sure to scan the facades of the buildings to your left. One of them sports the logo of Studebaker automobiles, a reminder of the businesses that helped tobacco workers spend their money. Bear in the mind that the last Studebaker rolled off the assembly line in 1966. Today, the Studebaker Building serves as office space.

As you near Corporation Street, you'll see what is today the Durham School of the Arts. On the former estate of Brodie L. Duke, another of Washington Duke's sons, the grounds once served as the campus for Durham Central High School. Since Durham city and county schools merged in 1992, the campus has served as a magnet school for grades six through twelve, emphasizing the arts.

Within one-and-a-half blocks, the old Durham Athletic Park comes into view. If you're a student of baseball movies, you know what lies ahead. If you're not, watch the movie *Bull Durham* when you return home.

Some people credit four movies with rekindling interest in major league baseball at a time when NASCAR's fan base was growing and interest in the NFL was exploding: *The Natural*, *Field of Dreams*, *A League of Their Own*, and, of course, *Bull Durham*. And, just as baseball fans travel to that little cornfield in Iowa where *Field of Dreams* was filmed, other fans travel to the historic Durham Athletic Park. (If you're looking for

The "old" Durham Athletic Park gained national fame in the movie Bull Durham.

the Bull, it's at the new DBAP, which is adjacent to the American To-bacco Complex on Blackwell Street.) Opened in 1926 as El Toro Stadium, the original stadium burned in 1939. Rebuilt and reopened in 1940, the park welcomed fans. Then, in 1988 the popularity of the old park went through the roof when the movie *Bull Durham*, which *Sports Illustrated* in 2003 dubbed the greatest sports movie ever, hit the silver screen.

Turn right to walk up Morris Street and begin the return trip to down-town. As you do, remember to look at the brick building that sits at the corner of Morris and Corporation Streets. At this writing the building currently houses Measurement, Inc., but back in the early 1900s the building was a factory that produced BC Powder, a headache remedy invented in Durham. As of this writing, mega-country music star Trace Adkins is the pitchman for the product.

When you reach Morgan Street, turn left. If you parked in the Durham Centre Parking Deck, your walk is now completed. If you parked in the deck at East Chapel Hill Street, cross Morgan Street, turn left, walk past the Carolina Theatre and turn right onto Rigsbee Avenue. You'll see the parking deck just another block away.

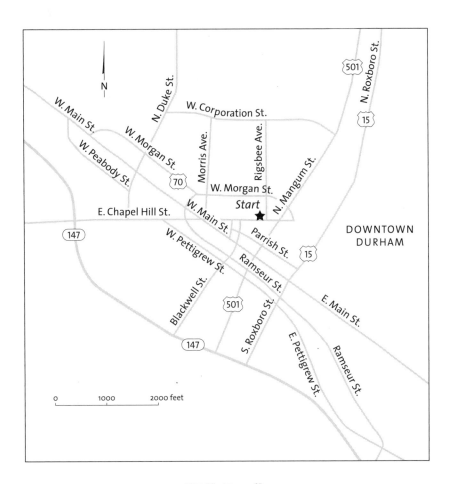

Walk Details

HOW TO FIND IT: Wedged between I-85 and I-40, in the center of the state, Durham looks harder to navigate than it is. Watch for signs that point you to the Downtown Loop, which makes use of several different streets. Once you're on the Downtown Loop, you can park in one of two city parking decks, depending on how much of the walk you want to take. If all you care to enjoy is the downtown stretch along Parrish Street, then park in the deck located at the intersection of Rigsbee Avenue and East Chapel Hill Street. If you want to include the jaunt by Brightleaf Square and the original Durham Athletic Park, you may want to park in the Durham Centre Deck located at the corner of Morris and Morgan Streets, across from the Carolina Theatre. You might like to consult the official city website at http://dcvb-nc.com/comm/downtown_guide.pdf, to understand how the streets connect and where parking is. The two decks are about one half-mile apart.

LENGTH: 2.5 miles if you walk the entire route

SURFACE: Sidewalk, except for a very brief stretch along North Duke Street

RESTROOMS: Located in the Durham Visitor Information Center (101 East Morgan Street), near McDonald's.

FOOTWEAR: Sneakers

PETS: OK on a leash

MAP: You can access an online map at http://www.durham-nc.com/visitors/maps/.

BEWARE: Make sure you can safely cross streets, regardless of what the pedestrian signals indicate. Durham's downtown core has many streets that are one-way or set at angles. This, combined with the many out-of-town visitors, means that a healthy percentage of drivers are unfamiliar with the traffic flow and directions.

GOOD TO KNOW: Step for step, this walk may have more good eateries than any other walk in the book. Be sure to go when you can allow time for a meal.

As you walk around downtown Durham, keep an eye out for murals celebrating the life of Pauli Murray, a noted writer and civil rights activist who in 1977 became the first African American woman ordained as an Episcopal priest. In 2012 Murray was canonized as an Episcopal saint.

For More Exploration

Duke Homestead: The best place to learn more about Washington Duke and the famous story of how he turned the last 50¢ left in his pocket after the Civil War into a multimillion-dollar fortune is to visit the Duke Homestead in northern Durham.

2828 Duke Homestead Road
Durham, N.C. 27705
Open Tuesday–Saturday 9 A.M.–5 P.M.
Closed Sunday and Monday
Phone: 919-477-5498
Email: duke@ncdcr.gov

Bennett Place: Here you see the reconstructed farmhouse where the largest surrender of Confederate troops took place.

4409 Bennett Memorial Rd.
Durham, NC 27705
Open Tuesday–Saturday 9 A.M.–5 P.M.
Closed Sunday, Monday, and most major state holidays
Phone: 919-383-4345
Email: bennett@ncdcr.gov

For more information about the American Tobacco complex, visit www.americantobaccohistoricdistrict.com/. This website contains videos telling the history, lists of restaurants, and maps to help you navigate.

Wilson

TOBACCO TOWN

Tobacco permeates our history, from Sir Walter Raleigh, who introduced tobacco to England through the court of Queen Elizabeth I, to Stephen Slade, the slave who accidentally discovered how to cure "bright leaf" tobacco. It includes the farmers who prayed for good weather and the families who worked the fields in the sweltering North Carolina summers, grateful for the icy-cold, sugar-filled, short Cokes that they greedily slurped down in the shade of a pickup truck.

To better appreciate the role of tobacco in North Carolina, travel east to Wilson, a town once called the "World's Greatest Tobacco Market." Go during July or August, and if you pass a tobacco field in full leaf, stop on the roadside and breathe deeply to smell of a way of life that, like fins on a '59 Cadillac, is never coming back. Then continue your way into Wilson, a town at the epicenter of tobacco's story in North Carolina.

Historical Context

This story starts with Jean Nicot, who served the King of France as the ambassador to Portugal in the mid-1500s. A botanist friend told Nicot about a South American plant that had healing properties. Intrigued, Nicot put the plant on a friend's face wound. The results impressed him. Nicot later sent snuff to Catherine de Medici, the Queen of France, to relieve her migraine headaches. Thrilled with the outcome, Queen Catherine decreed the plant be called *Herba Regina*. When scientists eventually discovered the addictive, stimulating alkaloid common across many varieties of the weed, they honored Nicot by using his name to coin a new word: "nicotine." In time, Europeans learned to like tobacco, and by the late 1500s, a pound of really good tobacco could cost $125. As Europeans colonized the New World, they hoped that their colonies would produce the plant, thereby increasing supply and lowering prices.

But New World tobacco had problems. Coastal soils produced a plant whose leaves tasted heavy, unappealing. Farmers thus experimented with soils, harvesting, and curing. Though they improved the product, they still couldn't produce something that Europeans really liked in their cigars.

In 1839, Stephen, a slave owned by Abisha Slade of Caswell County, fell asleep as he tended the wood fires used to cure the tobacco. He awoke to see the fire nearly out. Throwing hot charcoals into the embers to stoke the fire, Stephen produced a blast of heat that turned the leaves a bright yellow color, producing something few people had ever seen, smelled, or tasted. At the Lynchburg, Virginia, market, Slade's bright leaf tobacco became wildly successful. Over time, Abisha Slade perfected the curing process, and by 1857, he was making some of the highest profits on any farm product in North Carolina. Word spread, and farmers took notice. By 1860, two farm journals, the *North Carolina Planter* and the *Southern Planter*, were publicizing the technique of flue curing tobacco to interested farmers.

In the last days of the Civil War, local legend suggests that a second pivotal event occurred, the discovery of John Ruffin Greene's "Spanish-flavored" tobacco by Union soldiers who were garrisoned in Durham waiting for Generals Sherman and Johnston to come to surrender terms. (See chapter 21, Durham.) The popularity of the tobacco with residents above the Mason-Dixon Line boosted the market for the leaf, attracting the attention of farmers.

Then occurred a third pivotal development: eastern farmers who planted tobacco discovered that the thin, starved soils of the eastern North Carolina plain produced a wonderfully mild leaf. That mild leaf, coupled with the mildness derived from charcoal-based flue curing, wowed tobacco's audience, and combined with other factors, helped the crop's popularity explode. Towns such as Wilson became the beneficiary of such popularity.

The Walk

From Parking Lot #6 turn right to walk down to the Amtrak Station (401 East Nash Street). Step inside the building to see a well-preserved depot.

With the train station behind you, face Nash Street. From the start, this region faced challenges. The soils are poor. It lacks good river access. Although the area produced naval stores, Cumberland and Bladen Counties were far more productive. Subsistence farmers, many of them transplants from tired Virginia farms, nonetheless determined to make a life for themselves.

When the Wilmington-to-Weldon Railroad passed through Toisnot

This mural inside the old Atlantic Coast Line depot, still a working train station, speaks to the good life in Wilson after the tobacco markets started humming with commerce.

Depot (about three blocks in front of you) in the 1830s, life percolated a little more. Farmers were already having success growing cotton when Alpheus Branch, son of a Halifax planter, returned to Wilson in 1872 and opened a cotton-brokerage firm. After forming his business, Branch and Thomas Jefferson Hadley established Branch and Hadley, a private lending firm that would eventually become the town's first bank. Branch and Hadley was unusual for its time: it loaned directly to farmers based on their upcoming cotton harvests. Previously, farmers usually took their loans from the merchants with whom they did business. Branch bought his partner out in 1887, and two years later incorporated the Wilson Banking and Trust Company, known later as Branch Banking and Trust, and today as BB&T.

Like Branch, Willis Napoleon Hackney also sensed potential: farmers needed wagons to get their crops to the rail station. By the 1870s, his wagon company was one of Wilson's mainstay businesses.

Turn right to walk along Nash Street into town, to Goldsboro Street. Though the area's cotton farmers were surviving, they weren't thriving. In 1860, Wilson County produced 3,012 bales of cotton. By contrast, Edgecombe County produced 19,138 bales of cotton that year. After the Civil War, cotton prices started dropping. In 1880, farm income was

$55.76 per resident; in 1890, $41.71. Area·farmers started listening more closely to talk about tobacco.

Someone who talked about growing tobacco was Josephus Daniels, a young editor at the *Wilson Advance* who encouraged local farmers to grow bright leaf tobacco as a money crop. When H. Rountree, a prominent Wilson County farmer, crowed in 1889 that he could make more from five acres of tobacco than he could with the crops from his other sixty-five acres, farmers who had already been experiencing a general decline in cotton prices started replacing cotton with tobacco.

But where would they sell their tobacco? Wilson had no market. They could go to Danville, Virginia, which was the biggest market; or they could go to Oxford, Greenville, or Durham. Lafayette Lucas, a dry goods grocer in nearby Lucama, wrote in the *Wilson Advance* that a tobacco warehouse in Wilson would keep local tobacco local. He also speculated that it would draw tobacco from South Carolina, especially since the rail line ran from Wilson through Fayetteville to Florence, South Carolina.

The drumbeat touting the potential of tobacco grew louder, as did tensions in town. The result? A shoot-out between two of the town's most prominent men, Alpheus Branch and Frank Barnes, who also both happened to run the local banks. Barnes led the public bank in Wilson and backed the fledgling tobacco interests. Branch wanted to protect his cotton-based banking interests because he was on the verge of going public with his bank. Conflict ensued, and in January of 1890 Branch shot five times at Barnes. Although Barnes was unhurt, a local magistrate took one bullet in the heel. Eventually the men went to court, facing a judge who fined them $10.

Turn left, cross Goldsboro Street, and walk to Kenan Street toward the tobacco warehouse district. Eventually Frank Barnes and his investors raised $50,000 to build a tobacco warehouse. They hired E. M. Pace as promoter and warehouse manager. During the summer of 1890, Pace publicized best practices for growing tobacco in the *Wilson Advance*, making sure tobacco farmers knew about a beautiful new warehouse that would soon open in Wilson. One practice explained how to poison tobacco hornworms, cotton moths, and boll weevils with a lethal brew of molasses, vinegar, and Paris Green, a copper-based chemical once used to kill Paris sewer rats.

A week before the warehouse opened, Pace encouraged local farmers to come to Wilson to sell their tobacco. Complete with forty-four skylights, twenty-four windows, nine double doors, and an "elegant pair of Howe scales capable of weighing to the quarter ounce," the new warehouse was a trusty place to do business. Not surprisingly, Pace's ad copy targeted farmers' worst fear: corrupt pricing. "Come where you can, in person, superintend the weighing, see your tobacco handled, get your money and go home, before you can reach any other market," the ads declared. "Remember: PACE has promised you he will save you money in CHARGES. Proof of the pudding is chawin' the bag. Try him."

The day after the warehouse opened, September 11, 1890, the *Wilson Advance* rejoiced on the front page:

A Gala Day!
Fortune Again Smiles Upon
Favored Wilson

> From the east and from the west, from the north and from the south, from Edgecomb and Pitt, from Nash and Franklin, from Wilson and Wayne—in carts and wagons and rail it came. Capt. Pace stated in a business-like way that everything was ready and auctioneer Harriss began to cry that first pile.

Over a thousand people came that September day to sell, to watch, and to vend other wares, and during that first year, the Wilson Tobacco Warehouse sold 1,508 pounds of tobacco.

To further build success, Wilson offered free warehouse sites and no taxes for five years to induce investors to build more warehouses. The incentives worked: by 1899, farmers sold 18,078 pounds of tobacco in Wilson. Farmers throughout eastern North Carolina turned quickly away from cotton to tobacco. In 1890, farmers had cultivated 483 acres of tobacco in Wilson County, ten years later, that number was 9,465 acres.

Turn right onto Kenan Street and walk to Tarboro Street. This short section through part of the warehouse district is where a farmer was rewarded for his willingness to endure significant, and seemingly endless, manual labor. As farmers were fond of lamenting, "It takes thirteen months a year to raise that infernal crop."

In winter, the farmer started his seedlings. By March they would emerge. Come May, the farmer transplanted them in the fields. Then workers *hilled* the plants, cultivating the earth around the stalk. In late June or early July, *topping* started: workers removed the flower from the top of the plant to force the leaves to grow big. But topping produced suckers, volunteer stalks, so workers would comb the field again *suckering*, pinching off the volunteers. Later, someone had to pick off the green tobacco worms and either stomp them to death or pinch them in two. Every day the farmer prayed for good weather, especially during the summer. One fierce thunderstorm riddled with hail could ruin the leaves, making them unsellable.

Priming, snapping the leaves from the main stalk, started in mid-summer, as heat and humidity soared. The first pass of priming meant that the workers bent at the waist, cutting only the bottom two or three leaves. As the priming continued, workers could finally stand straight. After they cut the leaves, workers, their arms full of sticky tobacco, toted the leaves to a sled pulled by a mule, wearing long sleeves to limit their contact with the oozing sap. Too much exposure to the sap sickened a body. Farmers of course prized mules that would respond to voice commands: no one had to drive Old Red or Blackie or Maude, which meant that one more person could prime. If a farmer didn't have a mule, workers dragged a burlap bag near the rows.

Out in the sun, bending, cutting, toting, and sweating, workers looked forward to the mid-morning and mid-afternoon *set-up*. Usually an icy "Co-cola" or RC from the drink box and a Moon Pie from the local country store, the set-up pumped workers full of sugar so that they could continue their labor.

The next step, *looping*, referred to putting the leaves onto big sticks. The strongest workers then hung the tobacco sticks in the barn in neat, tightly spaced tiers. A barn typically held 400–700 sticks, each weighing 15–20 pounds. Only when the barn was full was the work day over.

Once the tobacco had been *barned*, *curing* started. Someone, usually an older adult whose back was too weak to work the fields, supervised the curing, a multiday process of yellowing the leaves at a temperature near 110 degrees and then raising the heat to about 180 degrees. Hand-adjustable curing thermometers made timing the rise in temperature into an art.

Curing was a hot job. But sitting up through the night with the barn had its rewards: usually a little bit of moonshine. But only a little bit because the sitter had to stay alert. If the barn caught fire, then the farmer would be utterly destroyed, ruined for the season. And tobacco barns burned regularly. Even as late as the 1960s when sirens wailed during the mid-summer across eastern North Carolina, people were apt to note "there goes someone's barn."

Once the tobacco was cured, work turned to the pack house, where the tobacco was put *in order*, bundling the leaves for display at the market and rehumidifying them if they were too dry and crumbly. Here, humid Carolina summers helped the farmers by providing moisture for leaves to gently absorb. Heavier leaves fetched a better price.

With the tobacco in order, farmers waited for the markets to open and worried about where to sell their leaves. The decision was fraught with variables. Should they sell their tobacco in the Old Belt, the New Belt, the Middle Belt, or the Border Belt? Should they go in August when the belts opened or wait until November when they were about to close? Should they go in September? Was October better? Which warehouse should they go to? The High Dollar? The Top Dollar? The Golden Leaf? The Liberty? The choice was worrisome. Tobacco was perishable and farmers needed to sell it quickly, but they all wanted to fetch the best price. Where was the best deal? And who wouldn't cheat them?

Warehouses competed for the farmer's business, advertising the availability of bunk rooms and showers and mule pens. They extolled covered docks that would keep tobacco out of the weather. They noted the number of skylights, for good lighting made the golden leaves glow.

When the farmer came to market, he often slept in the cart with his tobacco. That crop stood between him and ruin, and he had to protect it. Many were the farm families who cooked their meals by lamplight out at their carts.

Once sales started, they took place very quickly. If a farmer didn't have a practiced ear, the sing-song, sometimes humming, highly repetitive conversational chant of the auctioneer made no sense. Buyers indicated their bids with nods, winks, ear wiggles, and raised eyebrows. Farmers were forever suspicious that warehouse managers, auctioneers, and buyers were colluding against them. If a farmer didn't like the buyer's bid, he could *turn the ticket*, thereby rejecting the bid. But turning the ticket took courage, because farmers got their money within minutes after agreeing to sell. Turning the ticket also meant that a farmer now had to handle the fragile leaves to take them to another warehouse, risking damage to the tobacco.

Turn right onto Tarboro Street to return to Nash Street. Note the small buildings near the warehouse district that once sold goods to farmers who, after getting their long-awaited and worked-for payday—and after paying back their loans—could afford to buy things. The August 28, 1924, *Wilson Advance* rhapsodized about what the opening of the markets meant to Wilson: "The Garden of Eden is right here in Wilson . . . We shall open the fall season next Tuesday with a whoop and a bang, and our merchants and our business men will get busy and there will be plenty of trade and money to go around."

As you walk about the tobacco warehouse district, keep a sharp eye out for faded painted signs recalling the names of tobacco warehouses.

When you reach the corner of Nash and Tarboro Streets, pause to observe the commercial buildings that line the street, particularly Planters Bank (201 East Nash Street) and the BB&T building (124 East Nash), and think about how they compare with the smaller, older commercial buildings nearer the warehouses. In a matter of years, tobacco transformed Wilson. Several different measures indicate the growth. Between 1900 and 1940, the number of working mules tripled from about 2,100 to over 6,500. By 1920, Wilson had edged past Winston as measured by tons of tobacco sold: Winston warehouses sold a total of 60,581 tons; Wilson, 62,205 tons. (When R. J. Reynolds Tobacco saw this number, the company built a prizery, a place to re-dry leaves, in Wilson.) In 1880 Americans consumed 250 million pounds of tobacco. By the early 1950s they were consuming 1.5 billion pounds. Stores in town could now cater to a more affluent clientele.

After pausing at the corner, cross Nash Street. Then turn left to walk west. The stunning architecture of the downtown buildings attests to the life that the tobacco industry was breathing into Wilson. Indeed, newspapers from the 1930s report that when the markets opened, auctioneers competed in contests of skill and that department stores from Richmond, Virginia, advertised fur coats. The Wilson Hardware Company promised to have everything that a modern farm wife could want, especially the Hotpoint oven with thick insulating walls! Darlington Dress Shops advertised special prices on lingerie on opening day. Of course, cigarette ads made breathtaking claims:

> Others have found that good digestion and a sense of well-being are encouraged by Camels . . . SO, FOR DIGESTION'S SAKE, SMOKE CAMELS.

Sometime during the 1930s, a picture appeared in eastern North Carolina newspapers that would be repeated each year and forever define Wilson: inside a cavernous warehouse, anxious-looking farmers stand on one side of the tobacco, wearing open-collared shirts and their sleeves rolled up. Some study their tobacco, and others watch the men across the line. One of those men is the auctioneer, whose mouth is open. Behind him follows a gaggle of buyers in a hierarchy according to who bought the most poundage the year before.

In 1939, 91,007,768 pounds of tobacco were bought and sold in Wilson. In 1948, Arthur Godfrey and his Chesterfield Supper Club broadcasted live from Wilson, giving the town coast-to-coast radio coverage for the opening of its Tobacco Festival. Along with Godfrey were Perry Como and the Fontaine Sisters. Wilson, the World's Largest Tobacco Market, now contained seventeen warehouses, totaling a million square feet. Enough tobacco had been sold in Wilson to make 782,230,386,000 cigarettes.

As you walk Nash Street, look for the James Rountree House (206 West Nash Street). Frank Barnes bought this ornate Queen Anne Mansion in 1897.

Continue walking along Nash Street until you reach Whitehead Street. Turn right. This next series of turns lets you sample some of the historic homes of Wilson. **Turn right on Bruton Street. Turn left onto Gray Street. Turn right on Bragg Street. Then turn left onto Green Street.** See http://www.wilson-nc.com/WalkingTour.cfm for information about these homes.

Once you've arrived at Green Street, it's time to consider how tobacco's fortunes have impacted Wilson since the 1930s. Tobacco grew so well in eastern North Carolina that farmers planted too much of it, resulting in oversupply and lower prices. To cover their losses, tobacco farmers often planted even more tobacco, which caused prices to fall even more. As early as 1917, Governor T. W. Bickett complained that North

Carolina farmers were importing too much corn, wheat, and meat and choosing to grow tobacco instead. In 1922 Governor Cameron Morrison complained that no North Carolina county could completely feed itself because so many acres had been turned over to tobacco. In 1928, Governor O. Max Gardner enacted the "Live At Home" program to try to reduce tobacco surpluses by getting farmers to plant more corn, hay, and grain. In 1933 Governor John C. B. Ehringhaus closed the tobacco markets in North Carolina to lobby for higher prices for the product. In 1936, he urged farmers to voluntarily reduce tobacco crops. In 1938, the U.S. Government entered the fray by passing the Second Agricultural Adjustment Act and protecting the crop with quotas. Essentially, the government paid farmers not to plant tobacco.

As the economics of tobacco farming grew more tangled, the health risks grew more clear. In 1957, the U.S. Congress conducted hearings on the impact of tobacco use, and in 1964 the U.S. surgeon general issued the *Report on Smoking and Health*, which publicized the dangers of smoking. In 1970 tobacco advertising on television was outlawed.

Between the 1970s and 1995, 400 unsuccessful lawsuits were filed against the cigarette companies. In 1994 sixty law firms in five states representing 40 million smokers and 50 million ex-smokers filed a class action suit against the cigarette companies alleging that the companies knowingly addicted people to their products. In the mid-1990s, Florida, West Virginia, Minnesota, and Mississippi filed suits against the tobacco companies for the medical costs smokers were incurring (and states were paying in insurance claims) for smoking-related diseases.

Round and round the arguments flew: a way of life, tobacco farming had allowed thousands to prosper. Smoking was a choice; America is a free country. The government was paying farmers not to produce the weed. The federal government was picking up the tab for the medical care for smoking-related diseases.

In 1998 the states and the tobacco companies reached the Master Settlement Agreement. Chief among the provisions was that tobacco companies agreed to pay the states an estimated $206 billion and to finance a $1.5 billion antismoking campaign, to open previously secret industry documents, and to disband industry trade groups that attorneys general said conspired to conceal damaging research from the public. Farmers would find it less lucrative to farm tobacco.

Soon the Amtrak Station comes into view. When you reach the Amtrak Station, turn right to return to Lot #6. In 2001, only about 20 percent of

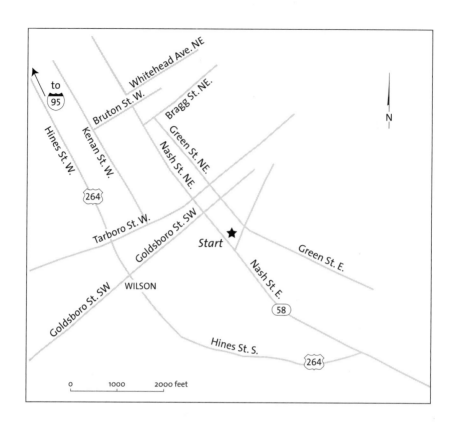

the tobacco produced in North Carolina went to auction; tobacco companies had started dealing directly with the tobacco growers. Though tobacco still comes to market in Wilson, only a few warehouses operate today.

Walk Details

HOW TO FIND IT: Wilson lies just east of I-95. Enter town via US 301, off US 264. Turn left onto Nash Street (NC 58). Signs will direct you to the Amtrak Station. You can park in Lot #6, which is on Nash Street about 40 yards beyond the Amtrak Station. If that lot is full, you can turn right onto Douglas Avenue and park in Lot #3.

LENGTH: 2 miles

SURFACE: Paved

RESTROOMS: Available in the Amtrak Station.

FOOTWEAR: Sneakers

PETS: OK on a leash

MAP: You can access an online map of Wilson at http://www.wilson-nc-downtown.com/map.html.

GOOD TO KNOW: To learn more about the job of a tobacco auctioneer, visit the Documenting the American South website at http://docsouth.unc.edu/sohp/R-0193/menu.html to find Oral History Interview with Edward Stephenson, September 21, 2002 (Interview R-0193. Southern Oral History Program Collection [#4007]).

If you've never heard a tobacco auctioneer at work, go to YouTube (http://www.youtube.com) and search "tobacco auction." Several good clips are available to acquaint your ear with the sing-song cadence of the auction.

You can tour the Growers Cooperative Warehouse between July and October. This warehouse is five football fields long. Call the Chamber of Commerce (252–237–0165) for more information.

The Tobacco Farm Life Museum in Kenly provides a further look into the tobacco heritage of North Carolina. Admission charged. Phone: 919–284–3431. http://www.tobmuseum.bbnp.com.

The namesake of Barnes Street is not Frank Barnes. It is Joshua Barnes, Wilson's first mayor. During his later service in the North Carolina state legislature, he pushed for the incorporation of the town of Wilson and for the formation of the county of the same name.

Pinehurst and Asheville

FAVORITE PLAYGROUNDS

Oh, to play in North Carolina! The North Carolina Department of Commerce says that in 2011 visitors to and within North Carolina spent a record $18 billion supporting more than 40,000 businesses. North Carolina is, according to 2011 statistics, the sixth-most-visited state in the country. And if you're curious about which part of the state draws more visitors—mountains? beach?—you'll be surprised to learn that the Piedmont sees the largest share of tourism spending.

Of course, Texas, Florida, Virginia, Georgia, Pennsylvania, Hawaii, Tennessee, South Carolina, Massachusetts, and New York are strong competitors. So what are North Carolina's trump cards? Like Massachusetts and Pennsylvania, we have colonial history. Like Texas and Florida, we have beautiful beaches. Like Pennsylvania and New York, we have gorgeous mountains. For most people, we're more convenient to visit than Hawaii. Our summers are a bit cooler than Georgia's and South Carolina's, and our winters are a bit warmer than Virginia's. Thus, some might argue that, from a travel and leisure point of view, North Carolina represents the best of all possible states.

While other walks speak to the ways in which our geography presented challenges, these two celebrate a bit of the history that helped North Carolina become one of America's favorite playgrounds.

Historical Context

You might suppose that the North Carolina tourist and resort business started in 1895 when James W. Tufts saw the pine barrens of the Sandhills and decided to establish a vacation spot there for people of modest means. Though internationally recognized as one of the best places in the country to enjoy a round of golf, Pinehurst wasn't our state's first resort.

Two locales vie for the title of first resort, and, unbelievably, one still operates today: Hot Springs. (The other, Shocco Springs in Warren County, no longer exists.) The Cherokee knew of the hot mineral water at Hot Springs, and history suggests that by 1778, lame and ailing settlers had discovered the 100-plus degree mineral water, too. In 1791, a man named William Nelson bought the hot springs property and started catering to travelers.

In 1824, future governor David Swain sponsored a bill to establish the Buncombe Turnpike, a public works project meant to help mountain farmers get their crops to markets in South Carolina and Georgia. The Buncombe Turnpike, which roughly followed today's US 25, did help farmers; it also opened the area to tourists. Asheville and Hendersonville were thus poised to grow, as was Hot Springs. In 1831, James Patton of Asheville bought the springs and built a 350-room hotel. By 1842, the St. John Hotel in Hendersonville was welcoming guests from Charleston, South Carolina, who needed to escape the sweltering coastal heat.

Railroads likewise boosted tourism. After the railroad arrived in Asheville in October 1880, yearly visitation spiked to about 50,000 visitors. Soon thereafter, the magnificent Battery Park Hotel was welcoming well-heeled guests including George W. Vanderbilt to Asheville.

The transition from farm life to industrial life also spurred travel: people were less tied to daily farm chores. Curiously, so did the Civil War: having seen North Carolina while in the Union army, entrepreneurial northerners devised ways to capitalize on the state's beauty. Union general John Wilder was one such visionary: he built the Cloudland Hotel at Roan Mountain, which held the distinction of having the highest elevation of any hotel east of the Mississippi River. Thomas Edison and Alexander Graham Bell visited there. A group of investors bought Ellerbe Springs, originally the summer home of South Carolinian Captain W. F. Ellerbe, and turned the property into a small resort of a dozen cottages and a boardinghouse.

By the mid-1880s, a fledgling tourist industry was finding its wings. In Blowing Rock, the Green Park was delighting guests such as Calvin Coolidge and John D. Rockefeller. In Hendersonville, the Kentucky Home and the Claddagh Inn were pampering rich South Carolinians. In Dillsboro, the tables at the Jarrett House were groaning under the weight of fried chicken. In 1875, two developers drew two straight lines on a map—one from New York to New Orleans and the other from Chicago to Savannah—and then built the Central House at the intersection. Travelers today recognize this spot as the Old Edwards Inn in Highlands.

The appeal of travel transcended rest and relaxation. People sought to restore their health. Just as Hot Springs had attracted tourists to its healing waters, so Asheville lured people with its clean mountain air. In the late 1800s, when tuberculosis was a leading cause of death, people flocked to Asheville for the air. While vacationing in Florida in 1893, Boston philanthropist James W. Tufts (cousin of Tufts University benefactor Charles Tufts), began thinking about creating a really big health retreat. As he rode the train through the pine forests near Aberdeen, at that time ruined by the naval stores industry, the idea came to him: buy this ground and re-create it. The winter climate was certainly more appealing than that in the Northeast. For $1 an acre, Tufts bought 648 acres of scarred pine thickets. To heal the land, he enlisted Frederick Law Olmsted, just as George Vanderbilt was doing in the mountains outside Asheville.

The likely tipping point for North Carolina tourism was December 1895, when the Holly Inn opened in Pinehurst. After struggling with what to call his resort, Tufts hit upon the name Pinehurst: *pine* for the trees and *hurst* referring to a plot of rising ground. Lodging was available for $12–$18 a week. The building boom across the state that followed Tufts's creation of Pinehurst was breathtaking. Lucius B. Moore created Lake Lure in 1902 and E. W. Grove built the Grove Park Inn in 1913.

As the century turned, promoters lured travelers to North Carolina. Advertisements for Pinehurst, the "healthiest Resort in the South," appeared in the *Harvard Crimson*, the *Yale News*, *Field and Stream*, *Vogue*, *Town and Country*, and *Banker and Financier*. This Shangri-la among the "pink mist of trembling" peach blossoms was only twenty-two and a half hours from Boston by rail and only sixteen hours from New York City. Advertising copy of the day reads like a hallelujah chorus of fun: "The click of a well-spanked golf ball . . . the twang of tightly strung tennis racquets . . . shouted good fellowship—these and other sounds carried on pine-scented breezes tell the story of outdoor pleasure at Pinehurst."

The "eight-day plan" to enjoy the splendor in Pinehurst cost only $97, which included rail fare, lodging, and golfing fees.

Richard Starnes, author of *Creating a Variety Vacationland: Tourism Development in North Carolina, 1930–1990*, notes that as early as 1925, North Carolina governors saw the potential our state had for tourism: Governor Angus McLean gushed that North Carolina rivaled Florida. In 1928, O. Max Gardner opined that visitors here would find us to be "a prototype of the New South." Having seen the enormous popularity of Great Smoky Mountains National Park, Gardner campaigned for the formation of Cape Hatteras National Seashore. (National seashore status came in

1953.) In 1937, former governors Gardner and Ehringhaus and the Carolina Motor Club led efforts to establish a Division of State Advertising. With a $125,000 appropriation, the division published a full-color tourist guide titled *North Carolina, A Variety Vacationland*. They hoped that tourism-generated revenues might exceed $50 million, which would be more than the revenue generated from North Carolina's corn crop and about one-third that of tobacco.

As the North Carolina tourism industry flexed its muscle, others joined in. State parks advocates used the visitation statistics to national parks and forests to promote more state parks. And why not? In the 1940s, over a million people visited Great Smoky Mountains National Park and Pisgah National Forest. Nantahala National Forest welcomed about half that many. Kill Devil Hills saw nearly 75,000 visitors, which a 1947 state report presumed "to be tourists, since it is unlikely that local persons would persist in climbing a hill so familiar to them."

After World War II, entrepreneurs once again looked for ways to court the tourist dollar. Hugh McCrae Morton built a mile-high swinging bridge at Grandfather Mountain. The ET&WNC train that once ran between Boone and Johnson City, Tennessee, became Tweetsie Railroad. Maggie Valley got its Ghost Town. And schoolchildren across the state helped purchase the USS *North Carolina* and park it in Wilmington. Outdoor dramas sprang up to tell important, if romanticized, stories of our history. Lodges that had once housed workers, notably Fontana Village and Tapoco Lodge, morphed into travel accommodations.

In 1972, North Carolina's outdoors again took center stage when three friends decided to launch the state's first adventure-travel business. Payson and Aurelia Kennedy and Horace Holden opened a rafting outfitter on the banks of the Nantahala River. The Nantahala Outdoor Center became the touchstone for a new type of outdoor fun. During the late 1970s and early 1980s, another transformation started. Old hotels such as the Balsam Mountain Inn and private homes such as the Mast Farm and Westglow were renovated into bed-and-breakfast inns and spas. Life-saving stations, such as the one at today's Sanderling Inn, became restaurants. Even the county home—the poorhouse—in Carteret County was changed into a bed-and-breakfast.

So how does this story end? If we're lucky, it doesn't. Playing is more fun than work, and North Carolina provides many different ways to go play. Take a day off from the grind and go see for yourself!

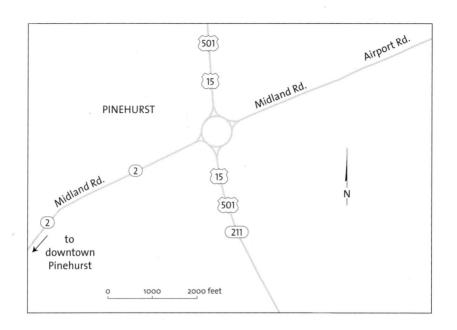

Walk Details

The walks below acquaint you with two of North Carolina's original resorts.

Pinehurst

HOW TO FIND IT: Pinehurst is located in central North Carolina. From "the circle," the intersection of US 15, US 501, and NC 211, follow Midland Road into the village. Look for the parking area near the center of town to begin this walk.

LENGTH: About 2 miles

SURFACE: Paved

RESTROOMS: None

FOOTWEAR: Sneakers

PETS: OK on a leash

MAP: Not available

THE ROUTE

From the sandy parking lot in the center of town, walk toward the Theater, but do not cross Village Green West. Follow the sand path at the edge of the pines, keeping the road and the Theater to your right. As you near the Village Chapel, bend left but stay near the perimeter of the pines.

OLD TOWN PATHS
Restored in 2006, the pathway extending down this block of Magnolia Road reflects America's preeminent landscape architect Frederick Law Olmstead's original vision for a "village in the trees." His plan consisted of a network of paths, using the local, natural materials of sand and clay to blend in with the environment.

Don't be surprised that part of the Pinehurst walk spans sandy surfaces: that's how Frederick Law Olmsted envisioned the village.

At Village Green East, bear left to walk past the Given Memorial Library and Tufts Archives (150 Cherokee Road). Inside the library a museum shows pictures of early Pinehurst. The Holly Inn (145 Cherokee Road) is across the street

Pass a small garden area on your left. A rock marks the original center of town.

Continue walking. Cross Cherokee Road and walk to Azalea Road. The Theater is to your left and the white clapboard department store is to your right. The cottages here were originally rental cottages. Today they are private homes.

At Azalea Road, bend right and walk to Magnolia Road. At Magnolia Road, turn left to walk the old path back to the center of town. The 1896 Magnolia Inn (65 Magnolia Road) appears to your left.

At the intersection, cross the streets. Lyne's Furniture Gallery is to your left. Pass Market Square. When Dogwood Road intersects from the right, make a hard right to walk along Dogwood Road. Pass Market Square again.

At Chinquapin Street, turn right to walk several yards to a crosswalk just beyond the department store. Cross the street, turn right, and continue walking Chinquapin, again passing the Magnolia Inn.

At Ritter Road, turn left to walk underneath the trees. Glimpses of the Carolina, built in 1901, appear through the trees on the right.

At the intersection of Carolina Vista turn right, cross Ritter Road, and make your way up to and around the circle. Step inside the Carolina to experience one of North Carolina's finest hotels. Return outside and follow the brick path to the right of the Carolina to walk past the Spa at Pinehurst. This walkway returns to Ritter Road, where you can cross and walk back into town.

Asheville

This walk, likely to be quite busy with many other people out enjoying downtown Asheville, follows the Urban Trail, which is marked by pink granite plaques or bronze sculptures. Temptation, in the form of shopping and neat restaurants, is as great as it ever was in the Gilded Age. You might also want to visit www.asheville-mountain-magic.com/asheville-architecture.html to print information about all of the buildings you'll pass along this walk because the text below mentions only a few.

HOW TO FIND IT: Asheville is located in western North Carolina, off I-40. Follow signs to Pack Square. You can find on-street parking. Several decks are also nearby as signage in the area indicates.

LENGTH: 1.7 mile loop

SURFACE: Concrete

RESTROOMS: Public restrooms available one block behind the Vance obelisk at Pack Place.

FOOTWEAR: Sneakers

MAP: Not available, but the Asheville Arts Council (www.ashevillearts.com; 828-258-0710) offers guided tours.

THE ROUTE

Begin at the obelisk commemorating Zebulon B. Vance, North Carolina's Civil War governor, a U.S. senator, and lawyer for Tom Dula (immortalized in the song "Tom Dooley"), at Pack Place (2 South Pack Square). If the spot feels like a natural intersection, you're right: some historians think that Cherokee trading paths once intersected here. The first white settler, believed to be William Davidson, arrived in 1784. Other settlers soon followed, and by 1793 this area was a public square punctuated with a wooden courthouse. The statuettes of pigs and turkeys near the base of the Vance monument recall the day when drovers led, poked,

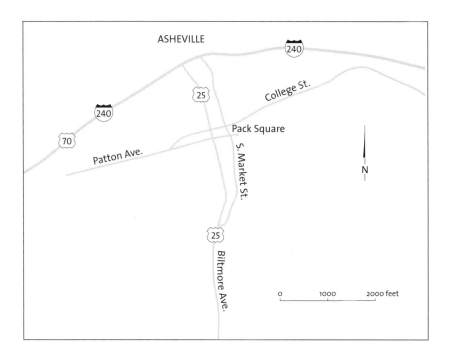

and prodded livestock to the markets south of town. The name of the square honors George Pack, a lumberman who arrived in Asheville in 1884 and was influential in modernizing the town.

With the Vance monument behind you, cross Biltmore Avenue to walk along Patton Avenue. Look for the O. Henry plaque that celebrates the famous short story all of us have read at least twice, "The Gift of the Magi." You may also see a sidewalk etching that recalls how the clear air of Asheville was once the hope of people stricken with tuberculosis and other respiratory diseases and how various sanitariums populated the area. One of the many people drawn here was E. W. Grove, whose impact on Asheville would be profound.

Turn right onto Haywood Street, which is marked by a small sign that also points the way to the Grove Arcade. Cross College Street. As you walk here, continue feasting your eyes on the wonderful architecture for which Asheville is famous. You'll be hard pressed to decide which building you like best, and you'll understand why, even on cold days, Asheville bustles with visitors.

Turn left onto Battery Park and walk a short block.

Turn left onto Wall Street. Here you traverse the Cat Walk, a bulkhead built to help stabilize Battery Hill.

Turn right onto Otis Street.

Turn right onto Battery Park. This series of turns takes you past the Grove Arcade, built in 1926–29. E. W. Grove, having grown rich on the sale of Grove's Tasteless Chill Tonic—a concoction designed to prevent malaria—was determined that Asheville would have the most "elegant building in America." The building is indeed jaw-dropping elegant, made especially so after its restoration in 2002. Make sure you step inside to admire its beauty and to marvel at what historians think is the last indoor shopping arcade built in America, before the advent of today's shopping malls.

Turn left onto Page Avenue. Walk up to Battle Square, bend to the right on Page Avenue to reach Haywood Street. Turn right onto Haywood Street. As you navigate the walk, be sure to admire the Basilica of St. Lawrence, which is thought to have the largest, free-standing, elliptical dome in North America and which is built entirely without wood or steel. Masonry and tile form the floors, ceiling and pillars.

When Walnut Street intersects at the left, turn left to walk down the hill to Lexington Avenue. At Broadway, turn left and walk to Woodfin Street. Turn right onto Woodfin. You may see that the design on the pink granite plaques changes: now you're following an angel, which commemorates one of Asheville's most famous citizens, Thomas Wolfe, most notably the author of *Look Homeward, Angel*. When you pass the sculpture memorializing Wolfe, take time to stand in the footprints. Like his expansive prose, his footprints are big.

Walk Woodfin Avenue to the sign signaling Thomas Wolfe Plaza. Turn right. Soon you'll pass by the Old Kentucky Home boarding house that inspired the Dixieland boarding house in *Look Homeward, Angel*. The original home burned in 2004, but has since been painstakingly restored.

Traverse Thomas Wolfe Plaza. At the top of the traverse, note that street signs indicate that you're now on Spruce Street. Cross Market Street, and as you do, look for the Asheville Community Theater (35 East Walnut Street). Charlton Heston and his wife once managed this theater. **Continue along Spruce Street to College Street.**

Make time to step inside the Grove Arcade to experience the grand building from within.

Cross College Street and re-enter Pack Place. The obelisk where the walk started is up to your right. By now, after enjoying all of the beauty Asheville has to offer, you may share the feelings Thomas Wolfe expressed in *Look Homeward, Angel*, "The mountains were his masters. They rimmed in life." And you may be thinking how you're going to find reasons to come here more often.

Separate, Not Equal, but Loved Anyway

JONES LAKE STATE PARK

Jim Crow–era thinking is, mercifully, receding into the past. But even if physical markers designating separate drinking fountains, building entrances, and waiting rooms have been banished to memory, you can see vestiges of segregation if you know what you're looking at. For example, take Umstead State Park outside Raleigh. It contains two sections. You may think, as I once did, that circumstance arises from US 70 bounding the park on the east side and I-40 on the west. I was wrong, and it wasn't until some research into the matter that I changed my thinking.

One fine November afternoon, I set out to walk both the Company Mill Trail in the park's Reedy Creek section (nearer the interstate) and the Sycamore Trail in the Crabtree Creek section (accessible off US 70). I have enjoyed hundreds of miles walking trails, and I found the "spur" or connector path linking these two trails just plain odd. My experience is that when trail builders want to link trails together, they simply link trails together. They don't use "spurs."

So I started poking into the past, learning how in the 1930s the federal Resettlement Administration purchased exhausted farmland from farmers to stimulate a depressed economy. The agency then sold or leased parcels to state governments for a nominal fee, often a dollar. I learned that many of our state's parks came about this way. The North Carolina legislature, following the "separate but equal" segregation practice of the day, designated Umstead State Park for white citizens and Reedy Creek State Park for black citizens. After civil rights legislation of the 1960s, however, the two state parks united, and other than the section designations, the "spur" trail is about all that's left as a reminder of that history.

These days, many of us can look the "separate but equal" phrase in the eye and see it for what it was. Time and again, we can recount examples of things that were separate—but far from equal. Yet the clear inequality of their designated public spaces and facilities did not cause North Carolina's black citizens to love and enjoy their spaces and facilities any less. Jones Lake State Park, the first state park set aside for North Carolina's black citizens, produced just as many good memories

On a calm winter's day, Jones Lake, one of the state's most notable Carolina bay lakes, can be positively glasslike.

for North Carolina's black citizens as any state park could. This walk invites you to consider those memories.

Historical Context

As the North Carolina Division of Parks and Recreation notes, the area of North Carolina now occupied by Jones Lake was settled during the 1700s. Had it not been for a large tract of land donated by Isaac Jones to accommodate the nearby town of Elizabethtown in 1773, the lake we know today as Jones Lake might have retained its original name of Woodward Lake, honoring Samuel Woodward, an area justice of the peace.

Jones Lake is a fine example of what are known today as Carolina bays—well-formed, usually shallow, undrained oval lakes that dot the Coastal Plain of North Carolina (and indeed the southeastern United States). They are something of a geologic mystery, and scientists don't agree on what created them. Native American legend offers the story of a fire that burned for thirteen moons, which tends to mesh with the popular but largely discredited theory that perhaps a meteor explosion of epic proportion occurred. Other scientists disagree; they suggest that underground springs or maybe even wind or wave action formed these bodies of water.

There is no such disagreement about the historic productivity of the land. Longleaf pines grew prolifically in the area, and the region soon became a powerhouse of naval stores production, sending barrel upon barrel of turpentine and pitch down the Cape Fear River to markets in Wilmington, along with thousands of board feet of timber. Later, cotton farming was added to the agricultural mix.

In time, however, planters and farmers had exhausted the land, and all the people had left were submarginal holdings, the kind of land the Resettlement Administration purchased and then leased or resold to state governments for use as parks. According to the Division of Parks and Recreation, the federal government bought up the property and managed the Jones Lake area for three years beginning in 1936. During this period, the Resettlement Administration developed a recreation center with a large bathhouse, beach, and refreshment stand. In 1939, the state of North Carolina took over the property and its management, opening it as a segregated state park.

The Walk

Before you walk through the visitor center and out to the beach and fishing pier, walk out to NC 242 along one of the park entrance roads. Today, a brown park sign that reads "Jones Lake State Park" alerts travelers to the facility. But the sign was not always worded this way.

On April 27, 2007, the *Raleigh News and Observer* published a story by David Cecelski titled "Mr. Dewitt's Lake." Cecelski interviewed Sallie Powell, who knew of the lake since her childhood and whose husband, Dewitt Powell, served as a park ranger there. Powell, who later taught math in the nearby Bladen County schools, remembered that the sign read: "Jones Lake State Park. Negroes Only." "I would have to go to Jones Lake and you would have been going to White Lake," Powell explained to Cecelski, referring to a larger lake just a few miles to the east on US 701 that remains home to a significant resort community.

Now walk to, and through, the visitor center, which is about ten years old. The park that Sallie Powell enjoyed offered a wooden bathhouse, a refreshment stand, and picnic grounds, and it drew people from as far away as Raleigh and Durham. Summer weekends were especially crowded, recalled Powell.

On weekends, oh my Lord! It would be crowded all weekend. There would be big groups of people.

They enjoyed the atmosphere there. . . . I worked in the refreshment stand as a teenager. I sold hot dogs, hamburgers, pork chop sandwiches. You just came to the window.

They had a place roped off for swimmers. They had life- guards. They would play volleyball, and some people would bring their tennis net and they would play tennis. Sometimes they played softball. You could rent rowboats there too, and they had a camping area.

When Jones Lake was at its peak as a tourist destination, ladies would often arrive in hats, the men in suits and ties, and the children in their Sunday clothes, recalls the *Bladen Journal*. Everyone would store their finery in lockers in the bathhouse and pay thirty-five cents for the privilege to go into the water. After enjoying a day swimming at the beach, they would shower and change back into their good clothes for the trip home.

And it wasn't just families that came out for weekend summer fun. Often, on Sundays, church groups might be conducting a baptism. "If they scheduled a baptism at, say, 10 o'clock in the morning," recalled Powell, "my husband would have people stay out of the water until after the baptism. . . . I saw many baptisms there. The preacher would wear a white robe, and the people being baptized would wear street clothes. They would sing." In the spring, school groups might come out.

Once you're on the lake side of the visitor center, walk out to the beach, which is slightly to the left. You'll notice quickly that the water of 224- acre Jones Lake is the color of tea. That's because of vegetation de- composing on the lake bottom. Nearby White Lake, however, is fed by underground springs, which meant that its white-only visitors could swim in clear water that allowed them to see the white sand of the lake bottom. But the difference didn't stop mothers like Sallie Powell from letting their babies enjoy the water. "My children loved the lake," she noted. "When they were diaper babies, I would take them after every- body was gone and set them in the water. They could splash around all they wanted." And it wasn't just mothers and toddlers who loved the water; men liked fishing on the lake for yellow perch, chain pickerel, catfish, and blue-spotted sunfish, all of which might be caught there today. Added Powell, "Oh, my husband loved working out there. He loved it to death. He liked outdoors."

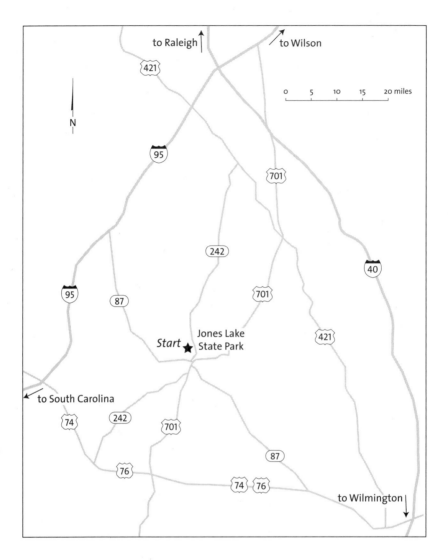

to Raleigh ↑   ↗ to Wilson

421

0   5   10   15   20 miles

N

95

701

242

95   40

87   701

Start ★ Jones Lake
         State Park   421

← to South Carolina

74   242   701

87

76

74 76

to Wilmington ↓

Beyond the beach, you'll see a sign pointing to the four-mile Bay Trail. This trail and the Cedar Loop Trail on the right side of the lake past the visitor center together form a five-mile loop around Jones Lake. In the beginning, there weren't any established trails to speak of, because none were built when the park was designed. But in time people made their own trails and, in some cases, used old logging roads to take a walk. These two trails likely result from those early walkers' trailblazing.

If you take the Bay Trail walk, you can immerse yourself in the often underappreciated beauty of a Carolina bay lake. As you might expect, the chorus of croaking frogs—or crickets, or both—provides its own symphony. During the cooler months, when the low sun brings out more colors in the tea-colored lake water, you might see purple and royal blue; and when the twilight sky begins to make inky silhouettes of the Spanish moss in the trees, you'll marvel at the way sunset falls on the Coastal Plain as you wind your way back to the trail's starting point. Before leaving Jones Lake State Park, look for photographs dating to the park's early days posted in and near the visitor center. As you study pictures of people enjoying the park, you'll also be able to glimpse the original facilities, which have been renovated and otherwise rebuilt twice since the park opened.

Walk Details

HOW TO FIND IT: Jones Lake State Park (4117 Highway 242 North) is located in eastern North Carolina, about four miles north of Elizabethtown.

LENGTH: About 5 miles if you hike the entire lake loop

SURFACE: Gnarled with roots, can be spongy or slippery after rain

RESTROOMS: At parking area

FOOTWEAR: Boots will be welcomed

PETS: Allowed on a leash

MAP: Available at Visitor Center

Beware: If you intend to enjoy the lake loop, hike in the cool months to avoid the snakes, gnats, mosquitoes, and ticks.

GOOD TO KNOW: To add another two miles to your walk, walk the one-mile trail out and back to Salters Lake, which received its name from Sallie Salter, a Revolutionary War heroine who spied on the Tories encamped in town. Salters Lake is one more example of a Carolina bay lake.

Fontana Dam

LUMBER, POWER, AND PERSONAL QUESTS

Some of the fastest, most furious change North Carolina has ever seen took place at Fontana Dam. In one generation, life went from being remote to supporting a global war effort. Lumber companies arrived and departed. The federal government, in the form of a TVA dam and, later, a national park, left its mark. The longest court case in U.S. history and a landmark decision against industrial monopoly, *Adams v. Wesfeldt*, concerned land here.

And that's not all. A second phase of history, a stark contrast to the noisy activity described above, speaks to restoration, preservation, and personal quest. After the federal government established Great Smoky Mountains National Park, second-growth forests reclaimed the mountainsides, restoring the natural serenity. That natural beauty attracted the outdoors lovers who seek personal challenge and restoration. It's nearly unbelievable what happened here in less than eighty years.

Historical Context

In the beginning, the Little Tennessee River carved a narrow gap between the mountains as it traveled west to join the 652-mile-long Tennessee River. The ancient town of the Cherokee, Nikwasi, stood where Franklin, about forty-five miles away, bustles today. Although forced removal of the Cherokee to Oklahoma was government policy, Cherokee settlements remained in the area (see chapter 9, Murphy). When white settlers moved in, land sold for five to ten cents an acre.

Opening these western mountains proved difficult. Not until 1875 would Jesse Gunter settle in Welch Cove, site of today's Fontana Village. (His cabin stands on the property.) NC 28, the road you travel today, was once a sled trail that Jesse Gunter used.

The Walk

Park in the lot closest to the dam, and walk to the dam. To the west lies what remains of the narrow mountain gap carved by the Little Tennessee. Across the lake, tree-covered ridges, the spine of Great Smoky Mountains National Park, rise up. Numerous creeks drain those ridges, flowing into Fontana Lake: Forney Creek, Scarlet Ridge, White Mans Glory, Bear Creek, Hazel Creek, and Eagle Creek, just to name a few. Once, they emptied into the Little Tennessee.

Timbering operations arrived here in the late 1880s. In those days, felling trees and turning them into boards was arduous work. First a man swung his axe again and again to fell the giant oaks, chestnuts, and poplars. Next, two men working together turned trees into boards. One man stood in a saw pit, a trench six or seven feet deep, beneath a tree while his sawing partner squatted above the pit. Together they hand-sawed their way through the tree, forming a single board. The man sawing above likely experienced piercing pain in his knees. The man below, sawing with his arms raised over his head, likely squinted as tiny wood chips and sawdust fell into his face. After the two men produced one board, they started again to make another board. Little wonder most pioneer cabins were a single room. Who would want more than 120 square feet of living space if turning trees into boards required such effort?

The pace of logging quickened when man learned how to harness creek water to create wooden splash dams to help haul out the trees. Splash dams occurred in a series, with each dam creating an impoundment pond behind it. These dams might be as large as 250 feet across and 18 feet high. Between the dams, loggers cleared the creek bed of boulders. Then they felled the best trees and dragged them to the nearest pond. There the logs collected. Some splash dams had gates, but sometimes the loggers simply exploded the dam when the pond had filled with logs. Either way, the accumulated force of water powered the trees down the creeks to the river. River hogs, men who walked alongside the creeks wearing spiked boots and carrying pike poles, dislodged any logjams. Once in the Little Tennessee, the logs floated to Chattanooga sawmills.

When machines arrived, the pace of logging quickened even more. Watered-powered saws could saw eighty strokes a minute and, unlike man, not become bone-tired. The geared Shay locomotive, and its competitors the Heisler and the Climax locomotives, could negotiate the grades and curves typical of mountain rail transportation. Loggers also harnessed steam engines to create skidders and log loaders. Where ground-skidding proved too difficult, loggers used overhead skidders, a cable system that hoisted logs through the air from more than half a mile away. Logging-industry historians note that although the work had become easier, it was not easy. The exertion was such that the average logger consumed 9,000 calories a day to fuel his body.

The effect of this industrialization? As Norwood Lumber Company felled trees along Forney Creek, Ritter logged Hazel Creek, Montvale went to Eagle Creek, Kitchens logged Twenty Mile Creek, and Whiting Manufacturing logged the south side of the Little Tennessee—2 billion board feet of lumber came out of the Smokies. Estimates suggest that if that lumber had been used to build three-bedroom houses, some 200,000 houses could have been built. Area farmers who once survived on subsistence farming became accustomed to paychecks from the lumber company. Meanwhile, the mountain ridges were stripped naked.

Towns sprang up on the creeks that drained the mountainside. Proctor, built on Hazel Creek by Ritter Lumber Company, boasted 1,000 residents, a post office, a school, a barbershop, and a movie theater. In the day, it rivaled Bryson City. A road, NC 288, ran at the base of the mountains along the river tying the communities together.

Just as trees were abundant above ground, so were minerals below. In the mid-1880s, Fonzie Hall discovered copper in the Eagle Creek area. Soon, Fontana Mining Corporation was operating there. Near Hazel Creek, two men, W. S. Adams and George Wesfeldt, both thought they owned the mineral-rich land and went to court to prove it. The case lasted twenty-six years; during one session twenty-two lawyers crowded the courtroom, eleven for each side. Ironically, both men died before a settlement was reached in 1927. Because of the prolonged lawsuit, Hazel Creek dodged the ills of open-heap roasting, a process that releases sulfuric acid into the air, killing vegetation and turning landscapes into moonscapes.

The industrial noise on the mountainsides must have been deafening! Power plants hummed, sawmills screamed, mining operations clanged, and trains whistled around the tracks that linked everything together. In September 1922, a Ritter Lumber Company newsletter crowed that the company had "11 band mills, 11 planing mills, 11 flooring units, 8 dimension mills, 6 dry kilns, comprising 14 logging operations, operated 187 miles of railroads, and its plants in the aggregate cover 96½ acres of floor space and its loading docks and piling spaces cover 407 acres of land. Its properties are scattered over five states and extend into nine counties. Its manufacturing capacity is 125,000,000 board feet annually."

By the late 1920s, however, the easy-to-get trees were gone, and the

Over 7,000 people worked round the clock to build Fontana Dam to help meet the country's rising need for aluminum during World War II.

lumber companies were leaving, taking the railroad tracks with them. Men were out of work.

Walk over Fontana Dam, away from the parking lot. While trees were falling, and the mountain vistas changing, twenty-two-year-old Charles Martin Hall discovered something in his woodshed in Oberlin, Ohio, that would forever change the narrows of the Little Tennessee River. Hall discovered that by passing an electrical current through a bath of cryolite and aluminum oxide, a semi-rare metal—aluminum— remained. Getting a patent and finding backers to turn the process into something commercially viable took nearly ten years, but by 1907, the Pittsburgh Reduction Company had formed. The Pittsburgh Reduction Company was the parent of the Aluminum Company of America, Alcoa.

Making aluminum required cheap electricity. Because locating aluminum plants close to a city typically raised the cost of that city's electric power, Alcoa started, in 1909, buying property along the Little Tennessee River, planning to build a dam. The land was cheap in large part because it was remote.

By 1914, Alcoa was eager to build an aluminum-smelting plant in Tennessee. Five years later, Cheoah Dam was supplying power to that plant. By 1929, Santeetlah Dam was operating too. As strong and light aluminum quickly became a staple in America, Alcoa became an American Goliath. To keep pace with demand, the company wanted to build two more dams on the Little Tennessee River.

As you near the far side of Fontana Dam, consider what had happened in thirty years. Subsistence farming was gone, or nearly so. Lumber barons had come and were gone, or nearly so. Mining was gone, or nearly so. The Great Depression was on the horizon, as was a world war.

The next forty years would be equally busy, but in a different way. People were advancing the idea that they needed the outdoors—national parks—to restore the sense of well-being that industrialism was taking away. Indeed, Yellowstone and Rocky Mountain National Parks, just to name two, already existed. In nearby Knoxville, Mr. and Mrs. Willis P. Davis had taken up the cause of creating a national park. Their advocacy, however, had its challenges: lumber companies owned much of the land where a park could be established. Moreover, because lumber companies were gone, people out of work wanted jobs. Many of them wanted a national forest, not a park, because national forest land could be timbered, mined, fished, and hunted. In a national park, those activities would cease. And then there was the money required to buy the land for park. Where would it come from? Speaker of the House Joseph G. Cannon, a Republican from Illinois, proclaimed that "not one cent" of federal money would be spent "for scenery." (Interesting fact: Cannon was born in Guilford County.)

Although departing, lumber companies still wanted a price for the tree-barren land. Push came to shove: North Carolina and Tennessee started filing condemnation suits to try to assemble parcels of land for cheap purchase even as neither state could explain where the money to purchase the land would come from. The purchase moved slowly until John D. Rockefeller donated $5 million. At last, the hoped-for Great Smoky Mountains National Park would become a reality. (For more of this story, read Michael Frome's wonderful book, *Strangers in High Places*.)

During this time, outdoors enthusiasts were joining ranks to support efforts to restore and preserve natural landscapes. The Smoky Mountains Hiking Club, formed by brothers George and Charlie Barber, took its first official hike on December 6, 1924. Later, when Judge Arthur Perkins and admiralty lawyer Myron Avery began championing Benton MacKaye's idea of an "Appalachian Trail," they sought the support of the Smoky Mountains Hiking Club to help build the Appalachian Trail. The original path of the AT, laid out in 1932–33, crossed the Little Tennessee River at Tapoco, near Cheoah Dam.

Then the Great Depression hit, changing life everywhere.

In 1933, Franklin D. Roosevelt and the New Deal would impact life near the narrows of the Little Tennessee. One New Deal program was the Tennessee Valley Authority. Operating in seven states, the TVA was the country's first attempt at regional planning and electrical production. The Tennessee River and its tributaries sat squarely in the sights of the TVA.

But a problem lurked: Alcoa owned the land and planned to build a dam to create electricity for its own purposes. Negotiations between business and government started immediately and were at first harmonious. Alcoa wanted to be in the aluminum business and not the power business, and thus agreed to sell its electrical interests in the unbuilt dam and be paid in electrical current. But three years later, with no agreement in sight, the relationship between Alcoa and the federal government had soured. According to historian Stephen Taylor, accusations of malfeasance "flew right and left." In 1937 in New York City, the off-Broadway play *Power* vilified electrical companies and extolled the virtues of the federal government with a folk tune called "TVA Song." By 1938, the Antitrust Division of the Justice Department had filed suit against Alcoa, attempting to break its monopoly on aluminum production. The trust-busting efforts rivaled those of the Standard Oil and U.S. Steel cases.

By 1939, the need for more aluminum was becoming urgent: Nazi Germany was rising, as was the age of air warfare. Still, business and government couldn't agree. Then, on December 7, 1941, after the Japanese attacked Pearl Harbor, both Alcoa and the federal government realized that progress was in everyone's interest, for not only did Alcoa need the electricity to make aluminum for the war effort, so did a secret group in Oak Ridge, Tennessee, known as the Manhattan Project. Work started on the dam five days later.

At the height of the effort, the TVA employed 7,000 people, working three shifts a day directly or indirectly on the dam. Jesse Gunter's Welch Cove, now called Fontana Village, hummed with people. Nineteen classrooms were built in village schools to accommodate workers' children. Posters of a smiling, bespectacled worker in a hard hat and overalls encouraged the furious pace with a caption that read:

A walk into the woods along Lakeshore Drive reveals remnants of the lives of people who lived in the area before Fontana Dam and Great Smoky Mountains National Park arrived.

We are Building the Dam
To Make the Power
To Roll the Aluminum
To Build the Bombers
To Beat the Bastards

The dam rose in the narrows of the Little Tennessee River, and the lake basin took shape. Almost immediately, people realized that much of NC 288, the road that connected all of the near-empty lumber towns, would go underwater. (The fate of NC 288 would be a sore point until 2007 when a settlement finally was reached.) Families who had stayed in the ghostly lumber towns were evicted. When the diversion tunnels of the dam closed on November 7, 1944, so that the reservoir could fill, many of the towns—even the Fontana Copper Mine—went underwater. Buildings that were not flooded were burned. The new dam went online on January 20, 1945, just over thirty-six months after work began. In 1946, the Smoky Mountains Hiking Club relocated the Appalachian Trail across Fontana Dam.

Across Fontana Dam, bear right to walk what remains of NC 288, today the trailhead for Lakeshore Drive. It follows a gentle grade through an area once harvested by the Whiting Manufacturing Company. After you cross Payne Branch, you'll be on old NC 288. About half a mile from the dam, you'll also see that the white-blazed Appalachian Trail splits to the left. If you opt to hike the AT here, you face a steady uphill grind. If you hike up Lakeshore Drive trail about 1.5 miles, you'll see remnants of old cars and the remains of an old homestead marked by four large shrubs. In early spring, you might also see daffodils blooming near what's left of the cabin foundation.

Return to the dam, cross it, and then walk the sidewalk near the parking lot up the hill and then down it to visit one of the Appalachian Trail's most beloved trail shelters: the "Fontana Hilton." The trail shelter bears this nickname because it is near enough the dam complex that grimy hikers can enjoy a welcomed hot shower in the tiled showers originally built for the round-the-clock dam builders.

After enjoying a respite at the Fontana Hilton, return to your car.

Walk Details

HOW TO FIND IT: From Asheville, take US 74 West to NC 28. Follow NC 28 to the entrance to Fontana Dam. Follow the drive down to the dam.

LENGTH: 4 miles roundtrip from the Fontana Hilton to the woods where Lakeshore Trail starts

SURFACE: Concrete, asphalt

RESTROOMS: Available at Fontana Dam and at a picnic area near the Fontana Hilton

FOOTWEAR: Sneakers OK unless you extend your walk to include the Appalachian Trail or Lakeshore Trail

PETS: Leave them at home. Bears frequent the area, sometimes as close as the Fontana Visitor Center. Having a pet along will invite trouble.

MAP: None available

GOOD TO KNOW: In March, April, and May, hikers who are attempting to hike the AT end to end (the northern terminus is in Baxter State Park in Maine) will be plentiful.

Don't let the relative proximity to gift shops and ice cream chests fool you: the last time I walked here I saw a mother bear and two cubs just on the far side of Fontana Dam.

Nearby Fontana Village once housed the workers who built Fontana Dam. American Express and Standard Oil both thought about buying

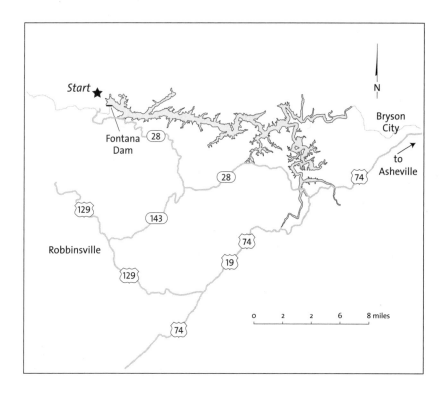

Fontana Village for company resort purposes but didn't. The little town now is a resort destination, and you can rent the houses where workers once lived.

For More Exploration

To see an original, untouched Appalachian forest, visit nearby Joyce Kilmer Memorial Forest outside Robbinsville. Follow US 129 North/NC 143 north and west out of town. When NC 143 and US 129 split, stay on NC 143. Turn right onto Joyce Kilmer Road. Follow signs to the parking area for Joyce Kilmer Memorial Forest. The two-mile trail starts just beyond the signboard. While walking this trail, you will see poplar trees that are old enough to predate the Revolutionary War.

Charlotte

BANK TOWN AND BEYOND

Say "Charlotte" and "history" in the same breath and people within hearing distance may likely scoff like Tom Hanks's crusty baseball manager from *A League of Her Own*: "Charlotte? History? There's no history in Charlotte!"

Charlotte, never a genteel town based on a planter's economy, does indeed ooze youth, independence, newness, and risk taking. NASCAR, the embodiment of mobility and risk taking, permeates the town. In addition, the other embodiment of Charlotte's modern attitude—the glass-and-steel canyon of the center city—suggests that the city won't offer much to those hunting for local antiques. Nonetheless, Charlotte's roots go deep, and the burg has an interesting history that culminates in its arrival as a "New South City" and one of the nation's major financial centers. The walk described below may surprise you more than any other urban walk in the entire book.

Historical Context

Honoring Queen Charlotte of Mecklenburg, the queen consort of King George III, Charlotte humbly began life where, local lore states, the Great Wagon Road intersected the Great Trading Path.

Thomas Polk, uncle of James Knox Polk, America's eleventh president, settled here in 1755, as did the Thomas Spratt family. (Polk, in love with Thomas Spratt's daughter, had followed the family south.) Charlotte Town was officially incorporated thirteen years later.

In those days, Revolutionary fever burned, creating a great controversy and a wonderful nickname for the settlement. Like many communities, Charlotte Town had a safety committee. Lore says that the committee produced a Mecklenburg Declaration of Independence on May 20, 1775, although a hard copy of the document did not appear until 1819. (The original supposedly burned in a fire.) Thomas Jefferson dismissed the 1819 document as a hoax, provoking a debate lasting to this day. Nonetheless, the May date earned a spot on our state flag.

Despite its big urban shoulders, Charlotte has an interesting colonial history.

And Charlotte's nickname? When British general Lord Cornwallis stopped here in 1780, his reception was hardly warm. Residents' angry reactions to the British army's presence led Cornwallis to write that the town was a "hornet's nest of rebellion." Charlotteans embraced Cornwallis's label, emblazoning a hornet's nest on both the Charlotte city and Mecklenburg County flags. Charlotte's independent spirit continued to burn long after the Revolutionary War, so much so that during the 1960s, state legislators called Charlotte the "State of Mecklenburg." Anyone growing up in Charlotte and points west always knew that, for Charlotte, Independence was more than a boulevard.

When gold was discovered in nearby Cabarrus County, the events that would morph Charlotte into Bank Town USA were set in motion. By the 1940s, Charlotte would muscle ahead to become North Carolina's largest, busiest, most modern city.

The Walk

Begin at Independence Square, often simply called "The Square," where Trade and Tryon Streets intersect. In 1770, Thomas Polk directed the platting of Charlotte's streets. According to local lore, the Great Wagon Road became Tryon Street to honor royal governor William Tryon, and the Great Trading Path became Trade Street. (One wonders if the Great Wagon Road would have been named for Tryon if the grid had been laid out a year later, after the Battle of Alamance, where Tryon put down a popular uprising by the Regulator movement.) Once the grid was set, Charlotte's ward system began.

The first courthouse, a log cabin atop an open-air market, sat here, as did Thomas Polk's house. The Mecklenburg Declaration was reportedly signed here, as was the Mecklenburg Resolves, a document that is sometimes mistakenly confused with the controversial "Meck Dec." When the British army marched up Tryon Street in September 1780, weeks before the battle of Kings Mountain, William Davie and a band of militiamen fired upon them from the courthouse. Later, in December, Nathanael Greene assumed command of the Continental army here, three months before the Battle of Guilford Courthouse.

While in the Square, study the bronze statues created by Raymond Kaskey. Erected in 1995, they tell Charlotte's history. The gold miner represents commerce; his pan spills gold onto the banker, whose face looks like Alan Greenspan's. The African American man clasping a maul represents transportation, railroading in particular. Beneath him, an eagle's face represents aviation. A female millworker represents industry: look for the spindle, the roller, and the hydroelectric bolts. Look too for the young child, symbolizing child labor. Most inspiring is the young mother who, holding her baby in the air, represents the future. She emerges from the branches of a dogwood tree, where a hornet's nest also sits.

From the corner where the Industry sculpture (the millworker) sits, walk along West Trade Street. Cross Church, Poplar, and Mint Streets. This stretch of West Trade Street contains Thomas Polk Park, where a stone marker signals the home of Captain James Jack. James Jack delivered the Mecklenburg Resolves to Philadelphia and the Continental Congress, after a thirty-eight-day, 1,100-mile (roundtrip) horse ride. When he arrived in Philadelphia and showed the document to the North Carolina delegation, they deemed it premature and chose not to disclose it to the other delegates. After the Revolutionary War, Jack was instrumental in creating the state of Tennessee. (At the corner of 4th Street and Kings Drive, outside the scope of this walk, a statue celebrates Captain Jack's ride.)

Across the street is the First Presbyterian Church (200 West Trade Street), established in 1815 as the Town Church and used by all denominations. One of Charlotte's earliest recorded banking transactions took place here when town commissioners borrowed money from the Bank of New Bern to build the church.

The African American man in one of the sculptures by Raymond Kaskey at the corner of Trade and Tryon Streets speaks to the labor of black citizens in building railroads and thereby helping Charlotte become a transportation hub. Below the sculpture, workers ready kiosks to celebrate the Coca-Cola 600, yet another manifestation of Charlotte's transportation heritage.

In 1841, Presbyterians bought the land. The front of the building you see dates from 1857. Notable church members included Daniel Harvey Hill, a West Point graduate, Davidson College mathematics professor, Confederate general, and namesake of the main library at North Carolina State University; Mary Anna Morrison Jackson, Hill's sister-in-law and wife of Stonewall Jackson; and Governor Zebulon B. Vance and his wife, Harriette. When Vance lived in Charlotte he worked as a lawyer. Legend says that when Vance argued a case, shopkeepers closed their stores because nobody was coming in to purchase anything: they were all in the courthouse listening to Vance.

Cross Mint Street and walk to the beautiful building on the left. This impressive building is not a branch of the U.S. Mint but a post office built where the Mint once stood. Charlotte became home to a branch of the U.S. Mint in 1838 due to gold strikes in nearby Cabarrus County and because the mint in Philadelphia was too far away from the gold mines. When the first coins were struck here on March 26, 1838, the *Charlotte*

Journal called the $5 half eagle gold pieces "the yellow boys." Over its twenty-four-year lifespan, the Charlotte Mint struck over $5 million in gold coins.

The day North Carolina seceded from the Union—May 20, 1861, and eighty-six years to the day of the infamous Mecklenburg Declaration—the Charlotte Grays, a local Confederate militia, occupied the mint. During the Civil War, the building served as a Confederate headquarters and as a hospital. Over time, the U.S. Post Office moved next door, and when the mint was bought for $950 by a citizen group in 1933, the U.S. Post Office built the structure you see today. Meanwhile, the mint was dismantled and moved to Randolph Road, where it now serves as the Mint Museum.

Return to Mint Street, cross it and then cross Trade Street to walk north on Pine Street. This area, the edge of Fourth Ward, was where Mrs. Stonewall Jackson lived. Her home was a popular spot for Confederate veterans to frequent. She is said to have kept Stonewall's saddle outside on a post as a welcome signal to the vets.

At the corner of Pine and Fifth Streets (in front of the Fifth and Poplar Condominiums), turn right to walk to the corner of Fifth and Poplar Streets. Look for the Bagley-Mullen House (129 North Poplar Street), a Victorian house illustrating the wealth of Fourth Ward residents in the late 1800s. The house has had many owners, but one owner merits special attention. Walter Mullen created a potion called *Hornet's Nest Liniment*. It supposedly could make the old look young and the fat look thin, put hair on a man's head and take it off a lady's face. Look, too, for earthquake rods stabilizing the house. In 1886, an earthquake struck Charleston, South Carolina; tremors were felt as far as Charlotte.

Cross Poplar Street. Then cross Fifth Street to enter the Settlers' Cemetery, Charlotte's first burial ground. Dating to the late 1700s, the cemetery was closed in 1867. A granite tablet on the upper-right corner of the cemetery explains who is buried here, including Thomas Polk.

To exit the cemetery, walk toward an old red-brick building toward the bottom-left corner. Opened at Davidson College in 1887, the North Carolina Medical College, the first chartered medical college in the state, called this building home until 1907. Dr. Annie Alexander, the first woman south of the Potomac to have a medical license, practiced medicine here. The school closed in 1907 when it was moved to Richmond, Virginia, to become the Medical College of Virginia.

Settlers' Cemetery served as Charlotte's first burial ground.

Continue walking along Poplar Street to 8th Street. To make a tiny loop through the Fourth Ward, turn left onto 8th Street and then right onto Pine Street. Here grand Victorian houses mix with luxury condos. As you walk along, note the small streets, unable to handle car traffic. Even though trolley service arrived in the 1890s, people usually walked to their downtown jobs. Look for the Overcarsh House (324 8th Street), believed to be the oldest frame structure uptown. Mainly physicians and merchants lived in Fourth Ward, as did Randolph Scott, a famous Hollywood leading man. Country music fans may remember that the Statler Brothers immortalized Scott in their song, "Whatever Happened to Randolph Scott?"

Turn right onto Settler's Lane and follow it to Poplar Street. Turn left onto 8th Street to walk to Tryon Street. Cross Church Street carefully, because you must do so without a traffic light. On your left appears the First United Methodist Church. James B. Duke worshipped here.

Turn right at Tryon Street to walk one block to St. Peter's Episcopal Church (115 West Seventh Street). Confederate president Jefferson Davis and his entourage worshipped here in April 1865, as they fled from the Yankees. The quiet little churchyard feels like an oasis of calm compared to the bustling downtown that stretches before you.

At the corner of 7th and Tryon Streets, cross Tryon. Now walk Tryon Street all the way to Stonewall Street to admire Charlotte in all of its modern, commercial glory. As you take in the bustling streets and observe how new buildings tower over old, the time has come to consider why, how, and when Charlotte became a major financial center. The answer stems in large measure from North Carolina's somewhat liberal banking laws and the competitive spirits of two men who headed rival banks: Hugh McColl and Ed Crutchfield.

Unlike other states' banking laws, North Carolina banking laws did not prevent banks from operating outside their county lines. Wachovia Bank, originally headquartered in Winston-Salem, was the first major North Carolina bank to capitalize on these laws. Founded in 1879, Wachovia was by 1911 the largest bank between Baltimore and New Orleans. During the 1950s, Wachovia held 20 percent of all bank deposits in North Carolina, and Robert Hanes enjoyed a national reputation for presiding over a well-run bank. When the fathers of today's Research Triangle Park sought financial backing, they went to Robert Hanes (see chapter 27, Research Triangle Park).

In 1957, American Trust Bank, a newcomer to Charlotte's banking choices, merged with Commercial National Bank, creating a resource of $234 million. In 1960, the company decided to change its name from American Commercial Bank to North Carolina National Bank (NCNB).

While banks were consolidating in the 1950s, something even more powerful appeared: the credit card. Writes Howard Covington in *The Story of NationsBank*, "before the bank credit card was introduced, one survey found that the people in the banking industry believed that the most exciting thing to happen in banking in post-war America was air conditioning."

In 1958, First Union National Bank, based in Charlotte, was the first in the state to introduce credit cards. These bank cards were good only in retail shops in Charlotte. Soon, however, all banks were offering a BankAmericard and, perhaps, a MasterCard. The profits to be made in credit were enormous.

Over time, banking consolidation intensified, and Charlotte's downtown grew taller. First Union grew by buying the Cameron-Brown Company in Raleigh in 1964 and then diversifying into brokerage services and into a corporate and investment banking entity. Seven years later, First Union built a thirty-two-story skyscraper in 1971 and, in 1973, named Ed Crutchfield its president. At the time, the thirty-two-year-old Crutchfield was the youngest president of a major bank in the country.

In 1974, NCNB named thirty-nine-year-old Hugh McColl its president, and, in 1975, the company built a forty-story building. In 1982, NCNB ventured outside state lines to buy First National Bank of Lake City, Florida.

In 1988, First Union built a forty-two-story tower. NCNB continued to grow, and in 1988 outmanuevered Wells Fargo and Citicorp to purchase First RepublicBank in Texas. Then, in 1991, NCNB acquired C&S/Sovran Bank in Atlanta, and in doing so, changed its name to NationsBank. In 1992, the organization moved into the Bank of America Corporate Center, which, at sixty stories, is North Carolina's tallest building, which soon earned the nickname "Taj McColl."

Bank consolidation continued into the early 1990s. In 1998, Nations-Bank acquired BankAmerica, becoming the second-largest bank in the country. Again the name of the company changed, this time to Bank of America. In 2001, Wachovia and First Union merged, keeping the name Wachovia and catapulting the new organization into the number four position. In December 2008, Bank of America bought Merrill Lynch, making Bank of America the largest U.S. banking and financial firm, with assets of $2.5 trillion. Wachovia merged with Wells Fargo. (These acquisitions weren't motivated by the desire to grow, however, as earlier acquisitions had been. Rather, the frenzied pace of consolidation came about because some banks were on the verge of failure. *Reckless Endangerment* by Gretchen Morgenson and Joshua Rosner and *Too Big to Fail* by Aaron Sorkin recount this slice of history.) Since then, the frenzied pace of mergers and acquisitions in the banking industry has understandably cooled, and other industries, notably energy and engineering, are now becoming stronger in Charlotte.

As you walk along Tryon Street, be sure to note the wonderful array of public art that appears at street level. In Transamerica Square, an open-air rotunda contains a domed fresco by Ben Long featuring the cycle of life. The fountain in front of the public library is a gift to Charlotte from its sister city, Arequipa, Peru. When you pass Bank of America Corporate Center, step inside to see the three panels of Ben

Long's first secular fresco. The first panel shows workers with gleaming golden shovels as they begin building the Bank of America building. The second, a representation of chaos and creativity, shows an unruly crowd. The third shows the calm that education and learning provide.

If you look closely, you will also see reminders of Charlotte's past, like the Latta Arcade (316 South Tryon Street), a building which began life in 1915 as both an office building and a place to grade cotton for nearby textile mills. The old Ivey's Department Store (corner of 5th and North Tryon Streets) now serves as luxury condominiums. The Merchants and Farmers Bank building (123 South Tryon Street) is the city's oldest surviving commercial structure. Also look for the 1929 Ratcliffe Floral Shop (431 South Tryon Street).

At St. Peter's Catholic Church (507 South Tryon Street), turn left onto Stonewall Street. As you do, you will pass the Gantt Center. Named for Charlotte's first black mayor, Harvey Gantt, the center preserves the historical legacy of Charlotte's black citizens, which was being jeopardized by urban renewal projects.

Walk two blocks to Brevard Street. Turn left. You are now in Charlotte's Second Ward, which is sometimes called the Government Ward. Early on, this area was called Logtown due to the number of log structures that sprang up here after the 1860s emancipation of slaves. Later the neighborhood was called Brooklyn and functioned as the center of Charlotte's black community. Many of the buildings in the neighborhood were razed beginning in the 1960s and throughout the 1970s to make way for several urban renewal projects that you see now. However, a few buildings do remain, as explained below.

Cross 3rd Street and then turn left. Before turning, look for the 1920s vintage Mecklenburg Investment Company building, the first building in Charlotte planned and built by black citizens to house black-owned businesses, offices, and organizations. Next door is the Grace AME Zion Church (219 South Brevard Street), built in 1902. This church was formed when members of the Clinton Chapel AME Zion Church broke away over the issue of abstinence in drinking alcohol. Grace AME Zion's motto became "God, Religion, and Temperance," which appears in Latin on the cornerstone of the building.

Turn right onto College Street. At 4th Street, turn left to walk one block back along Trade Street to return to Independence Square.

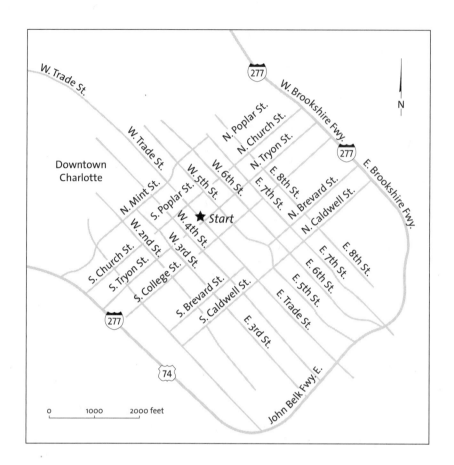

Walk Details

HOW TO FIND IT: Charlotte is located in the southern Piedmont, off
I-77, near the South Carolina border. If you are unfamiliar with
Charlotte, your best bet to navigating the city center is to go to
www.aboutparking.com and click on the link that will show you
where public parking is, as well as give a map to find your way to
the center of downtown, the intersection of Trade and Tryon Streets.

LENGTH: About 2.5 miles

SURFACE: Paved

RESTROOMS: At the visitor center (330 South Tryon)

FOOTWEAR: Sneakers

PETS: OK on a leash

MAP: See http://www.charlottesgotalot.com/maps for an online map of
Charlotte.

GOOD TO KNOW: Bank of America Stadium sits where the St. Catherine Mine, one of many important gold mines that operated in or around Charlotte during North Carolina's gold rush, once stood.

For more information about Ben Long's frescoes, see www.benlong frescotrail.org/.

To access Charlotte's public art tour, go to http://charlottein2012.com/ images/Public_Art_Walking_Tour.pdf. You might also wish to visit the Bechtler Museum of Modern Art and the Uptown Mint. You can get further information about these two museums at http://www.bechtler.org/ and http://www.mintmuseum.org/, respectively.

For information on visiting the Gantt Center, see http://www.gantt center.org/web/.

To find photographs of the Brooklyn neighborhood as it existed in the 1950s and descriptions of some of the now-razed buildings, visit www .cmstory.org and click on the African-American Community link.

For More Exploration

If this walk whets your appetite for more Charlotte history, visit the Levine Museum of the New South (200 E. Seventh Street). It highlights Charlotte's history since 1865. For more information, visit http://www .museumofthenewsouth.org/

For information about the NASCAR Hall of Fame, visit www.nascar hall.com.

Research Triangle Park

CRADLE OF NEW IDEAS

People who experience the traffic on I-40 between Raleigh, Durham, and Chapel Hill may think of Research Triangle Park only as the place where many people work. Yet the rest of the country, especially those who work in the technology or pharmaceutical industries, see Research Triangle Park as one of the most respected areas of our state. Following their professional dreams, people come from everywhere across the globe to work in RTP, the largest planned research center in the United States. Research clusters include pharmaceuticals, environmental sciences, telecommunications, computing, and nanotechnologies.

How did worn-out farmland help transform North Carolina from a tobacco-and-textiles state into a technology state ripe with entrepreneurial efforts? It didn't happen overnight. In fact, at a few critical points, it almost didn't happen at all.

Historical Context

In 1953, despite the end of the Korean War and a baby boom in full swing, life in North Carolina wasn't exactly on an upward trend. The state, eleventh in population and tenth in manufacturing, was forty-fourth in per capita income out of the forty-eight states. North Carolina had more farms than any state other than Texas, but those farms were small. Of our 288,000 farm families, only 44,000 had telephones. Over 62,000 lacked electricity. Only two television stations operated here: Channel 3 in Charlotte and Channel 2 in Greensboro. The state faced a brain drain; college graduates were leaving in droves.

Romeo Guest, a builder of textile mills in Greensboro, saw that the demand for new mills was slowing. A graduate of MIT and director of the Textile Foundation at State College in Raleigh, Guest had seen the development taking place along Route 128 outside Boston.

North Carolina didn't need to "borrow" industry, Guest suggested, as it had done when textile mills came south. Guest envisioned a place to breed new industry. One of Guest's associates, Dr. Paul Gross of Duke University, suggested a research institute where contract research could take place. Soon thereafter Guest coined a name: the Research Triangle Park. Robert M. Hanes, president of Wachovia Bank and a member of Guest's circle of associates, suggested that Guest arrange a lunch with Governor Luther Hodges.

Luther Hodges was unique as governors go: he was a business executive governor. He had retired from Marshall Field and Company in 1952 and then was elected lieutenant governor. When Governor William B. Umstead died two years into his term, Hodges assumed the helm. Lacking the political contacts of most governors, Hodges turned to his business contacts. When Guest and Hanes approached Hodges, Hodges listened. Moreover, he liked the idea: research is business, too, and it would attract industry. Hodges in turn promoted the idea and invited Gordon Gray of UNC and Hollis Edens of Duke University to get on board. About the same time, and unbeknownst to Hodges, the UNC Department of Physics had undergone an internal peer review conducted by people from Princeton and Cornell. Their advice? Strengthen the research so as to attract more scientists and industrial development.

Thus, the time seemed incredibly ripe to build what Hodges started calling the MIT of North Carolina. The initial vision was to have a research city populated by as many as 900 scientists. Word that the Southern Research Institute was forming in Birmingham, Alabama, prompted North Carolina to take action. If the Alabama facility took the lead, North Carolina would forever play catch-up in the South.

The Walk

The parking lot of the headquarters for Research Triangle Park, where this walk starts, is a good place to consider the beginnings of RTP.

On September 28, 1956, the Research Triangle Committee formed with a goal to raise $30,000 in five years to build a park—somewhere. But where? Someone proposed Camp Butner, up in Granville County: it already had the utilities, streets, and rail service. But the facility was too far from the university scientists and destroyed the notion of a "triangle." Someone suggested Umstead State Park. If the goal was to have a research park, then why not co-opt the park? But the state couldn't sell Umstead Park because it had bought the land from the federal government for $1 to use as a recreational park. Given the recent success in Raleigh and Durham agreeing to build a joint airfield, the committee believed that the farmed-out land between the two cities held potential.

With the farmland between Raleigh and Durham in their sight, Guest first tried to raise money by persuading paper companies to buy the land, operate most of it as a tree farm, and then make some acreage available for laboratories. Karl Robbins, a retired textile man (the town of Robbins is named for him), bought 4,000 acres of land and started a development company, Pinelands Incorporated. But hurdles arose, notably, stalled negotiations with Durham concerning water service. No water, no park. Moreover, scientists from state-funded universities felt queasy about participating in a for-profit venture. In addition, the recession of 1957–58 was setting in. The wondrous idea of a research park seemed destined to collapse.

From the Research Triangle Park Headquarters parking lot (12 Davis Drive), walk to Davis Drive. In 1958, the structure and leadership of the park's proponents changed. Archie K. Davis of Wachovia and George L. Simpson, a professor of sociology at UNC, re-formed the committee into the nonprofit Research Triangle Foundation. Simpson assembled a "sales" team of university professors to sell the idea of a scientific incubator. These professors talked to anyone who would listen. In sixty days, Davis and his team raised $1.5 million to acquire Pinelands stock and to found Research Triangle Institute.

At the paved greenway path at Davis Drive, turn left and walk to Cornwallis Road. Before RTP was born, only two roads existed in the area: NC 54 and Cornwallis Road. Governor Hodges allocated $150,000 to build a road to link NC 54 and Cornwallis and to celebrate Archie Davis's hard work. As you walk Davis Drive, look for a sign for the American Association of Textile Chemists and Colorists. AATCC was one of the earliest research companies to arrive in the park, as was the U.S. Forest Service. By 1961, reports were that—imagine this!!—long-range phone systems were about to connect each of the anchor cities. Though rooted, however, the research park wasn't thriving.

At the corner of Davis Drive and Cornwallis Road, turn left. Several IBM signs stand across the intersection. Their understated size belies the importance of IBM to the success of RTP.

In 1965, IBM announced that it would send thousands of people south to work in the Research Triangle Park. Jim Starnes, manager of IBM's Raleigh sales office and Luther Hodges, who had become the chairman of the Research Triangle Foundation, led the effort. Governor Dan Moore spearheaded the construction of I-40, reportedly needed so that IBMers could get to work quickly. Later that year, an announcement was made that the National Institute of Environmental Health Sciences would come to the Research Triangle Park. Their facility, on 500 acres, would employ 2,000 people.

RTP's future finally looked stable. Fourteen years later, on October 1, 1979, the *Raleigh News and Observer* ran a special supplement to celebrate the twentieth birthday of Research Triangle Park. The graphic design underscores the forward, scientific thinking taking place in RTP. A bearded man wears a hazmat suit. A young female wearing a white lab coat sits at her keyboard, her left hand displaying both an engagement ring and a pinkie ring. Tucked between the man and the woman are drawings of molecular and chemical structures, a mainframe computer, and one white rat. Perhaps none of these images rose to the popularity that NASA's "Mohawk Guy" garnered when the Mars rover Curiosity landed on the Red Planet, but they nonetheless spoke to a new world of work. Stories inside the supplement celebrate the salaries well-paid workers were earning. One story notes that bagels had arrived in area grocery stores! A picture of William Bennett shows the new director of the National Humanities Center sporting sideburns that Sonny Bono would have been proud of.

When you arrive at Institute Drive East, look left for a crosswalk and a sign designating Hanes Road, honoring Robert M. Hanes. Walk to the crosswalk and cross Institute Drive. Look through the trees for a sign signaling the offices of the USDA Forest Service Southern Research Station. Note that the U.S. Forest Service is within eyeshot of an IBM sign. This odd pairing of organizations is one of the few details in the park that speak to the park's beginnings.

Cross Institute Drive–West and follow the greenway to the headquarters sign for Research Triangle Institute, another of RTP's early arrivals. As you continue walking Cornwallis, look for another building, one quite unlike anything you usually see. The building? The original Burroughs Wellcome Building that today houses some, but not all, GlaxoSmith-Kline workers. For a time, this building symbolized the bright future RTP offered. Designed by Paul Rudolph, a former dean of architecture at Yale University, the architecturally bold building sports structural columns set at 22.5 degree angles. Fred Coe, then-president of Burroughs Wellcome, wanted the design to inspire forward thinking, which it certainly does. The building is so visually striking that when it served as a backdrop for the movie *Brainstorm*, a 1983 sci-fi thriller starring Natalie

The distinctive Burroughs Wellcome Building, now home to GlaxoSmithKline, is but one building in Research Triangle Park where workers explore the shape of the future.

Wood, it caught the attention of many who saw the movie—and convinced some movie-goers to seek jobs here.

At Alexander Road, turn around and retrace your steps to the parking lot. On the way back, note the diversity of businesses here: healthcare, technology, chemical and materials research, biotechnology, environmental science. More than 157 organizations are part of the 7,000-acre RTP community. Over 40,000 people work in RTP, in companies big and small. Nearly a third of the companies in the park have substantial global operations. The area is so rich with accomplishment that RTP now houses the home office for Sigma Xi, a scientific research society founded in 1886 to honor the work of more than 65,000 scientists. That's quite a transformation of a workforce that began with AstroTurf, one of the first scientific products created in the Research Triangle Park.

Walk Details

HOW TO FIND IT: Research Triangle Park is located off I-40 between Raleigh, Durham, and Chapel Hill. Park in the lot of the Research Triangle Park Headquarters (12 Davis Drive), in the heart of the original area of Research Triangle Park. Davis Drive connects I-40 to NC 54. This out-and-back walk traverses the oldest part of RTP.

LENGTH: About 4.5 miles

SURFACE: Paved

RESTROOMS: None

FOOTWEAR: Sneakers

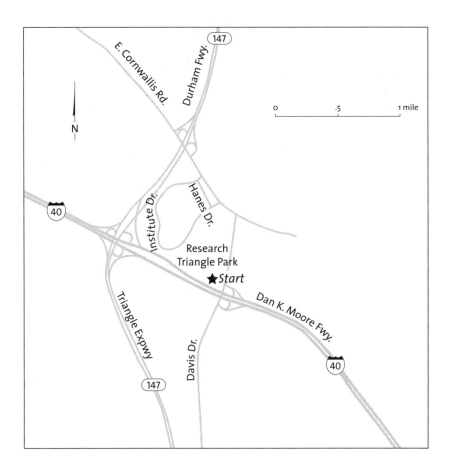

PETS: OK on a leash

MAP: Available at www.rtp.org

Beware: Watch for lush poison ivy at trailside. Be mindful of traffic when crossing streets.

GOOD TO KNOW: Research Triangle Park boasts over 14 miles of trails, so if you see a greenway and a place to park your car, get out and walk.

For More Exploration

Before you depart, you might like to walk Davis Drive to the right down to NC 54 to visit the RTP Commemorative Park. There, behind the facade signaling the entrance to RTP, several markers list the companies that have arrived, and continue to arrive, to do business here. You just might find your next employer emblazoned on the granite.

Our Favorite Export
NASCAR AND THE OCCONEECHEE SPEEDWAY

The beginning of motorsports may have been humble, but the impact the sport has had on North Carolina is huge. A study produced by the UNC Charlotte Belk College of Business Administration, *North Carolina Motorsports Economic Impact and Development Study*, put the total economic impact of the motorsports industry at just over $5 billion in 2003. At the time, the motorsports industry supported over 24,400 jobs. Moreover, between February and November each year, hundreds of thousands of people across the United States—and in 150 other countries—watch, either in the stands or at home via television, forty or so professional drivers race their cars around an oval at a very high rate of speed. As NASCAR writer Neal Thompson once observed, "try driving anywhere and not seeing NASCAR devotions glued to a car."

To walk—not drive!—the only surviving speedway from NASCAR's inaugural 1949 season, visit Historic Occoneechee Speedway in Hillsborough. Operating only until 1968, the track welcomed many of the fathers and grandfathers of drivers we root for today. It also welcomed Sarah Christensen, one of NASCAR's first women drivers. It is the third speedway to be placed on the National Register of Historic Places (the other two include Indianapolis Motor Speedway and the Bonneville Salt Flats).

Historical Context

Was NASCAR a natural outgrowth of the male competitive spirit? Or was it the natural outcome of the collision between the mass manufacturing of Fords and the rise of Prohibition? That's hard to say.

Certainly running moonshine figures heavily into NASCAR roots. When Junior Johnson, whom *Sports Illustrated* named in 1998 the greatest racecar driver of all time, spent time in an Ohio jail for running 'shine, then, yes, it's fair to say that NASCAR and moonshine share history. It's also hard to overlook stories about how Dawsonville, Georgia—home of NASCAR driver Awesome Bill Elliot—was a source of moonshine for Atlanta during Prohibition. Then there's the 1958 Hollywood

Climb the stairs to explore the old grandstand at the Occoneechee Speedway, one of the original "fast tracks" of NASCAR.

classic *Thunder Road*, which immortalized the driving skills of men who ran 'shine.

Yet before the Eighteenth Amendment attempted to curb drinking habits by outlawing the businesses that made, transported, and served alcoholic beverages, being in the distillery business was perfectly fine. In Salisbury alone, some sixteen distilleries operated into the late 1800s. Many of North Carolina's most prominent early political leaders ran distilleries. But as life changed from agrarian to industrial, drinking habits changed too: they rose. Prohibition was the response.

Meanwhile, Ford Motor Company was rolling cars off assembly lines, and men were discovering the car's racing potential. Could they make a business out of that potential? Bill France collected like-minded men in a hotel in Daytona, Florida, to answer that very question: was it possible to collect a winner's purse from something other than "pass the hat" contributions from curious spectators?

France was not the only one trying to answer that question, but he benefited from a flash of linguistic brilliance in naming his new baby. Among the names he considered was NCSCC, the National Champion Stock Car Circuit. Unfortunately the resulting pronunciation didn't sound very appealing: *Nic-Sic*? At one point the group considered calling the public face of the sport the Czar, but headlines about the Berlin airlift nixed that idea. How much better, then, was the name that stuck: National Association for Stock Car Auto Racing, or NASCAR. And why not entitle the public face the *Commissioner*?

Sixty drivers entered, and fifty appeared for, the first NASCAR race, held February 15, 1948, at Daytona Beach. Fourteen thousand spectators paid $2.50 to watch a race that became the stuff of legends. Atlanta native and World War II tail gunner Robert "Red" Byron won the race even though he had a permanently injured right foot and had to have his left foot fixed to a stirrup which was attached to the clutch. Byron won in a 1939 Ford owned by Raymond Parks, a convicted moonshiner.

That first season, fifty-two NASCAR races took place at twenty tracks. Originally a horse-training track, Occoneechee Speedway hosted its first race on June 27, 1948. Promotion hype was thick. Jack Horner, sportswriter for the *Durham Morning Herald*, quoted Al Jennings, Bill France's publicity man, as saying that the race will "be the greatest stock car race the fans have ever seen . . . and if you don't believe it's a thrill, you should come see for yourselves and be convinced."

Did the first Occoneechee race deliver the thrills? You bet. Winner Fonty Flock drove sixty-eight laps on the one-mile dirt oval in a 1939 Ford, reaching up to 120 miles per hour on the straightaways. Two cars went over the dirt wall in the second turn on lap fifty-two, and Thilbert Pierce, who flipped his car in the second lap, came back and continued racing, going off the track again in the home stretch.

In those days, cars fell into a "modified" stock division, meaning that the cars likely had parts that weren't original or standard to the car. World War II had caused a shortage of auto parts, and Bill France didn't think fans would appreciate new cars crashing when they were driving prewar rattletraps. By 1949, however, France decided that the war was enough of a memory and that parts were more plentiful so as to warrant a "strictly stock" car race. Predictably, as soon as the "strictly stock" moniker appeared, so did cheating. The first driver caught cheating was Glenn Dunnaway from Gastonia. In Charlotte, on June 19, he drove a Ford that had "spread" springs. Spreading the springs was a moonshiner's trick to help decrease a car's wiggle in the back end.

The *Charlotte Observer* race headline from that day speaks to shrewd promotion back then: "Woman Driver Tests Skill with Men Today in Stock Car Event." From the beginning, women competed with the men. Louise Smith wanted to race so badly that she acquired an engine, hid it in the trunk of the family car, and headed to Daytona. Later she said that France let her enter the race because he knew it would put fans in the seats. Did the fans turn out for the Charlotte race that June? Of course. It attracted 22,000 people who paid between $2.50 and $4.00 to watch thirty-three drivers. (To keep gatecrashers at bay, lore states that France strategically posted signs indicating that rattlesnakes lurked outside the track.) And did NASCAR deliver a show? Absolutely! Sara Christian drove with the men, and Lee Petty flipped his car—his neighbor's sedan, which Petty had borrowed—in the 107th lap. As for Lee Petty, he and his family had to hitchhike back home. What an impression was made that day on Petty's sons, Richard and Maurice, who would become big names in the sport.

Time proved Bill France right: people would pay to watch a race. The number of races each season rose. In 1949, NASCAR held eight sanctioned races; in 1950, nineteen; in 1951, forty-one. In 1950, the first 500-mile race took place in Darlington, South Carolina. Johnny "Madman" Mantz won it.

NASCAR was on its way to becoming a much-beloved sport. The nicknames of early racers—Fonty, Soapy, Speedy, Fireball, Cannonball, Crash—gave the sport its distinctive flavor. (NASCAR's Norm Froscher says Fireball's nickname came from sandlot baseball, not racing, but most NASCAR fans likely prefer instead to believe that Glenn Roberts earned his nickname in a fiery crash.) Fans loved the will, the daring, and the quirky personalities of the early drivers. Once, at Occoneechee Speedway, Louise Smith went airborne in the second turn. Rescuers needed thirty-six minutes with an acetylene torch to cut her out of the car. In 1952, Wendell Scott, a black racer from Danville, Virginia, broke the color barrier in NASCAR. Tim Flock raced with Jocko Flocko, a rhesus monkey, for eight races in 1953. Though popular with the fans, Jocko retired after a race in Raleigh. Recalled Flock, "During the Raleigh 300, Jocko got loose from his seat and stuck his head through the trap door . . . he went berserk! Listen, it was hard enough to drive those heavy old cars back then under normal circumstances, but with a crazed monkey clawing you at the same time, it becomes nearly impossible! I had to come into the pits to put him out. . . . The pit stop cost me second place and a $600 difference in my paycheck."

From the beginning, race fans felt like they were part of the race: the noise thundered in their heads, and dirt flung into the air by the cars spattered those sitting near the track. Unpredictable machinery increased the thrills. Wheels came off. Radiators burst, spewing steam everywhere. Suspensions might do anything due to the speed. At a race in August 1951 in Detroit, the front office "suits" were embarrassed to see how frequently mechanical failure occurred. But they also came to understand a pointed sales mantra: "Win on Sunday, sell on Monday."

Over time, cars became more reliable and drivers more knowledgeable. Tracks evolved, too. In 1959, twenty-seven of forty-four races were on dirt tracks. By 1969, only five of fifty-four races took place on dirt tracks. On September 15, 1968, Occoneechee Speedway saw its last NASCAR race. Richard Petty won it in a 1968 Plymouth, averaging 87.6 miles per hour. The next year, a newer superspeedway, Talladega, supplanted the Occoneechee track.

Despite the growth, NASCAR wasn't yet a mainstream sport. That metamorphosis occurred on February 18, 1979. A blizzard marooned millions of East Coast residents at home. CBS had already decided to televise the Daytona 500 live in its entirety. (The Indianapolis 500 was broadcast on tape delay.) With nothing else better to do, thousands tuned in to watch the season's first race.

They were not disappointed, and to this day, people still talk about that race. Early in the race Cale Yarborough and Donnie Allison spun each other out into a water-logged infield. On the last lap they battled again, repeatedly smashing into each other as they jousted to lead the final lap. Screeching sideways across the track, hitting the wall, and bouncing into the infield, the two men raced hard. Finally their two cars stopped. Then, a third car stopped: Bobby Allison wanted to see how brother Donnie was. Suddenly the three were out of their cars, swinging fists and helmets, pummeling each other in the mud. Richard Petty, racing against his doctors' advice, crossed the victory line first, one car length ahead of Darrell Waltrip. Fans, old ones and new converts alike, couldn't have asked for a better show.

NASCAR grew into the behemoth that it is today. Charlotte, and indeed North Carolina, became synonymous with NASCAR even though the business headquarters is in Daytona, Florida. In 1990, when Hollywood portrayed NASCAR as nothing but a redneck stereotype in the movie *Days of Thunder*, people were angry. Driver Alan Kulwicki complained, "I don't think they did us justice. They portrayed us like we're running bumper cars." Dale Earnhardt was so angry about the movie portrayals that he wouldn't even discuss it.

Today, NASCAR is anything but the province of rednecks. At North Carolina State University, many mechanical engineers participate in Wolfpack Motorsports, a student-run organization that designs and builds different forms of racecars and then competes in annual collegiate contests sponsored by the Society of Automotive Engineers. At UNC Charlotte, sophomore-level mechanical engineering students can apply for admission into the motorsports engineering curriculum. At the historically black Winston-Salem State University, students can enroll in a motorsports management curriculum. (Ironically, the Bowman Gray track in Winston-Salem is where Wendell Scott first tried to compete in a NASCAR race.) In Mooresville, students enroll in NASCAR Technical Institute, which opened in 2002. The Richard Petty Driving Experience, based at Lowe's Motor Speedway, takes many a skeptical person and turns him or her into a fan. I know, because it happened to me: after hurtling around the track at 167 miles per hour, I can assure you that the sport is for real.

The Walk

Walk at least one lap to study the construction techniques of the early tracks. Remnants of the safety fence still remain. Note, too, how close the track is to the Eno River and how low the walls are in the turns. Use the wooden stairs at either end of the track to traverse the dirt embankments. Go over to observe the walls from outside the track. Their height is more impressive from that vantage point than from inside the track. If you're curious to see what Mother Nature can do over 40 years or so, look at the infield. When races took place here, the in-field was completely devoid of trees.

As you lap the track a time or three, consider the excitement of those early races. On August 7, 1949, Sara Christian lost her right front wheel here. During that same race, Tim Flock lost a wheel and went over the wall. Fireball Roberts looked like a sure win for both that race and the season, but his engine gave out in lap 126. Movie star Jayne Mansfield was the guest of honor in 1963.

Walk Details

HOW TO FIND IT: Historic Occoneechee Speedway (320 Elizabeth Brady Road) is located off US 70 East, outside downtown Hillsborough in central North Carolina. Park in the lot and follow one of the mowed paths that lead to the track. In about half a mile, you'll reach the track, where you can then walk as many laps as you want.

LENGTH: 2 miles total, 1 mile of which is the track

SURFACE: Pine straw and leaves

RESTROOMS: None

FOOTWEAR: Sneakers

PETS: OK on a leash

MAP: Available at the signboard

GOOD TO KNOW: A clip of the 1979 Daytona 500 race fistfight is available on YouTube: http://www.youtube.com/watch?v=MXbHQtZH8dE.

Important Firsts

America's First State University
to Hold Classes

THE UNIVERSITY OF NORTH CAROLINA

Without doubt, North Carolina founding father William R. Davie stood tall among his peers. A native of Halifax, Davie served under George Washington. Later he served as Nathanael Greene's commissar, grumbling about being a "purveyor of beef and bacon." His orderly at the time was Andrew Jackson, a future president. Davie earned a degree from Princeton, studied law in Salisbury, represented North Carolina in the Constitutional Convention of 1787, served as the tenth governor of North Carolina, and served on a Peace Commission to France in 1800 at John Adams's request. And that's only a part of the man's résumé.

But few people remember any of those details. What they often remember is that Davie led the effort to establish a university that grew from the seven graduates taught by one professor in the class of 1798 to a school enrolling over 28,000 students taught by nearly 3,000 faculty, and worthy of its global stature. To see what happens when people fight for big ideas, walk the old section of campus, where Davie's magnificent legacy took shape.

Historical Context

In 1776, North Carolina founders wrote Article 41 of the North Carolina Constitution stating that North Carolina should have a university: "All useful learning shall be duly encouraged and promoted in one or more universities." But a war was at hand, and the effort ended. Thirteen years later, in 1789, William R. Davie resurrected the effort to charter a university; on December 11, 1789, the legislature approved Davie's bill.

With the bill approved, much work lay ahead. Just as state founders jousted over where to put the state capital (see chapter 8, Raleigh), they squabbled over where to put the university. They considered several towns: Hillsborough, Pittsboro, Smithfield, Williamsboro, and Goshen. Interestingly, as Joel Lane worked his deal to sell land for the soon-to-be-established state capital in Raleigh, he also angled to sell land for the university.

James Hogg, a Hillsborough resident, proved a better angler. Not only was Hillsborough roughly the center of the state—New Bern and Morganton are about 145 miles from Chapel Hill—but Hogg also convinced local landowners to donate 1,386 acres. Between the lure of donated land and Willie Jones's recommendation that the university be located with fifteen miles of New Hope Creek, the founders decided to put the university on a ridge where the road that ran from Petersburg, Virginia, to Pittsboro crossed the road that ran from New Bern to Greensboro. That place? New Hope Chapel Hill. Because only a thick forest stood on that high ridge, the founders also provided for a little village to support the university. Thus, the school and the town of Chapel Hill were a twin birth. The twenty-four, two-acre town lots fetched a handsome total of $3,000, seed money to build a university. Within six years, the University of North Carolina opened.

The Walk

This walk traverses the original part of campus.

From the Morehead Planetarium (250 East Franklin Street), walk toward Franklin Street. Follow the stone wall that borders campus and look for one of the several sidewalks that lead from Franklin Street into the quad. Turning left, walk to the Old Well, the heart of the original campus. When you reach the well, the street in front of you is Cameron Avenue. The Pittsboro-to-Petersburg road crossed New Hope Chapel Hill somewhere in the quad. Although the old roadbed has been lost, records indicate that the fourth campus building, Person Hall (right of the quad about midway between Franklin Street and the Old Well), once fronted the old road. Of the three buildings that opened in 1795— Old East, Stewards Hall, and the President's House—only Old East still stands.

Walk around the Old Well and face it, with Cameron Avenue behind you and Old East to your right. Davie's handprint abounds on campus. A Freemason, Davie laid the cornerstone of Old East on October 12, 1793 (it faces Cameron Avenue), placing inside it a brass plate to commemorate the event. In addition, Davie helped select the man who would initially comprise the entire faculty: David Ker, an immigrant from Ireland, whose starting salary was $300 a year. Davie wanted the school

The Old Well is the symbol of the University of North Carolina.

to focus on science, and as late as 1824 having theatrical performances on campus required written permission from three faculty members, ironic given the creative contributions of famous UNC alumni such as Thomas Wolfe, Paul Green, and Andy Griffith.

Old East, the oldest state university building in the nation, gets its name from its orientation to the sun. As was the habit of the day, important buildings faced the rising sun, a practice called "Orientalization." Both the North Carolina State Capitol and the U.S. Capitol face east.

Sometime between 1865 and 1875, Old East was vandalized and Davie's brass plate stolen. In 1916, however, the plate surfaced in a pile of scrap brass to be melted down by a foundry in Tennessee. The owner of the foundry, a UNC alumnus, saw the brass plate, recognized Davie's name, cleaned the plate, and returned it to the university. Today the

North Carolina Collection Gallery, housed just south of here in Wilson Library, guards it.

As you face the Old Well, look back toward Franklin Street. At a distance about the length of a football field beyond the well stands a large poplar tree—the Davie Poplar. It leans slightly. Lore says that Davie tied his horse here when he walked to one of the nearby creeks for water and announced, "This is it," referring to the site for the campus. Whether the story is true or not, UNC preserves the lineage of the Davie Poplar with other, younger Davie poplars grown from seeds or cuttings from the original tree.

Richard Dobbs Spaight, North Carolina's eighth governor, opened UNC on January 15, 1795, announcing to the public that "youth disposed to enter the University could come forward with the assurance of being received." Hinton James, the story goes, was the first youth so disposed. He arrived for class February 12, 1795, having walked the 150 miles from Wilmington. But he had to wait a few weeks for a class of young men to collect itself. One of the earliest students to enroll was Archibald Murphey, whose education plan survives. If Murphey's class load was typical, UNC students studied Latin, Greek, Aesop's fables, Virgil, Horace, Homer, arithmetick, rhetorick, geometry, trigonometry, conick sections, fluxions, natural philosophy, and lots of composition, theses, and declamations.

For twenty years Old East *was* UNC. As many as fifty-six students boarded there, four to a room. Students were rowdy: they kept whiskey kegs in their rooms and suffered the occasional penknife stabbing. Pranks were common, a favorite being to nail the classroom doors shut. Once, students attempted arson on a trustee's house. Room rent was $5 a year, and for this princely sum, students got a table and a bedstead. They had to provide their own mattresses, wood, candles, and washing stands. Servants brought the young men two buckets of water a day, one in the morning and one in the afternoon, from the Old Well.

Stewards Hall, the second building, no longer stands. If it did, it would be located in the middle of Cameron Avenue to the right of Old East. Stewards Hall was a dining hall, and, yes, complaints about campus food were legion. Meals were spartan: breakfast was milk or coffee and tea and one warm roll or, perhaps, cornbread and butter. The midday meal was bacon and turnip greens, sometimes accompanied by fresh meat or fowl and puddings and tarts. Students ate supper when the faculty prescribed it; usually it was coffee or tea or milk and bread or a biscuit, no butter. One letter home from two brothers indicated that "the meat generally stinks, and has maggots in it." Students occasionally hunted possums or sought meals with villagers to compensate. Some credit the bad food with inciting the Great Secession, a week-long student revolt in the spring of 1799.

South Building, behind you across Cameron Avenue, took sixteen years to build and prompted much controversy. Federalists, who thought the building too big, called it the "Temple of Folly." As construction plodded along, students living in Old East built study huts inside the unfinished shell. Finally, with the proceeds raised from a lottery, the building was finished. Behind South Building, where today students enjoy a shaded quad that stretches south to Wilson Library, open field lay. Union forces occupied South Building in the spring of 1865. Today it houses the Office of the Chancellor and other administrative offices.

From this core of buildings, the campus developed. Old West, left of the Old Well, opened thirty years after Old East. With two dorms, the students split into two debate societies. Students from eastern North Carolina formed the Philanthropic Society. They lived in Old East. Old West housed the Dialectic Society, made up of students from western North Carolina. Familiar North Carolina names populate the Di-Phi rosters: James K. Polk, Thomas Hart Benton, Thomas Bragg, William A. Graham, Thomas Clingman, Samuel Ervin Jr., John M. Morehead, Zebulon B. Vance, David L. Swain, Luther Hodges, Frank Porter Graham, Charles B. Aycock, J. C. B. Ehringhaus, William B. Umstead, Bryan Grimes, Elisha Mitchell, and Albert Coates, just to name a very few. The two societies gave Carolina its colors when the Dialectic Society adopted blue, the color of honor, and the Philanthropic Society chose white to signify truth and virtue. When football arrived at UNC in the 1880s, students knew that Wake Forest had adopted black and gold as their colors and that the University of Virginia used blue and orange. Posthaste, the two societies made their blue and white UNC's colors.

In 1897, UNC president Edwin Alderman invested $200 to replace the rustic original with the elegant, domed-roof version of the Old Well that you see today. A Greek shrine in the gardens of Versailles inspired him.

Return to Franklin Street, walking on the left side of the quad past Person Hall, the original campus chapel. Thomas Person, a university trustee, donated $1,050 in silver dollars to the campus (see chapter 8, Raleigh, for more information about Thomas Person). Here, students attended sunrise and sunset prayers daily and religious services on Sunday. Person Hall was also the first site of graduation ceremonies. For a short while, Person Hall served as the town hall for Chapel Hill. Here in 1831 William Gaston gave his graduation address condemning slavery, thirty years before the Civil War. Before you leave the building, look for the two stone gargoyles. They come from London's Big Ben.

The walk across the quad, formally known as McCorkle Place, is one of North Carolina's most beautiful strolls. In the early days, however, this area was "forbidden ground." Any student who crossed it had to pay a fine either to the Dialectic or Philanthropic Society. The two societies used the money they collected to buy books. Early on, the two societies had a better collection of books than did the library.

Look for a marble obelisk, the Caldwell Monument. This monument honors the first president of UNC, Joseph Caldwell. It does not, however, mention the nickname students gave him: "Diabolus." Apparently Caldwell was diabolically clever at catching students misbehaving. He also was responsible for changing the course of study at the university from the scientific one Davie wanted to a more classical program like that of Princeton. Just beyond the Caldwell Monument stands the Unsung Founders Memorial, honoring the enslaved and free people of color who helped build the university. Silent Sam, a third monument nearer Franklin Street, honors UNC's Civil War dead.

Pettigrew and Battle Halls stand on the left. James Johnston Pettigrew, an 1847 graduate, served as a brigadier general in the Confederate army. He led a charge up the left side of Cemetery Ridge at Gettysburg. The losses in Pettigrew's division were staggering: only 80 men of 800 survived the charge. A week later, Pettigrew died from wounds received during the Confederate retreat. Battle Hall honors Kemp P. Battle, a UNC president. Among Battle's many contributions is an exceptionally detailed, two-volume history of UNC.

At Franklin Street, use the crosswalk to reach the post office. Step inside to view two large murals that commemorate the laying of the cornerstone in Old East and the auctioning of lots in the village of Chapel Hill. In the auction mural, note the white square in the upper-right corner, a replica of the original town map of Chapel Hill.

Recross Franklin Street, and turn right to walk west to Columbia Street. At the corner of Franklin and Columbia Streets, turn left and walk back toward campus. Look on your left for Abernethy Hall, named for the first physician to attend to university students.

Murals in the post office depict some of the founding history of Chapel Hill.

At the corner of Cameron and Columbia Streets, look right to the Carolina Inn. Somewhere near here sat the original New Hope Chapel. Note how the inn resembles a plantation house. This is intentional, the result of a 1940s renovation that sought to present an image of tradition to allay fears that UNC professors were soft on communism. Also note the low dry-stack stone wall to your left. Elisha Mitchell, one of UNC's early professors, assumed landscaping duties around the school. Among his improvements were low stone walls to keep town livestock from wandering onto university grounds. These walls are not Mitchell's original walls, though later in the walk you'll pass some that are. (See chapter 31, Mt. Mitchell State Park, for more information about Elisha Mitchell.)

Turn left onto Cameron Street. The first home for UNC presidents sat to the left, roughly where Swain Hall sits today.

Swain Hall honors David L. Swain, North Carolina's twenty-sixth governor and UNC's third president. Swain's legacy is mixed. Students reportedly liked him; he was more lenient than Caldwell. Plus, he was serious about beautifying the campus. He was also instrumental in improving the university's library, in forming the Historical Society of North Carolina, and in preserving documents from UNC history. Were it not for the Civil War, his legacy might have been all positive. Against seceding from the Union, he nonetheless surrendered Raleigh to General Sherman. Then his daughter married the Union general who commanded the troops that occupied Chapel Hill. Moreover, during his term as university president, state support of the university dwindled due to the pressures of war. In 1862, a professor's salary was sixty barrels of flour. By the spring of 1865, it was down to four. Postwar economic troubles and Swain's diminished popularity further decreased enrollments for the university. The class of 1865 graduated fifteen students, only four of whom showed up for the ceremony. Thirty-five Union soldiers guarded them.

When Swain Hall first opened, it served as the dining hall. Apparently, the food wasn't much better here than it was in Stewards Hall; students nicknamed the building "Swine Hall."

The original name of Cameron Avenue was College Avenue. Paul C. Cameron, a student who did not graduate, loaned money to the university and gave the school two rows of maples to line the street. Today's maples along Cameron Avenue are mostly new plantings, but a significantly gnarly maple on the left almost in line with a crosswalk just beyond Swain Hall is thought to be one of Paul Cameron's original trees.

Cross Cameron Avenue. As you do, look for Phillips Hall. In 1938, when the university's engineering program was moved to North Carolina State College (today's North Carolina State University), a prankster put a tombstone in front of Phillips Hall proclaiming the death of the curriculum.

Walk to Memorial Hall, the second such structure in this spot. The first Memorial Hall, built in 1885 with bricks from the penitentiary, sported a German look. The auditorium had horrible acoustics, however, and became a gym in 1895. Eventually, the building was razed and rebuilt. The bronze book monument outside Memorial Hall contains the names of war dead who graduated from UNC, beginning with the Civil War and continuing to the Persian Gulf and Bosnia.

Across Cameron Avenue stands New West, home to today's Dialectic Society. In the late 1800s, students engaged in several notable hoisting pranks. At one point students hoisted a two-horse wagon to the top of New West. On another occasion, the village hearse was found on top of the Old Well. Inside the hearse was a coffin, and inside the coffin was a keg of beer.

From Memorial Hall, walk to Gerrard Hall. Gerrard Hall, opened in 1837, served as the second site of graduation ceremonies. A serious panic occurred there in 1846. The building was full of people; someone heard something snap. Thinking that the packed upper galleries were collapsing, people tried muscling their way out. No one was hurt, and the only explanation later offered for the sound was that perhaps someone heard a breaking tree limb outdoors. Nonetheless, when the 1847 graduation ceremonies took place, the gallery had been strengthened. The last class to graduate here was the class of 1884. One student's memoir notes that "academic mortality" was high that year: the class had ninety-seven members, but only sixteen received degrees that day.

Past Gerrard Hall, turn right to walk by the right side of the Campus YMCA Building. From the beginning at UNC, religious instruction was mandatory. However, in 1907, compulsory chapel services for students were deferred to the YMCA, which had been active on campus since 1860. The YMCA was the site of the first movie showing in Chapel Hill.

Walk through the quad past Hanes and Gardner Halls, angling left in front of the beautiful Wilson Library. Given the stateliness of the quad, it's hard to believe that when the university was new, this area was open field. Wilson Library, home to the North Carolina Collection, is a premier repository of state information. To visit the UNC Bell Tower, walk out and back between the Wilson Library and House Undergraduate Library across South Road.

Walk left past the Pit. If the Old Well serves as the heart of the campus, the Pit serves as the voice. No matter when you cross the Pit, you'll see copious remnants of student activity and communication.

After crossing the Pit, turn right and walk between the bookstore and the Student Union down the steps to South Road. At South Road, turn left to Country Club Road. Look for Woollen Gym and Carmichael Arena, where UNC began building its claim as the one of the best basketball programs in the country.

Look, too, for the Old Chapel Hill Cemetery, a final resting place for both white and black North Carolinians. Buried here are Charles Kuralt, Frank Porter Graham, Horace Williams, and William Coker.

When you reach the intersection of South and Country Club Roads, you might enjoy stepping into the Knapp-Sanders Building, home to the School of Government, where a collection of murals depict our state's history. An explanatory brochure is available at the reception desk.

At the corner of Country Club and South Roads, observe the ridge upon which the university is built.

Turn left onto Country Club Road and walk to where Country Club meets Raleigh Road and Cameron Avenue. The forested area to the right across from Playmakers Repertory is Battle Park. This wooded area, all that's left of original campus acreage, looks generally the way it did when William Davie and company climbed the ridge and explored the area. Kemp Battle, UNC's fifth president, created several trails through the area so that students could enjoy the forest.

At the intersection of Raleigh Road, Cameron Avenue, and Country Club Road, cross Raleigh Road. Then turn right to cross Cameron Avenue. Use the gravel path (not the trellis path) to walk through Coker Arboretum, where 580 species of trees and shrubs create a most serene spot. This ground was once a boggy pasture where faculty grazed their livestock. Dr. William C. Coker, the university's first botany professor, transformed the bog into a study garden with a university budget appropriation of $10 and one gardener. The garden won renown in 1923 when it was named the sixth-best medicinal garden in the country. Though the medicinal plant collection is no longer a feature of it, the arboretum is a pleasure to visit every season of the year. When the gravel path runs into another path, turn left to walk toward the trellis and emerge from Coker Arboretum at Davie Hall.

Walk to Cameron Avenue and turn right. Pass Davie Hall, and then cross Cameron Avenue. Look for a building that looks like a Greek temple. What look like standard Corinthian columns decorated with acanthus leaves are, in fact, columns styled of Indian corn and tobacco. Smith Hall, the building's original name, served as the university ballroom, the law school, a library, and a chemistry lab. Interestingly, the Michigan 9th Calvary stabled its horses here in the waning days of the Civil War.

At the Old Well, cross Cameron Avenue and return to Franklin Street. Past Alumni Hall, turn right toward the planetarium. Then walk diagonally past the sundial and through the rose garden. At Franklin Street, turn right and walk to the intersection of Franklin Street, Raleigh Street, and Hillsborough Street. Look for Spencer Hall. Named for Cornelia Phillips Spencer, Spencer Hall was the first dormitory for women. Spencer secured her place in UNC history when she climbed South Building on March 20, 1875, to ring the bell when the university reopened after the Civil War. (Some historians attribute the story about Davie tying his horse to the poplar tree to her.) Sitting diagonally across the intersection of the three roads is a small, somewhat exotic building, the first

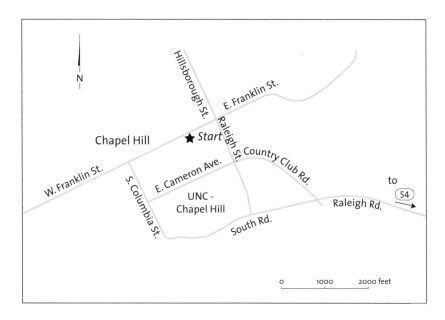

home of UNC's Law School. Note, too, the low stacked-stone wall. This is one of Elisha Mitchell's walls, although it has been restacked a time or two since the early 1800s.

Return to the parking lot at the planetarium. Many of UNC's accomplishments, such as North Carolina Memorial Hospital having created the country's first intensive care unit, sometimes go unnoticed. However, one of UNC's most prominent legacies stands before you in the form of the Morehead Planetarium. John Motley Morehead made his biggest scientific discovery in 1891, when he discovered calcium carbide. From this discovery came the creation of the acetylene gas industry and Union Carbide Corporation. From that success came wealth that found its way all over North Carolina by way of the Morehead Scholarship Foundation, which has supported over 2,700 students as they have pursued their degrees at UNC. These merits scholarships were the first of their kind in the country. Today the prestigious scholarship is known as the Morehead-Cain scholarship.

Walk Details

HOW TO FIND IT: Chapel Hill is located off I-40 in central North Carolina. After exiting onto Airport Road/Martin Luther King Jr. Boulevard, drive to the intersection of Columbia and Franklin Streets.

Turn left onto Franklin Street. The Morehead Planetarium (250 East Franklin Street), where you can park, is located on the right.

LENGTH: About 3.5 miles

SURFACE: Sidewalk

RESTROOMS: At the UNC Visitor Center, located on the side of the Morehead Planetarium

FOOTWEAR: Sneakers

PETS: OK on a leash

MAP: Available at the visitor center

BEWARE: Traffic on Cameron Avenue

GOOD TO KNOW: To celebrate University Day, visit here on October 12.

For more particulars about those buried in the Old Chapel Hill Cemetery, see www.ibiblio.org/cemetery/.

Gold!!!!!

REED GOLD MINE

The United States of America finally had a source of native gold when the nuggets discovered in the rolling Piedmont hills east of Charlotte became publicly known in 1802. North Carolina's importance to the Union soared, and the discovery of gold helped to further meld the new, sometimes balky, states into a country. Though we had a Constitution and a political system that was finding its legs, the lack of a standard currency system seriously hindered our country's ability to conduct commerce. A barter economy went only so far.

Robert Morris, a Pennsylvania Whig and one of America's first financiers, suggested a currency system in 1782, soon after the Revolution ended. But Congress didn't create the U.S. Mint in Philadelphia until 1792. Some founders fought the creation of a single currency because having such a tool smacked of Federalism, which they thought resembled too closely a monarchy. Moreover, they needed to work through many details. What would we call our currency? How would we divide it? Would it be like the Spanish eighths or would it be a decimal system? What would the coins look like? How much gold or silver would the coins contain? What was the punishment for counterfeiting?

Most important, however, was where the United States would find precious metals for coinage and to back the printed paper. Because of a John Dunsmore painting entitled *First Coinage Inspection*—it shows a seated Martha Washington surrounded by President Washington, Harry Voight (the first chief coiner), Thomas Jefferson, Secretary of the Treasury Alexander Hamilton, David Rittenhouse (the first director of the U.S. Mint), and others—historians believe that the United States' first coins were made from silverware that George and Martha Washington gave to the country. Thus, when John Reed took the large, yellow rock his son had found to a silversmith in Cabarrus County in 1802 to see what it was, the question of where the country would get precious metal from was answered: the country would get gold from North Carolina. Between 1802 and the Civil War, estimates indicate that North Carolina's total gold production ranged between $55 and $65 million.

Historical Context

In this day of debit cards and electronic transactions, it's almost impossible to believe how localized and fraught with problems our country's early commercial system was. Citizens bartered amongst themselves, determining relative value between livestock, vegetables, whatever. Colonial governments issued bills of credit from time to time, but those documents were easily forged, in part because they were handwritten. In North Carolina, the punishment royal governors exacted on forgers was severe: they had to publicly stand in the pillory for two hours and perhaps even have their ears cut off and nailed to the pillory. A second offense meant execution without benefit of clergy.

Even when printers received royal approval to print such documents, as James Davis did when he moved from Virginia to New Bern in 1749 to serve as royal printer, people were suspicious: just what, exactly, backed the printed paper? Citizens also feared the paper itself. The smallpox epidemic in New Bern in 1779 shifted the printing of bills of credit to Walker Davis of Wilmington because people were afraid that the pox contaminated the paper printed in New Bern. Yet against this backdrop of political debate, fear, and suspiciousness, an amazing story unfolded. In 1799, John Reed, an illiterate farmer in Cabarrus County, went to church while his son Conrad played hooky from services. (Reed, whose original name was likely Johannes Reith, was a deserter from the Hessian forces King George III hired to fight in the Revolution.) While shooting fish with a bow and arrow in Little Meadow Creek, Conrad found a seventeen-pound yellow rock. He brought it to his father, who used it for a doorstop for three years.

In 1802, John Reed took the large, yellow rock to a silversmith in Cabarrus County to see what it was. The silversmith didn't know. Reed then took his rock to Fayetteville, where a silversmith there recognized it and asked Reed to name a price. Reed did: he asked $3.50. The silversmith paid the tiny sum, and Reed left to buy some coffee beans and a dress for his wife. When Reed returned home, his friends chided him for his stupidity. Reed returned to Fayetteville to plead his case. The silversmith reportedly gave Reed $1,200. Reed returned home and began a life of farming in the spring and summer and mining in the winter.

Reed used the Placer method—stream panning—to mine, and he continued finding gold dust and nuggets in the stream. Then, in 1803, one of Reed's slaves found a twenty-eight-pound lump of gold. Reed then formed a business with two other partners. Word of the discovery

The machines used in mining may look fierce, but the rewards were sweet when miners found gold.

eventually reached Thomas Jefferson. William Thornton, architect of the U.S. Capitol, tried to buy land in the area. The landowners wouldn't sell.

By 1804, the U.S. Mint in Philadelphia had processed $11,000 of Cabarrus County gold, and the United States was seriously able to stand, financially speaking, on its own. A gold rush was on, and North Carolina received another nickname: The Golden State.

The Walk

Leave the Visitor Center, turn left, and cross Little Meadow Creek. Squint to see if you see any gold; between the time Conrad found the first nugget in 1799 and 1826, Little Meadow Creek produced $200,000.

Walk past an area called the Potato Patch. Between 1803 and 1825, people throughout Anson, Cabarrus, Davidson, Gaston, Guilford, Randolph, Rowan, Stanly Mecklenburg, Montgomery and Union Counties mined for gold by panning and digging. In 1821, the General Assembly asked

Denison Olmstead, a professor at UNC and close friend to Elisha Mitchell, to produce the state's first Geological and Mineralogical Survey for the Board of Internal Improvements. Because gold was being found in streams, Olmstead posited that gold was here due to a Great Flood.

In 1825, Matthias Barringer discovered that gold often appeared with quartz. His discovery gave rise to vein mining. Vein mining, or lode mining as it is sometimes called, required more manpower, machinery and, therefore, investment. Mining transformed into a full-fledged business, though John Reed wouldn't start vein mining until 1831.

Bear left to walk Upper Hill. Look for an engine shaft, 110 feet deep. The shaft had multiple uses: the first was to hoist men and gold-bearing, fist-sized quartz rocks via a device called a whim. (Seeing the device brings new meaning to the phrase, "on a whim.") It also provided a pumping function for a steam pump, should the hollowed out earth flood. As you walk to the remains of the engine house, home to a 50-horsepower steam engine, look for open shafts. No fewer than 15 shafts covered this area, along with several cabins that housed miners. Nearly 500 feet of tunnels lie beneath your feet. Also, notice the lush tree cover. When mining was active, this area was almost completely devoid of trees.

Also, keep a sharp eye for other unused paths that appear to intersect the path you're on. When the mines were operating, roads crisscrossed the area, and if you aren't watchful, it's easy to start walking them.

Between 1830 and 1850, more people mined in North Carolina than farmed. One reporter wrote that over 20,000 men speaking 13 different languages had come to the state to mine. As you descend Upper Hill, you will pass by some of the implements miners used to extract the metal—stamp mills, Chilean mills, and arresters, as well as explanations of the devices.

Descend to Lower Hill. Say you're a private citizen like John Reed and that you have found a 10 pound nugget of gold. What happens next?

The U.S. Mint in Philadelphia offered assay services. You could hire someone to take your nugget to Philadelphia, risking potential theft. Of course, you would have to wait for payment if the person you hired remained honest. Or you could go to Philadelphia yourself. A stagecoach ride reportedly cost between five and ten cents a mile, cheaper than today's cost per mile, but expensive in the day. But if you go, you're not mining. You're riding in a stagecoach, hoping that no one robs you. If robbers appear, you hope that the stagecoach driver is armed and good with his gun.

Wonder how much gold still remains in the shafts of Reed Gold Mine?

Into this business dilemma came two men, Christopher Bechtler and Andrew Jackson. Bechtler opened a private mint in Rutherfordton in 1831, strategically located between the North Carolina and Georgia gold mines. Bechtler's private mint made beautiful money, in part because he bought gold from Georgia mines. (Gold was discovered near Dahlonega in 1828. Georgia gold made very shiny coins and North Carolina gold made somewhat duller ones.) When Bechtler's coins drew the attention of the United States government, the U.S. Government learned that Bechtler coins had more gold in them than did U.S. coins. For some time the U.S. Government turned a blind eye to the private mint because the Philadelphia mint simply couldn't keep up with coinage demand.

By 1835, however, the country could no longer tolerate the private mint, and President Andrew Jackson signed legislation to open a US Mint in Charlotte, only 30 or so miles away from the North Carolina gold mines. By 1838, the Charlotte mint was producing coins with more gold in them than the Bechtler mint was. The 678 half eagles—at a face value of $5.00—are among the most collectible coins in America. Together the two North Carolina mints coined over eight million dollars before the Civil War.

At Lower Hill, you'll see the Ten-Stamp Mill, a Mechanical Engineering Landmark. This timber and cast iron behemoth was made at the Mecklenburg Iron Works.

Ore arrived at the mill via cart. Two 750-pound stamps, falling at a rate of 35 times a minute, crushed the rocks into dust. (Imagine the noise this action would cause.) Seventy-two gallons of water were needed every hour to help float the dust and to allow mercury to bind with gold to make an amalgam. A nearby marker indicates where Peter, Reed's slave, found the 28-pound gold nugget in 1803.

Descend Lower Hill and return to the Visitor Center. John Reed died in 1845, a wealthy man. Family inherited the mine but failed to make a profit. The mine changed hands several times, bought finally by the Kelly family in 1895. Soon thereafter a nugget once again made news. A 17-pound nugget, valued at $4866, was found just three and one-half feet beneath the surface of the ground. Nonetheless, the returns from the mine were usually small. In addition, gold fever had moved from California north to the Klondike. Excavation work dwindled, the last taking place in 1912.

Reports vary as to just how extensive gold mining was in North Carolina. Most generally agree that by 1830, at least 56 mines were operational. Other reports indicate 300 mines in 34 counties. Whichever number is right, or even close, the presence of gold mines helps explain how nearby Charlotte became the second largest banking center in the United States.

Walk Details

HOW TO FIND IT: Reed Gold Mine (9621 Reed Mine Road) is located in Midland, in central North Carolina. From NC 49, south of Concord, turn south onto US 601. Take NC 200 when it splits left from US 601. Signs point the remaining turns. In Locust, at the intersection of NC 24/27 and NC 200, turn north onto NC 200. Again, state historic site signs point the remaining turns.

LENGTH: About 1.5 miles

SURFACE: Sand, gravel

RESTROOMS: At the visitor center

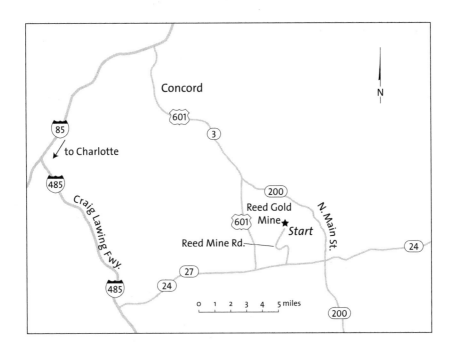

FOOTWEAR: Sneakers

PETS: OK on a leash

MAP: Available at park office

BEWARE: Heed warnings to stay on the trail. The ground is rumpled due to the effects of mining. Twisted ankles are a real possibility, and while unlikely, mine collapses are possible. On February 18, 2000, what is believed to be an abandoned mine shaft of the Phoenix mine collapsed in the yard of a home built on a golf course community in Cabarrus County.

GOOD TO KNOW: Reed Gold Mine is open Tuesday through Saturday. Spring and summer hours are 9 A.M. to 5 P.M.; fall and winter hours are 10 A.M. to 4 P.M.

The visitor center provides an underground tour of a shaft and shows a film of mining techniques. You can also pay a nominal fee and pan for gold.

The Charlotte Mint Museum, 2730 Randolph Road in Charlotte, is home to coins minted in Charlotte.

In May 2008, divers found Charlotte-minted coins in the SS *New York*, a shipwreck off the Louisiana coast; their value is thought to be worth $50,000 to $100,000 each.

Mt. Mitchell

NORTH CAROLINA'S FIRST STATE PARK

Why visit Mt. Mitchell, the mountain the Cherokee call *Black Dome?* Let Locke Craig, the North Carolina governor who led the effort in 1914 to transform the area into our first state park, explain why: "When on top of Mt. Mitchell, you feel that you are in a lofty altitude and amid the mighty upheavals of the primeval ages of the planet. Geologists tell us that this is the oldest land on earth. . . . Before Abraham, this mountain was. It was old when Sinai was built. It was dry land when Noah's deluge swept over Asia, for the waters did not rise above this summit. . . . Mitchell's best view is at sunrise. In the light of Dawn the world of mountains seems to rise out of the darkness of the infinite abyss; the chambers of the East are hung with crimson and cloth of gold, for the Majesty of Day is approaching with his escort of splendor."

And you thought the only reasons to come here were to escape the heat of July and August and to smell the fragrant evergreens, didn't you?

Historical Context

Does a dramatic landscape provoke human drama? In the case of Mt. Mitchell, it does.

The human drama seems to have started in 1803 when André Michaux asserted that the Black Mountains were the highest range in the United States. In 1828, Elisha Mitchell seconded Michaux's assertion. Mitchell was to be taken seriously: he was a Connecticut Yankee preacher who had joined the faculty at the University of North Carolina in 1818 to teach mathematics and natural philosophy. In 1835 and 1838 he returned to verify his measurements.

Despite Mitchell's scientific standing, the controversy wasn't over. The citizens of New Hampshire were convinced that Mt. Washington was higher than Black Dome. So, Mitchell measured the peak again in 1844—this time with better instruments—and decided that, yes, Black Dome was the highest peak in eastern America.

The controversy surrounding the mountain appeared over until 1855, when Thomas Clingman publicly asserted that Mitchell was

Seen from the Blue Ridge Parkway, Mt. Mitchell rises above the other peaks in the Black Mountains.

wrong. Clingman, Mitchell's former student, was not without standing himself. After graduating from the University of North Carolina in 1832, he began a meteoric political rise, serving in the North Carolina House of Commons in 1835, the North Carolina Senate in 1840, and the U.S. Congress in 1843. Some historians have dubbed Clingman the "Prince of Politicians." In addition, Clingman was an accomplished outdoorsman.

Thus, in 1857, Mitchell went to measure the peak again. On the morning of June 27, he struck out alone. A thunderstorm caught him and apparently caused Mitchell to fall to his death. Found several days later in a deep pool at the base of a waterfall by Big Tom Wilson, a hunting guide, Mitchell was buried on July 10, 1857, in Asheville. Within the year, citizens demanded that Mitchell be buried on the mountain that claimed his life. The highest peak in the eastern United States thus became a destination for those who wanted to honor Mitchell's life and accomplishments. In 1881, when the U.S. Geological Survey verified Mitchell's measurements yet again, Black Dome got a new name: Mt. Mitchell. Controversy and drama seemed truly to be over.

In 1910, however, another sort of drama started. Two groups were eyeing the area eagerly. Local citizens wanted to build a toll road to open the famous mountain to more tourism, as had happened at Mt. Washington. Lumbermen itched to log the magnificent fir and spruce trees. When the two groups joined forces in 1911, the pace of events quickened—breathtakingly so.

Some people thought that building a railroad and hauling out the trees would be a ten-year project, but they were wrong. Jeff Lovelace, author of *Mount Mitchell: Its Railroad and Toll Road*, notes that the railroad, which was both a passenger rail and a lumber hauler, opened a mere two years later on July 22, 1913, to the grand rhetoric of Governor Locke Craig who proclaimed, "This is the beginning of magnificent things."

The *Asheville Citizen* disagreed. S. Kent Schwarzkopf, author of *A History of Mt. Mitchell and the Black Mountains: Exploration, Development, and Preservation*, notes that an editorial appeared in August bemoaning the deforestation taking place across western North Carolina: "Think of it! Within another twelve months the magnificent forests of spruce and balsam on the slopes of Mt. Mitchell, the highest point east of the Rockies, 6711 feet and the pride of the entire eastern section of the United States will fall before the axe of the lumbermen to be turned into money!"

By 1914, thousands of trees were felled. Camp Alice, a tourist area about a mile below the summit, accommodated 250 people in the dining room, and the dining room was frequently full. Fortunately, Craig had evidently experienced a serious change of heart. Speaking to the North Carolina Forestry Administration, he issued a call to action: "when I looked around, where I had been bear hunting as a boy, and saw this vast desolation all below . . . I felt like a man that stood amidst the ruins of his home after the conflagration had destroyed it."

Was Locke Craig the right man at the right time with the right skill set to become active in preserving the environment? Perhaps. A native of Bertie County, Craig enrolled at UNC at age fifteen, the youngest student in the school at the time. While there, Craig distinguished himself as an orator and was elected commencement speaker. Later he enrolled in law school at UNC, and by 1883, at age twenty-three, Craig was living in Asheville, working first as a schoolteacher and then later practicing law. Surrounded by the natural beauty of Asheville, Craig fell in love with the out-of-doors.

When a local citizen, J. W. Dunn, wrote to Craig in June 1914 about how rapidly the lumbermen were felling trees on the west side of the range and how he, Dunn, was working to convince them to suspend operations, Governor Craig responded the next day to say that he was interested in joining the fight.

In his biennial message to the legislature in January 1915, Craig painted a bleak picture and asked the General Assembly to protect what was left of the original forests of the Black Mountains: "The lumberman is now denuding the mountains—mowing down their luxuriant coverings as the reaper mows a field of wheat. After him sweeps the conflagration, turning once magnificent slopes and peaks into a vast desolation of blackened ruin. We cannot expect the lumberman to sacrifice his individual interest to the public welfare. The State must exercise her power by proper regulation to save the forests."

The legislature agreed. By March 31, G. P. Deyton, a House representative from Yancey County, was leading the commission to buy out Pearley and Crockett, the lumber company. Nonetheless, acquiring the land had opponents, as an editorial from the *Asheville Citizen* shows: "It is greatly to be regretted that certain senators and representatives of the eastern section of the state fought the Mount Mitchell purchase bill with all of the energy they could summon." Yet the bill passed, providing $20,000 to buy the land. By 1916, the state owned a long, narrow, 525-acre tract at the top of the Black Mountains.

Ten thousand people visited Camp Alice between mid-May and mid-October that year to celebrate the action. Two years later, the state acquired more land, as it would again in 1935, 1962, and 1969. In 1947, the second-highest mountain in the Black Mountain range was named Mt. Craig. The railroad became a toll road, but eventually the state built a free road to the top so that anyone who wanted to make the trip could.

Today, the primary drama taking place here occurs when you walk the trails and marvel at the splendid views.

The Walk

Enough hiking trails traverse Mt. Mitchell State Park to delight even a frequent visitor. By putting together parts of these trails, you can create a moderately challenging loop hike of about seven miles. If you're not interested in an all-day excursion, hiking the Commissary Trail is the easiest of the hikes described below. If you want a somewhat-harder hike, but still not an all-day hike, opt for the Old Mitchell Trail, which will take you to the summit of Mt. Mitchell.

Increment 1: Commissary Trail

This easy, two-mile gravel trail, marked with orange diamonds, departs the Park Office at Stepp's Gap along the old railroad bed and toll road that once carried logging trains and passenger cars to Camp Alice. It provides stunning views of Pisgah National Forest as it snakes around the edge of the Black Mountain range. Look for Table Rock and Hawks-

Stepp's Gap, where gorgeous mountain views and cooling breezes prevail, is home to the park office for Mt. Mitchell State Park. Don't forget to take a jacket when you visit!

bill Mountain, two very distinct formations, to the east at Linville Gorge. This trail loses about 360 feet of elevation, meaning that if you use this trail for an out-and-back walk, your return trip will be a gradual uphill walk. Nothing remains of Camp Alice but a stream that once provided water.

Increment 2: Camp Alice Trail to the Intersection of the Old Mitchell Trail

This rigorous, half-mile uphill climb is one of the two oldest trails in the park. Hiking under the blackness of the fir and spruce trees helps you understand why these mountains are called the Black Mountains! Breathe deeply as you ascend the summit to enjoy the aroma of fir and spruce. Keep in mind as you hike up the slope that Elisha Mitchell did so at age sixty.

Increment 3: Old Mitchell Trail up to the Summit of Mt. Mitchell or down to Stepp's Gap

One-half mile up, the Camp Alice Trail intersects the Old Mitchell Trail, the other original trail in the park. To the right, the Old Mitchell Trail climbs steeply another half-mile to the summit. To the left, it descends about a mile and a half to return to the park office. At the summit, you can enjoy the views from the fifth Mitchell Observation Tower, opened in 2009. The first memorial to Elisha Mitchell was a bronze obelisk, which stood from 1888 until 1915. The second memorial was a wooden tower. In 1926 a stone, castle-like tower served as the third monument. The fourth Mt. Mitchell tower was built in 1960.

Increment 4: Summit Parking Area to Mt. Craig

Another increment you can add to your hike is the first mile of the twelve-mile Deep Gap Trail, which lies in the original section of the park and is the highest trail on the East Coast. If you arrived at the summit from the previous three increments, you can then follow the short footpath from the observation tower to the parking lot and walk past the concession area to the picnic area, where the trail begins. In addition to hiking on the rooftop of North Carolina, this increment lets you traverse Mt. Craig, where the views, especially in the fall, are stupendous. (If your legs feel lively, you can trek on to Big Tom, a peak that honors the guide who found Mitchell's body after his tragic fall. Be aware, however, that going to Big Tom adds two more miles to your hike.)

Increment 5: Old Mitchell Trail to the park office

From the summit parking lot, the Old Mitchell Trail descends two miles to the park office, bypassing the restaurant and the campground. Near the park office, the trail emerges from the cover of fir and spruce trees to an open area. When you reach this area, look straight across the mountain to the radio towers. First, find the road to the towers. Then look down and to the right to a less-distinct break in tree cover. This break is the remnant of the Big Tom Wilson Motor Road, a toll road that ascended Mitchell's peak from the Yancey County side.

Walk Details

HOW TO FIND IT: Mount Mitchell State Park (2388 NC 128) is located in Burnsville, 33 miles north of Asheville off the Blue Ridge Parkway at mile marker 355.
LENGTH: Varies according to the increments you choose
SURFACE: Gravel, roots, small boulders
RESTROOMS: At the park office and at the summit concession area
PETS: OK on a leash
MAP: Available at park office

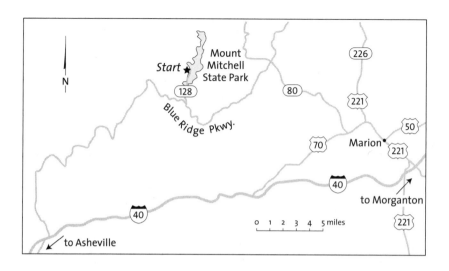

FOOTWEAR: Boots, especially if you hike any section other than the
  Commissary Trail
GOOD TO KNOW: Employees say that wildlife viewing is good along the
  Commissary Trail.

If you walk any trail other than the Commissary Trail, you might appreciate a hiking stick.

If time permits, drive the Blue Ridge Parkway north to Mt. Mitchell
overlook, milepost 350. From here you can see the crest of the Black
Mountains, almost from beginning to end.

In the 1920s, logging company Pearley and Crockett gave more than
100,000 fir and spruce seedlings to reforest the slopes of Mt. Mitchell.
Some are the trees you see today.

A New Profession for America

FORESTRY ALONG THE SHUT-IN TRAIL

Driving the mountain roads to see the leaves in the fall and stopping at overlooks along the Blue Ridge Parkway to feast your eyes on the interlocking, tree-covered ridges in the summer is a favorite pastime in North Carolina. To celebrate a man who played a significant role in creating the mountain vistas we love today, Gifford Pinchot, walk along the Shut-In Trail.

George Washington Vanderbilt made a simple but powerful decision as he contemplated how best to restore the acreage surrounding his stunning mansion, Biltmore House. The decision? To heed the advice of Frederick Law Olmsted. The advice? Hire then-unknown forester Gifford Pinchot and do more than beautify the grounds nearest his mansion. As Pinchot built a nursery, an arboretum, and a systematically managed forest to show the entire country what professional forest management could accomplish, he also built his résumé as well as the case for establishing the United States Forest Service, of which Pinchot served as first chief. Today the Forest Service manages over 193 million acres, including 155 national forests, 20 national grasslands, and 222 research and experimental forests.

Historical Context

Say "George W. Vanderbilt" and most people think Biltmore House. The Beaux Arts centerpiece of Vanderbilt's 125,000-acre estate is indeed stunning, especially the gardens and surrounding vistas.

But pictures taken of the estate before the house was built show a barren landscape. Forlorn tree stumps riddle the ground because farmers had girdled trees, causing them to die in place. (Girdling involves cutting a groove or notch into the trunk of a tree to interrupt the flow of sap between the roots and crown. It makes the tree look as if a beaver had started gnawing the tree but then quit. The purpose is to lessen the burden of removing heavy, sap-laden trees.) After the trees died and were removed, the space they occupied was usually called a "deadening."

Frederick Law Olmsted, the father of American landscape design, had already helped transform a treeless, rocky swampland into Central Park and Boston's noxious Back Bay Fens into a jewel in the string of parks known as the Emerald Necklace, so Vanderbilt sought him out to restore the beauty of his estate. But Olmsted encouraged Vanderbilt to a bigger purpose, recalling his conversation with Vanderbilt this way:

Vanderbilt: I have brought you here to examine it and tell me if I have been doing anything foolish.

Olmsted: What do you imagine you will do with all of this land? [At the time Vanderbilt had acquired 2,000 acres.]

Vanderbilt: Make a park on it I suppose.

Olmsted: You bought the place then simply because, from this point, it had a good distant outlook. If this was what you wanted you have made no mistake. There is no question about the air and none about the prospect. But the soil seems to be generally poor. The woods are miserable. . . . It's no place for a park.

Knowing that Vanderbilt was a man of substantial means, Olmsted then pointed out that "such land in Europe would be made into a forest; partly, if it belonged to a gentleman of large means, as a preserve for game, mainly with a view to crops of timber." Olmsted further indicated that forestry would be "a suitable and dignified business" for Vanderbilt to engage in. Moreover, it "would be of great value to the country to have a thoroughly well organized and systemically conducted attempt in forestry made on a large scale."

At the time, forest preservation was in its infancy. Historian Harold Pinkett notes that as early as 1864, George P. Marsh, an American diplomat, had warned, "it is certain that a desolation like that which has overwhelmed many once beautiful and fertile regions of Europe, awaits an important part of the territory of the United States, unless prompt measures are taken to check the action of destructive causes already in action." In describing the state of Vanderbilt's property, as well as the potential it had, Olmsted was describing the devastation of forests across America. Traditional timbering practices had destroyed so much.

In addition, the idea of returning beauty to people's lives was the zeitgeist of the day. American cities had grown exponentially during the latter half of the nineteenth century, as had the tenements. But the soulless tenements had prompted the idea of city beautification: if a city had elements that harkened to agrarian, natural beauty, then people would be happier to live in the city and continue their increasingly industrial lives. Olmsted championed this grand idea.

The idea that natural beauty had restorative powers manifested itself in other ways, both expected and surprising. It gave rise to the national park system, beginning with Yellowstone in 1872, and inspired a national tree-planting day, beginning in Nebraska with Arbor Day. Visionaries clamored for walking trails so people could enjoy the out-of-doors. But in 1890, not a single acre of public or private land came under systematic forest management.

During the Gilded Age, wealthy Americans such as Vanderbilt traveled to Europe to emulate the European aristocracy with regard to building and furnishing their estate homes. Olmsted's suggestion that Vanderbilt incorporate European ideas with regard to his private forests hit the mark. But neither Vanderbilt nor Olmsted was a forester. Whom, then, to hire? Olmsted suggested Gifford Pinchot, the son of a friend. Olmsted assured Vanderbilt that Pinchot would serve "with a degree of zeal that you could not expect from anyone else."

A New Englander, Pinchot had boldly gone with his education where no American had gone before. Forestry was not a recognized profession at the turn of the century; indeed, some considered it impractical. But Pinchot determined to make it acceptable and respected. He had already turned down an offer to work with Amos Eno, his grandfather, a wealthy real estate developer in New York City, because he considered forest conservation a higher calling.

On October 15, 1891, Vanderbilt and Pinchot met. In his diary, Pinchot later wrote, "Evening talk with V. about forest management in which he seemed to consider it certain it would be introduced, & spoke of building a distillery for wood acids etc. Has big ideas, anyhow."

Vanderbilt liked what he heard, and on December 6, 1891, extended the invitation to Pinchot to take charge. In February 1892, for a salary of $2,500, Pinchot began proving that forest-conservation practices could be both good for the forests and profitable. Later in his memoirs, Pinchot recalled his association with Vanderbilt and Olmsted this way:

> Mr. Olmsted was to me one of the men of the century. He was a quiet-spoke little lame man with a most magnificent head. . . .
> his knowledge was far wider than his profession. . . . George was

a lover of art and of the great outdoors, a slim, simple, and rather shy young man, too much and too long sheltered by female relatives, enormously rich, unmarried, but without racing stables or chorus girls in his cosmos. Biltmore was his heart's delight. To his very great credit, considering his association and his bringing up, he had a real sense of social responsibility and was eager to do more than merely live on his money.

Summarizing the moment, Pinchot acknowledged, "here was my chance."

The work wasn't easy, but Pinchot was inspired. Plus, he had Vanderbilt's full support: "Mr. Vanderbilt recognizes as fully as I do the educational value of the work and is disposed to do everything to give that side of it prominence and force." He also remarked that "North Carolina happens to be so situated that the Northern and Southern floras meet within the State. There is no other state in the union where so many of the valuable kinds of trees are to be found." Pinchot endured long days and later noted, "with my only technical advisers 3000 miles away across the ocean, it is not surprising that after many a hard day in the woods, I spent anxious hours over my French and German textbooks, when I ought to have been in bed."

Pinchot's work in turn inspired Vanderbilt. Soon Pinchot was roaming the surrounding woods, advising Vanderbilt about buying acreage on and near Mt. Pisgah and the Pink Beds. In August 1892, Pinchot wrote in his diary about going to see the new tract. Much of this acreage would become today's Pisgah National Forest, the first national forest in the eastern United States. Vanderbilt evidently valued his association with Pinchot; eventually he would address the man as "Dear Brother Pinch."

By 1893, Pinchot had proven his point about forest management: he netted Vanderbilt a profit of $1,200.56 after selling the timber in a market where he competed with farmers using traditional methods. Seeking to make Pinchot's accomplishments public, Vanderbilt asked Pinchot to distribute 10,000 of the pamphlets Pinchot had taken to the 1893 Columbian Exposition. The pamphlets contained the first formal illustration of scientific forestry. An editorial in *Garden and Forest*, the first American journal to address the new fields of horticulture, landscape design, and forestry, said that the Biltmore pamphlet "must be considered a most important step in the progress of American civilization as it records the results of the first attempt that has been made on a large scale in America to manage a piece of forest property on the scientific principles which prevail in France, Germany and other European countries."

Pinchot's star was rising, and by 1895, he had assumed the national stage. Serving as the first chief of the United States Forest Service, Pinchot worked for President Theodore Roosevelt, consolidating the federal government's fragmented attempts at forestry into the U.S. Division of Forestry. In 1923, Pinchot was elected governor of Pennsylvania. On June 15, 1949, the United States honored Pinchot's contributions by renaming the 1,407,791-acre Columbia National Forest in Washington the Gifford Pinchot National Forest. As for Olmsted, the work he did at Biltmore was his last great project; Olmsted died in 1895.

To replace himself at the Vanderbilt estate, Pinchot recommended that Vanderbilt hire Dr. Carl A. Schenck. A young forester from Germany, Schenck established the Biltmore School of Forestry, training over 300 professional foresters, sometimes known as the "Biltmore Boys." The one-year course of study was practical, focusing on silvicultural theory (the practice of controlling the establishment, composition, and growth of stands of trees to produce timber, pulp, energy, fruits, and fodder) and field training in forest management. The school remained open for about fifteen years. Today, the North Carolina State University Department of Forestry and Environmental Resources, the oldest forestry program in the United States, uses the 245-acre Carl A. Schenck Memorial Forest in Wake County as one of its many teaching forests.

In February 2007, a press release from the North Carolina Forestry Organization summarized the importance of the forestry industry to the state. The release noted that over 100,000 people worked in forest products, earning annual wages of $3.6 billion from the more than 17 million acres of forests.

In 1908, journalist Day Allen Willey wrote a story for *Broadway Magazine* about Vanderbilt. In the article, titled "The Greatest Estate in America: What George W. Vanderbilt Has Done for Himself and His North Carolina Farming Neighbors in Building His Vast Mountain Estate," Willey rhapsodized:

> The Vanderbilts ignore New York's smart set as they do the curious public, and the one who has their sesame must not only be a friend, but have done something. . . . he cares nothing for fox hunting, steeple chasing, or any of the horsy sports, and has no stable except of riders and drivers for his guests. He thinks little

of shooting. In his splendid library he spends much time reading. He is a student of Nature and when around the estate is continually suggesting ideas where the forester or landscape gardener may improve this or that vista. . . .

Their [the Vanderbilts] ability, their energy, their loyalty have made Biltmore the greatest country seat in America. But best of all, they themselves prove that a man of riches can thus spend his wealth and do a great uplifting educational work that pays in other coin than thanks.

The Walk

Pinchot's diary shows that he remained in contact with Vanderbilt after he left and notes that on November 30, 1896, he stayed at Vanderbilt's Buck Springs Lodge, which sat not too far from today's Pisgah Inn, a pleasant stopover on the Blue Ridge Parkway. Presumably, he traveled to the lodge along the Shut-In Trail.

Thick rhododendrons overhead inspired the trail name, but the trail is anything but dark and spooky. In fact, along the section suggested below, you can glimpse Vanderbilt's mansion if the leaves aren't too thick. Because this stretch of trail parallels the Parkway—in fact, the building of the Parkway obliterated some stretches of the trail—you'll likely hear some car noise from passing motorists. You may also see local residents who like to walk their dogs. If you've never walked much in the woods, this is a great stretch of trail to begin to develop your hiking skills because, except for roots and rocks, it isn't very difficult. In spring, wildflowers are said to be abundant. Be aware that it is not out of the realm of possibility, however, to see a bear! And, if you hike here in warm weather, keep a sharp eye out for poison ivy.

The entire length of today's trail spans about sixteen miles, so if you want to add more distance to this walk, you can. However, some of those sections are more strenuous than the one noted below.

Walk Details

HOW TO FIND IT: This easy section of trail begins at Walnut Cove Overlook on the Blue Ridge Parkway (milepost 396.4, elevation 2,915 feet) and ends at Chestnut Cove Overlook (milepost 398.3, elevation 3,035). The blaze is a white hiker symbol, which is not to be confused with the white circle that signals the Mountains-to-Sea Trail.

To walk in George Vanderbilt's footsteps, enjoy a hike along the Shut-In Trail. When the trees are bare, you can enjoy long-distance views of the Biltmore House.

LENGTH: 3.8 miles, round trip

SURFACE: Woods trail

RESTROOMS: None

FOOTWEAR: Boots; hiking stick recommended

PETS: OK on a leash

MAP: Not available per se. Findable on most forest service maps relevant to the area.

GOOD TO KNOW: A few steep switchbacks ascend to and from the Parkway.

Shut-In Trail begins at NC 191 near the North Carolina Arboretum and runs to the site of the Buck Spring Lodge.

For a full history of the original trail and its location see the book *Trail Profiles: The Mountains to Sea Trail from Beech Gap to Black Mountain Campground*, produced by the Carolina Mountain Club.

For More Exploration

You might also visit the Forest Discovery Center at the Cradle of Forestry Historic Site in Pisgah Forest, reached from the Parkway by US 276

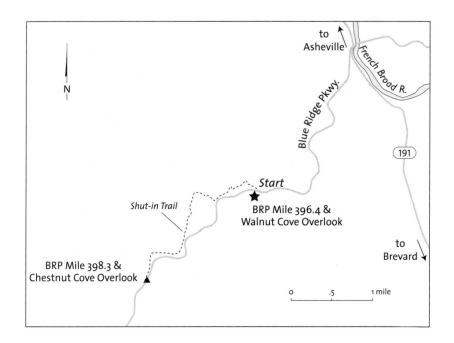

South toward Brevard. The Forest Festival Trail covers 1.3 paved miles and goes past a logging locomotive and an old portable sawmill. The one-mile Biltmore Campus Trail passes through the campus of the Biltmore Forestry School, America's first forestry school. The facility is open from mid-April until early November.

Kitty Hawk

WHERE MEN SOARED

To walk the 852 feet of the Wright brothers' fourth and longest flight on December 17, 1903, is to celebrate dogged determination. Seldom have two visionaries had such odds stacked against them. They disproved accepted knowledge, created devices to help them create a flying machine, and found the courage to leave the bounds of earth. Amazing.

The moment was magnificent for the few spectators who watched that cold December day. "They done it! They done it! Damned if they ain't flew!" exclaimed the adolescent Johnny Moore upon watching Orville fly. In that moment when Orville left the ground, life changed forever. The National Air Traffic Controllers Association says that on any given day, 70,000 flights are in the skies over America. It's almost a sure bet that these millions of people board their planes without giving a thought to the physics of flying, an ironic contrast to all of the energy the Wright brothers invested in proving that man could fly.

Did the Wright brothers see the future they ushered in? Apparently Wilbur Wright did. Speaking to the Aero Club of France in November 1908, Wilbur Wright said, "it is not really necessary to look too far into the future; we can see enough already to be certain it will be magnificent. Only let us hurry and open the roads."

Historical Context

Who flew first? Icarus and his father, Daedalus, as they tried to escape King Minos's prison with wings made of wax and feathers? Ibn Firnas, a Spanish Berber, who jumped off the minaret of the Mezquita mosque in Cordoba, Spain, in 852, sustaining, but surviving, minor injuries? Giovanni Battista Danti, who, in 1499, jumped off a roof of a church, crashing and breaking his leg? It's hard to say, in part because what constituted flying wasn't clear.

Eventually men quit trying to be birds and started thinking of machines that could fly. Leonardo da Vinci drew plans for a flying machine, but he never attempted flight. In 1783 in Annonay, France, Jean-Fran-

The shortest walk in the book is, for many, the most inspiring, for here the Wright brothers demonstrated that man could indeed fly.

çois Pilatre de Rozier and François Laurent d'Arlandes flew in a hot-air balloon made by the Montgolfier Brothers. In 1871, Alphonse Penaud flew the first powered, stable model aircraft. In 1891, Otto Lilienthal, the German "Glider King," made his successful piloted glider flight. In 1896, Samuel P. Langley watched his steam-powered model, Aerodrome Number 5, achieve sustained flight, and Octave Chanute flew a manned glider. As the 1800s ended, much progress had been made: men had successfully flown model aircraft that carried an engine but no man and gliders that carried a man but no engine.

Into this whirlwind of activity the Wright brothers were born, Wilbur in 1867 and Orville in 1871. The brothers' mechanical aptitude surfaced publicly when they worked as printers in Dayton, Ohio. Unsatisfied with presses of the day, they built better ones for themselves. When the "merry wheel" appeared and put Dayton in a frenzy over bicycles, the brothers went into the bicycle-repair business. The triangular frame, safer to ride than high-wheelers, enticed the public to ride, and soon the brothers were building custom bikes. When not repairing and building bicycles, the brothers were devouring the stories local magazines and newspapers carried about aeronautics achievements. Curiously, it was the 1896 notice of Otto Lilienthal's death in a glider crash that spurred the brothers to read all they could about heavier-than-air flying machines.

Their interest became their obsession, and within three years, the Wright brothers were writing the Smithsonian, asking Secretary Samuel P. Langley for papers published on flying. On their own, they found and absorbed everything known about the basics of lift, propulsion, and control. As they did, they wondered if what they knew about cycling had any bearing on flying. Why? Because bicycling required a rider to operate an unstable vehicle moving at a high rate of speed. And although riding a bicycle at first seems daunting—with the need to simultaneously pedal, balance, and steer—it soon becomes second nature. Could flying be the same?

They watched how birds twisted their wings to control their flight. One night in the bike shop, Wilbur twisted the ends of an inner-tube box, discovering "wing warping," the beginning of human-controlled flight. The brothers then built a biplane kite with controllable wings and observed what happened when it flew. They sought advice from Octave Chanute, a civil engineer and early aviation pioneer, who had published table data based on the experiments of Otto Lilienthal. The table contained mathematical values detailing the amount of lift and drag on various wing shapes. With this data, the brothers determined how big a wing would have to be to lift the weight of a glider. They realized they would need a headwind of at least fifteen miles per hour.

After studying wind data from the *Monthly Weather Bulletin*, published by the U.S. Weather Bureau, the brothers located William Tate, a Kitty Hawk resident, to confirm what they suspected about the weather there. Mr. Tate assured the brothers that Kitty Hawk would welcome them. Yet Kitty Hawk wasn't the Wright brothers' first choice. It was sixth on the list of the likely windiest places. However, it was remote and out of the public eye—and the sand made for a slightly softer landing than did the dirt of the other choices.

In September 1900 the brothers came to North Carolina. Wilbur came first, traveling with glider parts and lumber he had purchased in Norfolk to build wings. He was lucky to have survived the nine-day trek, which included trains, a steamer, a skiff, and a rotten, leaky, flat-bottomed schooner so rat infested that he refused to descend to the cabin. As the schooner sailed from Elizabeth City to Kitty Hawk, a storm blew in and rolled the boat until it started taking on water. Miraculously, Wilbur kept the gilder materials from sinking into the Albemarle Sound.

In late September Orville arrived, and the brothers started living in a tent. For two weeks they worked, building a fifty-pound glider they would fly as a kite. When Wilbur tried a tethered flight, he couldn't get off the ground. Something was wrong with their calculations.

Frustrated, they tested various scenarios: the machine as empty kite, the machine loaded with sand bags or chains, the machine loaded with Tom Tate, William Tate's son, a test that allowed the brothers to measure wind resistance. As they collected data, they realized that the glider wings were generating only two-thirds of the lift predicted by the Lilienthal tables. Were the tables wrong? Maybe. But how to know?

They then tried free glides from the biggest of the Kill Devil Hills, the hill where the Wright Brothers National Memorial stands today. Wilbur logged about two minutes of air time in about twelve glides, an average of ten seconds per flight. Afterward, they abandoned the craft where it landed the last time and returned to Dayton to apply what they had learned. Mrs. Tate, mother of young Tom, salvaged the French sateen wing fabric to make dresses for her two daughters.

When the Wright brothers returned to Kitty Hawk in July 1901, they continued to face frustration, with more than one test flight ending in an episode of "well digging," a reference to the small crater left by a glider impacting sand. The wing was seriously deforming under light loads, so much so that Wilbur said to Orville that "not within a thousand years would man ever fly." Still, the brothers remained determined. When Wilbur spoke to the Western Society of Engineers in Chicago later that year, he explained his undaunted attitude: "If you are looking for perfect safety, you will do well to sit on a fence and watch the birds; but if you wish to learn, you must mount a machine and become acquainted with its tricks."

Over the next year, the Wright brothers started disproving accepted wisdom by designing a wind tunnel to collect aeronautic data. Using a bicycle as their apparatus, they methodically collected enough data to prove the Lilienthal table wrong. After testing over 200 wing shapes, they decided that shape number twelve would yield the best results.

In 1902, on their third trip to Kitty Hawk, the brothers made somewhere between 700 and 1,000 glides with their new machine. Still plagued by adverse yaw—a back-and-forth motion in the tail that causes an aircraft to move like a fish—the brothers added a controllable rudder. Applying for a patent of their glider control system, the Wright brothers were confident that they would build the first airplane. All that remained now was to add power to the craft. But ten car companies turned them down. Still the Wright brothers remained resolute: they would build their own engine.

But the Wright brothers were not alone in trying to discover if man could fly. Other aviation pioneers had been busy, Samuel Langley in particular. Feeling a sense of urgency due to the Spanish-American War, the federal government had awarded Langley $50,000 to produce a piloted version of the 1896 steam-powered craft. By October 1903, Langley had built a quarter-sized model of a gasoline-powered airplane that successfully flew. On October 7, Langley publicly tested the craft. Catapulted from the roof of a houseboat in the Potomac River, the craft and its pilot dropped straight into the water like, a Washington reporter observed, "a handful of mortar." The next day, after repairs, Langley and his pilot tested the craft again. This time, it nosed straight up, flipped on its back, and again fell into the water. Having escaped death twice, the pilot, Langley's assistant, refused to fly again. Langley went back to his drawing board.

When, in 1903, the Wright brothers arrived in Kitty Hawk a fourth time with their custom-built, one-of-a-kind engine, much work lay before them. They had propellers to attach, test, redesign, and test again. They had rudders to remake. They had the engine to attach and test. They had to repair vibration damage that the engine wrought upon tubular propeller shafts. Unlike Langley, they were completely out of the public eye.

On Saturday, December 12, they tested their flying machine by running it down a track. Unfortunately, they damaged the rudder. Sons of a Methodist bishop, the boys respected their father enough not to work on Sunday. By Monday afternoon, they had repaired the craft. Then, as Wilbur tried to put the craft on the rail, he held it at too sharp an angle. The wind caught it and slammed it to the ground, damaging the forward elevator, a component that helped elevate the plane. Over the next two days, the brothers repaired the additional damage.

On the morning of December 17, 1903, the winds were blowing between twenty and twenty-seven miles per hour. The temperature was close to freezing and had produced "low-density," that is, thick, air. The Wright brothers signaled their friends at the lifesaving station (home today to a Kitty Hawk restaurant called the Black Pelican) that they needed a hand. John T. Daniels, a surfman from the lifesaving station, arrived and agreed to take pictures. Johnny Moore, a local teen, happened by. Orville set up the camera where he thought the craft might leave the ground and asked Daniels to stand underneath the drape of the glass-plate camera and squeeze the bulb when the plane left the ground. What Orville wouldn't know until later was that Daniels had never seen a camera, let alone operated one. This detail may have been the only one the brothers overlooked.

Wilbur steadied the right wingtip of the 605-pound craft. Orville climbed into the pilot's position and released the restraining wire that held the craft in place.

The airplane clacked down the rail.

Twelve seconds and 120 feet later, Johnny Moore was shouting and Wilbur asked Daniels if he got the picture. "I don't know," came Daniels's reply. Nor would they know until Christmas when the brothers returned home to Dayton to develop the negatives. Wisely, the brothers decided not to double-expose the glass plate on the second attempt.

A historic flight would be front page news the next day, right? Wrong. The Wright brothers had instructed their younger brother Lorin to deliver to the Dayton newspaper their notification telegram when it arrived. However, between Orville and Wilbur at Kitty Hawk and Lorin in Dayton were a telegraph operator and newspaper reporter in Norfolk who picked up the Wright brothers' plainly worded telegram, revising it into a wildly different story. The *Dayton Journal* reporter to whom Lorin took the simple story remarked that if the Wright brothers had flown for fifty-nine minutes, "it might have been a story." Instead, the *Cincinnati Enquirer* broke the story concocted by the telegraph operator and reporter.

Not until 1904 was the true story reported. Even then, the place of publication is unbelievable—*The Gleanings in Bee Culture*. Amos Root, a beekeeper, had heard about the Wright brothers and came to the flying field outside Dayton where the brothers had later relocated their experiments. When he saw what the Wright brothers had accomplished, he wrote in a journal he published for beekeepers that it was "the grandest sight of my life."

To date, the brothers have been awarded forty-eight medals of honor, including ones from the city of Dayton, the French Legion of Honor, the International Peace Society, and the American Society of Mechanical Engineers, as well as the Prince Albert Medal, the Langley Medal, the

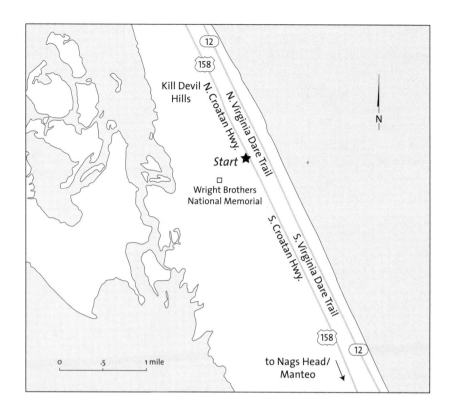

U.S. Distinguished Flying Cross, and the U.S. Congressional Medal of Honor. Not bad for brothers who did not graduate from high school.

Curiously, North Carolina has not awarded the Wright brothers a medal.

The Walk

Twenty-five years after the historic flight, three of the four original witnesses gathered to identify the point of lift-off. The National Aeronautic Association placed a granite marker to mark that spot. Begin your walk here, as hundreds of visitors to the Wright Brothers National Memorial do each year.

This walk includes all four points to which the Wright brothers flew, from the first 12-second, 120-foot distance to the 59-second, 852-foot last flight. To mimic the speed at which the Wright Brothers flew in their final flight walk the path as if you are about to miss a plane, something close to jogging speed.

Walk Details

HOW TO FIND IT: Kill Devil Hills is on the Outer Banks. Wright Brothers National Memorial is located at mile post 7.5 on US 158. The walk starts near the wooden sheds.

LENGTH: 852 feet

SURFACE: Sand

RESTROOMS: In the visitor center

FOOTWEAR: Sneakers

PETS: OK on a leash

MAP: Not needed

BEWARE: Stay on the sidewalks. The area is full of low-growing, thorny cacti that can easily pierce a sneaker as well as your foot.

GOOD TO KNOW: If you'd like to try your luck with hang-gliding, nearby Jockey's Ridge State Park is the place to try. If you decide to try, wear long pants. Landing in the sand can be painful. You can rent gear from nearby outfitters.

The Call for Civil Rights

THE GREENSBORO FOUR

Four young men enrolled at North Carolina A&T in the fall of 1959, not suspecting that five months later they, *as college freshmen*, would take a stand—actually a seat—in what would become a pivotal moment in American history.

When asked many years later about the experience, Franklin Mc-Cain, who was threatened by mail and by phone and subject to surveillance by the FBI and SBI because of the experience, replied, "I learned something early in life. February 1 taught us this: if you really want to do something you cannot wait—and we had tried—but you cannot wait for anybody else."

The moment this walk traces occurred like so many important acts: slowly and then suddenly. Nonetheless, the short walk described here taken by Ezell Blair Jr. (now Jibreel Khazan) and David Richmond of Greensboro, Franklin McCain of Washington, D.C., and Joseph McNeil of Wilmington, helped change a nation.

Historical Context

Since his early teens, Franklin McCain had been acutely aware of discrimination and of the lie that was desegregation at that time. Having been taught the same lessons as white children of the day—mind your manners, do a good deed every day, work hard—McCain saw that neither he nor his parents were reaping the same rewards as white people. "It was business as usual," he observed.

Business as usual in the late 1950s and early 1960s in North Carolina meant separate drinking fountains for the races, separate doors, separate schools that weren't really "equal" when you look at funding data, less real opportunity for work, less real opportunity for dignity.

"And I didn't think it was right," remarked McCain. "I knew in my heart what Christians did and how Christians behave and that wasn't happening. And what my parents promised me wasn't happening. And I thought, 'My goodness, isn't there any justice at all for doing what you're supposed to do? Isn't there some kind of payback?' There didn't appear to be so."

Franklin McCain found three friends who shared his point of view that democracy was not fully open to black citizens. In their dorm rooms in Scott Hall, they talked often and at length about what they saw.

Finally, on a Sunday evening, they realized that being armchair activists was no longer enough. "We owed more to ourselves than just talk," observed McCain. Spontaneously, they put together their plan. No one else was involved. "Students would sit in on our bull sessions. They were aware of the caste system, but they accepted it grudgingly. They thought, 'this is what the system is; yes, it's unjust; no, we don't like it; but what can we do about it?'"

So, said McCain, "we went on our own."

The Walk

Begin at the statue of the Greensboro Four in front of the Dudley Building on the campus of North Carolina A&T. The plan the four freshmen devised was simple: after attending classes on Monday, February 1, 1960, they would meet at Scott Hall (no longer standing) around three o'clock and then walk the short distance from the campus to F. W. Woolworth's, where they would first buy some small items. Then after making their purchases, they would sit down at the lunch counter and ask for coffee. Their logic was flawless: having been allowed to purchase something at one counter, they would ask to purchase something else at another counter, the lunch counter, a mere ten feet away.

The bronze statue of the Greensboro Four remarkably captures the moment they set out. Their clothing—ties, buttoned-down shirts, overcoats, hats—speaks also to the seriousness of their purpose. The now-famous picture published by the *Greensboro Daily Record* captures a very solemn look on the young men's faces and makes them look older than their seventeen or eighteen years.

Walk to Dudley Street, a surface street running in front of the campus. Turn left and walk to Market Street. The weather that day was cool and mild after a rainy evening the day before. As they walked, they talked very little. "The mood was serious and somber," recalled McCain in a March 2004 interview with Gloria Pitts and Gail McCain.

At Market Street turn right to walk downtown. You're following the path the four followed. Look for the ornate, seventeen-story Jefferson Stan-

When you visit the statue of the Greensboro Four, remember that these young men were only seventeen or eighteen years old when they helped change the world.

dard Building. In 1923, this building was the tallest skyscraper in the state. Note, too, the railroad tracks that served, in the 1960s, as a psychological as well as physical divide between black and white neighborhoods.

Turn left onto Elm Street. The intersection of Elm and Market Streets marks the original center of Greensboro.

Walk left to Woolworth's. Once in Woolworth's the four milled about for five, maybe ten, minutes making their purchases. Reports disagree on whether they bought toothpaste or school supplies or both. "It felt like an hour," McCain reports. Their purchases complete, with receipts in hand, the time had arrived to sit. And sit they did.

Recalling the euphoria of that moment, of doing what his conscience said to do, McCain says that he "had the most wonderful feeling of my life. . . . I had complete self-acceptance, complete peace. And all I had done was sit on a dumb stool. That's all. Nothing else."

Several conversations ensued: first between the four students and the waitress, then between the students and Geneva Tisdale, a black dishwasher; the lunch-counter manager; and, finally, a policeman who arrived about thirty minutes after the men had sat down.

The conversation fell into a repetitive loop: the four asked for service, and the waitress explained that "we just don't do that." When asked why not, the waitress replied that "it is our custom." Joseph McNeil, attempting to show that the custom was contradictory and arbitrary, offered to show the waitress the receipt he had for the earlier purchase he'd been able to make.

As the waitress left to seek help from the lunch-counter manager, Tisdale berated the students, calling them stupid and saying, "It's Negroes like you who create problems for us." When the manager arrived, more of the same took place. Finally, the manager blamed the corporate headquarters in New York for the lack of service.

When the policeman arrived, he began slapping his nightstick into his hand and pacing back and forth. The message may have been wordless, but the four heard what the nightstick said. The fate of Emmett Till, brutalized to death by white Mississippi men, hung heavily in their minds. Recalled McCain, "We weren't breaking any laws, we weren't creating any confusion. But I knew what was going to happen. I just didn't know when. I had no notions about coming back to campus on February 1. I envisioned jail—or a pine box."

What McCain hadn't anticipated was the response of a little old white lady. "I wondered what her thoughts were," mused McCain. "I was invading her space, where I didn't belong." As she left, she patted McCain's shoulders saying, "Boys, I'm so proud of you. I only regret you didn't do this ten years ago." "I had expected the very worst," said McCain, "and I got the very best."

At an impasse, Woolworth's closed for the day, and the students went home. They were, however, prepared to go the distance, "several days, several weeks . . . until something is done." That night on campus, the four tried to enlist the help of fellow students. Most of their classmates thought the story was a hoax and did not join in. "They thought we were playing a trick on them," said McCain.

Reports vary as to what happened Tuesday morning. The *Greensboro Daily Record* says that twenty students came to Woolworth's to make small purchases and try to get service at the lunch counter. McCain says that only he, two other students from NC A&T, and three white girls from Greensboro College joined in. Regardless of the number, the same quiet demand took place. The *Record* reported that the "students appeared to study." Dr. Harold Hutson, Greensboro College president, issued a statement threatening his students with expulsion if they participated in the sit-in.

On Wednesday, the numbers of students taking part grew dramatically; they occupied sixty-three of the sixty-five seats at the lunch counter.

By Thursday, with the movement showing no sign of stopping, Woolworth's president in New York City had issued a statement saying that the store would support whatever the local custom turned out to be. State Attorney General Malcolm Seawall took the predictable legal stance, saying that "no law would prohibit service to both races at a single counter, but that there was also no law that said a business had to serve anyone it didn't want to serve." On Friday, the numbers swelled to 300; on Saturday, to somewhere between 1,000 and 3,000. On Sunday, the movement spread to Winston-Salem. According to the *New York Times*, whenever the students went in, lunch-counter managers "responded with their own form of resistance: counters were closed."

On Monday, February 8, the *Greensboro Daily News* published an editorial titled "A Just and Honorable Answer," indicating that the human need to save face shouldn't stand in the way of solving the impasse. "It can be done," the paper said.

The next week, the movement spread to Durham and Raleigh. In Raleigh, forty-three people were arrested, and the *Raleigh News and Observer* called the local custom "complicated hospitality." Raleigh mayor William G. Enloe said that it was "regrettable that some of our young Negro students would risk endangering these relations by seeking to change a long-standing custom in a manner that is all but destined to fail." Claude Sitton, the *New York Times* reporter who brought the story to national attention, described the local custom of integration: the Negro was a "guest invited into the house," he said, "but definitely not to the table."

Soon the sit-in movement, which had served as a protest tactic since the 1940s, spread to Virginia, South Carolina, Florida, and Tennessee. Reports differ on exactly how many cities saw sit-ins of their own, but some list the number as high as 215.

Parents of the students were terrified for their children. "My mother said 'come home now,' and threatened to come get me," recalls McCain. It was only by daily phone calls home that McCain was able to calm his mother.

Spencer Love, CEO for Burlington Industries, stepped in, hoping to help city and university leaders find a way out; increasing tension and the specter of violence would be bad for business. A two-week cooling off period ensued between the students and the local business in

Greensboro. Still, during the next six months, students and interested others continued their sit-ins with both patience and persistence until July, when the Woolworth's lunch counter was desegregated. Other businesses came around, albeit slowly, opening their doors to black Americans. Today the Woolworth's is the home of the International Civil Rights Center and Museum. Exhibits here describe the struggle for civil rights in addition to housing the original lunch counter and stools where the four young men sat.

Retrace your steps to North Carolina A&T.

Walk Details

HOW TO FIND IT: Greensboro is located in the central Piedmont, near the intersection of I-85 and I-40. Street parking is available near North Carolina A&T, which is located just off Market Street. From I-40, exit onto Lee Street toward town. When Lee Street intersects Dudley Street, turn right. You will soon see the university and areas open for parking.

LENGTH: About 3 miles

SURFACE: Sidewalk

RESTROOMS: You can find restrooms at the Greensboro Historical Museum, 130 Summit Avenue.

FOOTWEAR: Sneakers

PETS: OK on a leash

MAP: For online maps, see http://www.greensboro-nc.gov/index .aspx?page=995.

GOOD TO KNOW: James Benson Dudley, the second president of North Carolina A&T and the man for whom the Dudley Building is named, was born a slave in 1859 in Wilmington. In addition to graduating from Shaw University in Raleigh, Dudley was principal of the Peabody School in Wilmington and served as editor of the *Wilmington Chronicle*.

To learn more about the International Civil Rights Center and Museum, visit www.sitinmovement.org.

For More Exploration

As you take the walk described above, you may want to delve further into Greensboro's history and soak in the wonderful architecture, par-

ticularly along South Elm Street. If so, consider visiting the Carolina Theatre Box Office (310 South Greene Street, one block to the right from Elm Street) where you can rent MP3 players and listen to a 90-minute recording that guides you through some of Greensboro's other historical areas. For more information, call 336–333–2605 or visit www. greensboronc.org and enter "walking tour" in the search box. The Visitor Information Center at 317 S. Greene St. (near the Carolina Theatre) can also answer questions for you. Contact the information center at 336–274–2282.

To print your own information about the downtown buildings and design your own route, visit www.greensboro-nc.gov/departments/Library/Downtown/.

If you do walk along South Elm Street, pause at the intersection of Elm and McGee Streets. This area was once known as Hamburger Square because at some point in Greensboro's past history hamburger and hot dog joints sat at all four corners. Look, too, for the old Southern Railway Building (400 South Elm Street) and Fordham's Drug Store (514

A stop at the Greensboro Historical Museum, housed in the 1892
Presbyterian Church is certainly worth the time.

South Elm). One interesting story from Fordham's Drug Store concerns Coca-Cola. In 1913, a salesman tried to persuade Dr. Fordham to sell the stuff. Dr. Fordham sipped it—and decided it would never sell.

If you walk north along Elm Street from the Woolworth's, you will approach the Greensboro Historical Museum, housed in what was the First Presbyterian Church, built in 1892. Collections inside the museum highlight the Greensboro sit-ins as well as such Greensboro and Guilford County notables as O. Henry and Dolly Madison.

Sources

Generally Used Sources

Crow, Jeffrey, Paul D. Escott, and Flora J. Hatley Wadelington. *History of African-Americans in North Carolina*. Raleigh: Division of Archives and History, North Carolina Department of Cultural Resources, 2002.

Grundy, Pamela. *A Journey through North Carolina*. Salt Lake City: Gibbs Smith Publisher, 2008.

John Locke Foundation. North Carolina History Project. www.northcarolinahistory .org/North Carolina Business History. www.historync.org.

North Carolina Department of Cultural Resources. Office of Archives and History. www.ah.dcr.state.nc.us/org.htm.

———. Office of Archives and History. Division of Historical Resources. State Historic Preservation Office. www.hpo.dcr.state.nc.us/.

———. Office of Archives and History. North Carolina Literary and Historical Association. www.ah.dcr.state.nc.us/affiliates/lit-hist/lit-hist.htm.

———. State Library of North Carolina. *NCpedia*. http://statelibrary.dcr.state .nc.us/nc/cover.htm.

———. State Library of North Carolina. Government and Heritage Library. North Carolina Newspapers. www.statelibrary.dcr.state.nc.us/TSS/newspape.htm.

Powell, William S., ed. *Dictionary of North Carolina Biography*. Chapel Hill: University of North Carolina Press, 1986.

———. *Encyclopedia of North Carolina*. Chapel Hill: University of North Carolina Press, 2006.

Powell, William S., and Michael Hill. *North Carolina Gazetteer: A Dictionary of Tar Heel Places*. Chapel Hill: University of North Carolina Press, 1968.

University of North Carolina at Chapel Hill, University Library. *Documenting the American South*. http://docsouth.unc.edu/nc.

United States Census Bureau. "State and County QuickFacts." http://quickfacts .census.gov.

Chapter 1. Fort Raleigh and the Freedmen's Colony

Click, Patricia. *The Roanoke Island Freedmen's Colony*. http:// www.roanokefreemenscolony.com/map1.html. Accessed October 14, 2007.

———. *Time Full of Trial: The Roanoke Island Freedmen's Colony, 1862–1867*. Chapel Hill: University of North Carolina Press, 2001.

Emery, Theo. "Map's Hidden Marks Illuminate and Deepen Mystery of Lost Colony." *New York Times*. http://www.nytimes.com/2012/05/04/us/map-markings -offer-clues-to-lost-colony.html.

The Lost Colony Center for Science and Research. "List of Participants in the Roanoke Voyages." http://www.lost-colony.com/namelist.html. Accessed August 13, 2008.

Powell, William S. "Roanoke Colonists and Explorers: An Attempt at Identification." *North Carolina Historical Review* 34 (April 1957): 202–26.

U.S. Department of Interior. National Park Service. *Fort Raleigh.* Reprint. Washington, D.C.: GPO, 2003.

———. Fort Raleigh National Historic Site Visitor Center. Permanent Exhibits.

Chapter 2: Edenton: Colonial Capital

About.com. "Nat Turner's Rebellion." http://afroamhistory.about.com/od/natturner/a/turnerrebellion.htm. Accessed January 1, 2009.

Bath Harbor Marina and Motel. www.bathharbor.com. Accessed September 1, 2008.

Camp, Louis Van. *Edenton and Chowan County.* Charleston, S.C.: Arcadia Publishing, 2001.

Cheeseman, Bruce. "The Survival of the Cupola House: A Venerable Old Mansion." *North Carolina Historical Review* 63 (January 1986): 40–73.

Chowan County Heritage Development Council. *Community, Family, Church: African-American Life in Edenton 1700s to the Present.* Edenton, N.C.: Chowan County Heritage Development Council.

Chowan County Tourism Development Authority. *Visitor's Guide to Edenton, NC, and Chowan County.* Edenton, N.C.: Chowan County Tourism Development Authority, 2006

Connor, H. G. *James Iredell: Lawyer, Statesman, Judge.* Raleigh: Edwards and Broughton Printing, 1912.

Edenton-Chowan County Tourism Development Authority. "Edenton Cotton Mill Historic District." http://visitedenton.com/edenton-cotton-mill-historic-district.html. Accessed September 25, 2008.

Edenton Gazette. 1830–31 extant issues.

Edenton Historical Commission. *Roanoke River Lighthouse.* Edenton Historical Commission.

Edenton Woman's Club. *Historic Edenton and Countryside.* Chowan Herald, 1953.

Fulton, Gary, Reverend. "A Short History of St. Paul's Episcopal Church." http://stpauls-edenton.org/history.html.

Haywood, Marshall Delancey. *Governor George Burrington of the Colony of Carolina.* Raleigh: Edwards and Broughton Printing, 1896.

"Insurrection in Southampton." *Edenton Gazette,* August 31, 1831.

Lefler, Hugh T., and William S. Powell. *Colonial North Carolina: A History.* New York: Charles Scribner's Sons, 1973.

McPherson, Elizabeth Gregory. "Nathaniel Batts, Landholder on Pasquotank River, 1660." *North Carolina Historical Review* 43 (January 1966): 66–81.

North Carolina Historic Sites. *Chowan County Courthouse.* Raleigh: Office of Archives and History, North Carolina Department of Cultural Resources.

———. *Harriet Ann Jacobs, 1813–1897: Self-Guided Tour of Her Edenton Years.* Raleigh: Office of Archives and History, North Carolina Department of Cultural Resources, 1998.

————. *Historic Bath: North Carolina's First Town*. Raleigh: Office of Archives and History, North Carolina Department of Cultural Resources.

————. *Historic Bath Walking Tour*. Raleigh: Office of Archives and History, North Carolina Department of Cultural Resources, 2004.

————. *Historic Edenton*. Self-guided map. Raleigh: Office of Archives and History, North Carolina Department of Cultural Resources.

North Carolina Wildlife Resources Commission. *Coastal Boating Guide*. http://www.ncwildlife.org/Boating/BoatersGuides.aspx.

Powell, William S. *The Proprietors of Carolina*. Raleigh: Carolina Charter Tercentenary Commission, 1963.

Reed, C. Wingate. *Beaufort County: Two Centuries of Its History*. Raleigh: Edwards and Broughton Printing, 1962.

Watson, Alan. *Bath: The First Town in North Carolina*. Raleigh: Office of Archives and History, North Carolina Department of Cultural Resources, 2005.

Watts, Gordon P. *Edenton Harbor Wrecks: Underwater Archaeology in America*. New York: Archaeological Institute of America, 1981.

Whichard, Willis P. *Justice James Iredell*. Durham: Carolina Academic Press, 2000.

Chapter 3: New Bern: Royal Capital

Cecelski, David. *The Waterman's Song*. Chapel Hill: University of North Carolina Press, 2001.

Craven County Convention and Visitors Center. *New Bern Walking Tours: African-American, Churches and Cemeteries, Civil War, and Historic Homes*. New Bern: Craven County Convention and Visitors Center.

Dill, Alonzo Thomas, Jr. "Eighteenth Century New Bern." *North Carolina Historical Review* 22 (July 1963): 1–21.

————. "Public Buildings in Craven County, 1722–1835." *North Carolina Historical Review* 20 (October 1943): 301–26.

Garden Club of North Carolina. *New Bern: Cradle of North Carolina*. Raleigh: Garden Club of North Carolina, 1941.

Gilmore, Glenda Elizabeth. "Gender and Jim Crow: Women and the Politics of White Supremacy in North Carolina, 1896–1920." *Washington Post*. http://www.washingtonpost.com/wp-srv/style/longterm/books/chap1/genderandjimcrow.htm.

Hand, Bill. *A Walking Guide to North Carolina's Historic New Bern*. Charleston: History Press, 2007.

Reed, C. Wingate. *Beaufort County: Two Centuries of Its History*. Raleigh: Edwards and Broughton Printing, 1962.

Watson, Alan. *A History of New Bern and Craven County*. New Bern: Tryon Palace Commission, 1987.

Wilson, Emily Herring. *Memories of New Bern: An Oral History*. New Bern: New Bern Historical Society Foundation, Inc., 1995.

Wright, Robert K., Jr., and Morris J. Macgregor Jr. "Richard Dobbs Spaight." In *Soldier-Statesmen of the Constitution*. Washington, D.C.: Center of Military

History, U.S. Army, 1987. http://www.history.army.mil/books/RevWar/ss/
spaight.htm.

Chapter 4: Hillsborough: Colonial Town of the Piedmont

Caswell County Historical Association. "Archibald Debow Murphey: Father of
North Carolina Public Schools." http://www.rootsweb.com/~ncccha/
biographies/archibaldmurphy.html. Accessed December 7, 2007.

Cemetery Census. "Orange County North Carolina Cemeteries." *http://
cemeterycensus.com/nc/orng/index.htm*. Accessed December 7, 2007.

generalnash.org. "General Francis Nash Biography." http://generalnash.org/.
Accessed August 23, 2008.

Hillsborough Historical Society. *Welcome to Historic Hillsborough*. Hillsborough
Historical Society, 2003.

The Society of the Cincinnati. "Inception of General Society."
www.pasocietyofthecincinnati.org. Accessed February 28, 2008.

Lloyd, Allen Alexander, and Pauline Lloyd. *History of the Town of Hillsborough,
1754–1966*. Hillsborough: Allen Alexander Lloyd and Pauline Lloyd, 1966.

Nash, Francis. *Hillsboro: Colonial and Revolutionary*. Raleigh: Edwards and
Broughton Printing, 1903.

North Carolina Department of Cultural Resources. Division of Archives and
History. North Carolina Historic Sites. "John Lawson, Explorer, Historian,
and Co-Founder of Bath." www.ah.dcr.state.nc.us/sections/hs/bath/
Lawson.htm. Accessed February 12, 2008.

*Occaneechi Band of the Saponi Nation. Occaneechi Homeland Project Preservation
Project: Bringing the Past and Future Together*. www.obsn.org. Accessed
February 17, 2008.

"UNC-CH Archaeologists Move 1,000 Tons of Earth to Establish
Hillsborough History." *Science Daily*. www.sciencedaily.com/
releases/1998/07/980710081223.htm. Accessed February 12, 2008.

Chapter 5: Halifax: With Resolve

Allen, W. C. *A History of Halifax County*. Boston: Cornhill Company, 1918.

Barringer, Rufus. "History of North Carolina Railroad." *Papers of the North Carolina
Historical Society*, May 10, 1894.

Gordon, Armistead. "John Paul Jones' Name." *New York Times*, March 23, 1901.

North Carolina Historic Sites. *Historic Halifax: The Early River Port Town of the
Roanoke Valley*. Raleigh: Office of Archives and History, North Carolina
Department of Cultural Resources.

Chapter 6: Building Infrastructure: Holden Mill Trail

Ammon, Christopher. Ranger, Eno River State Park. Telephone interview, August
2008.

Anderson, Jean. "A Community of Men and Mills." *Eno Journal* 7 (July 1978).
http://www.enoriver.org/eno/Shop/Journals/MillJournal/EnoMills.htm.

Anderson, Jean, and Margaret Nygard. "The Story of West Point on the Eno."

Eno Journal 3 (July 1975). http://www.enoriver.org/eno/Shop/Journals/
1975/storyofwestpoint.html.

Hazen, Theodore. "Flour Milling in America." http://www.angelfire.com/folk/
molinologist/america.html.

Heron, Duncan. "Mill Sites on the Eno River: A Geological Viewpoint." *Eno
Journal* 7 (July 1978). http://www.enoriver.org/eno/Shop/Journals/
MillJournal/Geos.htm.

House-Autry Mills website. www.house-autry.com.

MeasuringWorth. *Six Ways to Compute the Relative Value of a US Dollar Amount,
1774 to Present.* www.measuringworth.com. Accessed September 7, 2008.

North Carolina Division of Parks and Recreation. *Eno River State Park.* Raleigh:
North Carolina Department of Environment, Health, and Natural
Resources.

———. *Merchants Millpond State Park.* Raleigh: North Carolina Department of
Environment, Health, and Natural Resources.

———. *North Carolina State Parks.* "Size of the North Carolina Parks System."
http://www.ncparks.gov/About/docs/protection_acreage.pdf.

———. *Trails of Western Eno River State Park.* Raleigh: North Carolina Department
of Environment, Health, and Natural Resources.

World Almanac. "Most Common Last Names." www.worldalmanac.com.
Accessed September 7, 2008.

Chapter 7: Guilford Courthouse: Where a Defeat Became a Victory

Baker, Thomas. *Another Such Victory: The Story of the American Defeat at Guilford
Courthouse That Helped Win the War for Independence.* 2nd ed. Fort Washington, Pa.: Eastern National, 2005.

BritishBattles.com. "The Battle of Monmouth 1778." www.britishbattles.com/
battle-monmouth.htm. Accessed August 24, 2008.

Harris, Michael. Museum educator, Brandywine Battlefield, Brandywine,
Pennsylvania. Email interview, October 15, 2007.

U.S. Department of Interior. National Park Service. *Bicycle and Pedestrian Trails in
Parks Fact Sheet.* Washington, D.C.: U.S. Department of Interior, 2003.

———. "Guilford Courthouse: Administrative History." http://www.nps.gov/
history/history/online_books/guco/adhi/adhi1.htm.

———. *Guilford Courthouse National Military Park.* Washington, D.C.: U.S. Department of Interior, 1994.

———. *Moores Creek Bridge.* Washington, D.C.: U.S. Department of Interior, 1976.

———. *Walking Guide to Guilford Courthouse National Military Park.* Washington,
D.C.: U.S. Department of Interior.

Chapter 8: Raleigh: The Debate Ended Here

Capital City Trail: A Field Guide to Raleigh Historic Points of Interest. Raleigh Historic
Districts Commission, Greater Raleigh Convention and Visitors Bureau,
2000.

City of Raleigh. *Our History and Our Flag.* 2007.

College Foundation of North Carolina. *North Carolina State Capitol*. College
　　Foundation of North Carolina.
Estey Organ Company. "History." www.esteyorgan.com/history.html. Accessed
　　October 9, 2008.
First Baptist Church, Salisbury Street. "History." www.fbcraleigh.org.
First Baptist Church, Wilmington Street. "Our History." www.raleighfirstbaptist
　　.org. Accessed October 9, 2008.
Greater Raleigh Convention and Visitors Bureau. *Raleigh Walking Tour*.
　　www.visitraleigh.com.
Ligon Historians, Ligon GT Magnet Middle School. *Ligon History Project*. "John
　　Chavis." www.ncsu.edu/ligon/about/history/chavis.htm. Accessed
　　November 1, 2008.
Moses, Amis. *Historical Raleigh with Sketches of Wake County*. Raleigh: Commercial
　　Printing, 1913.
Murray, Elizabeth Reid. *Wake: Capital County of North Carolina*. Vol. 1. Raleigh:
　　Capital County Publishing Company, 1983.
Raleigh: Capitol of North Carolina. Raleigh Sesquicentennial Commission, 1942.
Raleigh City Museum. *Businesses That Built Raleigh*. Raleigh City Museum, 2001.
Raleigh City Museum and the Raleigh Arts Commission. *Fayetteville Street: A
　　Walking Guide*. Raleigh City Museum and the Raleigh Arts Commission,
　　2006.
Shaw University. "Historical Perspective." www.shawuniversity.edu. Accessed
　　May 19, 2008.

Chapter 9: Murphy: The Trail of Tears

About North Georgia. "Winfield Scott." http://ngeorgia.com/ang/Winfield_Scott.
　　Accessed December 28, 2012.
Cherokee County, North Carolina. http://main.nc.us/cherokee/
Cherokee Nation. Constitution of the Cherokee Nation.
　　http://www.cherokee.org.
Duncan, Barbara, and Brett Riggs. *Cherokee Heritage Trails Guidebook*. Chapel Hill:
　　University of North Carolina Press, 2003.
Freel, Margaret. *Our Heritage: The People of Cherokee County, NC, 1540–1955*.
　　Murphy, N.C.: Cherokee County Historical Museum, 1956.
Holland, Lance. *Fontana: A Pocket History of Appalachia*. Robbinsville, N.C.:
　　Appalachian History Series, 2001.
Kane, Sharyn, and Richard Keeton. *Beneath These Waters: Archaeological and
　　Historical Studies of 11,500 Years along the Savannah River*. Web version, 2000.
　　http://www.nps.gov/seac/beneathweb/ch11.htm#11
North Carolina Department of Cultural Resources. North Carolina Arts
　　Council. Cherokee Heritage Trails. http://ncculturaltrails.org/Default.
　　aspx?alias=ncculturaltrails.org/cherokeeheritage.
Public Broadcasting System. "People and Events: Indian Removal, 1814–1858."
　　www.pbs.org/wgbh/aia/part4/4p2959.html. Accessed December 31, 2007.

Sturgis, Amy H. *The Trail of Tears and Indian Removal*. Westport, Conn.: Greenwood Press, 2007.

The Tennessee Encyclopedia of History and Culture. "Overhill Cherokees." http://tennesseeencyclopedia.net/entry.php?rec=1026. Accessed December 28, 2012.

Trail of Tears Association. *The Story*. www.nationaltota.org/the-story/. Accessed December 31, 2007.

Trail of Tears Interpretive Center. Permanent Exhibits. Cherokee County Historical Museum, Murphy, N.C.

U.S. Department of Interior. National Park Service. Trail of Tears National Historic Trail. "What Happened on the Trail of Tears." http://www.nps.gov/trte/historyculture/stories.htm.

White, Alice D., and Nell A. White, eds. *The Heritage of Cherokee County, North Carolina*. Vol. 1. Winston-Salem, N.C.: Hunter Publishing, 1987.

Chapter 10: Cataloochee: Ghost of a Remote Mountain Community

Asbury Trail Award. SEJ Commission on Archives and History, United Methodist Church, Lake Junaluska, N.C.

Clark, Elmer T., ed. *Francis Asbury: The Prophet of the Long Road*. Lake Junaluska: General Commission on Archives and History, United Methodist Church, 1989.

Davis, Hattie Caldwell. *Reflection of Cataloochee Valley and its Vanished People in the Great Smoky Mountains*. Hattie Caldwell Davis, 1999.

Great Smoky Mountains Natural History Association. *Hiking Trails of the Smokies*. Gatlinburg, Tenn.: Great Smoky Mountains Natural History Association, 1994.

———. *Historic Areas: Great Smoky Mountains National Park*. Gatlinburg, Tenn.: Great Smoky Mountains Natural History Association, 1994.

Powers, Elizabeth, and Mark Hannah. *Cataloochee: Lost Settlement of the Smokies*. Charleston, S.C.: Powers-Hannah Publishers, 1982.

Strutin, Michal. *History Hikes of the Smokies*. Gatlinburg, Tenn.: Great Smoky Mountains Association, 2003.

U.S. Department of Interior. National Park Service. *Cataloochee Auto Tour*. Great Smoky Mountains National Park, U.S. Department of Interior, n.d.

———. *Return of the Elk*. Great Smoky Mountains National Park, U.S. Department of Interior, n.d.

Chapter 11: Mountain Discoverers: The Magnificent Wanderers

Appalachian Voices. "Asa Gray: Legendary Botanist and Pioneering Appalachian Naturalist." http://appvoices.org. Accessed March 7, 2008.

Bartram, William. *The Travels of William Bartram: Naturalists' Edition*. Athens: University of Georgia Press, 1998.

Daniel Stowe Botanical Garden. *André Michaux*. www.michaux.org. Accessed January 6, 2008.

Dugger, Shepherd. *The Balsam Groves of Grandfather Mountain*. Philadelphia: John C. Winston Company, 1907.

Ellison, George. "Early WNC Botanists Encountered Plethora of Plants." *Smoky Mountain News*, October 23, 2002. www.smokymountainnews.com. Accessed March 7, 2008.

Frome, Michael. *Strangers in High Places*. New York: Doubleday and Company, 1966.

Kephart, Horace. *Camping and Woodcraft: A Handbook for Vacation Campers and For Travelers in the Wilderness*. Knoxville: University of Tennessee Press, 1988.

———. *Our Southern Highlanders*. New York: Outing Publishing Company, 1913.

Kranyik, Jay. "Asa Gray: Legendary Botanist and Pioneering Appalachian Naturalist." http://appvoices.org/2007/03/31/2673/

North Carolina Bartram Trail Society. Trail brochures. Highlands, N.C.: North Carolina Bartram Trail Society.

Slaughter, Thomas P. *The Natures of John and William Bartram*. New York: Alfred A. Knopf. 1996.

Strutin, Michal. *History Hikes of the Smokies*. Gatlinburg, Tenn.: Great Smoky Mountains Association, 2003.

Thomas' Legion. "Clingman's Brigade." http://thomaslegion.net/clingman.html. Accessed January 6, 2008.

U.S. Congress. "Thomas Clingman," *Biographical Dictionary of the United States Congress*. http://bioguide.congress.gov/scripts/biodisplay.pl?index=C000524. Accessed January 6, 2008.

Chapter 12: Colonial Industry of the Sandhills: Naval Stores

Butler, Carroll B. *Treasures of the Longleaf Pines*. Shalimar, Fla.: Tarkel Publishing, 1998.

Directorate of Public Works. *Longleaf Pine-Wiregrass Ecosystem*. IMSE-BRG-PWE-Endangered Species Branch. U.S. Army. Fort Bragg, N.C.

Martin, Donald Fraser, Jr. "The Naval Stores Industry in the United States." M.A. thesis, University of North Carolina, 1931.

North Carolina Division of Parks and Recreation. State Parks. Weymouth Woods–Sandhills Nature Preserve. Exhibits.

North Carolina General Assembly. *North Carolina General Statutes*. State Song and Toast. www.ncleg.net/gascripts/Statutes/StatutesTOC.pl?Chapter=0149. August 12, 2008.

Powell, William S. "What's in a Name? Why We're All Called Tar Heels." North Carolina Collection: Online Exhibits. http://www.lib.unc.edu/ncc/tarheel.html. August 12, 2008.

Chapter 13: Wilmington: A Grand Port City

Black Loyalists: Our History, Our People. "Thomas Peters." http://www.blackloyalist.com/canadiandigitalcollection/people/secular/peters.htm.

Christensen, Rob. *The Paradox of Tar Heel Politics*. Chapel Hill: University of North Carolina Press, 2008.

Cissnia, Bill. "North Carolina Waterfront Town Has History—and Star Power."
     http://www.capefearcoffee.com/wilmingtoncoffee.htm.
Conser, Walter H., Jr. *Sacred Space: Architecture and Religion in Historic Wilmington.*
     Wilmington: Bellamy Mansion Museum of History and Design Arts, 1999.
Division of Community Planning. *Wilmington, North Carolina Historic Area.*
     Raleigh: North Carolina Department of Conservation and Development,
     1962.
1898 Wilmington: Debunking the Myths. "Georgia Community Activist Rebecca
     Felton Calls for Lynching of Rapists." www.1898wilmington.com. Accessed
     December 10, 2008.
Fryar, Jack. *The Yellow Death: Wilmington and the Epidemic of 1862.* Wilmington:
     Dram Tree Books, 2008.
Gamache, Sue. "Showboat." From *Memoirs of Francis E. Tellier EM3/C-E-Div.* http://
     usswashington.com/showboat.htm. Accessed December 29, 2012.
Gregory Elementary School and Williston Industrial School. http://cdm15169.
     contentdm.oclc.org/cdm/singleitem/collection/p15169coll6/id/637/rec/1.
     Accessed October 2012.
Graham, Nicholas. "February 1971: The Wilmington 10." *This Month in North
     Carolina History.* North Carolina Collection, UNC Libraries. www.lib.unc.edu/
     ncc/ref/nchistory/feb2005/.
Greater Wilmington Chamber of Commerce. *History of the Lower Cape Fear:
     Early Exploration to the American Revolution 1524–1775, New Hanover County.*
     1976. www.nhcgov.com/AgnAndDpt/LIBR/LocalHistory/Pages/
     HistoryoftheLowerCapeFear. Accessed December 12, 2008.
Hirchak, John. *Ghosts of Old Wilmington.* Charleston, S.C.: The History Press.
     2006
Howell, Andrew J. *The Book of Wilmington, 1730–1930.* Wendell: Broadfoot's
     Bookmark, 1979.
Lennon, Donald R., and Ida Brooks Kellam, eds. *The Wilmington Town Book.*
     Raleigh: Division of Archives and History, North Carolina Department of
     Cultural Resources, 1973.
McRee, Griffith J. "An Imperfect Sketch of the History of the Town of Wilming-
     ton," *Wilmington Chronicle.* September 2, 1846.
Prather, H. Leon. *We Have Taken a City: The Wilmington Racial Massacre and Coup
     of 1898.* Wilmington: Dram Tree Books, 2006.
Reaves, Bill. *Brief History of Wilmington, NC.* Wilmington: B. Reaves, 1977
Sprunt, James. *Derelicts: An Account of Ships Lost at Sea in General Commercial
     Traffic and a Brief History of Blockade Runners Stranded along the North Carolina
     Coast, 1861–1865.* Baltimore: Lord Baltimore Press, 1920.
N.C. State Ports Authority. *The Transition of North Carolina Ports at Wilmington
     and Morehead City from Colonial Days to the Present.* Raleigh: N.C. State Ports
     Authority, 1971.
Warren, James Robert. "History in Towns: Wilmington, NC." *Antiques.* December
     1980.
Warships Associated with World War II in the Pacific. "USS North Carolina." http://

www.cr.nps.gov/history/online_books/butowsky1/northcarolina.htm.
Accessed December 28, 2012.

Wilmington Daily Journal. 1858.

Chapter 14: The Roanoke Canal Trail: North Carolina's First Business Corridor

Braswell, Peggy Jo Cobb. *The Roanoke Canal: A History of the Old Navigation and Water Power Canal of Halifax County, North Carolina.* Halifax: Roanoke Canal Commission, 1987.

Kopp, Katherine. "Taming the Roanoke." *Our State,* July 2006.

Roanoke Canal Museum and Trail. http://www.roanokecanal.com/.

Chapter 15: Warrenton: Antebellum Town

Agriculture Adjustment Act of 1938. WebRef.org. http://www.webref.org/agriculture/a/agricultural_adjustment_act_of_2.htm. Accessed February 28, 2008.

"Bell, Ella Reeves (Rives) Eaton Dickens." Texas State Cemetery. http://www.cemetery.state.tx.us/pub/user_form.asp?step=1&pers_id=268. June 8, 2008.

Cigarette Tax (political cartoon). *Warren Record,* March 9, 1934.

Coulling, Mary P. *The Lee Girls.* Winston-Salem: Blair Publishing, 1987.

Daniel, James C. "North Carolina Tobacco Marketing Crisis of 1933." *North Carolina Historical Review* 61 (July 1964): 370–82.

DeCock, Luke. "Sir Archie's Family Ties." *Raleigh News and Observer,* May 3, 2008, C1.

Dirksen, Everett M. *The Congressional Front* (newsletter). June 22, 1935.

Faith, Stanley L. "The Warrenton Female Academy of Jacob Mordecai, 1809–1818." *North Carolina Historical Review* 35 (July 1958): 281–98.

"The Greek of Homer: A Living Language." *Warren Weekly,* March 24, 1853.

Hill, Michael, ed. *The Governors of North Carolina.* Raleigh: Office of Archives and History, North Carolina Department of Cultural Resources, 2007.

Mangum, William Preston, II. Speech Presented to North Carolina Thoroughbred Breeders Association in March 2002. www.tryonhorsecountry.org/History_of__Horse_Racing_in_NC.doc. Accessed February 28, 2008.

McFarland, Kenneth. *The Architecture of Warren Country, North Carolina 1770s to 1860s.* Warrenton: Warren County Historical Association, 2001.

Montgomery, Lizzie Wilson. *Sketches of Old Warrenton.* Raleigh: Edwards and Broughton Printing, 1924.

Nature Conservancy. *Coastal Plain: Roanoke River.* http://nature.org/wherewework/northamerica/states/northcarolina/preserves/art5631.html. Accessed March 6, 2008.

North Carolina Department of Cultural Resources. North Carolina Highway Historical Marker Program. "Kerr, John H." http://www.ncmarkers.com. Accessed February 28, 2008.

"North Carolina to $10,000,000 for Farmers." *Warrenton Record,* April 20, 1934.

Office of Environmental Education. *Roanoke River Basin.* Raleigh: North Carolina

Department of Environment, Health, and Natural Resources, 2007. www.eenorthcarolina.org.

Office of the Command Historian. "Bragg, Braxton." XVIII Airborne and Fort Bragg. Fort Bragg. http://www.bragg.army.mil/Pages/History.aspx Accessed January 6, 2008.

Preservation Warrenton. "Warrenton North Carolina—A Walking Tour." http://preservationwarrenton.com/Warrenton%20Walking%20Tour.html.

Price, William S., Jr. "Nathaniel Macon, Antifederalist." *North Carolina Historical Review* 81 (July 2004): 288–312.

———. "Nathaniel Macon, Planter." *North Carolina Historical Review* 78 (April 2001): 187–214.

"Rules for Summer Health." *Warrenton Reporter*, August 16, 1825.

Smith, Jason. "Horsepower Heaven." *Endeavors*. http://endeavors.unc.edu/spr2002/fulghum.html.

U.S. Congress. House of Representatives. Subcommittee of the Committee of Ways and Means. 73rd Congress, 2nd session, March 27–31 and April 10, 1934.

"Warrenton Male Academy." *Warrenton Reporter*, May 30, 1840.

Warrenton News, February 26, 1858; March 22, 1861

Weldon, Elsie. Register of Deeds, Warren County. Telephone interview, June 9, 2008.

Wellman, Manly Wade. *The County of Warren, North Carolina, 1586–1917*. Chapel Hill: University of North Carolina Press, 1959.

Chapter 16: Fayetteville: Vibrant Queen of the Coastal Plain

"After Many Years." *Fayetteville Observer*, February 8, 1883, 1.

Barrett, John J. *Sherman's March through the Carolinas*. Chapel Hill: University of North Carolina Press, 1956.

Broadwater, Robert P. *Battle of Despair: Bentonville and the North Carolina Campaign*. Macon, Ga.: Mercer University Press, 2004.

"By the Governor: A Proclamation." *Fayetteville Observer*, February 20, 1865

Crittenden, Charles Christopher. *North Carolina Newspapers before 1790*. Chapel Hill: University of North Carolina Press, 1928.

Elliot, Robert. "North Carolina Newspapers in the Federal Period, 1789–1800." M.A. thesis, University of North Carolina, 1948.

"Failure of the Peace Commission." *Fayetteville Observer*, February 13, 1865, 1.

Famous Scots. "Flora MacDonald." http://www.rampantscotland.com/famous/blfamflora.htm. Accessed August 24, 2008.

"Fayetteville." *Carolina Observer*, August 22, 1816.

Fayetteville Observer. www.fayobserver.com.

Fayetteville State University. http://www.uncfsu.edu/pr/about-fsu.

Fort Bragg. www.bragg.army.mil/.

GlobalSecurity.org. "Fort Bragg." www.globalsecurity.org/military/facility/fort-bragg.htm. Accessed August 24, 2008.

Graham, Nicholas. "August 1751—North Carolina's First Newspaper." *This Month* in *North Carolina History*. North Carolina Collection, UNC Libraries. www.lib.unc.edu/ncc/ref/nchistory/aug2004/index.html. Accessed December 11, 2007.

"The Great Fire." *Carolina Observer*, June 7, 1831.

Huddle, Mark A. "To Educate a Race: The Making of the First State Colored Normal School, Fayetteville, North Carolina, 1865–1877." *North Carolina Historical Review* 74 (April 1997): 135–60.

Hughes, Nathaniel Cheairs. *Bentonville: The Final Battle of Sherman and Johnston.* Chapel Hill: University of North Carolina Press, 1996.

Irwin, R. B, Lt. Col., and Col. S. M. Bowman. *Sherman and His Campaign.* New York. Charles B. Richardson, 1865.

Neal, Larry K., Jr. "How Did We Get Here from There?" *Tar Heel Junior Historian* (Spring 2006).

"The News." *Fayetteville Observer*, March 6, 1865, 1.

Oates, John. *The Story of Fayetteville and the Upper Cape Fear.* Charlotte: Dowd Press, 1950.

"The Peace Commission." *Fayetteville Observer*, February 6, 1865, 1.

Powell, Joey. *Cumberland County.* Mount Pleasant: Arcadia Publishing, 1999.

"RS&N History." TrainWeb.org. www.trainweb.org/roc/htm/rocrsntxt.htm. Accessed January 24, 2008.

Sherman, W. T. *Memoirs of General W. T. Sherman.* Vol. 2. New York: D. Appleton and Company, 1875.

"Sherman's March to the Sea." *New Georgia Encyclopedia.* www.georgiaencyclopedia.org/nge/Article.jsp?id=h-641

"Ten Costliest Battles of the Civil War." www.civilwarhome.com/Battles.htm.

U.S. Department of Interior. National Park Service. Heritage Preservation Services. American Battlefield Protection Program. "Civil War Battle Summaries by State." www.nps.gov/history/hps/abpp/battles/bystate.htm.

Whitted, Fred. *Fayetteville, NC.* Black America Series. Mount Pleasant: Arcadia Publishing, 2000.

www.visitfayetteville.com.

Chapter 17: Winston-Salem: Religious Freedom and Industry Side by Side

Bricker, Michael. *Winston-Salem: A Twin City History.* Charleston: The History Press, 2008.

Fries, Adelaide. *Forsyth: The History of a County on the March.* Chapel Hill: University of North Carolina Press, 1976.

Home Moravian Church. www.homemoravian.org.

Niven, Penelope, and Cornelia B. Wright. *Old Salem: The Official Guidebook.* Winston-Salem: Old Salem, Inc., 2000.

Old Salem. www.oldsalem.org.

Old Salem Museum and Gardens. *African-American Walking Tour in Salem.*

Rouse, Parke, Jr. *The Great Wagon Road from Philadelphia to the South.* New York: McGraw-Hill, 1973.

Salem College. www.salem.edu.

Chapter 18: Salisbury: Piedmont Emblem

Brawley, James. *The Rowan Story, 1753–1953.* Salisbury: Rowan Printing Company, 1953.

Fowler, Tom. "Retracing the Great Indian Trading Path." www.tradingpath.org.

Hartley, Michael O., and Martha B. Hartley. "The Great Philadelphia Wagon Road." *Tar Heel Junior Historian* (Spring 2006). www.ncmuseumofhistory.org/collateral/articles/So6.great.wagon.road.pdf.

Livingstone College. "Dr. Joseph Charles Price, Founder and President of Livingstone College." www.livingstone.edu.

McKown, Harry. "Salisbury Bread Riot." *This Month in North Carolina History.* North Carolina Collection, UNC Libraries. www.lib.unc.edu/ncc/ref/nchistory/mar2005/index.html. Accessed December 14, 2008.

North Carolina Office of Environmental Education. *Yadkin–Pee Dee River Basin,* North Carolina Department of Environment, Health and Natural Resources. www.ee.enr.state.nc.us/public/ecoaddress/riverbasins/yadkin.pdf.

Rumple, Reverend Jethro. *A History of Rowan County, North Carolina.* Salisbury: J. J. Bruner, 1881.

Salisbury Confederate Prison Association. *Prison History.* www.salisburyprison.org/PrisonHistory.htm.

"Salisbury Heritage Walking Tour." Historic Salisbury, N.C. http://www.visitsalisburync.com/things-to-do/family-fun/default.aspx?id=129 January 22, 2008.

"Salisbury Historic District." Rowan County Library. http://www.rowancountync.gov/GOVERNMENT/Departments/PublicLibrary/tabid/145/Default.aspx. January 22, 2008.

Salisbury History and Art Trail. Salisbury Community Appearance Commission.

"Salisbury NC Confederate Prison." Salisbury National Cemetery. http://salisburyprison.gorowan.com/. Accessed January 8, 2008.

Salisbury's African-American Heritage Trail. Livingstone College and the Rowan County Convention and Visitors Bureau.

"Salisbury's Historic Home Showcase: Treasures Inside and Out." Historic Salisbury Foundation. www.historicsalisbury.org. Accessed January 22, 2008.

Salisbury's Mural: Cross Roads: Past into Present. Mural Preservation, Inc.

Searching for the Confederacy in Rowan County. Rowan County Convention and Visitors Bureau.

"Theo. Buerbaum's Salisbury." Rowan County Public Library http://www.rowancountync.gov/GOVERNMENT/Departments/PublicLibrary/tabid/145/Default.aspx

Yadkin/Pee Dee River Basin Association. "General Info." www.yadkinpeedee.org. Accessed January 22, 2008.

Chapter 19: Walk the Walk of the Surfmen

Caffey's Inlet Station. www.thesanderling.com. Accessed October 6, 2008.

Charlet, James. Site Manager and Programs Director, Chicamacomico Life-Saving Station Historic Site. Interview, October 2007

Chicamacomico Life-Saving Station, Chicamacomico Historical Association. http://www.chicamacomico.net/index.htm.

Duffus, Kevin. *The Graveyard of the Atlantic: 400 Year of Shipwrecks, Mysteries and Heroic Rescues.* DVD. www.lookingglassproductions.org. Raleigh, N.C.

Graveyard of the Atlantic Museum. Permanent exhibits. Hatteras, N.C.

Mobley, Joe A. *Ship Ashore! The U.S. Lifesavers of Coastal North Carolina.* Raleigh: Division of Archives and History, North Carolina Department of Cultural Resources, 1994.

Molloy, Linda. Site Operations Manager, Chicamacomico Life-Saving Station Historic Site. Interview, October 2007.

Mosher, Kate. "Treasures of Chicamacomico: Architectural Gem Yields Rich Historical Beauty." *Coastwatch.* North Carolina Sea Grant. www.coastalguide. com/nc/seagrant/chicamacomico01.htm. Accessed October 14, 2007.

"Rodanthe: Chicamacomico Lifesaving Station," www.hatteras-nc.com/chicamacomico/. Accessed October 14, 2007.

U.S. Department of Interior. National Park Service. "Cape Hatteras." http://www.nps.gov/caha/index.htm.

Chapter 20: Cooleemee: Mill Hill

Cooleemee Mill Town Museum and exhibit markers. Cooleemee, N.C.

DePriest, Joe. "Textile Tales Retold at Reunions." *Charlotte Observer,* October 7, 2007. Hall, Jacquelyn Dowd, et al. *Like a Family: The Making of a Southern Cotton Mill World.* Chapel Hill: University of North Carolina Press, 1987.

Rumley, Jim. Cooleemee Historical Association. Interview. October 29, 2007.

Textile Heritage Initiative. www.textileheritage.org/. Accessed October 14, 2007.

Chapter 21: Durham: The Bull City

Duke University Libraries. "Washington Duke." http://library.duke.edu/uarchives/history/histnotes/duke_washington.html.

Durham Athletic Park. http://www.milb.com/team5/page.jsp?ymd=20121023& content_id=40001812&vkey=team5_t234&fext=.jsp&sid=t234

"Lincoln Hospital of Durham, North Carolina: A Short History." *Journal of the National Medical Association.* http://www.ncbi.nlm.nih.gov/pmc/articles/ PMC2610830/?page=1.

North Carolina Mutual Life. http://www.ncmutuallife.com/newsite/pages/ about.html.

Shestak, Elizabeth. "The Lasting Legacy of Lincoln Hospital." *Durham News.* Reissued by the Duke Endowment. http://www.dukeendowment.org/ health-care/lincoln-hospital-spotlight-durham-news.

UNC Libraries. "Historic Parish Street." http://mainstreet.lib.unc.edu/projects/ parrish_st_durham/index.php.

Chapter 22: Wilson: Tobacco Town

Badger, Anthony J. *Prosperity Road: The New Deal, Tobacco, and North Carolina.* Chapel Hill: University of North Carolina Press, 1980.

Biles, Roger. "Tobacco Towns: Urban Growth and Economic Development in Eastern North Carolina." *North Carolina Historical Review* 84 (April 2007): 156–90.

Brandt, Allan M. *The Cigarette Century: The Rise, Fall, and Deadly Persistence of the Product That Defined America.* New York: Basic Books, 2007.

Fun Starts Here! Wilson Walking Tour. Wilson Downtown Development Corporation, c. 1990.

Master Settlement Agreement. Office of the Attorney General, State of California. http://ag.ca.gov/tobacco/msa.php.

McAdams, Robert C. "The Tobacco Culture of Wilson County, North Carolina." Ph.D. diss., University of Tennessee, 1996.

UNC-TV. "North Carolina Tobacco Timeline." *History of Tobacco.* http://www.unctv.org/content/nctobacco/history/. Accessed September 5, 2008.

Valentine, Patrick. *The Rise of a Southern Town: Wilson, North Carolina, 1849–1920.* Baltimore: Gateway Press, 2002.

Wilson, N.C. www.wilsonnc.org.

Wilson Advance, June 26, 1890; August 28, 1890; September 11, 1890.

Wilson Chamber of Commerce. *Come to Wilson, N.C.* Greensboro: Bradham and Company, 1949.

Wilson Daily Times, June 1924; August 28, 1924; July 13, 1924; August 28, 1936; July 1961.

Wilson Visitors Bureau, www.wilson-nc.com.

Chapter 24: Pinehurst and Asheville: Favorite Playgrounds

Asheville Architecture and History Walk. www.asheville-mountain-magic.com/asheville-architecture.html. Accessed January 28, 2013.

Barrett, J. S. "The History of Tapoco." http://tapocolodge.com/Tapoco-Story/The-History-of-Tapoco.aspx. Accessed December 28, 2012.

Bearden, James. *The Travel Industry in North Carolina: Proceedings of the Governor's Travel Information Conference, October 28–30, 1964.* Greenville: Bureau of Business Research, School of Business, East Carolina College, 1964.

Claddagh Inn. www.claddaghinn.com. Accessed October 9, 2008.

Green Park Inn. www.greenparkinn.com. Accessed October 6, 2008.

Greystone Inn. www.greystoneinn.com. Accessed October 7, 2008.

Grove Park Inn. www.groveparkinn.com. Accessed October 31, 2008.

History of Asheville. www.ashevillenc.com/area_info/history_of_asheville. Accessed January 28, 2013.

History of Hot Springs. www.hotspringsnc.org/. Accessed October 14, 2008.

History of Pinehurst. Pinehurst, Inc., 2003.

Jarrett House. www.jarretthouse.com. Accessed October 9, 2008.

National Park Service. *Asheville, NC: A National Register of Historic Places Travel Itinerary.* http://www.nps.gov/nr//travel/asheville/. Accessed October 6, 2008.

North Carolina Department of Commerce. "North Carolina Tourism." www.nccommerce.com/en/TourismService/PromoteTravelAndTourismIndustry/. Accessed October 7, 2008.

Old Edwards Inn. http://www.oldedwardsinn.com/. Accessed October 7, 2008.

Sharpe, Bill. *The Travel Industry in North Carolina*. Raleigh: State Division of Advertising News, 1947.

Starnes, Richard D. "Creating a Variety Vacationland: Tourism Development in North Carolina, 1930–1990." In *Southern Journeys: Tourism, History and Culture in the Modern South*, ed. Richard D. Starnes. Tuscaloosa: University of Alabama Press, 2003.

Town of Lake Lure. www.townoflakelure.com. Accessed October 7, 2008.

Tufts Archives, Pinehurst, N.C. 1923 collection.

Wellman, Manly Wade. *The Story of Moore County*. Southern Pines: Moore County Historical Association, 1974.

Chapter 24: Separate, Not Equal, but Loved Anyway: Jones Lake State Park

Cecelski, David. "Mr. Dewitt's Lake." *Raleigh News and Observer*, April 27, 2007.

Current, Richard N., ed. "Reconstruction in Retrospect: Views from the Turn of the Century." In *The Reconstruction of Southern States*. Atlanta: 1901.

Gavins, Raymond. "North Carolina Black Folklore and Song in the Age of Segregation." *North Carolina Historical Review* 66 (October 1989): 414–15.

Moses, Amis. *Historical Raleigh with Sketches of Wake County*. Raleigh: Commercial Printing, 1913.

North Carolina Division of Parks and Recreation. "Hammocks Beach State Park." www.ncparks.org/Visit/parks/habe/history.php.

———. *Hanging Rock State Park*. North Carolina Department of Environment, Health, and Natural Resources.

———. *Jones Lake State Park*. North Carolina Department of Environment, Health, and Natural Resources.

———. *William B. Umstead State Park*. North Carolina Department of Environment, Health, and Natural Resources.

Thomas, Larry Reni. *The True Story behind the Wilmington Ten*. Hampton, Va.: UB & US Communications Systems, Inc., 1993.

Weaver, Jefferson. "Major Renovations Underway at Jones Lake." www.bladenjounral.com. August 20, 2012.

Zipf, Karin. "Different Colored Current of the Sea: Reconstruction, North Carolina, Mutuality and the Political Roots of Jim Crow, 1872–1875." In *North Carolinians in the Era of the Civil War and Reconstruction*, edited by Paul D. Escott. Chapel Hill: University of North Carolina Press, 2008.

Chapter 25: Fontana Dam: Lumber, Power, and Personal Quests

Appalachian Trail Conference. www.appalachiantrail.org.

Appalachian Trail Guide to North Carolina–Georgia. Harpers Ferry, W.Va.: Appalachian Trail Conservancy, 2011.

Boydon, Lucile Kirby. *The Village of Five Lives*. Fontana Dam: Government Services, 1964.

Catton, Bruce, *Michigan: A History*. New York: Norton, 1984.

DeHart, Allen. *North Carolina Hiking Trails.* 2nd ed. Boston: Appalachian Mountain Club, 1982.

Douty, H. M. "Wage Rates and House of Labor in North Carolina Industry." *Southern Economic Journal* 3 (October 1936).

"Electricity in the Limelight: The Federal Theater Project Takes on the Power Industry." New Deal Network. http://newdeal.feri.org/power/essay01.htm. Accessed August 23, 2008.

Fontana Village Resort. "About Fontana Village Resort." www.fontanavillage. com. Accessed October 6, 2008.

Holland, Lance. *Fontana: A Pocket History of Appalachia.* Robbinsville, N.C.: Appalachian History Series, 2001.

Oliver, Duane. *Hazel Creek from Then til Now.* Maryville, Tenn.: D. Oliver, 1989.

Pierce, Daniel, *Logging in the Smokies.* Gatlinburg, Tenn.: Great Smoky Mountains Association. 2003.

Size of the North Carolina State Park System. http://www.ncparks.gov/About/ docs/protection_acreage.pdf.

Smoky Mountains Hiking Club. http://www.smhclub.org/.

Taylor, Stephen Wallace. "Building the Back of Beyond." Diss., University of Tennessee, 1996.

U.S. Forest Service. "Joyce Kilmer Memorial Forest." http://www.fs.fed.us/ wildflowers/regions/southern/JoyceKilmer/index.shtml.

Chapter 26: Charlotte: Bank Town and Beyond

Alexander, J. B. *The History of Mecklenburg County from 1740 to 1900.* Charlotte: Observer Printing House, 1902.

Blackwelder, Ruth. *Old Charlotte and Old Mecklenburg Today.* Charlotte: Mecklenburg Historical Association, 1973.

Blythe, LeGette, and Charles Rave Brackman. *Hornet's Nest: The Story of Charlotte and Mecklenburg County.* Charlotte: McNally, 1961.

Charlotte Branch American Association of University Women. *Making a Difference: Women of Mecklenburg.* Charlotte Branch American Association of University Women, 1980.

Charlotte Chamber of Commerce. *Charlotte's Advancing Economy 1968–1970.* Charlotte: Charlotte Chamber of Commerce, [1970?].

Charlotte–Mecklenburg Historic Landmarks Commission. www.cmhpf.org. Accessed August 19, 2008.

Charlotte-Mecklenburg Story. www.cmstory.org. Accessed August 19, 2008.

Charlotte Skyscraper Diagram. http://skyscraperpage.com. Accessed August 19, 2008.

Covington, Howard E. *The Story of NationsBank.* Chapel Hill: University of North Carolina Press, 1993.

Davidson, Chalmers J. "Independent Mecklenburg." *North Carolina Historical Review* 46 (1969): 122–29.

Fitzpatrick, Dan. "As Steel Shaped Pittsburgh, Banking Defines Charlotte."

Pittsburgh Post-Gazette, June 27, 2006. www.post-gazette.com/
   pg/06176/701039-28.stm. Accessed May 27, 2008.

———. "How Charlotte Became a Banking Giant, Outpacing Pittsburgh's
   Banks." *Pittsburgh Post-Gazette*, June 25, 2006. www.post-gazette.com/
   pg/06176/701039-28.stm. Accessed May 27, 2008.

Kratt, Mary Norton. *A Little Charlotte Scrapbook*. Davidson: Briar Patch Press,
   1990.

Lester, Carl. "A Brief History of the United States Branch Mint at Charlotte."
   Southern Gold Society. www.southerngoldsociety.org/charlotte.html.
   Accessed June 6, 2008.

The Mint Museum. "Crafting North Carolina." www.mintmuseum.org/
   craftingnc/02-02-001-a.htm. Accessed June 6, 2008.

North Carolina in the Global Economy. "Banks and Finance." www.soc.duke.
   edu/NC_GlobalEconomy/banks/corporations.shtml . Accessed August 19,
   2008.

Public Art Tour. "Charlotte Center City Partners." www.charlottecentercity.org.
   Accessed August 19, 2008.

Schweikart, Larry. *Banking in the American South from the Age of Jackson to
   Reconstruction*. Baton Rouge: Louisiana State University Press, 1987.

"Wachovia to Move Top Execs to New Building." *Charlotte Business Journal*,
   August 31, 2007. http://charlotte.bizjournals.com/charlotte/
   stories/2007/08/27/daily53.html. Accessed August 19, 2008.

Wells Fargo. "Wachovia Company History." https://www.wellsfargo.com/about/
   corporate/wachovia. Accessed August 19, 2008.

Williams, Stephanie Burt. *Wicked Charlotte: The Sordid Side of the Queen City*.
   Charleston: The History Press, 2006.

Yockey, Ross. *McColl: The Man with America's Money*. Atlanta: Longstreet
   Publishing, 1999.

Chapter 27: Research Triangle Park: Cradle of New Ideas

AstroTurf. http://www.astroturf.com/ Accessed August 18, 2008.

Freeze, Gary. *North Carolina Society in 1953 and in 2003*. Raleigh: North Carolina
   Museum of History, Office of Archives and History, North Carolina
   Department of Cultural Resources, 2005.

Hamilton, W. B. "The Research Triangle of North Carolina: A Study in Leadership
   for the Common Weal." *South Atlantic Quarterly* 65 (Spring 1966): 254–78.

Historical markers. Research Triangle Commemorative Park. Davis Drive and
   NC 54.

Little, William F. "Research Triangle Park." *The World and I* 3 (November 1988):
   178–85.

Martin, D. G. "Our Governors—How Quickly We Forget." *Chatham Journal Weekly*,
   June 20, 2005. www.chathamjournal.com/cgi-bin/moxiebin/
   bm_tools.cgi?print=1143;s=6_3;site=1. Accessed May 2, 2008.

"North Carolina Attempts Unique Experiment—The Research Triangle." *Lawyers
   Title News*, April 1961.

Park, Fred M. "Turning Poor Dirt into Pay Dirt." *METRO Magazine.* http://www.metronc.com/article/?id+421. Accessed May 2, 2008.

"Research Triangle Park 20th Anniversary." *Raleigh News and Observer,* Supplement. October 1, 1979.

RTI History. www.rti.org/page.cfm?objectid=E4550DC8-C1E5-4A9D-A4EF B3CF60379343

Raleigh-Durham International Airport. http://www.rdu.com/authority/history.html. . Accessed May 2, 2008.

Research Triangle Park. www.rtp.org/main/.

Sellars, Linda. "Origins of Research Triangle: Acquiring a Park." Paper read to the Historical Society of North Carolina. March 8, 1991.

Southern Research. http://www.southernresearch.org. Accessed May 1, 2008.

Vollmer, Sabine. "RTP Was 'a Leap of Imagination." *Raleigh News and Observer,* May 2007. http://www.newsobserver.com/1542/v-print/story/581711.html.

———. This Area Was Just Ripe." *Raleigh News and Observer,* September 9, 2007.

Weddle, Rick, Elizabeth Rooks, and Tina Valdecanas. "Research Triangle Park: Evolution and Renaissance." Presented to 20006 IASP World Conference, June 2006.

"Welcome." Research Triangle Park Chapter of Sigma Xi Scientific Research Society. www.rtp-sigmaxi.org. Accessed August 18, 2008.

Chapter 28: Our Favorite Export: NASCAR and the Occoneechee Speedway

"Bob Flock Cops Top Prize in Stock Car Race in Hillsboro." *Durham Morning Herald,* August 8, 1949, section 11, 2.

Eno River Association. "Occoneechee Speedway." www.enoriver.org/eno/parks/occspdwy.htm. Accessed July 31, 2006.

"Fonty Flock Takes Top Honors in Hillsboro Speedway Event." *Durham Morning Herald,* June 28, 1948, section 11, 2.

Froscher, Norm. "The 'Fireball' Myth: Did 'Fireball' Really Get His Name From Baseball? www.fireballroberts.com/Fireball2StoriesC.htm. Accessed August 23, 2008.

Garner, Joe. *Speed, Guts, and Glory: 100 Unforgettable Moments in NASCAR History.* New York: Warner Books, 2006.

Howell, Mark D. *From Moonshine to Madison Avenue: A Cultural History of the NASCAR Winston Cup Series.* Bowling Green, Ohio: Bowling Green State University Popular Press, 1997.

Historic Occoneechee Speedway Trail, 2006.

Jack Horner's Sports Corner. *Durham Morning Herald,* June 23, 1948, section 11, 2.

Latford, Bob. *NASCAR: A Celebration.* Carlton Books Ltd, 1998.

Louise Smith. http://www.evi.com/q/facts_about_louise_smith.

McGee, Ryan. *ESPN Ultimate NASCAR: 100 Defining Moments in Stock Car Racing History.* New York: ESPN Books, 2007.

North Carolina Motorsports Association. "North Carolina Motorsports Facts." http://northcarolinamotorsportsassociation.org/about-ncma/north-carolina-motorsports-facts/.

"Once Blue Collar, NASCAR Now a Sport of Tycoons." *Raleigh News and Observer,* January 25, 2008, 6D.

NASCAR. www.nascar.com

The Official Tim Flock Homepage. "The Story of Jocko Flocko." http://www.legendsofnascar.com/Tim_Flock.htm. Accessed August 23, 2008.

Ohio State University. Department of History. *Temperance and Prohibition.* http://prohibition.osu.edu/.

Thompson, Neal. *Driving with the Devil: Southern Moonshine, Detroit Wheels and the Birth of NASCAR.* New York: Crown Publishers, 2006.

Vance, Bill. "Junior Johnson: Legend of Moonshine Running and Race Car Driving." *Canadian Driver.* www.canadiandriver.com/articles/bv/junior.htm. Accessed August 23, 2008.

Wendell Scott Organization. "Wendell Scott." http://www.wendellscott.org/.

Wolfpack Motorsports. http://www.wolfpackmotorsports.com/.

"Woman Driver Tests Skill with Men Today in Stock Car Event." *Charlotte Observer,* June 19, 149, 12-B.

Women in the Winner's Circle Foundation. "Sara Christian." http://www.thehenryford.org/exhibits/racing/wiwc/bios/trailblazers/SaraChristian.pdf. Accessed January 19, 2008.

Chapter 29: America's First State University to Hold Classes:
The University of North Carolina

Battle, Kemp P. *The History of UNC.* Raleigh: Edwards and Broughton Printing Company, 1907.

———. *Sketches of the History of the University of North Carolina.* Chapel Hill: University of North Carolina, 1889.

Blackwelder, Ruth. *The Age of Orange: Political and Intellectual Leadership in North Carolina, 1752–1861.* Charlotte: William Loftin, 1951.

Chapel Hill Historical Society. *Historic Buildings and Landmarks of Chapel Hill.* Chapel Hill: Chapel Hill Historical Society, 1973.

Chapel Hill/Orange County Visitors Bureau. *Chapel Hill, with Carrboro and Hillsborough: Official Visitor's Guide.*

The Chapel of the Cross. "History of the Chapel of the Cross." https://thechapelofthecross.org/welcoming-all/who-is-chapel-of-the-cross/. Accessed August 17, 2008.

Faris, Jane Corey. *North Carolina Firsts.* Poster. Raleigh: Provincial Press, 1971.

Fordham, Christopher C., III. "University of North Carolina at Chapel Hill: The First State University." Address delivered to the North Carolina meeting of the Newcomen Society of the United States, held in Chapel Hill, April 18, 1985.

The Dialectic and Philanthropic Societies. http://diphi.web.unc.edu/. Accessed January 3, 2013.

Henderson, Archibald. *The Campus of the First State University.* Chapel Hill: University of North Carolina Press, 1949.

Kapp, Paul. Campus Historic Preservation Manager, University of North
    Carolina at Chapel Hill. Interview, June 4, 2008.
Love, James Lee. 'Tis Sixty Years Since: A Story of the University of North Carolina in
    the 1880s. Chapel Hill: University of North Carolina Press, 1945.
Morehead-Cain Scholars Program. "What Is the Morehead-Cain?" http://
    moreheadcain.org/about. Accessed August 17, 2008.
North Carolina Botanical Garden. Coker Arboretum: A Walking Tour. University of
    North Carolina, November 2005.
Schumann, Marguerite. The First State University: A Walking Guide. Chapel Hill:
    University of North Carolina Press, 1985.
Silent Sentinels of Stone: Old Chapel Hill Cemetery. "History of the Cemetery."
    www.ibiblio.org/cemetery/history.html. Accessed December 7, 2007.
Town of Chapel Hill. "Old Chapel Hill Cemetery." http://www.townofchapelhill
    .org/index.aspx?page=1407. Accessed May 17, 2008.
University of North Carolina. "A Self-Guided Tour of Campus: Landmarks."
    www.unc.edu/tour. Accessed August 14, 2006.
————. Visitor's Guide. 2009.
University of North Carolina at Chapel Hill. University Library and UNC
    Center for the Study of the American South. The Carolina Story: A Virtual
    Museum of University History. http://museum.unc.edu. Accessed February
    12, 2008.

Chapter 30: Gold!!!!! Reed Gold Mine

Brake, Cindy. "Charlotte Mint Has 'Golden' History: Area Gold Discovery
    Prompts Coinage." Coin World. www.usrarecoininvestments.com/
    coin_articles/charlotte_mint.htm. Accessed August 12, 2008.
"Centuries-Old Charlotte Coins Found." Charlotte Observer. May 15, 2008.
    www.charlotte.com/115/story/624974.html. Accessed June 6, 2008.
Chappell, John. "All That Glitters: Warm Weather Brings Out Gold Prospectors."
    The Pilot http://archives.thepilot.com/April 2004/04-18-04/041804Gold.html.
    April 18, 2004.
Coinage Act of 1792. www.constitution.org/uslaw/coinage1792.txt. Accessed
    June 6, 2008.
Fulghum, Neil. "A Brief History of North Carolina Money." Historic Moneys in
    the North Carolina Collection. www.lib.unc.edu/dc/money/ncmoney.html.
    Accessed June 6, 2008.
Funk, Linda. Reed Gold Mine Guidebook. Raleigh: North Carolina Division of Ar-
    chives and History, North Carolina Department of Cultural Resources, 1979.
Gold! Ten-Stamp Mill, Reed Gold Mine, Stanfield, North Carolina. Piedmont-Carolina
    Section of the American Society of Mechanical Engineers. April 25, 1983.
Jones, H. G. The First Gold Rush: A Master Plan for Reed Gold Mine. National Park
    Service, 1972.
————. "Prelude to Sutter's Mill and the Klondike: The First Mining of Gold in
    the United States, 1799–1896." Northern Review 19 (Winter 1998): 84–92.

Knapp, Richard. "Golden Promise in the Piedmont: The Story of John Reed's Mine." *North Carolina Historical Review* 52 (January 1975): 1–19.

LaPoint, Dennis. "The Gold Rush in North Carolina." *Geotimes* (December 1999): 14–18.

Mobley, Joe, ed. *The Way We Lived in North Carolina.* Chapel Hill: University of North Carolina Press, 2003.

North Carolina Department of Cultural Resources. North Carolina State Historic Site. Reed Gold Mine. Permanent Exhibits.

———. "Reed Gold Mine." http://www.nchistoricsites.org/reed/reed.htm. Accessed June 6, 2008.*North Carolina Paper Currency.* http://newbern .cpclib.org/digital/money.htm. Accessed June 6, 2008.

Stevenson, Jed. "Coins: A Bite of Gold." *New York Times*, September 1, 1991. http://www.nytimes.com/1991/09/01/news/coins.html Accessed June 4, 2008.

———. "Coins: An Honest Man and His Gold Dollar." *New York Times*, September 12, 1993.http://www.nytimes.com/1993/09/12/style/coins-an-honest -man-and-his-gold-dollar.html. Accessed December 31, 2012.

United States Mint. "Coin Production." http://www.usmint.gov/ historianscorner/?action=production. Accessed June 6, 2008.

———. "The Mint's Roles in History." http://www.usmint.gov/education/ historianscorner/?action=roles. Accessed June 6, 2008.

———. "Timeline of the United States Mint." http://www.usmint.gov/education/ historianscorner/?action=timeline. Accessed June 6, 2008.

valuable-coin-stories.com. "First Federal Mint—Making Money the Old Fashioned Way." http://valuable-coin-stories.com/first-federal-mint.html. Accessed June 6, 2008.

"Virtual Tour of Philadelphia: United States Mint." http://www.ushistory.org/ tour/tour_mint.htm. Accessed June 6, 2008.

Chapter 31: Mt. Mitchell: North Carolina's First State Park

"Buying Mt. Mitchell." *Asheville Citizen*, April 2, 1915, 4.

Jones, May, ed. *Memoirs and Speeches of Locke Craig, Governor of North Carolina, 1913–1917: A History, Political and Otherwise, from Scrap Books and Old Manu- scripts.* Asheville: Hackney and Mosie, 1923.

———. *Public Letters and Papers of Locke Craig, Governor of North Carolina 1913– 1917.* Raleigh: Edwards and Broughton Printing Company, 1916.

Lovelace, Jeff. *Mount Mitchell: Its Railroad and Toll Road.* Johnson City, Tenn.: Overmountain Press, 1994.

North Carolina Department of Environment and Natural Resources. "State Parks Make Significant Contribution to Local Economies" (press release). May 22, 2008.

North Carolina Parks and Recreation. *Dr. Elisha Mitchell and the Measuring of Mt. Mitchell.* North Carolina Department of Environment, Health, and Natural Resources, 2006.

———. *Mount Mitchell State Park.* North Carolina Department of Environment, Health, and Natural Resources.

Schwarzkopf, S. Kent. *A History of Mt. Mitchell and the Black Mountains: Exploration, Development and Preservation*. North Carolina Division of Archives and History, North Carolina Department of Cultural Resources, 1985.

Chapter 32: A New Profession for America: Forestry Along the Shut-In Trail

Alexander, Bill. "Biltmore Estate's Forest Legacy." http://www.ces.ncsu.edu/nreos/forest/feop/Agenda2003/symposium/proceedings_2003/PDFs/Alexander.pdf. Accessed December 31, 2012.

Carpenter, Cindy. Education/Interpretation Program Manager, U.S. Forest Service, Cradle of Forestry in America Historic Site. Interview. November 14, 2007.

Forest History Society Library and Archives. "Guide to Forestry Lectures of Carl Alwin Schenck, 1904–1909." http://www.foresthistory.org/research/Biltmore_Project/Schenck_Lectures.html. Accessed August 24, 2008.

"Forest Products Industry Emerges as North Carolina's Largest Manufacturing Industry." Press Release, NC Forestry Association. February 9, 2007. www.ncforestry.org. Accessed October 14, 2007.

Frederick Law Olmsted.com. http://www.fredericklawolmsted.com. Accessed December 8, 2007.

North Carolina State University. College of Natural Resources, Department of Forestry and Environmental Resources. "Department History." http://cnr.ncsu.edu/for/dept/depthis.html. Accessed August 24, 2008.

Pennsylvania Historical and Museum Commission. "Governor Gifford Pinchot." http://www.portal.state.pa.us/portal/server.pt/community/1879-1951/4284/gifford_pinchot/469112. Accessed October 14, 2007.

Pinchot, Gifford. *Breaking New Ground*. New York: Harcourt, Brace, 1947.

Pinkett, Harold T. *Gifford Pinchot: Private and Public Forester*. Urbana: University of Illinois Press, 1970.

———. "Gifford Pinchot at Biltmore." *North Carolina Historical Review* 34 (July 1957): 346–57.

Rickman, Ellen E. *Biltmore Estate*. Images of America. Charleston, S.C.: Arcadia Publishing, 2005.

Steen, Harold K. *The Conservation Diaries of Gifford Pinchot*. Durham: Forest History Society, 2001.

U.S. Forest Service. www.fs.fed.us/. Accessed August 24, 2008.

Volk, Victoria Loucia. "The Biltmore Estate and Its Creators," M.A. thesis, University of North Carolina at Chapel Hill, 1984.

Weber, Walt. *Trail Profiles: The Mountains to Sea Trail From Beech Gap to Black Mountain Campground*. Alexander, N.C.: WorldComm, 1999.

Chapter 33: Kitty Hawk: Where Men Soared

"Celebrating the Success of the Wright Brothers." www.wrightstories.com. Accessed October 25, 2007.

Crouch, Tom. *First in Flight: The Wright Brothers and the Invention of the Airplane*.

National Park Handbook #159. Washington, D.C.: U.S. Department of the
Interior, [2002?].

Federal Aviation Administration. "Passenger Boarding (Enplanement) and
All-Cargo Data." http://www.faa.gov/airports_airtraffic/airports/planning_
capacity/passenger_allcargo_stats/passenger/index.cfm?year=2006.
Accessed August 23, 2008.

Kachurek, Lynda. Wright State University, Special Collections and Archives.
Interview, October 25, 2007.

National Air Traffic Controllers Association. "Air Traffic Control: By the
Numbers." www. natca.org. Accessed August 23, 2008.

Outer Banks Sentinel. Commemorative Edition. The First Flight Centennial.
December 17, 2003.

White, Tom. National Park Ranger, Wright Brothers Memorial. Interview,
October 20, 2007

Chapter 34: The Call for Civil Rights: The Greensboro Four

City of Greensboro. "Historical Walking Tour." http://www.greensboro-nc.gov/
index.aspx?page=995

Gaillard, Frye. *The Greensboro Four: Civil Rights Pioneers.* Charlotte: Main Street
Rag Publishing, 2001.

"Movement by Negroes Growing." *Greensboro Daily News,* February 4, 1960.

"Needed: A 'Just and Honorable' Answer." *Greensboro Daily News,* February 8,
1960.North Carolina A&T University. "History and Mission." http://
www.ncat.edu/about/history-mission.html. Accessed October 11, 2007.

———. F. D. Bluford Library. "The A&T Four: February 1st, 1960." http://www
.library.ncat.edu/resources/archives/four.html. Accessed October 11, 2007.

Public Broadcasting System. *February One: The Story of the Greensboro Four.*
www.pbs.org/independentlens/februaryone/till.html. Accessed October 12,
2007.

Raines, Howell. Interview with Franklin McCain, 1960. From *My Soul Is Rested*
(1977). http://stuff.mit.edu/afs/athena/course/21/21h.102/www/
Primary%20source%20collections/Civil%20Rights/Sit_in_interview.htm.

Sitton, Claude, "Negro Sitdowns Stir Fear of Wider Unrest in South," Reporting
Civil Rights—Part One, *American Journalism Literary Classics of the US,* 431–32
and 433–39.

Sykes, Marvin. "Negro College Students Sit at Woolworth's Lunch Counter."
Greensboro Record, February 2, 1960.

University of North Carolina at Greensboro. UNCG Public History Program.
"Walking Through Greensboro's Past: Chaos and Collapse in Confederate
Greensboro." http://library.uncg.edu/dp/walkingtours/.

About the Author

A native North Carolinian, Lynn Setzer started reading historical markers before she was six years old. On trips across the country, her family would stop at notable places—the OK Corral, Fort Phantom Hill, Big Rock Candy Mountain, Little Big Horn, just to name a very few—to soak in the local stories, songs, and tall tales. Later, when walking and hiking became her exercise of choice, it seemed natural to blend the enjoyment of physical exertion with the excitement of learning something new. Whether she's walking on a trail used by the French Voyageurs or looking for Horace Kephart's favorite campsite in Great Smoky Mountains National Park, Lynn believes that there's nothing quite like experiencing life and history at walking speed. To date, Lynn has logged literally thousands of miles in North Carolina and across the country, still visiting the reminders of lives lived long ago, writing stories, and snapping pictures. Today, she lives in Winston-Salem and is happily wearing out yet another pair of walking shoes and looking forward to all of the walks that still await her.

Other **Southern Gateways Guides** you might enjoy

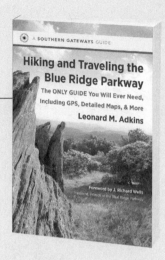

Hiking and Traveling the Blue Ridge Parkway
The Only Guide You Will Ever Need, Including GPS, Detailed Maps, and More

LEONARD M. ADKINS

The most up-to-date resource for Blue Ridge Parkway travelers

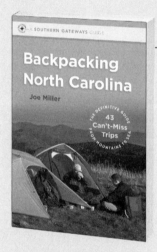

Backpacking North Carolina The Definitive Guide to 43 Can't-Miss Trips from Mountains to Sea
JOE MILLER

From classic mountain trails to little-known gems of the Piedmont and coastal regions

Farm Fresh North Carolina
The Go-To Guide to Great Farmers' Markets, Farm Stands, Farms, Apple Orchards, U-Picks, Kids' Activities, Lodging, Dining, Choose-and-Cut Christmas Trees, Vineyards and Wineries, and More

DIANE DANIEL

The one and only guidebook to North Carolina's farms and fresh foods

MIX
Paper from
responsible sources
FSC® C013483

FSC
www.fsc.org